"In the coming years, important regulations for major online platforms will likely arise from Council of Europe member states. European Court of Human Rights rulings will shape a complex global jurisprudence on online speech. Natalie Alkiviadou deserves praise for pioneering scholarship in this challenging and evolving field."

—**Eric Heinze,** *Professor of Law and Humanities,*
Queen Mary University of London, UK

"This important book presents an incisive analysis of the decisions concerning hate speech under the European Convention on Human Rights, offering a constructive critique of the case law's historic trajectory. In our interconnected world, the book's insightful analysis should inform debates far beyond Europe."

—**Nadine Strossen,** *John Marshall Harlan II Professor of Law Emerita,*
New York Law School, USA

Hate Speech and the European Court of Human Rights

This book argues that the European Court of Human Rights (ECtHR) should reconsider its approach to hate speech cases and develop a robust protection of freedom of expression as set out in the benchmark case of *Handyside v the United Kingdom*. In that case, the ECtHR determined that Article 10 of the European Convention on Human Rights (ECHR), safeguarding the right to freedom of expression, extends protection not only to opinions which are well received but also to those deemed offensive, shocking, or disturbing. However, subsequent rulings by the Court have generated a significant amount of contradictory case law. Against this backdrop, this book provides an analysis of hate speech case law before the ECtHR and the now-obsolete European Commission on Human Rights. Through a jurisprudential analysis, it is argued that these institutions have adopted an overly restrictive approach to hate speech, which fails to provide adequate protection of the right to freedom of expression. It also demonstrates that there are stark inconsistencies when it comes to the treatment of some forms of 'hate speech' versus others. The study further contends that, in reaching its decisions on hate speech cases, the Court disregards empirical evidence on matters related to free speech restrictions. Viewing the ECHR as a 'living instrument,' the book places this analysis within the current state of affairs vis-à-vis the handling of hate speech, particularly online, by European countries, the European Union itself and social media platforms, actions which the author argues are contributing to a free speech demise. The book will be a valuable resource for academics, researchers and policymakers working in the area of law, political science, European studies and sociology.

Natalie Alkiviadou is Senior Research Fellow at the Future of Free Speech at Vanderbilt University, USA. Her research interests lie in the freedom of expression, the far right, hate speech, hate crime and non-discrimination.

Routledge Research in Human Rights Law

Bulk Surveillance, Democracy and Human Rights Law in Europe
A Comparative Perspective
Marcin Rojszczak

Surveillance Law, Data Retention and Human Rights
A Risk to Democracy
Matthew White

Domestic Abuse and the European Court of Human Rights
Ronagh J.A. McQuigg

Human Rights Law and Corporate Regulation
A Neo-Concession Approach
Jonathan Barrett

Refugee Displacement, Disability and Human Rights
The Production, Processing and Power of Data
Philippa Duell-Piening

Detention and the Right to Liberty
Addressing Gaps in Protection at the European Court of Human Rights
Sabina Garahan

Transitional Justice Archives
Documenting Human Rights Violations in Latin America
Edited by Anita Ferrara and Beatrice Canossi

Hate Speech and the European Court of Human Rights
Natalie Alkiviadou

For more information about this series, please visit: www.routledge.com/Routledge-Research-in-Human-Rights-Law/book-series/HUMRIGHTSLAW

Hate Speech and the European Court of Human Rights

Natalie Alkiviadou

Routledge
Taylor & Francis Group
LONDON AND NEW YORK

First published 2025
by Routledge
4 Park Square, Milton Park, Abingdon, Oxon OX14 4RN

and by Routledge
605 Third Avenue, New York, NY 10158

Routledge is an imprint of the Taylor & Francis Group, an informa business

British Library Cataloguing-in-Publication Data
A catalogue record for this book is available from the British Library

Library of Congress Cataloging-in-Publication Data
Names: Alkiviadou, Natalie author
Title: Hate speech and the European Court of Human Rights / Natalie Alkiviadou.
Description: Abingdon, Oxon [UK] ; New York, NY : Routledge, 2025. | Series: Routledge research in human rights law | Includes bibliographical references and index.
Identifiers: LCCN 2025004703 | ISBN 9781032909240 hardback | ISBN 9781032909257 paperback | ISBN 9781003560548 ebook
Subjects: LCSH: Hate speech—Law and legislation—Europe | Hate speech—Law and legislation—Europe—Cases | European Court of Human Rights | Convention for the Protection of Human Rights and Fundamental Freedoms (1950 November 5) | Council of Europe | Freedom of expression—Europe
Classification: LCC KJC8781.I63 A45 2025 | DDC 341.4/833094—dc23/eng/20250208
LC record available at https://lccn.loc.gov/2025004703

ISBN: 978-1-032-90924-0 (hbk)
ISBN: 978-1-032-90925-7 (pbk)
ISBN: 978-1-003-56054-8 (ebk)

DOI: 10.4324/9781003560548

Typeset in Galliard
by Apex CoVantage, LLC

In memory of my grandfather Andreas Alkiviades, the kindest of souls.
Αιωνία σου η μνήμη

And of course, for my little munchkins, Andreas and Markella. Forever and always.

Contents

Table of Cases

About the Author

Dr Natalie Alkiviadou is Senior Research Fellow at the Future of Free Speech at Vanderbilt University. Her research interests lie in the freedom of expression, the far right, hate speech, hate crime and non-discrimination. She holds a PhD (law) from the Vrije Universiteit Amsterdam. She has published three monographs, namely, *The Far-Right in International and European Law* (Routledge 2019), *Legal Challenges to the Far-Right: Lessons from England and Wales* (Routledge 2019) and *The Far-Right in Greece and the Law* (Routledge 2022). She is the author of a forthcoming (2025) Routledge monograph *Hate Speech and the European Court of Human Rights* and co-editor of the *Oxford Handbook of Hate Speech*. She has published, reviewed and edited journal articles on hate speech, free speech, and the far right in a wide-range of journals. Natalie has extensive experience in working with civil society, educators and public servants on human rights education and has participated in European actions such as the High-Level Group on Combatting Racism, Xenophobia and Other Forms of Intolerance. In 2020, she chaired the United Nations Minority Forum on 'Hate Speech, Social Media and Minorities.' Natalie was the country researcher for the 2019 European Network Against Racism report on hate crime and the 2022 report on structural racism. She has drafted handbooks, strategy papers and shadow reports for projects funded by the Anna Lindh Foundation, the European Commission and the European Youth Foundation on themes such as hate speech. She is a trained mediator (conflict resolution and mediation) by OCN Northern Ireland and was the lead author on a handbook on social mediation. Natalie was an international fellow (2022/23) of the ISLC–Information Society Law Centre of the Università degli Studi di Milano. She is currently on the advisory board of the Forum for Humor and the Law (ForHum) and DELIAH: Democratic Literacy and Humour. She is a member of the International Press Institute.

Introduction

This book critically examines the hate speech jurisprudence of the former European Commission on Human Rights (EComHR/Commission) and the European Court of Human Rights (ECtHR/Court). The themes that will be assessed include speech targeting protected characteristics, such as racist or homophobic speech and speech within the sphere of totalitarianism, genocide denial and violent speech, exploring the legal, theoretical and practical dimensions of their approach. It must be noted that the focus of this book is the ECtHR, but relevant cases from the obsolete EComHR are also considered. However, when discussing broader themes related to notions, concepts and contexts of hate speech, references are made solely to the Court for clarity, unless the EComHR is of relevance.

The ECtHR has consistently affirmed that Article 10, which provides for the right to freedom of expression, protects not only speech that is well received but also that which 'offends, shocks or disturbs.'[1] This was decided in the 1976 landmark case of *Handyside v the United Kingdom*, in which the applicant, owner of a publishing firm, was convicted of possessing obscene publications after he published a book with the title *The Little Red Schoolbook*, a book on sex education for teenagers. The book included sections on issues such as pornography and abortion. However, when it comes to the very broad notion of hate speech, the Court has shown a concerning willingness to curtail free speech, invoking limitations under Article 10(2) of the European Convention on Human Rights (ECHR/Convention), as well as ousting speech from protection under the 'prohibition of abuse of rights' clause in Article 17. To illustrate this, cases involving anti-immigrant speech, such as *Féret v Belgium* (2009),[2] and homophobic and/or transphobic speech, such as *Vejdeland v Sweden* (2012)[3] and *Lilliendahl v Iceland* (2020),[4] have all noted

1 *Handyside v the United Kingdom* (1976) App no 5493/72 (ECHR, 7 December 1976) para 49
2 *Féret v Belgium* App no 15615/07 (ECHR, 16 July 2009)
3 *Vejdeland v Sweden* App no 1813/07 (ECHR, 9 February 2012)
4 *Lilliendahl v Iceland* App no 29297/18 (ECHR, 12 May 2020)

DOI: 10.4324/9781003560548-1

that insults, ridicule or defamation without the calling to a specific act of violence fall within the ambit of hate speech and can be prohibited. It is worth noting that all three aforementioned cases involved the imposition of criminal penalties. This group of cases, along with some others, falls under the prism of what I refer to as the low-threshold hatred paradigm. Holocaust denial is categorically excluded from Article 10 protection through Article 17, with the latter used alone or in conjunction with the former as an interpretative aid for Article 10's limitation grounds. The exclusion of Holocaust denial has been justified by the ECtHR due to its role in fostering anti-Semitism and the Holocaust's status as a 'clearly established historical fact.'[5] In contrast, *Perinçek v Switzerland* (2015) treated the denial of the Armenian genocide differently, finding that Article 17 played no role in this case as a result of, *inter alia*, a lacking unified consensus on the facts.[6] The section dealing with genocide denial reveals an implicit hierarchy of historical suffering. When it comes to totalitarianism, the Court and the former Commission have consistently excluded Nazi propaganda from Article 10 protection via Article 17, as seen in *Kühnen v Germany* (1988), reflecting Europe's historical commitment to preventing fascist resurgence. By contrast, in *Vajnai v Hungary* (2008)[7] and *Fáber v Hungary* (2012),[8] the Court adopted a robust protection of Article 10, allowing symbols linked to Communism and a Hungarian fascist regime, respectively. However, in *Nix v Germany* (2018),[9] restrictions on Nazi imagery were upheld even though they were presented on a blog dedicated to the debate of racial discrimination in Germany. In terms of violent speech, the cases examined primarily involve expressions critical of governments or institutions, rather than hate speech targeting protected groups. For instance, in *Özgür Gündem v Turkey* (2000)[10] and *Dink v Turkey* (2010),[11] the Court addressed state obligations to protect journalists from violence, focusing on safeguarding democratic discourse. While the Turkish cases and an additional case of violent speech in Russia are significant, their inclusion under hate speech appears misaligned, as the expressions involved do not fall within the sphere of hate speech. For example, even in cases of revisionism, the overarching objective underlying the prohibition of revisionist speech is that it is considered by the Court as a form of anti-Semitism and, therefore, targets Jewish people. In relation to totalitarianism, Nazi symbols in particular are prohibited for the same reason. The inclusion of violent speech cases which do not target protected characteristics reflects the Court's occasional categorisation of

5 *Lehideux and Isorni* (1998) App no 24662/94 (ECHR, 23 September 1998) para 53
6 *Perinçek v Switzerland* App no 27510/08 (15 October 2015)
7 *Vajnai v Hungary* App no 33629/06 (ECtHR, 8 July 2008)
8 *Fáber v Hungary* App no 40721/08 (ECHR, 24 July 2018)
9 *Nix v Germany* App no 35285/16 (ECHR, 13 March 2018)
10 *Özgür Gündem v Turkey* App no 23144/93 (ECHR, 16 March 2020)
11 *Dink v Turkey* App nos. 2668/07, 6102/08, 30079/08, 7072/09 & 7124/09 (ECHR, 14 September 2010)

such cases as hate speech rather than their relevance to the broader analysis of the book's themes. Nevertheless, the inclusion of such cases is valuable for comparative analysis, as it highlights the heightened protection the Court has afforded even to statements that include violent elements, especially when contrasted with its treatment of cases involving insults or ridicule targeting protected characteristics.

Hate speech is a contentious field, where the ECtHR's rulings have often revealed weaknesses, such as adjudicative inconsistencies between similar cases, a lacking definitional framework and a low threshold of severity when ascertaining what constitutes hate speech which falls outside the protection of the ECHR. These issues not only undermine the clarity and predictability of the Court's jurisprudence but also raise broader concerns about its impact on the right to free expression and the democratic principles enshrined in the Convention more generally.

Turning to the definitional framework, on a Council of Europe level, the 2022 Committee of Ministers Recommendation on Combating Hate Speech adopts a relatively narrow definition, focusing on incitement to violence, hatred or discrimination. It understands *hate speech* to be

> all types of expression that incite, promote, spread or justify violence, hatred or discrimination against a person or group of persons, or that denigrates them, by reason of their real or attributed personal characteristics or status such as 'race,' colour, language, religion, nationality, national or ethnic origin, age, disability, sex, gender identity and sexual orientation.[12]

However, in some cases, the ECtHR applies much broader interpretations of what it considers to be hate speech without adopting a definition of hate speech *per se*. The previous Recommendation could be an opportunity to fill this definitional gap, but we have yet to see this formally constitute the definitional benchmark for the Court's legal analysis. The closest we have come to furthering the conceptualisation of hate speech is in *Lilliendahl*, in which the Court offered a severity hierarchisation of unprotected speech under Article 10 and Article 17, but not a substantive definition of hate speech. Closely tied to the absence of a clear definition and the broad array of concepts attributed to what the Court deems hate speech is the issue of thresholds, particularly the Court's tendency to apply low thresholds for restricting speech. For example, following its *Féret* paradigm, when faced with speech targeting protected characteristics, the Court has systematically ruled that hate speech includes expressions of insult or ridicule, even in the absence of direct incitement

12 The CM/Rec (2022) 16 on Combating Hate Speech was adopted by the Committee of Ministers on 20 May 2022 <https://www.coe.int/en/web/combating-hate-speech/recommendation-on-combating-hate-speech> accessed 1 September 2024

to violence, as will be discussed in Chapter 4. In reaching its decisions, the Court makes fleeting references to allegations regarding the nature and harm in hate speech that do not go beyond normative. For example, in *Féret*, the Court, with no extrapolation of the issues in question, held that the applicant's speech 'clearly incited discrimination and racial hatred,'[13] without explaining what it understands as discrimination or hatred or how the speech in question constituted this form of discrimination. In this case, it also made several comments regarding racist and xenophobic speech in an electoral context, noting that 'such a context contributed to stirring up hatred and intolerance'[14] and that 'slogans or stereotypical formulas come to prevail over reasonable arguments.'[15] Again, it does not conduct any substantial analysis before making these statements, while it seldom looks at scholarship to assist it in its process. In the sphere of hate speech in particular, the rare occasions of references to scholarship are found in individual opinions. In the core of the judgement, the closest we have come is in an Article 11 case, namely, *Alekseyev v Russia* (2010), which involved the repeated ban on gay rights marches in Moscow, where the Court noted:

> [T]here is no scientific evidence of sociological data at the Court's disposal suggesting that the mere mention of homosexuality or open public debate about sexual minorities' social status, would adversely affect children or 'vulnerable adults.' On the contrary, it is only through fair and public debate that society may address such complex issues as the one raised in the present case. Such debate, backed up by academic research, would benefit social cohesion by ensuring that representatives of all views are heard, including the individuals concerned.[16]

Therefore, in *Alekseyev*, the Court looked at scholarly work and data to establish whether the harm alleged by the government was pragmatic. This case and its finding were subsequently referenced in a concurring opinion in *Vejdeland*.[17]

Relying on scholarship in hate speech cases by the Court in its analysis rather than by individual concurring or dissenting judges, particularly when cases involve low thresholds of hate, such as insults, ridicules and prejudice, would lead to more principled and coherent judgements and ensure that the threshold of prohibited speech is legitimately placed at a level which is neither too low nor too high. Considering that national laws across the countries of the Council of Europe vary, and while hate speech laws are inherently subjective either in their design or application, the ECtHR is under the duty as

13 *Féret* (n 2) para 78
14 *Féret* (n 2) para 76
15 *Féret* (n 2)
16 *Alekseyev v Russia* (2010) App no 4916/07 (ECHR, 21 October 2010) para 86
17 *Vejdeland* (n 3) Concurring Opinion of Judge Yudkivska joined by Judge Villiger, para 5

European supervisor to conduct a substantive assessment of impact and harm and adopt a functional definition of hate speech if Article 10 is to be protected adequately. These two changes would reduce, but not diminish, the risks brought about by restricting speech based on viewpoints and establish a more stringent threshold of what hate speech should fall outside the scope of Convention protection. As it stands, eliminating insulting and prejudicial speech, for example, does not bode well with the Court's own finding that speech extends to that which 'shocks, offends or disturbs.'[18] In addition to the fundamentality of speech and its protection are the issues that arise from restricting it. Studies discussed in Chapter 2 highlight how silencing offensive speech can elevate speakers into martyrs, drive their rhetoric underground, make it more difficult to counteract hate through public debate and, also, exacerbate social tension, and even, violence. Despite these findings, the ECtHR has shown no substantial engagement with scholarship when assessing the necessity and proportionality of speech restrictions. This gap underscores the need for the Court to adopt a more evidence-based approach to hate speech regulation, one that considers the broader societal impacts of its rulings. While the Court may refer to ECRI reports on particular themes or surveys pertaining to the issue at stake, this is not sufficient. There is a plethora of academic work developed over time that delves into the intricate themes that need to be explored before making assertions that something *is* hate speech, that this *does* cause x types of harm and that, as a result, it *should be* prohibited, even if that prohibition is of a criminal nature, as we see in the large majority of cases.

This book argues for a recalibration of the ECtHR's approach, emphasising the need for clear and stringent thresholds of harm based on principles of international human rights law (IHRL), research-informed reasoning and a robust definition of hate speech. This combination would allow for the prohibition of speech which could incite harm, such as incitement to violence or hatred, established on a case-by-case basis through the application of a strict scrutiny test emanating from a sound definitional framework. This is essential for redressing the speech-restrictive approach taken in hate speech cases to date, which, as demonstrated in Chapter 2, can be of damage not only to free speech but also to minorities and social cohesion, which the Court, through its judgements, tries to protect. This change will also prove particularly useful for addressing the complexities of hate speech in an increasingly pluralistic and digital world.

The Proliferation of Hate Speech Regulation

The advent of social media and digital platforms has dramatically transformed the dissemination of information, allowing instantaneous global communication. In fact, the global reach of the internet has enabled hate speech to transcend

18 *Handyside* (n 1) para 49

national boundaries, creating serious challenges for traditional legal systems that were established to regulate conduct within geographically defined societies. The digital revolution has fundamentally transformed the nature of hate speech, turning it from a localised phenomenon into a global challenge. Social media platforms such as Facebook, YouTube and X are central forums for public discourse, offering unprecedented opportunities for expression while also amplifying the possibility, visibility and/or engagement with hate speech across a very broad spectrum of severity. This dual role has prompted governments worldwide to enact increasingly stringent laws targeting online hate speech. Germany's Network Enforcement Act (NetzDG) of 2017, now being replaced by the European Union's Digital Services Act (DSA),[19] was a pioneering effort to combat online hate speech, mandating the removal of illegal content within as little as 24 hours to up to 1 week, with such content including insult, defamation and malicious gossip.

In 2024, the European Union introduced the DSA, which imposes obligations on platforms to, *inter alia*, remove 'illegal content,' which includes 'illegal hate speech.' The DSA avoids defining 'illegal content,' and therefore 'illegal hate speech,' but it notes that content may be deemed illegal under national or European law, leaving it to platforms to interpret and apply these legal standards, granting them substantial discretion in the process. The DSA's failure to define hate speech highlights a recurring issue in global regulation, specifically the lack of a definition, the interlinked risk of overreach and the suppression of legitimate discourse.

In terms of global impact of legislation such as those mentioned, it is noteworthy that the NetzDG's influence has extended beyond Europe, with more than 20 countries, including Turkey, Russia and Venezuela, adopting similar models, citing the NetzDG at some point in the legislative process.[20] Authoritarian regimes have essentially weaponised the language of hate speech

19 For a discussion on the DSA, see, amongst others, Joan Barata, 'The Digital Services Act and Its Impact on the Right to Freedom of Expression: Special Focus on Risk Mitigation Obligations' *DSA Observatory* (2021) <https://dsa-observatory.eu/2021/07/27/the-digital-services-act-and-its-impact-on-the-right-to-freedom-of-expression-special-focus-on-risk-mitigation-obligations/> accessed 1 October 2024; Joan Barata and Jordi Calvet-Bademunt, 'The European Commission's Approach to DSA Systemic Risk is Concerning for Freedom of Expression' *Tech Policy Press* (2023) <https://www.techpolicy.press/the-european-commissions-approach-to-dsa-systemic-risk-is-concerning-for-freedom-of-expression/> accessed 1 October 2024; Joan Barata, 'Joan Barata on the EU's Digital Services Act' *CEU Democracy Institute* (2022) <https://cmds.ceu.edu/article/2022-05-27/joan-barata-eus-digital-services-act> accessed 15 November 2024; Joan Barata, 'The Out-of-court Settlement Mechanism under the DSA: Questions and Doubts' *DSA Observatory* (2023) <https://dsa-observatory.eu/2023/10/26/the-out-of-court-settlement-mechanism-under-the-dsa-questions-and-doubts/> accessed 10 October 2024

20 Jacob Mchangama and Natalie Alkiviadou, 'The Digital Berlin Wall: How Germany (Accidentally) Created a Prototype for Global Online Censorship—Act Two' *Justitia* (2020) <https://futurefreespeech.org/wp-content/uploads/2020/09/Analyse_Cross-fertilizing-Online-Censorship-The-Global-Impact-of-Germanys-Network-Enforcement-Act-Part-two_Final.pdf> accessed 1 October 2024

to suppress dissent, further complicating the global dynamics of free speech. Although Putin, Maduro, Erdogan or the likes are unlikely hanging around, anticipating a European law to justify suppressing dissent, the existence of a European framework that they can subsequently misuse serves to legitimise their actions. The risks of overreach are not confined to authoritarian regimes. Even in liberal democracies, hate speech laws can have unintended consequences, suppressing legitimate expression and chilling public debate. A 2024 study revealed that the vast majority (87.5% to 99.7%) of comments deleted on Facebook and YouTube in France, Germany and Sweden were legally permissible.[21] Legislative developments which aim at imposing enhanced liability on internet intermediaries such as social media platforms underscore the double-edged nature of hate speech regulation. Special Rapporteur on Opinion and Expression Irene Khan cautioned:

> The trend that sees States delegating to online platforms 'speech police' functions that traditionally belong to the courts has continued. The risk with such laws is that intermediaries are likely to err on the side of caution and 'over-remove' content for fear of being sanctioned.[22]

As such, online platforms are increasingly held accountable for third-party content, a trend reinforced by the ECtHR's jurisprudence. In *Delfi AS v Estonia* (2015), the ECtHR held that finding an online news portal liable for hate speech posted by readers on the comment sections of articles was not a violation of Article 10, establishing a precedent that blurs the boundaries of free speech protection in the digital age.[23] In *Sanchez v France* (2023), the Court upheld the criminal conviction of a politician for failing to delete hateful comments made by others on his Facebook post.[24] With these two cases, 'hate speech by proxy' is born, with liability imposed even on those not uttering the hate speech.[25]

In the previously described rapidly evolving and glocal[26] environment, the ECtHR's role in upholding free speech and in handling hate speech is more critical than ever, not only for re-setting the tone for Europe, but also for providing a framework for governments and private actors worldwide.

21 'Preventing "Torrents of Hate" or Stifling Free Expression Online?' *The Future of Free Speech* (2024) <https://futurefreespeech.org/preventing-torrents-of-hate-or-stifling-free-expressiononline/> accessed 8 October 2024

22 UNHRC, 'Report of the Special Rapporteur on the Promotion and Protection of the Right to Freedom of Opinion and Expression' (13 April 2021) UN Doc A/HRC/47/25, para 58

23 *Delfi AS v Estonia* App no 64569/09 (ECHR, 16 June 2015)

24 *Sanchez v France* App no 45581/15 (ECHR, 15 May 2023)

25 Natalie Alkiviadou, 'Hate Speech by Proxy: Sanchez v France and the Dwindling Protection of Freedom of Expression' (2021) <https://opiniojuris.org/2021/12/14/hate-speech-by-proxy-sanchez-v-france-and-the-dwindling-protection-of-freedom-of-expression/> accessed 8 November 2024

26 Reflecting or characterised by both local and global considerations

Legislative developments that can affect the offline and online world include, for example, the Scottish Hate Crime and Public Order (Scotland) Act. Enacted in 2021, the Act criminalises a broad spectrum of conduct, including 'stirring up hatred' against protected groups. It has been described as 'vague and broad, establishing hierarchies amongst certain groups in terms of what protection they are offered and integrating speech and violence together, without adequate thought given to the ramifications on the freedom of expression.'[27] The Act's implications resonate with broader concerns about the definitional ambiguities surrounding *hate speech* but also reflect the challenges of adopting viewpoint-based restrictions to speech. The issue of viewpoint-selective prohibitions of speech is of particular concern when assessing hate speech legislation and, subsequently, the ECtHR's approach to hate speech restriction. To demonstrate the challenges that arise from the imposition of viewpoint-selective bans, we will briefly look at several laws in force which, while discriminatory in nature, were developed and are applied under the guise of protecting "family values." Nevertheless, in essence, they serve as powerful tools for institutionalising prejudice and silencing vulnerable communities. These are the so-called "gay propaganda" laws, which have proliferated in several countries and turned discriminatory ideologies into legally sanctioned repression. These laws do not merely limit speech; they weaponise societal biases to entrench homophobia and marginalise LGBTQ+ individuals and groups under the pretext of safeguarding traditional norms. Given the geographical scope of the book, and for the purposes of demonstrating that this abuse of hate speech laws is taking place in the Council of Europe region, only examples from member states will be given. Hungary has followed a similar trajectory to Russia's 2013 law, updated over the years. In 2021, it enacted its own propaganda law, *Act LXXIX*, which prohibits content that 'propagates divergence from self-identity corresponding to sex at birth, sex change or homosexuality' from being accessible to minors. Hungary incorporated its restrictions into a range of existing laws, including those on child protection, education and broadcasting. By embedding discrimination into a broader legislative framework, Hungary has created legal mechanisms that curtail visibility of LGBTQ+ individuals while using the rhetoric of child protection to justify the measures. The law has had a chilling effect on public discourse and deepened the invisibility of LGBTQ+ people within Hungarian society.[28] Bulgaria has recently followed suit, adopting its own version of a 'gay

27 Jacob Mchangama and Natalie Alkiviadou, 'Hate Crime and Public Order (Scotland) Bill (21 August 2020) Rights!' <https://rightsblog.net/2020/08/21/hate-crime-and-public-order-scotland-bill/> accessed 10 November 2024

28 Amnesty International, 'Hungary: Propaganda Law has "Created Cloud of Fear" Pushing LGBTI+ Community into the Shadows' (27 February 2024) <https://www.amnesty.org/en/latest/news/2024/02/hungarypropaganda-law-has-created-cloud-of-fear-pushing-lgbti-community-into-the-shadows/> accessed 14 October 2024

propaganda' ban in August 2024.[29] This legislation, which prohibits LGBTQ+ content in schools, has sparked widespread protests and condemnation from human rights organisations. Rights groups have warned that such measures exacerbate stigma and discrimination, pushing LGBTQ+ individuals into further marginalisation. By framing their objectives in emotionally charged and vaguely defined terms, such as 'propaganda' or 'family values,' legislators enable the suppression of discourse that challenges heteronormative or patriarchal norms. These examples, in their more extreme form, highlight the inherent issues with viewpoint restrictions, demonstrating how laws regulating speech can ultimately undermine the very principles of equality and free expression they are intended, on a Council of Europe level at least, to protect. In their current form, the "gay propaganda laws" serve as stark reminders of the dangers inherent in legislating viewpoints without clear definitions and robust safeguards.

Turning to the past[30] also gives us an ominous tale of viewpoint restrictions. During British colonisation, the Indian Penal Code criminalised 'feelings of enmity or hatred between different classes of Her Majesty's Subjects.'[31] This provision was invoked in 1934. The author of a leaflet advocating for exploited labourers to protest against the wealthy was deemed to incite class hatred, leading to his six-month prison sentence.[32] Further, reflecting that hate speech laws are 'prone to majoritarian bias in enforcement'[33] is the example of the 1965 British Race Relations Act, where some of the first few people to be prosecuted under this law were members of minority groups. A leader of the Black Power movement and four members of the Universal Coloured People's Association were convicted for stirring hatred against White people.[34]

The Structure and Purpose of the Book

The book seeks to provide a comprehensive analysis of hate speech regulation through the lens of ECtHR's jurisprudence, contextualised within broader societal and regulatory trends. The first chapter lays the groundwork by

29 Seb Starcevic, 'Rights groups slam Bulgaria for Banning LGBTQ+ "Propaganda"' *Politico* (8 August2024)<https://www.politico.eu/article/bulgaria-lgbtq-rights-far-right-europe-russia-human-rights/> accessed 14 October 2024

30 For a detailed discussion on this, see Jacob Mchangama, *Free Speech: A History from Socrates to Social Media* (1st edn, Basic Books 2022); Jacob Mchangama and Nadine Strossen, 'Hate-Speech Laws are No Friend of Minorities' *Spiked* (26 June 2020) <https://www.spiked-online.com/2020/06/02/hate-speech-laws-are-no-friend-of-minorities/> accessed August 2024

31 Jacob Mchangama, 'The Sordid Origin of Hate-Speech Laws' (2011) 170 Policy Review 45 accessed 28 July 2024

32 Mchangama (n 31)

33 Mchangama (n 31)

34 *R v Malik* (1968) 1 WLR 353, *R v Sawh*, The Times, 29–30 November 1967, Mchangama and Strossen (n 31)

exploring the definitional and conceptual frameworks of hate speech across international, regional and domestic contexts and the evolution of IHRL in this field. The analysis highlights the varying thresholds and protections afforded to speech across jurisdictions, including at the Council of Europe, the United Nations and the European Union. The chapter also examines thematic inconsistencies in addressing hate speech, including hierarchies of protected characteristics, and explores the unique challenges posed by digital platforms and their corporate definitions and policies. It also looks at the hate speech–free speech debate, and how this has shaped the handling of hate speech across supranational and inter-governmental organisations. Through a critical engagement with academic perspectives and institutional practices, the chapter underscores the definitional ambiguity of hate speech and its implications for free expression. The second chapter explores the multifaceted effects of hate speech and critically examines the suitability of regulation as a response to this phenomenon. Through an assessment of empirical and theoretical work, it looks at the impact of hate speech on individuals, groups and society, critically analysing research and its limitations. It also looks at free speech through the ambit of a marketplace of ideas, considering arguments for and against this theoretical framework for purposes of placing speech in a normative setting, through which subsequent analysis of its restriction can be effectuated. The chapter also engages with the ongoing debate surrounding hate speech regulation, contrasting arguments for safeguarding dignity and equality with concerns about free expression. Critics of restrictive measures warn of potential risks to the fundamental right of freedom of expression, but also to societal impacts, such as driving hate groups underground, elevating perpetrators to the status of martyrs, silencing dissenting voices and counter-speech and, ultimately, adopting a superficial 'plaster' approach to a problem rooted in deep structural inequalities. Further, through a critical analysis of militant democracy, the chapter discusses the theory underpinning the Court's overly and overtly restrictive approach to freedom of expression in hate speech cases. The chapter argues that the Court inadequately engages with theoretical and empirical studies on hate speech, its impact and the effects of its overly restrictive approach, calling for a more structured, substantive perspective to be adopted that is research-informed. Ultimately, the chapter aims to give food for thought to the highly complex and intertwined questions of (1) what, if any, are the real-life harms in hate speech and (2) if regulating speech is an appropriate response to hate speech. The third chapter focuses on the role of the Council of Europe in shaping hate speech regulation. It commences with an overview of the Council of Europe, its establishment, its history and the articulation of Article 10 and Article 17 through the Convention's *Travaux Préparatoires.* These are the two articles which are of direct relevance to hate speech cases, since most applications are brought forth by speakers. Chapter 3 provides an overview of the central tenets of Article 10 and Article 17 for purposes of setting the scene for the jurisprudential analysis that will be conducted in the following two chapters. In providing an overview of the two articles, as well as their history, cross reference is made to counterparts on a United Nations scale. Due to the book's focus on hate speech, the chapter will also look at the Additional Protocol to the Convention on Cybercrime, Concerning the Criminalisation of Acts of a Racist and Xenophobic Nature Committed Through Computer Systems as the only Council of Europe instrument which criminalises some forms of hate speech. The fourth chapter examines the jurisprudence of the ECtHR and the former EComHR concerning hate speech directed at protected characteristics, including race, religion, ethnicity, sexual orientation and gender identity. It explores the EComHR's and, for the most part, the ECtHR's approach to hate speech, ranging from expressions involving insult or ridicule, to direct calls for hostility or violence. It critically analyses their interpretation and application of Article 10 and, where relevant, Article 17, highlighting challenges regarding the threshold of severity and the impact of the impugned speech, as well as judicial inconsistencies in similar cases. In a handful of ECtHR cases invoked by victims of hate speech or people belonging to the victim group, Article 8 and the right to private life were invoked alone or in conjunction with the non-discrimination clause found in Article 14 of the ECHR. These will be developed further in this chapter. The chapter looks at the doctrine of the margin of appreciation, arguing that the in-depth evaluation of core themes pertaining to the case in question is often disregarded under the shield of the margin of appreciation granted to states. The chapter also assesses developments in the sphere of speech digitalisation, evaluating the Court's findings that third-party entities and individuals bear liability for online speech uttered by others. Chapter 5 explores the jurisprudence of the EComHR and the ECtHR on speech related to totalitarianism, genocide denial and violence. The analysis highlights the consistent exclusion of Nazi-related speech and symbols from Article 10 protection, while demonstrating that other totalitarian regimes, such as Communism, but also fascist spin-offs, are not dealt with in the same way. It also scrutinises the Court's differential treatment of genocide denial beyond the Holocaust, referring to its controversial handling of the Armenian genocide in *Perinçek v Switzerland* (2015). Finally, the chapter addresses violent speech cases, highlighting the interplay between incitement to violence, political expression and hate speech. By analysing the aforementioned categories, the chapter reveals legal inconsistencies and implicit hierarchies in hate speech jurisprudence, raising critical questions about the balance between freedom of expression, historical memory and democratic values.

This book addresses a critical gap in existing literature by examining the ECtHR's and the EComHR's hate speech jurisprudence. Ultimately, the book aspires to contribute to the ongoing debate on the boundaries of free speech in a pluralistic society, cognisant always of European history and its approach to hate speech. By critically examining the ECtHR's jurisprudence and situating it within contemporary regulatory trends, it argues for a recalibrated approach that balances the imperatives of combatting harm with the foundational right to free expression. Through a combination of jurisprudential analysis with broader contextual, normative and empirical insights, the book aims to provide readers with a nuanced understanding of the ECtHR's approach to hate speech and its implications for free expression. It is intended for a wide readership, including academics, civil society, journalists, policymakers, legal practitioners, IT companies and anyone interested in the matter.

Food for Thought

In Europe, the foundational approach to hate speech regulation involves balancing the right to free speech against broader concerns, such as group protection, social cohesion and the preservation of democracy. This book does not aim to theorise if, whether or how this binary framework is suitable or not or whether it should remain the same. It focuses on jurisprudential analysis, raising critical concerns on key issues that could relate to the current approach, including the very low threshold attached to speech that is deemed unprotected by the Convention. Chapter 2 gives space for the author to put forth several ideas that could be interesting for readers in terms of the harm in hate speech and whether this justifies its regulation. The chapter seeks to provide readers with a lens of varying possibilities through which they can perceive the subsequent jurisprudential analysis. After that, it delves into a black letter analysis of hate speech jurisprudence, which constitutes the bulk of the book, in Chapters 4 and 5. On one level, this analysis is hopefully useful for the reader in terms of the collection of hate speech cases, including very old ones, into one book. In addition to this, the core of the analysis demonstrates (1) a lacking definitional benchmark that systematically marks the Court's jurisprudence and which has contributed to a very low threshold of hate being deemed prohibitable by the Court, such as ridicule or insult, and which has contributed to inconsistencies in the adjudication of hate speech cases, and (2) a lack of engagement with scholarship by the Court. Furthermore, the book argues that viewpoint-based restrictions on hate speech are open to abuse, so it is of the utmost urgency that the Court adopts a well-articulated approach to hate speech cases, particularly given the margin of appreciation which states enjoy. In a rapidly evolving landscape marked by the proliferation of digital platforms, sweeping regulatory frameworks and a resurgence of authoritarian tendencies, the balance between combatting harmful speech and safeguarding freedom of expression finds itself in precarity. Developments such as the NetzDG, and now the DSA, embolden private platforms to over-remove content and authoritarian regimes to replicate such models to suppress dissent. Against this backdrop, the ECtHR's role as Europe's human rights arbiter is pivotal. Its jurisprudence shapes the normative boundaries of permissible speech, influencing not only domestic laws but also other courts across the globe. As such, a coherent and principled stance is essential to prevent a chilling effect on legitimate expression and to counter the instrumentalisation of hate speech laws for political suppression. By setting clear, evidence-based thresholds for hate speech which emanate from a sound definitional framework that is based on principles of IHRL, the ECtHR can reaffirm its commitment to protecting fundamental human rights in addition to the foundational principles of the ECHR, such as protecting democracy and the public space. At a time when the line between protecting vulnerable groups and stifling dissent grows increasingly blurred, the Court's guidance is indispensable in upholding a vision of Europe that values both inclusivity and freedom.

1 Hate Speech

Definitional and Conceptual Framework

Introduction

Although widely used in legal, academic and public discourse, *hate speech* remains an elusive term, and its precise definition remains contested. Debates continue over the balance between protecting free expression and preventing speech that incites harm. These debates are influenced by differing legal standards and cultural attitudes towards free speech and the evolving nature of communication in a digital world. In this sphere, Chapter 1 seeks to provide an understanding of hate speech by giving an overview of its contemporary historical roots in international human rights law (IHRL) and various legal interpretations of hate speech and the challenges that emanate therefrom. Through an examination of thematic inconsistencies, including hierarchies of protected characteristics, the analysis of the tensions between free speech and hate speech in institutional settings and the emergence of digital platforms as arbiters of acceptable speech, this chapter lays the groundwork for understanding the European Court of Human Rights' (ECtHR's/Court's) approach to hate speech, which grapples with definitional and conceptual ambiguities as well as emerging trends and challenges in the ambit of hate speech.

This chapter is divided into seven main subsections. Section 1 provides a brief overview of the evolution of hate speech laws following World War II, commenting particularly on the position of European states during the drafting of relevant documents under IHRL. Section 2 delves into the international and European definitional frameworks of hate speech, focusing on the absence of a universal definition and the varying thresholds for its regulation. The analysis looks at ECtHR jurisprudence and how it conceptualises hate speech, underlining the lack of a definitional framework in the Court's jurisprudence. It explores key legal instruments, including the Council of Europe's Additional Protocol to the Convention on Cybercrime, Concerning the Criminalisation of Acts of a Racist and Xenophobic Nature Committed Through Computer Systems (Additional Protocol); Article 20(2) of the International Covenant on Civil and Political Rights (ICCPR); the European Union's Framework Decision on Combating Certain Forms of Expression of Racism and Xenophobia by Means of Criminal Law (Framework Decision); and its Code of Conduct on

DOI: 10.4324/9781003560548-2

Countering Illegal Hate Speech Online (Code of Conduct/Code). Section 3 gives an overview of the treatment of hate speech in selective national legislations. By looking at how legislation approaches the question of hate speech in various jurisdictions, the section illustrates the diversity of strategies employed to regulate it. Section 4 turns to the contemporary challenges posed by digital platforms in defining and regulating hate speech. In the digital age, social media platforms have become both enablers of harmful rhetoric and arbiters of acceptable speech, developing their own expansive definitions and enforcement mechanisms. The section looks at the policies of major platforms, including Meta (Facebook), X (formerly Twitter), Reddit and YouTube, highlighting their broad conceptualisation of hate speech. Section 5 gives a brief insight into varying definitions of hate speech in academic discourse. Section 6 looks at how the free speech–hate speech debate is tackled on an international and European scale, reflecting key tensions pertaining to this debate, which also marks the jurisprudence of the ECtHR. Section 7 explores thematic hierarchies in hate speech regulation, analysing the prioritisation of certain protected characteristics over others. It identifies a clear hierarchy within international and regional frameworks, where speech related to race, ethnicity and xenophobia is systematically given greater prominence and legal protection than speech targeting characteristics such as sex, gender orientation and sexual orientation. This section highlights the gaps and inconsistencies in addressing homophobic, transphobic and sexist hate speech, emphasising the need for a more inclusive and intersectional approach to hate speech regulation.

1 Hate Speech After World War II: A Short Commentary

The concept of hate speech, while widely recognised today, has evolved in response to historical events, social movements and the ongoing struggle to balance freedom of expression with the protection of individuals and groups from harm. In pre-modern societies, laws, such as those of sedition or blasphemy, reflected societal concerns about speech that could disrupt public order or offend prevailing religious or moral standards.[1] In the aftermath of World War II, IHRL began to address the issue of hate speech within the realm of incitement. Article 20(2) of the ICCPR calls for the prohibition of 'any advocacy of national, racial or religious hatred that constitutes incitement to discrimination, hostility, or violence.' This marked one of the pivotal moments where international law explicitly addressed what would later be broadly understood as hate speech.[2] Whilst the ICCPR was formally adopted

1 For a detailed discussion on this, see Jacob Mchangama, *Free Speech: A History from Socrates to Social Media* (1st edn, Basic Books 2022)

2 Note that the historical background of Article 10, on the right to freedom of expression, and Article 17, on the prohibition of abuse of rights of the European Convention on Human Rights (ECHR), will be discussed in Chapter 3

in 1966, its initial draft was completed by 1949.[3] This document influenced the drafting of the ECHR. The text of Article 20 of the ICCPR explicitly prohibits the advocacy of war propaganda and 'advocacy of national, racial or religious hatred that constitutes incitement to discrimination, hostility or violence.' When Article 20 of the ICCPR was put to a vote, no member of the Council of Europe at that time supported its adoption,[4] and no other Western democracy aligned with the majority vote in favour of its adoption.[5] Numerous concerns were raised regarding the implications of Article 20 on freedom of expression. The Norwegian representative, speaking on behalf of the Scandinavian delegations, argued that freedom of expression was already endangered by the wording of Article 19 of the ICCPR, and that Article 20 further exacerbated those concerns.[6] Delegates expressed apprehension about the potential ambiguities in determining what constitutes war propaganda and warned that the provision prohibiting advocacy of national hatred that incites hostility could easily be misinterpreted, potentially leading those it aimed to protect to become its unintended victims.[7] Despite these concerns, the majority voted to adopt the text of Article 20(2) ICCPR, with 50 votes in favour, 18 against and 15 abstentions.[8]

The adoption of the International Convention on the Elimination of All Forms of Racial Discrimination (ICERD) in 1965 marked the broadest international treaty–based effort to prohibit hate speech rooted in racial discrimination. The drafting process of the ICERD revealed significant political divisions between Eastern and Western states regarding the implications of the Convention on freedom of expression. This divide was particularly evident in the contentious debate over Article 4 of the ICERD, acknowledged as one of the most 'difficult and controversial'[9] provisions of the Convention. Article 4 criminalises, among other things, the dissemination of racist ideas and incitement to racial violence. Communist states like Czechoslovakia and Poland advocated strongly for the broad criminalisation of racist ideas under Article 4(a), without requiring actual incitement to violence as a precondition.[10]

3 Fact Sheet No 2 (Rev. 1) The International Bill of Human Rights <https://www.ohchr.org/sites/default/files/Documents/Publications/FactSheet2Rev.1en.pdf> accessed 28 July 2024

4 Against: Belgium, Denmark, The Netherlands, Sweden, UK, Iceland, Ireland, Turkey. Abstained: France, Italy, Greece, Cyprus, Austria

5 UN General Assembly, 16th Session, Third Committee, Agenda Item 35, 5 December 1961, A/5000, 16 <https://documents-dds-ny.un.org/doc/UNDOC/GEN/N61/295/95/PDF/N6129595pdf?OpenElement> accessed 28 July 2024

6 Comments of Mr. Leiro to UN General Assembly, 16th Session, Third Committee, 26 October 1961, UN Doc. A/C.3/SR.1084, para 4 <https://undocs.org/A/C.3/SR.1084> accessed 28 July 2024

7 Comments of Mr. Leiro to UN General Assembly (n 6)

8 UN General Assembly (n 5)

9 Natan Lerner, *The U.N. Convention on the Elimination of all Forms of Racial Discrimination* (1st edn, Brill 1980) 43

10 Lerner (n 9) 46; Three Proposals: A/C.3/L.1208 (Ukraine); A/C.3/L.1220 (Czechoslovakia); A/C.3/L.1210 (Poland); Lerner (n 9) 46

In contrast, several Western and Southern American states expressed reservations about the expansive scope of Article 4 as initially proposed, fearing its potential severely to restrict freedom of speech.[11] For instance, the British delegate argued that freedom of expression was so fundamental that restrictions should only apply in cases directly inciting violence. In response to these concerns, the 'due regard' clause was introduced, stipulating that Article 4 of the ICERD should be implemented while respecting the principles of the Universal Declaration of Human Rights and the rights outlined in Article 5 of the ICERD itself, which includes a set of rights, such as the right to freedom of opinion and expression. As elaborated on further later, several Western states issued declarations or reservations affirming their commitment to enacting measures against racist activities covered by the provision, but only to the extent necessary and without jeopardising the right to freedom of expression. Several liberal democracies emphasised their cautious approach to implementing criminal measures under Article 4 ICERD.[12]

In relation to the drafting of the Universal Declaration of Human Rights (UHDR), Council of Europe states and the United States engaged in discussions with the Soviet Union and its allies, who advocated for the Declaration to include not only protection for freedom of expression but also specific obligations to prohibit 'fascism.'[13] Despite repeated efforts by the Soviet delegation to impose restrictions on free speech, no explicit prohibition of hate speech was ultimately adopted.[14] This does not imply that European states advocated for unrestricted freedom of speech but, rather, that they were receptive to limitations on rights, such as freedom of expression, viewed, however, as a blanket prohibition of what is now recognised as hate speech under IHRL as susceptible to misuse.[15] The Soviet Bloc's proposal was particularly contentious as Western nations perceived it as an attempt to justify extensive censorship prevalent in that geopolitical region at that time, rather than to advance equality and non-discrimination. Instead of endorsing a complete ban, Articles 29(2) and 30 of the UDHR were considered adequate safeguards against the abuse of freedom of expression, corresponding respectively to Article 10(2) and Article 17 of the ECHR.

Article 29(2) provides:

> In the exercise of his rights and freedoms, everyone shall be subject only to such limitations as are determined by law solely for the purpose of

11 Lerner (n 9)

12 ICERD Reservations and Declarations <https://treaties.un.org/Pages/ViewDetails.aspx?src=TREATY&mtdsg_no=IV-2&chapter=4&clang=_en#EndDec> accessed 28 July 2024

13 Jacob Mchangama, 'The Sordid Origin of Hate-Speech Laws' (2011) 170 Policy Review 45 <https://www.hoover.org/research/sordid-origin-hate-speech-laws> accessed 28 July 2024

14 Jacob Mchangama and Natalie Alkiviadou, 'Hate Speech and the European Court of Human Rights: Whatever Happened to the Right to Offend, Shock or Disturb?' (2021) 21(4) Human Rights Law Review 1012

15 Mchangama and Alkiviadou (n 14)

> securing due recognition and respect for the rights and freedoms of others and of meeting the just requirements of morality, public order and the general welfare in a democratic society.

Article 30, meanwhile, provides:

> Nothing in this Declaration may be interpreted as implying for any State, group or person any right to engage in any activity or to perform any act aimed at the destruction of any of the rights and freedoms set forth herein.

2 Hate Speech: The International and European Definitional Framework

While universally recognised as a form of harmful expression, *hate speech* eludes a singular, universally accepted definition,[16] while the conceptualisation of its harm varies across countries and regions.[17] As noted by the 2019 United Nations Strategy and Plan of Action on Hate Speech, 'there is no international legal definition of hate speech, and the characterization of what is "hateful" is controversial and disputed.'[18] The European Parliament has acknowledged the deficiencies resulting from the lack of a unified definition of *hate speech* and has urged the Commission to explore the feasibility of establishing a common legal definition of hate speech within the European Union,[19] which has yet to happen. As such, on an international and European level, definitions of hate speech are scarce.

The ICCPR, the ICERD, the European Union's Framework Decision and the Additional Protocol are the international/regional laws which directly prohibit forms of hate speech without referring to the term itself.[20] As reflected in the footnotes to each document, these have been referred to by the ECtHR in hate speech case law. The ECtHR has also referred

16 See, amongst others, Natalie Alkiviadou, 'Regulating Hate Speech in the EU' in Stavros Assimakopoulos, Fabienne H. Baider and Sharon Millar (eds), *Online Hate Speech in the EU: A Discourse Analytical Perspective* (1st edn, Springer Briefs in Linguistics 2017); Audun Fladmoe and Marjan Nadim, 'Silenced by Hate? Hate Speech as a Social Boundary to Free Speech' in Arnfinn H. Midtbøen, Kari Steen-Johnsen and Kjersti Thorbjørnsrud (eds), *Boundary Struggles: Contestations of Free Speech in the Norwegian Public Sphere* (Cappelen Damm Akademisk 2017); Iginio Gagliardone and others, *Countering Online Hate Speech* (UNESCO 2015)

17 See, amongst others, Erik Bleich, *Freedom of Expression versus Racist Hate Speech: Explaining Differences between High Court Regulations in the USA and Europe* (1st edn, Routledge 2015), Michel Rosenfeld, 'Hate Speech in Constitutional Jurisprudence: A Comparative Analysis' (2002–2003) 24 Cardozo Law Review 4

18 United Nations Strategy and Plan of Action on Hate Speech <https://www.un.org/en/hate-speech/un-strategy-and-plan-of-action-on-hate-speech> accessed 2 September 2024

19 Motion for a European Parliament Resolution on Establishing a Common Legal Definition of Hate Speech in the EU B8–0172/2017 (2017)

20 *Lenis v Greece* App no 47833/20 (ECHR 27 June 2023) para 15

to jurisprudence of the Court of Justice of the European Union (CJEU) and to soft law, such as recommendations/resolutions of the Parliamentary Assembly of the Council of Europe,[21] the Council of Europe Committee of Ministers, the European Commission Against Racism and Intolerance (ECRI), the United Nations Special Rapporteur on the Promotion and Protection of the Right to Freedom of Opinion and Expression (SROFE), as well as jurisprudence or General Comments of the Human Rights Committee (HRC), which is the monitoring body of the ICCPR and the Committee on the Elimination of Racial Discrimination (CERD), which is the monitoring body of the ICERD.[22] Both committees receive individual complaints on alleged violations of articles found in the ICCPR and the ICERD, respectively.

2.1 *Hate Speech and the Council of Europe*

The ECHR does not contain a 'hate speech' clause, as is the case with Article 20(2) of the ICCPR, which prohibits 'any advocacy of national, racial or religious hatred that constitutes incitement to discrimination, hostility or violence.' Nevertheless, the Council of Europe does have the Additional Protocol. This document entered into force in 2006. At the time of writing, 36 countries have ratified the Additional Protocol, and 10 have signed it. It calls parties to adopt measures to criminalise the dissemination of racist and xenophobic material, racist and xenophobic threat, racism- and xenophobia-motivated insult and denial, gross minimisation, approval or justification of genocide or of crimes against humanity.

Article 2 defines *racist and xenophobic material* as

> [a]ny written material, any image or any other representation of ideas or theories, which advocates, promotes or incites hatred, discrimination or violence, against any individual or group of individuals, based on race, colour, descent or national or ethnic origin, as well as religion if used as a pretext for any of these factors.

Several provisions of the Protocol reflect considerations of free speech. Regarding the dissemination of racist and xenophobic material, a state party may reserve the right not to impose criminal liability if the material is neither hateful nor violent and if other effective remedies are available. For racist and xenophobic insults, a state party may require that the insult expose individuals to hatred, contempt or ridicule, or it may opt not to apply this article in

21 These have been particularly referred to in cases involving online hate speech: *Sanchez v France* App no 45581/15 (ECHR, 15 May 2023) para 74 and *Delfi AS v Estonia* App no 64569/09 (ECHR, 16 June 2015) para 147

22 For an example of a case referring extensively to different international/regional documents, see *Sanchez v France* App no 45581/15 (ECHR, 15 May 2023)

whole or in part. Additionally, a safeguard is included for the denial or minimisation of genocide or crimes against humanity, allowing states parties to criminalise such speech only if it incites hatred, discrimination or violence, or to choose not to apply this article in whole or in part. Furthermore, the Protocol's Explanatory Note clarifies that, with the exception of insults, all acts covered by the Protocol must be public in order to comply with Article 8 of the ECHR on the right to private and family life.[23] The enhanced free speech protections found in the Protocol are assumingly linked to the fact that it is dedicated to the use of criminal law to deal with online racism and xenophobia, an approach which may result in fines and/or prison sentences. Nevertheless, the criminalisation of speech is inherently dangerous and amplified when the threshold for severity, as established in the Protocol, is set as low as mere insults. While states parties retain the discretion to invoke the Protocol in cases where speech incites hatred, discrimination or violence, its provisions permit the criminalisation of simple insults, even without incitement.

There are also some non-binding documents on a Council of Europe level which provide some sort of definitional overview of hate speech. General Policy Recommendation 15 on Combatting Hate Speech (2015) of the ECRI notes that *hate speech* is

> the advocacy, promotion or incitement, in any form, of the denigration, hatred or vilification of a person or group of persons, as well as any harassment, insult, negative stereotyping, stigmatization or threat in respect of such a person or group of persons and the justification of all the preceding types of expression, on the ground of race, colour, descent, national or ethnic origin, age, disability, language, religion or belief, sex, gender, gender identity, sexual orientation and other personal characteristics or status.

This definition was offered by ECRI for the purposes of the Recommendation, while recognising that *hate speech* is understood in different ways on a national and international level. It is often cited in ECtHR hate speech case law.

Moving to the judicial level, neither the ECtHR nor the former European Commission on Human Rights (EComHR) defined *hate speech*. The actual term *hate speech* is referred to in some cases but not in others. A 2020 study which looked at 60 hate speech cases before the now-defunct EComHR and the ECtHR between 1979 and 2020 found that the actual term 'hate speech' was referred to in 21 out of the 60 cases.[24] The first case in which *hate speech* was used as a term was that of *Sürek v Turkey* (1999), in which the applicant, a major shareholder in a weekly review, was prosecuted for two letters published in 1997 on Kurdistan, which were deemed by Turkish authorities to propagate

23 Explanatory Report <https://rm.coe.int/16800d37ae> accessed 1 September 2024 para 29
24 Future of Free Speech: Hate Speech Database <https://futurefreespeech.org//hate-speech-case-database/> accessed 20 September 2024

anti-state propaganda and incite enmity and hatred. However, the Court has yet to provide any substantial definition of *hate speech* that systematically constitutes the conceptual framework of its adjudication on hate speech. The first time it referred to a definition was in *Gűndűz v Turkey* (2003), a case involving speech calling for the implementation of Sharia. The Court understood *hate speech* as 'all forms of expression which spread, incite, promote or justify hatred based on intolerance (including religious intolerance).'[25] The definition referred to in this case was based on ECRI's Recommendation No. R (97) 20 of the Committee of Ministers on Hate Speech, also referred to in the judgement. The inclusion of merely justifying hatred demonstrates the low threshold attached to unacceptable speech. The Court also noted that there 'can be no doubt that concrete expressions constituting hate speech, which may be insulting to particular individuals or groups, are not protected by Article 10 of the Convention.'[26] This low threshold of harm was then further embedded in the 2009 case *Féret v Belgium* (2009). Building on *Gűndűz*, the Court in *Féret* embraced an expansive understanding of *hate speech*, maintaining that it was not necessary for speech to incite violence or other crimes. Instead, the presence of insult, ridicule or slander within the speech is deemed harmful in and of itself, resulting in a particularly low threshold of free speech protection. This allows for the restriction of insulting, ridiculing or slanderous speech, which, for the Court, falls within the ambit of legitimately prohibitable hate speech.

The element of insult in the ambit of hate speech is interesting to look at because the ECtHR has given it varying treatment across cases. For example, *Ibragim Ibragimov and Others v Russia* (2018) concerned the banning of a book authored by Muslim scholar Said Nursi, which had been prohibited on the grounds of allegedly constituting extremist literature. The Court determined that the restriction was unjustified, emphasising that the book conveyed a moderate and non-violent interpretation of Islam. Crucially, the Court observed that:

> [M]erely because a remark may be perceived as offensive or insulting by particular individuals or groups does not mean that it constitutes 'hate speech.' Whilst such sentiments are understandable, they alone cannot set the limits of freedom of expression. The key issue in the present case is thus whether the statements in question, when read as a whole and in their context, could be seen as promoting violence, hatred or intolerance.[27]

Insult was handled differently in *Atamanchuk v Russia* (2020), a case which concerned a journalist and politician who sought relief after being convicted

25 *Gűndűz v Turkey* App no 35071/97 (ECHR, 4 December 2003) para 40
26 *Gűndűz* (n 25) para 41
27 *Ibragim Ibragimov and others v Russia* App nos. 1413/08 and 28621/11 (ECHR, 4 February 2019) para 115

for making derogatory statements against non-Russians, describing them as criminals without inciting violence. The Court followed the *Féret* paradigm, where

> inciting hatred does not necessarily involve an explicit call for an act of violence, or other criminal acts. Attacks on persons committed by insulting, holding up to ridicule or slandering specific groups of the population can be sufficient for the authorities to favour combating xenophobic or otherwise discriminatory speech in the face of freedom of expression exercised in an irresponsible manner.[28]

As such, in the former case, mere insult did not justify restricting speech, whereas, in the latter, the Court permitted restrictions on insulting remarks, framing them within the context of inciting hatred, even without clearly defining the link between insult and hatred. As will be extrapolated on in Chapter 4, it could be reasonably assumed that the distinguishing factor contributing to the varying approaches was that, in the latter case, the speech targeted a specific group based on ethnicity, while the former was a particular depiction of Islam.

Lilliendahl v Iceland (2020), a case involving transphobic and homophobic speech, was the first time in its jurisprudence in which the Court attempted to tackle the question of hate speech directly, posing the following question:

> *Did the applicant's comments amount to 'hate speech' within the meaning of the Court's case-law?*[29]

Unfortunately, the Court provided an overview of hate speech through a hierarchical classification rather than a substantive look into what hate speech entails. The first 'category' of speech includes what the Court described as the 'gravest forms of hate speech,'[30] which is excluded from any protection under Article 17 of the ECHR on the prohibition of abuse of rights. The second category encompasses 'less grave forms of hate speech,'[31] which remains within the scope of Article 10 but can be restricted by contracting states. For the ECtHR, this category includes not only calls for violence or other criminal acts but also insults, ridicule and slander aimed at combatting 'prejudicial speech within the context of permitted restrictions on freedom of expression.'[32] The Court concluded that determining whether speech is hate speech depends

28 *Atamanchuk v Russia* App no 4493/11 (ECHR, 11 February 2020) para 52
29 *Lilliendahl v Iceland* App no 29297/18 (ECHR, 12 May 2020) para 32
30 *Lilliendahl* (n 29) para 34
31 *Lilliendahl* (n 29) para 35
32 *Lilliendahl* (n 29) para 36

on an assessment of both the content of the expression and the manner of its delivery. As we will see in Chapters 4 and 5, this assessment has not been substantially effectuated in the large majority of cases.

Strasbourg's lacking definitional framework of hate speech has been deemed 'unsatisfactory from the point of judicial interpretation, doctrinal development and general predictability and foreseeability.'[33] It could also be argued that the absence of this definition has contributed to the rather-controversial judgements discussed in Chapters 4 and 5, which arguably go against the very notion of free speech.

2.2 *Hate Speech and the United Nations*

Article 20(2) of the ICCPR prohibits 'any advocacy of national, racial or religious hatred that constitutes incitement to discrimination, hostility or violence.' The Rabat Plan of Action on the Prohibition of Advocacy of National, Racial or Religious Hatred (RPA), which was adopted in 2012 by a group of experts appointed by the United Nations, emphasises that the application of Article 20(2) requires a high threshold.[34] The RPA clarifies that in order to assess the severity of hatred and determine whether the high threshold is met, factors to be considered include 'the cruelty of what is said or the harm advocated and the frequency, amount, and extent of the communications.'[35] This is further supported by the 2012 Report of the SROFE, which asserts that 'the threshold of the types of expression that would fall under the provisions of Article 20(2) should be high and solid.'[36] The dual nature of Article 20, addressing both the prohibition of war propaganda in Part 1 and the prohibition of advocacy of national, racial, or religious hatred in Part 2, suggests that it involves particularly severe forms of speech.

Article 4 of the ICERD prohibits, amongst other things, 'all dissemination of ideas based on racial superiority or hatred, incitement to racial discrimination as well as acts of violence or incitement to such acts against any race or group of persons of another colour or ethnic origin.' General Recommendation 35 of

33 Tarlach McGonagle, 'The Council of Europe against Online Hate Speech: Conundrums and Challenges. Expert Paper. Belgrade: Ministry of Culture and Information' *Council of Europe* (2013) 10 <https://rm.coe.int/16800c170f> accessed 1 November 2024

34 'Rabat Plan of Action on the Prohibition of Advocacy of National, Racial or Religious Hatred that Constitutes Incitement to Discrimination, Hostility or Violence' (2002) para 22 <https://www.ohchr.org/sites/default/files/Rabat_draft_outcome.pdf> accessed 30 November 2024

35 Rabat Plan of Action (n 34) para 22

36 'Report of the Special Rapporteur on the Promotion and Protection of the Right to Freedom of Opinion and Expression' (2012) A/67/357, para 45 <https://documents.un.org/doc/undoc/gen/n12/501/25/pdf/n1250125.pdf> accessed 10 November 2024

the CERD extrapolates on who is considered part of a racial group, including, amongst others

> [I]ndigenous peoples, descent-based groups, and immigrants or non-citizens, including migrant domestic workers, refugees and asylum seekers, as well as speech directed against women members of these and other vulnerable groups . . . [including] persons belonging to certain ethnic groups who profess or practice a religion different from the majority.[37]

Unlike the Additional Protocol and the Framework Decision discussed later, which function exclusively as instruments of criminal law, the legal approaches under the two United Nations articles differ in their chosen mechanisms. In terms of Article 20(2) ICCPR, General Comment 11 of the HRC provides that states parties are obliged to adopt necessary legislative measures prohibiting the actions referred to in Article 20 of the ICCPR.[38] The General Comment asserts that to guarantee the efficient and effective enforcement of Article 20, states parties should enact legislation that classifies the advocacy described in Article 20(2) as contrary to public policy, while also establishing appropriate sanctions for any violations of this law.[39] In relation to the appropriate sanctions reference, 'the article, thus, does not require criminal penalties, at least not for less serious forms of hate advocacy,'[40] since the word 'appropriate' is used rather than 'criminal.'

Article 4 has been characterised as 'the most important article in the Convention'[41] and should be applied through 'criminal laws and other legal provisions.'[42] CERD's General Recommendation 35 provides that

37 CERD General Recommendation 35, 'Combatting Racist Hate Speech' (2013) CERD/C/GC/35, paras 6, 9 <https://documents.un.org/doc/undoc/gen/g13/471/38/pdf/g1347138.pdf> accessed 15 November 2024

38 HRC General Comment 11, 'Article 20—Prohibition of Propaganda for War and Inciting National, Racial or Religious Hatred' (1994) HRI/GEN/1/Rev.1 at 12, para 1 <https://www.ohchr.org/sites/default/files/Documents/Issues/Opinion/CCPRGeneralCommentNo11.pdf> accessed 1 November 2024

39 HRC (n 38) para 2

40 Sandra Coliver, *Striking a Balance: Hate Speech, Freedom of Expression and Non-Discrimination* (1st edn, Article 19, International Centre against Censorship, University of Essex 1992) 31

41 Drew Mahalic and Joan Gambee Mahalic, 'The Limitation Provisions of the International Convention on the Elimination of all Forms of Racial Discrimination' (1987) 9(1) Human Rights Quarterly 89

42 *Gelle v Denmark*, Communication no 34/2004 (CERD, 15 March 2006) CERD/C/68/D/34/2004, para 7.3. This was reiterated in *Jama v Denmark*, Communication no 041/2008 (CERD, 21 August 2009); *Adan v Denmark*, Communication no 43/2008 (CERD, 13 August 2010) and *TBB-Turkish Union v Germany*, Communication no 48/2010 (CERD, 26 February 2013)

'as a minimum requirement and without prejudice to further measures, comprehensive legislation against racial discrimination, including civil and administrative law as well as criminal law, is indispensable to combating racist hate speech effectively.'[43] When it comes to this article, the very low threshold of speech incorporated therein renders the use of criminal law unsuitable. Nevertheless, in *Gelle v Denmark* (2006), the CERD observed:

> [I]t does not suffice, for purposes of Article 4 of the Convention, merely to declare acts of racial discrimination punishable on paper. Rather, criminal laws and other legal provisions prohibiting racial discrimination must also be effectively implemented by the competent national tribunals and other State institutions. This obligation is implicit in Article 4 of the Convention.[44]

As such, neither Article 20(2) nor Article 4 is *solely* a criminal law provision, as is the case with the nature of the Framework Decision and the Additional Protocol, but criminal law is an option for the articles' implementation. Hence, justifications for the varying thresholds and speech protection, particularly when comparing instruments, cannot extend too far.

When it comes to non-binding documents, the United Nations Strategy and Plan of Action on Hate Speech describes it as

> any kind of communication in speech, writing or behaviour, that attacks or uses pejorative or discriminatory language to a person or a group on the basis of who they are, in other words, based on their religion, ethnicity, nationality, race, colour, descent, gender or other identified factors.[45]

The preceding text is a rather broad definition, which raises issues regarding the threshold for identifying hate speech, particularly where vague terms like 'pejorative' are concerned. 'Other identified factors' adds flexibility but introduces interpretative ambiguity, potentially leading to inconsistent interpretation. It makes no mention of actual incitement to, for example, violence or hatred. In fact, the term 'hatred' or 'hate' is missing from its conceptualisation of hate speech.

43 CERD, General Recommendation no 35 (n 37) para 8

44 *Gelle v Denmark*, Communication no 34/2004 (CERD, 15 March 2006) CERD/C/68/D/34/2004, para 7.3. This was reiterated in *Jama v Denmark*, Communication no 041/2008 (CERD, 21 August 2009) *Adan v Denmark*, Communication no 43/2008 (CERD, 13 August 2010) and *TBB-Turkish Union v Germany*, Communication no 48/2010 (CERD, 26 February 2013)

45 *Gelle* (n 44)

2.3 *Hate Speech and the European Union*

In 2008, following extensive deliberation, the European Union adopted the Framework Decision. The Framework Decision does not provide a definition of *hate speech*, nor does it refer to the term. Instead, it prohibits

> public incitement to violence or hatred directed against a group of persons or a member of such a group defined by reference to race, colour, religion, descent or national or ethnic origin.

Article 1(2) grants member states the liberty to punish the aforementioned actions and/or expressions only when they are carried out in a way 'likely to disturb public order or which is threatening, abusive or insulting.'

Article 1 also punishes conduct which publicly condones, denies or grossly trivialises crimes of genocide, crimes against humanity and war crimes, as set out in the Statute of the International Criminal Court as well as the Charter of International Military Tribunal, when such actions are directed towards a group or an individual identified by race, colour, religion, descent or national or ethnic origin and when expressed in a manner that is likely to incite violence or hatred against the group or its members.

The Framework Decision punishes the public incitement to violence or hatred and does not extend to discrimination, as referred to in Article 20(2) ICCPR, discussed in the following. The threshold is further elevated by incorporating provisions that allow states to restrict speech that disturbs public order and/or is threatening, abusive or insulting, thereby incorporating further conditions to what can be prohibited or not, adding further free speech safety nets. This heightened threshold of protection is likely reflective of the necessity for a clear and specific intent to incite violence or hatred, recognising the serious implications of criminal penalties and the need to avoid overly broad or vague restrictions that could unduly infringe on free speech rights in a criminal law setting. As such, the Framework Decision is tailored in such a manner as to ensure that only the most severe forms of hate speech, those that directly incite violence or hatred against specific groups, are subject to criminal sanctions. By setting a higher bar for criminal liability, the Framework Decision seeks to ensure that criminal law interventions are reserved for the most harmful expressions and, as such, maintain a stringent standard that respects the principles of legal certainty and proportionality in the application of criminal law. Nevertheless, the combination of criminal law and 'speech crimes' is inherently problematic. For example, the Rabat Plan of Action notes that 'criminal sanctions related to unlawful forms of expression should be seen as last resort measures to be applied only in strictly justifiable situations.'[46] So despite the elevated free speech protection, care should still be taken with the

46 Rabat Plan of Action (n 34) para 34

treatment and use of the Framework Decision. The same reasoning applies to the heightened protection of speech provided by the Council of Europe's Additional Protocol, which is also a criminal law instrument, and to national criminal laws on hate speech.

Despite the Framework Decision, the understanding, and treatment, of hate speech is not equal across the European Union, with some examples given in Section 3 of this chapter. The obligations for content removal in the co-regulatory framework established by the European Union's Code of Conduct on Countering Illegal Hate Speech Online emanate from the Framework Decision's understanding of *hate*. The Code notes that, in order to prevent the spread of illegal hate speech, it is essential to ensure that relevant national laws transposing the Framework Decision are fully enforced by member states in both the online and the offline environment. It underlines that, while the effective application of provisions criminalising hate speech is dependent on a robust system of sanctions against perpetrators of hate speech, this work must be complemented with actions geared towards ensuring that illegal hate speech online is expeditiously acted upon by online intermediaries and social media platforms upon receipt of a valid notification and in an appropriate time frame.

As such, the Code endorses a high threshold of harm, requiring severe and demonstrable effects before intervention is warranted. The European Union's choice of reference to the Framework Decision in the Code of Conduct is peculiar in that the former is a criminal law instrument, and the latter a co-regulatory document requesting removal of online content. The consequences of the two documents are thus very different. This could simply emanate from its lack of a better document for referral. However, nothing was stopping the European Commission from adding its own definition in the Code. By contrast, as demonstrated in Section 4, platform standards/guidelines often set a lower bar for content moderation, allowing for the removal of speech that might not reach the level of harm envisaged by the Framework Decision's definitional complexity. Pertaining to the Digital Services Act (DSA), no effort was made for a definition, and no direct reference was made to the Framework Decision as a benchmark for defining *hate speech*, as was the case in the Code of Conduct. The DSA imposes a duty on platforms swiftly to assess and remove illegal content, including 'hate speech,' but also 'unlawful discriminatory content.'[47] However, the DSA refrains from clearly defining 'illegal content,' instead delegating significant discretion to platforms to determine the illegality of specific material. Such illegality may stem from either national law which complies with EU law or EU law which platforms are

47 Press Release, 'Digital Services: Landmark Rules Adopted for a Safer, Open Online Environment' *European Parliament* (2022) <https://www.europarl.europa.eu/news/en/press-room/20220701IPR34364/digital-services-landmark-rules-adopted-for-a-safer-open-online-environment> accessed 24 November 2024

required to interpret and apply. The disparities in national approaches generate substantial legal uncertainty and pose significant challenges for digital content providers operating within Europe.[48] The reference to EU law incorporates the Framework Decision in the context of hate speech without specifically stipulating it in its text or footnotes. The DSA does refer to platforms' obligations under the Code of Conduct, which, in turn, works around the definition of the Framework Decision. The particularly contentious nature of hate speech necessitates some kind of definition/conceptualisation, at least in major pieces of legislation, such as the DSA.

The Fundamental Rights Agency (FRA) has referred to *hate speech* as

> the incitement and encouragement of hatred, discrimination, or hostility towards an individual that is motivated by prejudice against that person because of a particular characteristic.[49]

This definition highlights core elements, such as incitement and encouragement. The focus on incitement suggests that for speech to be considered hate speech, it must reach a certain threshold of harm, potentially inciting discriminatory actions or fostering a hostile environment, rather than merely offending or perpetuating stereotypes. Similar to Article 20(2) of the ICCPR, discussed later, but offering lower protection than the Framework Decision, the FRA's definition sets a relatively high threshold which reflects a concern to protect freedom of expression while targeting speech that directly harms or marginalises individuals and groups. The FRA's approach in terms of who is incorporated as a protected group is broad, referring to the targeting of a 'particular characteristic' without specifying the nature of such characteristics. This open-ended phrasing provides flexibility, allowing the definition to encompass various grounds of discrimination, such as race, ethnicity, religion, gender, sexual orientation, disability and other social identities without being exhaustive. This broadness can be seen as a strength, enabling the definition to adapt to new forms of prejudice and societal changes. However, it may also lead to challenges in application, as it requires further interpretative guidance to ensure consistent enforcement and understanding across jurisdictions. It also necessitates careful consideration of context, intent and impact when determining whether speech constitutes hate speech, ensuring that only genuinely harmful expressions are captured under this definition. As such, the FRA has established a relatively high threshold for the protection of free speech, particularly considering that this definition, unlike those of the Framework Decision and the Additional Protocol, is not exclusively designed for a criminal law instrument.

48 Ronan Ó Fathaigh, Natali Helberger and Naomi Appelman, 'The Perils of Legally Defining Disinformation' (2021) 10(4) Internet Policy Review 14

49 Fundamental Rights Agency, 'Hate Speech and Hate Crimes against LGBT Persons' <https://fra.europa.eu/sites/default/files/fra_uploads/1226-Factsheet-homophobia-hate-speech-crime_EN.pdf> accessed 10 October 2024

3 The Meaning of Hate Speech in Selective National Legislation[50]

Following World War II, hate speech bans were incorporated into several European criminal statutes under the heading of 'incitement to hatred.'[51] This was rarely incorporated into constitutional texts in older democracies.[52] This changed, with some newer constitutions directly prohibiting hate speech, even if it was not defined as such. This section gives a brief overview of provisions in criminal law and constitutional provisions for purposes of demonstrating the variations of dealing with hate speech and related themes. In terms of criminal law, in Germany, hate speech (although not referred to as such) is regulated under Section 130 of the German Criminal Code (Strafgesetzbuch), which criminalises incitement to hatred:

> Whosoever, in a manner capable of disturbing the public peace, incites hatred against a national, racial, religious group or a group defined by their ethnic origins, or against segments of the population, or calls for violent or arbitrary measures against them; or assaults the human dignity of others by insulting, maliciously maligning, or defaming segments of the population shall be liable to imprisonment.[53]

French law, under the Law on the Freedom of the Press of 1881, addresses hate speech by criminalising 'speech that incites discrimination, hatred or violence against a person or group of persons on the grounds of their origin or their membership or non-membership of a particular ethnic group, nation, race or religion.'[54] France criminalises the denial of crimes against humanity as defined in the Charter of the International Military Tribunal by the 1990 Gayssot Act.[55] The Spanish Criminal Code is particularly broad. It prohibits conduct including directly or indirectly fostering, promoting or inciting hatred, hostility, discrimination or violence against people due to certain protected characteristics, the distribution of hateful material and public revisionism,

50 For a comparative study on the criminalization of speech in 24 jurisdictions, see Eric Heinze (ed), *Criminalising Hate Speech: A Comparative Study* (T.M.C Asser Press 2024)

51 For example, Czech *propagace hnutí*, French *incitation à la haine*, German *Volksverhetzung*, Russian *возбуждение ненависти* and Swedish *hets mot folkgrupp*. For more on this, see: Uladzislau Belavusau, 'Hate Speech' in Raine Grote, Rüdiger Wolfrum and Frauke Lachenmann (eds), *The Max Plank Encyclopedia of Comparative Constitutional Law* (OUP 2017)

52 Belavusau (n 51)

53 Criminal Code in the version published on 13 November 1998 (Federal Law Gazette I, p 3322) as last amended by Article 2 of the Act of 22 November 2021 (Federal Law Gazette I, p 4906) <https://www.gesetze-im-internet.de/englisch_stgb/englisch_stgb.html> accessed 2 September 2024

54 Article 24, Law of July 29, 1881 on the Freedom of the Press <https://www.legifrance.gouv.fr/loda/id/LEGITEXT000006070722> accessed 4 October 2024

55 Law no 90–615 of July 13, 1990, Aimed at Suppressing all Racist, Anti-Semitic or Xenophobic Acts <https://www.legifrance.gouv.fr/loda/id/JORFTEXT000000532990> accessed 4 October 2024

negationism and denialism. While it is beyond the scope of this book to conduct an extensive analysis of Article 10, interesting elements include the fact that incitement to hatred can be direct or indirect. The element of 'indirectness' is speech-restrictive in that even indirect speech can be criminally punishable. The inclusion of ***indirect incitement*** in the Spanish Criminal Code represents an expansive scope of criminal liability in hate speech regulation. This provision criminalises not only explicit calls to hatred or violence but also more subtle forms of communication that may indirectly foster such outcomes. The concept of indirectness captures conduct where the connection to harm is less immediate but still deemed influential. While this broadens the capacity to address hate speech, it also raises significant concerns regarding potential overreach and the risk of chilling effects on freedom of expression. By extending liability to indirect acts, the provision underscores the tension between safeguarding societal values and maintaining robust protections for speech. This expansive approach raises significant questions about the balance between preventing harm and safeguarding free expression. It also illustrates how different jurisdictions, even within the Council of Europe region, interpret the threshold for harmful speech, a theme that resonates throughout the ECtHR's jurisprudence, as explored later in this book. Further, the Spanish Criminal Code incorporates a broad range of protected characteristics ranging from ethnicity to illness, while negationism and revisionism are only punishable if they promote or encourage a climate of violence, hostility, hatred or discrimination. The part on negationism and revisionism contains elements of harm similar to those found in Article 20(2) of the ICCPR. All elements of the Spanish hate speech clause must occur for reasons of racism, anti-Semitism or others related to ideology in order for them to be criminally punishable.[56] The Norwegian Criminal Code is one of the few legal documents that directly refer to the term 'hate speech.'[57] Section 185 therein provides for a prison sentence of up to three years for any person who 'with intent or gross negligence publicly makes a discriminatory or hateful statement.' Such a statement is defined in the Code as 'threatening or insulting a person or promoting hate, persecution or contempt for another colour based on protected characteristics, specifically, skin colour or national or ethnic origin, religion or life stance, homosexual orientation or reduced functional capacity.'

As noted earlier, the reference to hate speech (or related terms) in constitutional text is rare, but not completely absent. The Constitution of Slovenia addresses hate speech in Article 63, titled 'Prohibition of Incitement

56 Article 510, Criminal Code of Spain, Official State Gazette Number 281, 25 November 1995 <https://documents.law.yale.edu/sites/default/files/criminal_code_spain.pdf> accessed 4 October 2024

57 The Penal Code, Part II. Criminal Acts, Section 185 'Hate Speech' <https://lovdata.no/dokument/NLE/lov/2005-05-20-28/KAPITTEL_2#KAPITTEL_2> accessed 30 October 2024

to Discrimination and Intolerance,' which provides that 'any incitement to national, racial, religious, or other discrimination, and the inflaming of national, racial, religious, or other hatred and intolerance, are unconstitutional.' There are also some interesting examples beyond Europe, particularly because constitutional provisions are found in newer constitutions. For example, Article 57 of the Venezuelan Constitution, on freedom of expression, includes a limitation paragraph which provides, amongst others, that 'discriminatory messages or those promoting religious intolerance are not permitted.'[58] Article 19 of the Constitution of Ecuador, on media freedom, notes that 'it is forbidden to broadcast advertisements that foment violence, discrimination, racism, drug addiction, sexism, religious or political intolerance and all that undermines rights.'[59] A more detailed look is now given to South Africa due to a recent case by the country's constitutional court. The South African Constitution specifically addresses hate speech in Section 16, which deals with freedom of expression. While the Constitution broadly protects freedom of expression, it explicitly excludes certain forms of speech from this protection. According to Section 16(2) of the Constitution:

> The right in subsection (1) does not extend to . . .
> (c) advocacy of hatred that is based on race, ethnicity, gender, or religion, and that constitutes incitement to cause harm.[60]

This South African definition of *hate speech* emphasises that not all forms of expression are protected, particularly those that advocate hatred and incite harm based on specified grounds. The clause establishes a narrow but clear boundary for what constitutes hate speech, focusing specifically on advocacy of hatred that directly incites harm. The constitutional provision is further operationalised through legislation, like the Promotion of Equality and Prevention of Unfair Discrimination Act (PEPUDA), which provides additional details and mechanisms for addressing hate speech in South Africa. Section 10 therein prohibits hurtful, hateful and harmful speech. Relevant to this section is the case of *Qwelane v South African Human Rights Commission* (2019), which involved a 2008 publication by Jon Qwelane, a well-known anti-apartheid activist and journalist in the *Sunday Sun*. The article was titled 'Call me names but gay is not okay . . .' and used homophobic language and was accompanied by a cartoon comparing homosexuality to bestiality. The Supreme Court of Appeal found that Section 10

58 Venezuela (Bolivarian Republic of) 1999 (rev. 2009) <https://www.constituteproject.org/constitution/Venezuela_2009> accessed 1 September 2024

59 The Constitution of Ecuador 2008 (rev. 2021) <https://www.constituteproject.org/constitution/Ecuador_2021> accessed 1 September 2024

60 'The Constitution of the Republic of South Africa 1996' <https://www.justice.gov.za/constitution/SAConstitution-web-eng.pdf> accessed 20 October 2024

of the PEPUDA went beyond what was constitutionally permissible under Section 16(2) of the Constitution. However, the Constitutional Court of South Africa subsequently ruled that Section 10 was, in fact, constitutional, apart from its reference to 'hurtful.'[61] It noted that 'if speech that is merely hurtful is considered hate speech, this sets the bar rather low.'[62] *Qwelane* highlights the difficulties in ensuring that hate speech laws remain proportional, and thresholds robust. This case sets a good paradigm of how courts must carefully balance free expression and societal harm, a challenge that is equally prominent in ECtHR jurisprudence.

4 The Meaning of Hate Speech on Selective Social Media Platforms

In recent years, the proliferation of digital platforms has reshaped the landscape of hate speech, challenging traditional definitions and regulatory frameworks. Online hate speech differs significantly from its offline counterpart, due to the unique affordances of digital platforms, such as (semi-)anonymity/pseudonymity, possibility of a vast reach and accessibility.[63] Social media platforms play a crucial role in setting the boundaries of acceptable speech, often with significant consequences for public discourse,[64] with tech companies like Meta, X, YouTube and Reddit establishing their own policies to combat hate speech. The algorithms used by digital platforms to identify and moderate hate speech introduce further complexity as automated systems struggle to capture the nuances of context and intent. This technological revolutionalisation of hate speech has prompted scholars to question how definitions are operationalised in practice, highlighting a gap between theoretical understanding and the realities of enforcement.[65]

At the platform level, definitions of *hate speech* can be particularly extensive. Meta states that hateful conduct encompasses

> direct attacks against people—rather than concepts or institutions—based on what we call protected characteristics: race, ethnicity, national origin,

61 *Qwelane v South African Human Rights Commission and Another* (CCT 13/20) [2021] para 139

62 *Qwelane* (n 61)

63 Koustuv Saha, Eshwar Chandrasekharan and Munmun De Choudhury, 'Prevalence and Psychological Effects of Hateful Speech in Online College Communities' (2019) WebSci Proceedings of the 10th ACM Conference on Web Science <https://dl.acm.org/doi/10.1145/3292522.3326032> accessed 1 October 2024

64 See, for example, Tarleton Gillespie, 'The Politics of Platforms' (2010) 12 New Media and Society 3; Tarleton Gillespie, *Custodians of the Internet: Platforms, Content Moderation, and the Hidden Decisions that Shape Social Media* (1st edn, Yale University Press 2018); Blake Hallinan, Rebecca Scharlach and Limor Shifman, 'Beyond Neutrality: Conceptualizing Platform Values' (2021) 32 Communication Theory 2

65 See, for example, Gillespie (n 64)

> disability, religious affiliation, caste, sexual orientation, sex, gender identity, and serious disease.[66]

Note that the term 'hate speech' was replaced by 'hateful conduct' in major changes which were made to Meta's policy on 7 January 2025.

Additional characteristics, such as age and occupation, are considered protected under the preceding clause if targeted in combination with other protected characteristics, while the policy also protects refugees, migrants, immigrants and asylum-seekers from the 'most severe attacks.' Prohibited content is divided into two tiers, with the first tier incorporating what Meta considers to be the most severe attacks, such as dehumanisation, calls for harm, harmful stereotypes historically linked to intimidation or violence, but also content such as slurs. Tier 2, the less-severe attacks include, amongst others, calls for support for exclusion or segregation, social exclusion, insults and others. As such, Meta's policy protects a wide array of characteristics, including race, religion, gender identity, sexual orientation and lesser-seen categories, such as caste and serious disease, but as will be demonstrated later, it does not provide equal protection amongst such characteristics. By incorporating two tiers of severity, Meta attempts to net a broad spectrum of harmful speech. However, this categorisation introduces complexity, raises free speech concerns, while also making it challenging for users to understand the boundaries of permissible speech. It is beyond the scope of this book to delve into the changes made in 2025 to Meta's policy on hateful conduct. However, a few points are noted as they are relevant to the discussion I put forth regarding the hierarchisation of harm in several instruments. For example, before the 2025 changes, it was prohibited to say that someone has a mental illness due to their gender identity or sexual orientation. The updated policy now allows such allegations and notes thus:

> We do allow allegations of mental illness or abnormality when based on gender or sexual orientation, given political and religious discourse about transgenderism and homosexuality and common non-serious usage of words like 'weird.'

However, for all other protected characteristics, mental characteristics such as allegations of stupidity, intellectual capacity and mental illness is prohibited. Removing the LGBTQ community from this protection on the grounds of religious or political discourse essentially denotes an arbitrariness in the perception of when discourse counts as public discourse and when it does not. Also, when it comes to objectifying speech, the new policy has removed the prohibition of the use of the term 'it' for transgender and non-binary persons, while references to women as household objects or property, or objects more generally, are permissible. At the same time, however, objectifying Black

66 Meta—Hateful Conduct Policy <https://transparency.meta.com/policies/community-standards/hateful-conduct/> accessed 8 January 2024

persons by referring to them, for example, as farm equipment continues to be prohibited. In addition, content which is exclusionary or insulting in the context of discussing political or religious topics, such as trans rights, immigration or homosexuality is now permissible speech. Had Meta undertook a rigorous amendment to its policy based on free speech principles, the discussion on the company's policy changes could be positive in that this could have contributed to a more open public space. However, despite some generic changes, such as the replacement of the term *hate speech* with *hateful conduct* and the removal of self-admission to intolerance based on protected characteristics from the framework of prohibited content, the policy shift is marked by changes which are specifically tailored to permitting content that targets the LGBTQ community and women, thereby creating a hierarchy of protection rather than a more open civic space.

X's policy on hateful conduct incitement includes, *inter alia,* stereotypes, discrimination and harassment, slurs and tropes, dehumanisation and hateful imagery, such as the swastika. Incitement to violence is dealt with under a separate policy. Importantly, the rules note that 'some posts may appear to be hateful when viewed in isolation but may not be when viewed in the context of a larger conversation.' Here it refers to the use of slurs by minority communities themselves for purposes of 'reclaim[ing] terms that were historically used to demean individuals.' The interesting characteristics of X's policy are the nuances when it comes to how terms are used and the context in which they are used. The protected characteristics set out under X's policy are race, ethnicity, national origin, caste, sexual orientation, gender identity, religious affiliation, age and disability or serious disease.[67]

Rule 1 on Reddit notes that 'everyone has a right to use Reddit free of harassment, bullying and threats of violence. Communities and users that incite violence or that promote hate based on identity or vulnerability will be banned.'[68]

Reddit's hate speech policy is rooted in its community-driven ethos, prioritising the prevention of harassment, bullying and threats of violence, while also banning groups that promote hate based on identity or vulnerability. Unlike other platforms, Reddit relies heavily on community self-regulation, with individual subreddits enforcing these policies alongside site-wide rules. This decentralised model can foster strong community standards in some areas but may also lead to variable enforcement due to differing interpretations of the rules by community moderators.

The policy on YouTube states:

> [H]ate speech is not allowed on YouTube. We don't allow content that promotes violence or hatred against individuals or groups based on any of the following attributes, which indicate a protected group status

67 X, Hateful Conduct Policy <https://help.x.com/en/rules-and-policies/hateful-conduct-policy> accessed 8 December 2024

68 Reddit Content Policy <https://redditinc.com/policies/content-policy> accessed 8 December 2024

> under YouTube's policy: Age, caste, disability, ethnicity, gender identity and expression, nationality, race, immigration status, religion, sex/gender, sexual orientation, victims of major violent events and their kin, veteran status.[69]

So YouTube's policy against hate speech includes a long list of protected categories, including immigration status, veteran status and victims of violent events, alongside more commonly recognised characteristics, like race and gender. The broadness of scope marks YouTube's hate speech policy and was the subject of a 2023 report which assessed the hate speech policies of eight social media platforms (including all the aforementioned). The report found a significant expansion in the scope of these policies in terms of the types of content and the list of protected characteristics over time across all platforms examined, including all the previously mentioned ones. It found that during the mid-2000s and early 2010s, platforms primarily prohibited the promotion of hatred and racist speech. In recent years, however, these bans have been extended to include a broad range of potential hate speech, such as harmful stereotypes, conspiracy theories and slurs against protected groups.[70] While the 2025 changes to META's policy may have some elements of a broadening of the scope of protected speech, such as the fact that it now allows for the self-admission of intolerance based on protected characteristics, the changes which target particular groups rather than deal with the entire spectrum of how hate speech should be dealt with do not sit comfortably with the principle of equality and raise issues pertaining to Volokh's 'censorship envy,'[71] discussed in Chapter 2.

As such, in light of legislative developments, such as the DSA, and judicial decisions, such as *Delfi AS v Estonia* (2012), discussed in Chapter 4, corporate actors have become key players in defining and enforcing hate speech norms. Platforms have essentially adopted expansive definitions of *hate speech*, often far exceeding legal standards and principles of IHRL.[72] These private regulations lead to several concerns. Profit-making, private companies who are not subject to IHRL have a key role in deciding what hate speech is and deciphering the boundaries of our freedom of expression, which often

69 YouTube Hate Speech Policy <https://support.google.com/youtube/answer/2801939?hl=en> accessed 9 January 2024

70 Jacob Mchangama, Abby Fanlo and Natalie Alkiviadou, 'Scope Creep: An Assessment of Eight Social Media Platforms' Hate Speech Policy' *Justitia* (2023) <https://futurefreespeech.org/wp-content/uploads/2023/07/Community-Guidelines-Report_Latest-Version_Formated-002.pdf> accessed 17 October 20424

71 Eugene Volokh, 'Censorship Envy' *The Volokh Conspiracy—Reason* (13 November 2023) <https://reason.com/volokh/2023/11/13/censorship-envy-2/> accessed 15 November 2024

72 For more on this, see Jacob Mchangama, Natalie Alkiviadou and Raghav Mendiratta, 'A Framework of First Reference—Decoding a Human Rights Approach to Content Moderation on Social Media' *Justitia* (2021) <https://futurefreespeech.org/a-framework-of-first-reference-decoding-a-human-rights-approach-to-content-moderation-on-social-media/> accessed 2 October 2024

takes place in their digital *agoras.* This could contribute to their adopting a cautious, better-safe-than-sorry approach to regulation, especially when fines are at stake, prioritising the protection of their business models and financial interests. Furthermore, in order to meet such regulatory obligations imposed by laws such as the DSA, and given the sheer quantity of online content, private companies increasingly employ artificial intelligence (AI) for purposes of content moderation. The use of AI in enforcing content removal obligations places free speech at risk, as automated mechanism cannot pick up the nuance of language in the same way that a human moderator can.[73] Also, it risks leading to biased outcomes due to inadequate data and prejudiced datasets, which disproportionately silence members of minority communities. For example, an assessment of AI tools for regulating harmful text found that African American English tweets are twice as likely to be labelled offensive compared to others.[74] This raises serious concerns regarding violations of both the right to freedom of expression and the right to non-discrimination.[75]

5 Hate Speech: Selective Academic Definitions and Conceptualisations

Scholars have grappled with defining hate speech in ways that capture its multifaceted nature while acknowledging the context-dependent boundaries of harmful expression. In academic discourse, numerous definitions have been proposed to describe hate speech. Matsuda conceptualised *hate speech* as containing three central elements, these being that the message is 'of racial inferiority,' is 'directed against historically oppressed groups' and is 'persecutory, hateful, and degrading.'[76] McGonagle suggests that 'virtually all racist and related declensions of noxious, identity-assailing expression could be brought within the wide embrace of the term.'[77] Smolla goes beyond the sphere of racism and defines *hate speech* as a 'generic term that has come to embrace the use of speech attacks based on race, ethnicity, religion, and sexual orientation or preference.'[78] In 'Only Words,' MacKinnon draws parallels between hate speech

73 See, for example, 2021 developments at META <https://about.fb.com/news/2021/12/metas-new-ai-system-tackles-harmful-content/> accessed 14 November 2024

74 Maarten Sap and others, 'The Risk of Racial Bias in Hate Speech' [2019] Proceedings of the 57th Annual Meeting of the Association of Computational Linguistics 1671

75 See, amongst others, Natasha Duarte and Emma J. Llansó, 'Mixed Messages? The Limits of Automated Social Media Content Analysis' [2018] Proceedings of the 1st Conference on Fairness, Accountability and Transparency, PMLR 81; Thiago Oliva Dias and others, 'Fighting Hate Speech, Silencing Drag Queens? Artificial Intelligence in Content Moderation and Risks to LGBTQ Voices Online' (2021) 25(2) Sexuality and Culture

76 Mari J Matsuda, 'Public Response to Racist Speech: Considering the Victim's Story' (1989) 87(8) Michigan Law Review 2357

77 Tarlach McGonagle, 'Wresting Racial Equality from Tolerance of Hate Speech' (2001) 23(21) Dublin University Law Journal 4

78 Rodney A Smolla, 'Academic Freedom, Hate Speech and the Idea of a University' 53(3) Law and Contemporary Problems (1990) 195

and pornography, arguing that hate speech is a tool of control perpetuating racial and gender oppression, entrenching the control of one social group over another.[79]

In light of these sections, although common elements can be identified among various understandings of hate speech, it could be said that 'hate speech seems to be whatever people choose it to mean.'[80] The concept of hate speech remains fraught with definitional ambiguity across international, regional and domestic frameworks, as well as academic circles, reflecting divergent cultural, legal and philosophical traditions. While institutions such as the European Union, the Council of Europe and the United Nations address related phenomena such as racism, xenophobia, incitement to hatred, violence or discrimination, the term 'hate speech' is absent, apart from in non-binding documents and opinion. This lack of definitional clarity is mirrored within organisations themselves. For instance, while the ECtHR references hate speech in select rulings, it has yet to articulate a coherent, universally applicable definition. Instead, the ECtHR identifies contextual markers of hate speech, sometimes applying varying thresholds of severity, as evidenced in the contrasting approaches to insult in *Ibragim Ibragimov and Others* and *Atamanchuk*.

Internationally, pivotal legal instruments further illustrate this fragmentation. Article 20(2) of the ICCPR adopts a relatively stringent test requiring that advocacy of hatred incites discrimination, hostility or violence. Its accompanying RPA further embeds this rigour. Conversely, the ICERD prohibits the mere dissemination of ideas predicated on racial superiority or hatred, thereby casting a broader regulatory net. So even within the same institution, there is a divergence of harm thresholds. On an EU level, the Framework Decision is essential in combatting hate speech but does not include the term itself, focusing instead on incitement to violence or hatred linked to specific protected characteristics. The Code of Conduct and the DSA reference 'illegal hate speech,' drawing an implicit yet significant distinction between actionable and permissible expressions of hate.

Academically, hate speech has been examined through diverse and often conflicting lenses. Matsuda and Delgado characterise hate speech as a vehicle of systemic oppression which targets historically marginalised groups. Others, such as McGonagle and Smolla, adopt a broader range of protected characteristic beyond race, including gender and sexual orientation. These perspectives reflect that while definitions converge on certain core elements, such as incitement to hatred or violence, their application remains highly context-dependent and open to interpretative variability. Digital platforms have further complicated the definitional landscape. Companies like Meta and YouTube adopt

79 Catherine A MacKinnon, *Only Words* (1st edn, Harvard University Press 1996)

80 Roger Kiska, 'Hate Speech: A Comparison Between the European Court of Human Rights and the United States Supreme Court Jurisprudence' (2012) 25(1) Regent University Law Review 110

expansive definitions of *hate speech*, encompassing dehumanising language and exclusionary practices. These policies, driven by corporate priorities of private, profit-making entities rather than legal imperatives, often exceed the thresholds articulated in legislative or treaty frameworks. The fact that these companies are not bound by IHRL raises further concern when it comes to the protection of free speech.

In conclusion, the fragmented and often inconsistent approaches to hate speech across legal, institutional and academic domains reflect a broader struggle to reconcile the right to free expression with the need to mitigate harm. This is further perplexed by the digital age, where the global reach of harmful rhetoric requires adaptability on a practical side and certainty when it comes to the aspect of legitimacy.

6 Defining Hate Speech: The Free Speech–Hate Speech Debate in International and European Law

While international instruments such as the ICCPR explicitly address hate speech through Article 20(2), the ECHR does not include a comparable provision. Nevertheless, the ECtHR has actively engaged with hate speech cases interpreting the Convention's provisions to navigate this issue. As will be further demonstrated in Chapters 3, 4 and 5, according to established ECtHR jurisprudence, the rights enshrined in Article 10(1) are to be interpreted broadly. In *Handyside v the United Kingdom* (1976), the Court affirmed:

> [F]reedom of expression constitutes one of the essential foundations of [a democratic society], one of the basic conditions for its progress and for the development of every man. Subject to paragraph 2 of Article 10 (art. 10–2), it is applicable not only to 'information' or 'ideas' that are favourably received or regarded as inoffensive or as a matter of indifference, but also to those that offend, shock or disturb the state or any sector of the population. Such are the demands of that pluralism, tolerance and broadmindedness without which there is no 'democratic society.'[81]

The Court has consistently highlighted the central importance of free expression in a democratic and pluralistic society, systematically reiterating the *Handyside* principle set out earlier. However, as will be discussed later in this book, the Court has also been assertive in limiting speech it deems harmful. In fact, the Court has developed a considerable body of case law that permits restrictions on 'hate speech' in ways that cast significant doubt on the degree to which offensive, shocking and disturbing speech, as set out in *Handyside*, is genuinely safeguarded under the ECHR. This reality features emphatically in Chapter 4 in particular and is a clear demonstration of the dynamics of the free speech/hate speech link on an ECtHR level.

81 *Handyside v the United Kingdom* App no 5493/72 (ECHR, 7 December 1976) para 49

On a United Nations level, the free speech/hate speech issue has been extrapolated on by the HRC, the CERD and the SROFE. Article 19 of the ICCPR provides that:

1. Everyone shall have the right to hold opinions without interference.
2. Everyone shall have the right to freedom of expression; this right shall include freedom to seek, receive and impart information and ideas of all kinds, regardless of frontiers, either orally, in writing or in print, in the form of art, or through any other media of his choice.
3. The exercise of the rights provided for in paragraph 2 of this article carries with it special duties and responsibilities. It may therefore be subject to certain restrictions, but these shall only be such as are provided by law and are necessary:

   (a) For respect of the rights or reputations of others;
   (b) For the protection of national security or of public order (ordre public), or of public health or morals.

In this realm, the HRC has been faced with cases involving hate speech, for example, in *Faurisson v France* (1996),[82] which was brought by a revisionist who complained that his Article 19 (freedom of expression) rights were violated after he was prosecuted for making, *inter alia*, the following claims:

> I would wish to see that 100 per cent of all French citizens realize that the myth of the gas chambers is a dishonest fabrication ('est une gredinerie'), endorsed by the victorious powers of Nuremberg in 1945–46 and officialized on 14 July 1990 by the current French Government, with the approval of the court historians.[83]

The historian, prosecuted under the anti-revisionist Gayssot Act, presented his case to the HRC, alleging a violation of his freedom of expression. The Committee concluded that anti-Semitic speech could justifiably be restricted to safeguard the rights and freedoms of others, specifically to protect Jews from religious hatred. More specifically, the Committee held thus:

> 'he restrictions placed on the author did not curb the core of his right to freedom of expression, nor did they in any way affect his freedom of research; they were intimately linked to the value they were meant to protect—the right to be free from incitement to racism or anti-semitism; protecting that value could not have been achieved in the circumstances by less drastic means.

82 *Faurisson v France*, Communication no 550/1993 (HRC, 8 November 1996), CCPR/C/58/D/550/1993, para 9.6
83 *Faurisson* (n 82) para 2.6

Article 20(2) of the ICCPR provides that 'any advocacy of national, racial or religious hatred that constitutes incitement to discrimination, hostility or violence shall be prohibited by law.' Seven countries have imposed reservations/declarations on Article 20 generally or Article 20(2) specifically. These are Australia, Belgium, Luxembourg, Malta, New Zealand, the United Kingdom and the United States. Thus, such reservations do not only happen in the free speech 'absolutist' USA. An indicative European example is the reservation of Luxembourg:

> The Government of Luxembourg declares that it does not consider itself obligated to adopt legislation in the field covered by article 20, paragraph 1, and that article 20 as a whole will be implemented taking into account the rights to freedom of thought, religion, opinion, assembly and association laid down in articles 18, 19 and 20 of the Universal Declaration of Human Rights and reaffirmed in articles 18, 19, 21 and 22 of the Covenant.

The HRC highlighted that Article 19 on the right to freedom of expression and Article 20(2), the UN's 'hate speech clause' are 'compatible with and complement each other. The acts that are addressed in Article 20 are all subject to restriction pursuant to Article 19, paragraph 3.'[84] In comparing Article 19 and Article 20, the HRC noted that 'it is with regard to the specific forms of expression indicated in Article 20 that States Parties are obliged to have legal prohibitions.'[85] *Ross v Canada* (2020) involved a former teacher who had been transferred to a non-teaching post as a result of his publication of books and leaflets which were deemed discriminatory against Jews. Here, the HRC underlined that 'restrictions on expression which may fall within the scope of Article 20 must also be permissible under Article 19, paragraph 3.'[86]

In relation to Article 4 of the ICERD, which prohibits, amongst others, the dissemination or racist ideas, 18 countries[87] have imposed declarations/reservations on Article 4 of the ICERD, which, amongst others, mandates that states parties must criminalise the dissemination of ideas grounded in racial superiority or hatred, as well as the incitement of racial discrimination and

84 Human Rights Committee General Comment 34, 'Article 19—Freedom of Opinion and Expression' (2011) CCPR/C/GC/34, para 50 <https://www2.ohchr.org/english/bodies/hrc/docs/gc34.pdf> accessed 16 November 2024

85 Human Rights Committee (n 84) para 52

86 *Ross v Canada*, Communication no 736/1997 CCPR/C/70/D/736/1997 (HRC, 18 October 2000) para 10.6

87 Antigua and Barbuda, Australia, Austria, Bahamas, Belgium, France, Grenada, Ireland, Italy, Japan, Malta, Monaco, Nepal, Papa New Guinea, Switzerland, Tonga, United Kingdom, United States

acts of violence, or the incitement to such acts targeting individuals or groups based on their race, colour or ethnic origin.

The reservation of the USA on Article 4 ICERD provides that:

I. The Senate's advice and consent is subject to the following reservations:

(1) That the Constitution and laws of the United States contain extensive protections of individual freedom of speech, expression and association. Accordingly, the United States does not accept any obligation under this Convention, in particular under articles 4 and 7, to restrict those rights, through the adoption of legislation or any other measures, to the extent that they are protected by the Constitution and laws of the United States.

The CERD has responded to country reservations on Article 4. For example, in the 2018 Concluding Observations to Japan, the CERD held thus:

> The Committee regrets that the State party continues to maintain its reservation to subparagraphs (a) and (b) of article 4, which may affect the full implementation of the Convention (art. 4). Recalling its general recommendation No. 35 (2013) on combatting racist hate speech, which outlines diverse measures to combat racist hate speech effectively while protecting the legitimate right to freedom of expression, the Committee recommends that the State party examine the possibility of withdrawing its reservation to article 4 of the Convention and provide information to the Committee on the precise effect of the reservation.[88]

In its General Recommendation 15 on Measures to Eradicate Incitement to or Acts of Discrimination, the CERD emphasised that 'the prohibition of the dissemination of all ideas based upon racial superiority or hatred is compatible with the right to freedom of opinion and expression.'[89] The CERD's readiness to restrict free speech to protect the rights and freedoms of others, particularly in the context of regulating hate speech, was also evident in *Jewish Community of Oslo et al. v Norway* (2005). This case, which involved a march commemorating Rudolf Hess, considered the interpretation of the 'due regard clause' in Article 4. Specifically, the prohibition of racist speech and activity as delineated in Article 4 must have 'due regard to the Universal Declaration of Human Rights and the rights expressly set forth in Article 5 of this

88 CERD, 'Concluding Observations on the Combined Tenth and Eleventh Periodic Reports of Japan' (2018) CERD/C/JPN/CO/10–11

89 CERD General Recommendation 15, 'Measures to Eradicate Incitement to or Acts of Discrimination' (1994) A/48/18 at 114, para 4

Convention,' which include, among other rights, the freedom of expression. In this case, the CERD held that

> to give the right to freedom of speech a more limited role in the context of Article 4 does not deprive the due regard clause of significant meaning, all the more so since all international instruments that guarantee freedom of expression provide for the possibility, under certain circumstances, of limiting the exercise of this right.[90]

In fact, the CERD held that the 'freedom of speech has been afforded a lower level of protection in cases of racist and hate speech.'[91]

This section has briefly explored the interplay between international and regional legal frameworks on hate speech and free expression, highlighting the varying thresholds of harm and levels of speech protection. These differences underscore the complex role of any institution, including the ECtHR, when seeking to balance freedom of expression with the need to combat hate speech, since ascertaining thresholds is not, in any way, easy. This is rendered even more complicated in the absence of a hate speech clause in the ECHR. This tension forms the core of the book's analysis of the ECtHR's jurisprudence, which will be examined in Chapters 4 and 5.

7 Hate Speech: The Issue of Thematic Hierarchies

Studies have consistently highlighted the prevalence of hate speech against LGBTQ individuals in Europe. For example, ILGA Europe's Annual Review 2024 found that there has been a growing surge of homophobic and transphobic rhetoric, particularly prevalent on social media platforms, where online communities have emerged advocating for the so-called protection of traditional family values and shielding children from sexual education.[92] A 2021 report by the Council of Europe Parliamentary Assembly found that, in recent years, there has been a 'marked increase in hate speech'[93] targeting the LGBT community. In 2020, the United Nations Independent Expert on Sexual Orientation and Gender Identity noted that in the context of the

90 *The Jewish Community of Oslo and others v Norway* Communication no 30/2003, (CERD/C/67/D/30/2003) (CERD, 15 August 2005) para 10.3

91 *The Jewish Community of Oslo and others* (n 90) para 10.5

92 ILGA-Europe, 'Annual Review of the Human Rights Situation of Lesbian, Gay, Bisexual, Trans and Intersex People in Europe and Central Asia' (2022) <https://www.ilga-europe.org/report/annual-review-2022/> accessed 30 October 2024

93 Council of Europe Parliamentary Assembly, 'Combating Rising Hate against LGBTI People in Europe' (2021) <https://assembly.coe.int/LifeRay/EGA/Pdf/TextesProvisoires/2021/20210921-RisingHateLGBTI-EN.pdf> accessed 1 October 2024

pandemic, 'hate speech inciting violence against LGBT persons has been on the rise.'[94]

Notwithstanding this data, sexual orientation and gender identity do not receive equal footing in international and European legislation. However, the ECtHR, through its case law, has underscored the equal severity of homophobic and transphobic speech to racist speech. In *Vejdeland v Sweden* (2012), the ECtHR stipulated that homophobic speech should be prohibited in the same manner as racist speech, stressing that 'discrimination based on sexual orientation is as serious as discrimination based on race, origin or colour.'[95] In *Lilliendahl v Iceland* (2020), it dealt with homophobic and transphobic speech, extending, therefore, protections in the ambit of transphobia as well. However, on a Council of Europe level, amongst others, there is still no legal tool equivalent to the Additional Protocol to the Convention on Cybercrime that incorporates/deals with homophobic and/or transphobic speech. The Additional Protocol only addresses online speech related to racism and xenophobia. The drafters of the Protocol, created in 2003 and adopted in 2006, did not expand the scope of hate speech to include homophobic and transphobic speech.

The Framework Decision represents the first document of its legal magnitude developed and adopted at a European Union level to address hate speech, albeit limited to the areas of racism and xenophobia. While the Framework Decision aims to penalise both hate speech and hate crime, these terms are conspicuously absent from its title and text. Moreover, this document exclusively criminalises specific types of speech which targets race, colour, religion, descent and national or ethnic origin and only considers racist and xenophobic motivations as aggravating circumstances. It does not extend protection to other characteristics, such as sex, gender identity or sexual orientation. Recognising this shortcoming, the European Parliament recommended that the European Commission propose a 'recast' of the Framework Decision to include 'other forms of bias crime and incitement to hatred, including on grounds of sexual orientation and gender identity.'[96] Expressing its general dissatisfaction with the European Union's approach to homophobia, Parliament passed a 2014 resolution addressing homophobia

94 Statement by Victor Madrigal-Borloz 'UN Independent Expert on Protection against Violence and Discrimination based on Sexual Orientation and Gender Identity at the 75th UN General Assembly' (2020) <https://www.ohchr.org/en/statements/2020/10/statement-victor-madrigal-borloz-un-independent-expert-protection-against> accessed 1 September 2024

95 *Vejdeland and others v Sweden* App no 1813/07 (ECHR, 9 February 2012) para 55

96 European Parliament: Joint Motion for a Resolution on Strengthening the Fight against Racism, Xenophobia and Hate Crime (11 March 2013) (2013/2543(RSP)) <https://www.europarl.europa.eu/doceo/document/RC-7-2013-0121_EN.html?redirect> accessed 4 November 2024

and discrimination based on sexual orientation and gender identity.[97] In this Resolution, Parliament argued that the EU currently lacks a comprehensive policy for protecting the fundamental rights of LGBTI people.[98] Consequently, it called on the European Commission, member states and relevant agencies to collaborate on a comprehensive multiannual policy to safeguard the fundamental rights of LGBTI persons. In 2019, the European Parliament adopted a resolution on the issue of public discrimination and hate speech against LGBTI people, including LGBTI free zones in Poland. Amongst others, the 2019 resolution condemned hate speech by public authorities and elected officials against hate speech.[99]

In her 2020 State of the Union address, the president of the European Commission noted that the Commission would extend the list of EU-level crimes to include all forms of hate crime and hate speech, whether based on race, religion, gender or sexuality. The president also mentioned that the European Commission would work to strengthen racial equality laws without acknowledging the existing imbalances and gaps in equality laws concerning other protected characteristics, which urgently need reconfiguration to ensure the same level of protection provided to race.[100] Nevertheless, since 2000, the *status quo* is that homophobia (but not transphobia) has only been addressed within the employment framework,[101] while it was entirely overlooked in the 2008 Framework Decision concerning hate speech and hate crime.

As previously noted, the mechanisms that exist on a United Nations level to tackle hate speech are Article 4 ICERD and Article 20(2) ICCPR, as well as Article 19 of the ICCPR, which provide for restrictions on the freedom of expression for the respect of the rights or reputations of others, the protection of national security or of public order or of public health or morals. These articles collectively cover speech targeting ethnic, racial and religious characteristics. There are no equivalent conventions or articles which seek to protect victims who are targeted due to other characteristics, such as sexual orientation or gender identity.

In a 2021 report, the SROFE dealt with the aspect of sexist hate speech for the first time in the mandate of this position. Specifically, Khan looked at

97 European Parliament Resolution of 4 February 2014 on the EU Roadmap against Homophobia and Discrimination on Grounds of Sexual Orientation and Gender Identity (2013/2183(INI)) <https://www.europarl.europa.eu/doceo/document/TA-7-2014-0062_EN.html> accessed 14 November 2024

98 European Parliament Resolution (n 97)

99 European Parliament: Resolution on Public Discrimination and Hate Speech against LGBTI People, including LGBTI Free Zones, 2019/2933 (RSP)

100 European Commission, 'The Commission Proposes to Extend the List of 'EU Crimes' to Hate Speech and Hate Crime' (2021) <https://ec.europa.eu/commission/presscorner/detail/en/ip_21_6561> accessed 14 October 2024

101 Employment Equality Directive (Directive 2000/78/EC)

issues which restrict women's right to freedom of expression and noted hate speech as one of them, referring to it as 'gendered hate speech.'[102] Her report underlines that such speech must be tackled under IHRL and refers to Article 20(2) of the ICCPR, noting that

> although gender and sex are not mentioned in article 20(2), they can and should be considered grounds for protection in view of the gender equality clauses elsewhere in the Covenant and the broader intersectional approach to non-discrimination that international human rights law has consistently taken in recent decades.[103]

While the SROFE refers to 'gendered hate speech,' as discussed in the preceding text, the Council of Europe refers to sexist hate speech, defining it as

> one of the expressions of sexism, which can be defined as any supposition, belief, assertion, gesture or act that is aimed at expressing contempt towards a person, based on her or his sex or gender, or to consider that person as inferior or essentially reduced to her or his sexual dimension. Sexist hate speech includes expressions which spread, incite, promote or justify hatred based on sex.[104]

Sękowska-Kozłowska, Baranowska and Gliszczyńska-Grabias argue that delineating between sexist hate speech and other statements which may be 'oppressive and hurtful'[105] but which do not amount to hate speech is central in determining when speech targeted towards women and girls is, in fact, hate speech.[106] They refer to Richardson-Self, who distinguishes between 'sexist speech,' which is not hateful, and 'misogynistic speech,' which is hate speech.[107] The aforementioned authors recognise the blurry lines between the different types of speech against women and girls and highlight that context should play a role in distinguishing between what is hate speech and what is

102 United Nations General Assembly, 'Report of the Special Rapporteur on the Promotion and Protection of the Right to Freedom of Opinion and Expression' (2021) A/76/258, para 68 <https://documents.un.org/doc/undoc/gen/n21/212/16/pdf/n2121216.pdf> accessed 8 October 2024

103 United Nations General Assembly (n 102) para 69

104 'Combating Sexist Hate Speech' *Council of Europe* 2 <https://edoc.coe.int/en/gender-equality/6995-combating-sexist-hate-speech.html>

105 Katarzyna Sękowska-Kozłowska, Grażyna Baranowska and Aleksandra Gliszczyńska-Grabias, 'Sexist Hate Speech and the International Human Rights Law: Towards Legal Recognition of the Phenomenon by the United Nations and the Council of Europe' (2022) 35 International Journal for the Semiotics of Law 2328

106 Sękowska-Kozłowska and others (n 105) 2327

107 Louise Richardson-Self, 'Woman-Hating: On Misogyny, Sexism and Hate Speech' (2018) 33 Hypatia: A Journal of Feminist Philosophy 2

not in that sphere.[108] They make an interesting observation in that if speech is racist, 'it almost automatically identifies as hate speech.'[109]

While the equality element in terms of sexist hate speech or gendered hate speech is partially satisfied by the 2021 SROFE's report on gendered hate speech, what is the situation in relation to other characteristics not covered by Article 20(2)? Of concern here is that neither Article 20(2) nor Article 2 of the ICCPR, the Convention's non-discrimination clause, explicitly refers to other characteristics which are common targets of hate, such as sexual orientation and gender identity. Although no reference is made in Article 2 of the ICCPR to sexual orientation and 'gender identity,' these characteristics could be incorporated in 'other status', and as held by the HRC in *Toonen v Australia*, 'sex' must include sexual orientation.[110] At the same time, Article 2 of the ICCPR extends the principle of non-discrimination to 'other status,' which could encompass a broad range of characteristics, assumingly subject to interpretation by national courts or, for example, by the HRC itself. It must also be noted that, when it comes to sex and gender, these fall within the general framework of IHRL, which also includes the Convention on the Elimination of all Forms of Discrimination Against Women (CEDAW). Noteworthy is the fact that neither the CEDAW nor the Council of Europe Convention on Preventing and Combating Violence Against Women and Domestic Violence (The Istanbul Convention) mentions sexist hate speech/gendered hate speech or other notions that fall within the ambit of hate speech. When it comes to sexual orientation and gender identity, there is no equivalent convention which could be referred to. The implicit conclusion from the overview of the aforementioned documents is that international and European legislation (not ECtHR case law) dictates that racist and xenophobic material and speech should be prohibited, even through criminal law, whereas sexist, gendered, homophobic and transphobic speech and material are not dealt an equal glove of protection.

One may argue that the previously described gap is a major omission of the European and United Nations frameworks and sets a distressing precedent for states parties, indicating that steps do not have to be taken to punish or prohibit homophobic or transphobic speech. Essentially, the legislation available on United Nations, European Union and Council of Europe levels has completely disregarded certain characteristics that are vulnerable to haters beyond the ones described, such as race, establishing, therefore, a hierarchy of importance when it comes to what ought to, and what ought not, be protected. The initial objectives of preventing the recurrence of

108 Sękowska-Kozłowska and others (n 105) 2328

109 Sękowska-Kozłowska and others (n 105)

110 *Toonen v Australia* (HRC, 31 March 1994) Communication no 488/1992, U.N. Doc CCPR/C/50/D/488/1992, para 8.7

World War II atrocities and the gradual development of the human rights movement post-ICCPR and post-ICERD may justify the narrow focus of older documents. These justifications cannot extend to newer documents, particularly the Framework Decision and the Additional Protocol.

In relation to sexual orientation and gender identity, it could be said that the United Nations faces significant challenges in legislating on LGBTQ+ issues, primarily due to the diverse composition, objectives and historical context of the organisation. The United Nations structure and function, which rely on the collective agreement of its member states, often hinder the development of inclusive frameworks that address LGBTQ+ rights. In this scope, many countries, especially those with strong religious or cultural objections, resist initiatives perceived as contrary to their traditional values. With member states ranging from liberal countries, such as Denmark, Canada or the United Kingdom, to conservative ones, such as Saudi Arabia and Pakistan, achieving consensus on LGBTQ+ rights is particularly difficult. The 2008 Framework Decision of the European Union, which emerged in an era when the notion of equality had significantly broadened, is a document of a European Union of shared values and not a culturally, religiously and politically unmatched consortium of states, as is the case of the United Nations. As such, it is argued that the selective approach adopted in the Framework Decision underscores a clear hierarchy of hate within the European Union framework,[111] which opted to develop a law addressing only racist and xenophobic speech and crime rather than a comprehensive document addressing all forms of hate speech and hate crime. While the Council of Europe is a broader geographical and cultural region than the European Union, it does not have the variations witnessed at the United Nations as described earlier. As such, the incorporation of homophobic and transphobic speech into the Additional Protocol could have been achieved.

Conclusion

The findings of this chapter underscore the persistent and multifaceted ambiguities surrounding the concept of hate speech across international, regional and domestic frameworks. The definitional uncertainty, highlighted by institutions such as the Council of Europe, the European Union and the United Nations, reflects the ongoing tension between safeguarding free expression and mitigating the harms of hateful rhetoric, while the severity of such harms is not agreed upon. This definitional ambiguity is not only a theoretical issue

111 For more on this see: Natalie Alkiviadou, 'The Hierarchy of Hate: Mixed Signals in the Combat against Hate Speech' (*VerfBlog*, 2018) <https://verfassungsblog.de/the-hierarchy-of-hate-mixed-signals-in-the-combat-against-hate-speech/> accessed 2 September 2024

for academic discussion but also a central theme that resonates throughout this book, shaping the analysis of the ECtHR's jurisprudence on hate speech. Despite efforts to address hate speech through legal, institutional and corporate mechanisms, a unified conceptualisation remains elusive, often shaped by cultural, historical and socio-political considerations.

The Council of Europe's approach, particularly through the jurisprudence of the ECtHR, reflects low thresholds of speech protection. While the Court has not provided a definitive definition of *hate speech*, its decisions have gradually outlined contextual markers. In *Gündüz v Turkey* (2003), the Court incorporated the element of insult in its hate speech narrative, and in *Féret*, the ECtHR expanded the scope further, asserting that hate speech 'does not necessarily entail a call for an act of violence or other criminal acts' but can include 'insulting, holding up to ridicule, or slandering specific groups of the population.'[112] This jurisprudential ambiguity undermines the principle of necessity of restrictions, raising concerns about the scope and limits of free expression under the ECHR. Regionally, the European Union's Framework Decision avoids the term 'hate speech,' as is the case with the ICCPR and the ICERD, focusing instead on incitement to violence or hatred linked to specific protected characteristics. By setting a high bar for criminal liability, the Framework Decision reflects a cautious approach to balancing harm prevention with free speech protections. However, the Framework Decision is the definitional setting of the Code of Conduct, which operationalises platform accountability through co-regulation rather than criminal law. The DSA leaves significant discretion to platforms in determining illegality, as they must interpret relevant European Union law or national laws which are in line with European Union law, while failing to articulate a coherent definition of hate speech. These fragmented regulatory efforts and a lacking definition of hate speech, despite the term's reference in the Code or the DSA, expose inherent tensions within the European Union framework. At the international level, the ICCPR sets out the important provision of Article 20(2), prohibiting advocacy of hatred that incites discrimination, hostility or violence. This threshold is high when compared to Article 4 of the ICERD, but also high when compared to ECtHR judgements, as will be reflected in Chapters 4 and 5. The ICERD establishes broader prohibitions, criminalising even the mere dissemination of racist ideas. While such approaches aim to protect vulnerable groups, they also raise concerns about overreach and potential infringements on legitimate speech.

Domestic legislative frameworks further exemplify the diversity of approaches in defining and regulating hate speech. For instance, Spain criminalises indirect incitement to hatred, whereas the United States maintains a libertarian stance under the First Amendment, where courts consistently protect even offensive or hateful speech unless it incites imminent lawless

112 *Féret v Belgium* App no 15615/07 (ECHR, 16 July 2009) para 73

action.[113] Meanwhile, jurisdictions like South Africa and Slovenia incorporate hate speech prohibitions directly into their Constitutions, balancing protections for free expression with safeguards against harmful rhetoric. *Qwelane v South African Human Rights Commission* (2019) exemplifies the judicial struggle to delineate hurtful speech from constitutionally impermissible hate speech, reinforcing the importance of contextual assessments. These comparative insights provide critical context for the ECtHR's jurisprudence, demonstrating both its distinct approach and its potential for learning from other frameworks.

The role of digital platforms adds another layer of complexity to the definitional and regulatory challenges surrounding hate speech. Companies like Meta, YouTube and X (formerly Twitter) have developed expansive policies that exceed legal thresholds, incorporating broad conceptualisations of hate speech that encompass, amongst others, slurs and harmful stereotypes. These expansive standards, coupled with automated enforcement mechanisms, often lead to inconsistencies and raise questions about transparency and accountability within the broader framework of the privatisation of speech regulation. As noted in this chapter, platform policies frequently diverge from legal frameworks, exacerbating the fragmentation of hate speech definitions in the digital age, while the use of AI to moderate hate speech leads to a myriad of problems pertaining to free speech and non-discrimination. The definitional and regulatory challenges raised by digital platforms exemplify the broader ambiguities the ECtHR must navigate.

The chapter further highlights the critical contributions of academic scholarship to understanding what hate speech is through its roots and impact. Such perspectives are integral to understanding the ECtHR's jurisprudence, as it often falls short of engaging with broader structural critiques which mark academic definitions.

In conclusion, the definitional and conceptual ambiguities surrounding hate speech reflect broader societal struggles to reconcile the competing imperatives of free expression and the prevention of harm and the varying significance institutions and countries attach to the freedom of expression. While international and regional frameworks offer valuable insights, their fragmented and often inconsistent approaches highlight the challenges of establishing a universal definition, but also workable institutional definitions. In relation to ECtHR's jurisprudence, the book argues that, at times, it reflects a concerning lack of restraint and allows for overreach that risks undermining the foundational principle of freedom of expression enshrined in the ECHR. A lacking definitional framework, a broad range of national laws and viewpoint bases, restrictions deemed permissible by the ECtHR, as will be demonstrated in Chapters 4 and 5, render the right to freedom of expression vulnerable in Europe. The first step towards a more robust

113 *Brandenburg v Ohio*, 395 U.S. 444 (1969)

approach to hate speech cases is to build a sound definitional setting against which all hate speech cases are assessed. In addition, the proliferation of digital platforms further complicates this landscape, exposing the limitations of traditional regulatory models in addressing online hate speech. As this book will argue, the ECtHR's jurisprudence must rise to meet these challenges with greater consistency and clarity.

2 The Effects of Hate Speech and How Best to Deal With Them

Introduction

Hate speech occupies a deeply contentious position in contemporary legal, social and political discourse. It evokes significant concerns regarding human dignity, equality and societal cohesion, while simultaneously raising fundamental questions about the boundaries of the freedom of expression and democracy's ability to regulate harmful speech. This chapter seeks to explore the effects of hate speech, examining its potential harms at individual, group and societal levels, while critically engaging with the debate on whether these harms justify legal restrictions. It also takes a critical look at the European Court of Human Rights' (ECtHR/Court's) militant democratic stance to free speech in the sphere of hate speech cases for the purposes of putting forth the theoretical framework through which the Court adopts a speech-restrictive approach to hate speech.

The chapter's first section looks at how hate speech affects people, communities and society more broadly. It looks at the psychological impact on the individual, but also the effects at group and societal levels, where some argue that hate speech reinforces stereotypes, deepens societal divisions and perpetuates systemic discrimination, often amplifying patterns of historical oppression. Many of the scholars discussed believe that hate speech fosters division and erodes social cohesion, undermining the democratic values of tolerance, respect and equality.[1] On a broader societal scale, the link between incitement to violence and mass atrocities will be assessed with examples, including the role of the radio in the Rwandan genocide[2] and the dissemination of hate

1 See, for example, Mari J Matsuda and others, *Words That Wound: Critical Race Theory, Assaultive Speech, and the First Amendment* (1st edn, Westview Press 1993); Jeremy Waldron, *The Harm in Hate Speech* (1st edn, Harvard University Press 2012)

2 See, for example, David Yanagizawa-Drott, 'Propaganda and Conflict: Evidence from the Rwandan Genocide' (2014) 129 The Quarterly Journal of Economics 4, Christine L. Kellow and H. Leslie Steeves, 'The Role of Radio in the Rwandan Genocide' (1998) 48 *Journal of Communication* 3; Darryl Li, 'Echoes of Violence: Considerations on Radio and Genocide in Rwanda' (2004) 6(1) Journal of Genocide Research

DOI: 10.4324/9781003560548-3

rhetoric through social media during the persecution of the Rohingya Muslims in Myanmar.[3] This section also makes reference to the variability in hate speech's impact as influenced by contextual, societal and historical factors and considers the position of critics, who emphasize the complexities of proving a causal link between hate speech and real-world harm. The second section critically engages with the debate surrounding hate speech regulation, highlighting the competing perspectives on whether the harms of hate speech warrant legal restrictions. Proponents of regulation, such as Waldron, Matsuda and Tsesis, argue that hate speech inflicts profound harm by undermining dignity, equality and inclusiveness. For these scholars, legal intervention is essential to protect marginalised groups and preserve social cohesion. On the other hand, it discusses the approach of critics such as Heinze and Strossen, who do not believe in the efficacy of regulating hate speech and raise significant concerns about the serious consequences of such practice. Critics argue that restrictions risk, *inter alia,* endangering the fundamental right of freedom of expression,[4] suppressing dissent and counterspeech,[5] elevating perpetrators to martyrs,[6] further entrenching extremist narratives and may even lead to social unrest.[7] This part underscores the tension between protecting individuals and groups from harm while safeguarding freedom of expression as a cornerstone of democracy. Additionally, it discusses the 'marketplace of ideas,' engaging with contemporary critiques that expose its limitations in the ambit of hate speech. Section III examines the ECtHR's approach to hate speech through the lens of militant democracy, a doctrine that permits pre-emptive restrictions on the rights to protect democratic systems from anti-democratic threats. This discussion lays the groundwork for the analyses in Chapters 4 and 5, which highlight significant shortcomings in the Court's jurisprudence on Article 17's prohibition of abuse of rights in hate speech cases. Notably, the Court has consistently failed to substantiate the actual harm caused by hate speech, marking a substantial departure from the original objectives of Article 17.

3 See, for example, Anamika Modok, 'Role of Social Media in Inciting the Genocidal Acts: A Case Study on Myanmar's Rohingya' (2023) 4 Contemporary Challenges: The Global Crime, Justice and Security Journal 7; Matt Schissler, 'Beyond Hate Speech and Misinformation: Facebook and the Rohingya Genocide in Myanmar' (2024) 26 Journal of Genocide Research 1

4 See, for example, Eric Heinze, *Hate Speech and Democratic Citizenship* (1st edn, OUP 2016); Enes Kulenović, 'Should Democracies Ban Hate Speech? Hate Speech Laws and Counter-speech' (2023) 26 *Ethical Theory and Moral Practice*; Nadine Strossen, *Hate: Why We Should Resist it with Free Speech, not Censorship* (1st edn, OUP 2018); James Weinstein, 'Hate Speech Bans, Democracy, and Political Legitimacy' (2017) 32 Constitutional Commentary

5 Maxime Lepoutre, 'Hate Speech in Public Discourse: A Pessimistic Defense of Counterspeech' (2017) 43 *Social Theory and Practice* 4; Strossen, *Hate* (n 4); Weinstein (n 4)

6 Nadine Strossen, 'Regulating Racist Speech on Campus: A Modest Proposal?' [1990] Duke Law Journal 559; Jonathan Rauch, *Kindly Inquisitors: The New Attacks on Free Thought* (expanded edn, University of Chicago Press 2013) 70

7 Christian Bjørnskov and Jacob Mchangama, 'Freedom of Expression and Social Conflict' (2023) IFN Working Paper No 1473

1 Hate Speech and Its Effects

Comprehending the impact of hate speech on a micro (individual), meso (group) and macro (societal) level is essential when attempting to understand what it is. In the context of targets, Scanlon has focused on the extent to which a particular expression affects the rights and interests of those it targets. He contends that for a state to regulate speech legitimately, it must first assess whether, and to what extent, the rights and interests of the affected groups are compromised. These groups encompass not only the direct participants and the immediate audience but also bystanders and broader societal members who may be harmed by the speech.[8]

One of the central arguments of this book is that ECtHR jurisprudence has not yet provided an adequate assessment of the purported harm hate speech causes, even though it has decided that even insulting or defaming speech has been harmful. The need for a substantial harm assessment is centrifugal in hate speech cases since the right which is restricted in the name of hate speech is the fundamental right to freedom of expression. Commencing with identifying the various groups who may be harmed by hate speech is a good starting point for achieving the aforementioned.

1.1 Psychological, Societal and Systemic Harm

Hate speech occupies a deeply contentious position in contemporary legal, social and political discourse. While this book does not delve deeply into theoretical and empirical debates concerning the meaning, impact and regulation of hate speech, it presents key scholarly perspectives and findings to facilitate a comprehensive understanding of the phenomenon and variations. These perspectives serve to illustrate the breadth of issues surrounding hate speech, issues that the Court should, at the very least, critically engage with in its jurisprudence. Whether hate speech causes harm and the extent to which it does so both remain questions of scholarly debate. Some contend that there is a clear causal connection between hate speech and injury, while others dispute this, arguing that there is insufficient empirical support for such statements. This section critically examines these competing perspectives.

Matsuda argues that racist speech operates as 'a mechanism of subordination reinforcing a historical vertical relationship,'[9] which results in negative effects which are 'real and immediate'[10] to those it targets. Scholars such as Tsesis highlight hate speech's destructive potential, not only as a tool of individual harm but also as a mechanism for entrenching societal divisions and systemic oppression. Tsesis views hate speech as the dissemination of harmful messages with a destructive impact on society at the group level, rather than merely

8 Thomas Scanlon, *The Difficulty of Tolerance* (1st edn, CUP 2003) 86, 99, 151, 92, 155

9 Mari J. Matsuda, 'Public Response to Racist Speech: Considering the Victim's Story' (1989) 87(8) Michigan Law Review 2358

10 Matsuda (n 9) 2236

affecting individuals. He links hate speech to the emergence of dangerous movements and critiques of prevailing free speech theories by highlighting the violent experiences of historically marginalised groups. He illustrates how hate speech becomes ingrained in mainstream discourse through its systemic development, using instances like slavery and genocide to demonstrate this process.[11] A significant example of mass destructiveness is the role hate speech had in the 1994 Rwandan genocide. Hutu extremists used hate speech to dehumanise their targets and incite mass murders, while radio broadcasts that spread anti-Tutsi propaganda were a major factor in inciting violence. According to Yanagizawa-Drott's quantitative research, areas with more radio penetration had noticeably higher rates of violence, which may indicate a clear correlation between the spread of hate speech and the genocide that followed.[12] Further, using Facebook's extensive reach to disseminate hate speech and false information, Myanmar's military planned a propaganda campaign in October 2016 to encourage mass violence against Rohingya Muslims. Facebook was slow to act despite multiple warnings about the worsening situation, which allowed the violent rhetoric to spread unchecked for a considerable amount of time.[13] A report by the United Nations Independent International Fact-Finding Mission on Myanmar (2018) found that the spread of hate speech on social media platforms played a critical role in facilitating the mass violence and atrocities committed against the Rohingya, including acts of genocide, ethnic cleansing and other crimes against humanity.[14]

Outside the framework of mass atrocities, there has been interesting research on the impact of hate speech on crimes. For example, in the United States, a study found that states with a higher engagement with Donald Trump's tweets during the 2016 election experienced a statistically significant increase in hate crimes. The researchers used machine learning techniques to analyse patterns of online hate speech and its impact on real-world behaviour and concluded that inflammatory rhetoric on social media platforms can have direct and harmful consequences.[15] A 2019 study which examined whether there was a link between online hate speech and hate crime in London over an eight-month

11 Alexander Tsesis, *Destructive Messages: How Hate Speech Paves the Way for Harmful Social Movements* (1st edn, New York University Press 2002)

12 Yanagizawa-Drott (n 2)

13 Evelyn Douek, 'Facebook's Role in the Genocide in Myanmar: New Reporting Complicates the Narrative' *Lawfare* (2022) <https://www.lawfaremedia.org/article/facebooks-role-genocide-myanmar-new-reporting-complicates-narrative> accessed 14 September 2024; Matt Schissler, 'Beyond Hate Speech and Misinformation: Facebook and the Rohingya Genocide in Myanmar' (2024) 26 Journal of Genocide Research 1

14 United Nations Human Rights Council, 'Report of the Independent International Fact-Finding Mission on Myanmar' (12 September 2018) UN Doc A/HRC/39/64 <https://www.ohchr.org/en/documents/country-reports/report-independent-international-fact-finding-mission-myanmar-0> accessed 5 October 2024

15 Karsten Müller and Carlo Schwarz, 'From Hashtag to Hate Crime: Twitter and Anti-Minority Sentiment' (2020) SSRN <https://papers.ssrn.com/sol3/papers.cfm?abstract_id=3149103> accessed 21 December 2024

period found that there was a strong correlation between spikes in online hate speech and subsequent increases in hate crimes.[16] Matsuda contends that hate speech undermines the sense of identity and self-esteem of the victim and the feeling of personal safety.[17] A 2024 empirical study also demonstrated that victims of online hate speech had a heightened concern regarding their sense of security.[18] Lawrence highlights the 'injurious impact' of direct racial insults, equating them to a 'slap in the face' that hinders opportunities for response, often resulting in silence or retreat due to the fear, anger and shock they provoke.[19] Some research has found that hate speech may lead to psychological effects on victims,[20] which vary according to exposure and endurance[21] but also increased hate crimes.[22] It is important to underline that 'the exact individual impact of speech varies depending on content.'[23] While research has established significant links between hate speech and real-life harm, the evidence is not without its counterarguments and limitations. For instance, Dworkin recognises the 'malign, chilling force'[24] of hate speech but argues that claims about its harms are often 'inflated and some are absurd.'[25] In the framework of long-standing and prosperous democracies (LSPDs), which Heinze defines in his book *Hate Speech and Democratic Citizenship*, he argues that 'despite decades of pro-ban law and policy. . . no empirical evidence has, in any statistically standard way, traced hatred expressed within general public discourse to specifically harmful effects.'[26]

I want to make a short intervention when it comes to the handling of empirical work. When discussing empirical findings on hate speech, it is important to recognise certain limitations that, while not detracting from the value of the specific research cited in this chapter or similar studies, are relevant to the broader discourse. The knowledge gap between academic disciplines often

16 Matthew L. Williams and others, 'Hate in the Machine: Anti-Black and Anti-Muslim Social Media Posts as Predictors of Offline Racially and Religiously Aggravated Crime' (2020) 60(1) British Journal of Criminology 3
17 As she discusses in Matsuda and others (n 1) and Matsuda (n 9)
18 Arne Dreißigacker and others, 'Online Hate Speech Victimization: Consequences for Victims' Feelings of Insecurity' (2024) 13 Crime Science 4
19 Charles R. Lawrence III, 'If He Hollers Let Him Go: Regulating Racist Speech on Campus' (1990) 40 Duke Law Journal 452
20 Dreißigacker and others (n 18)
21 Koustuv Saha, Eshwar Chandrasekharan and Munmun De Choudhury, 'Prevalence and Psychological Effects of Hateful Speech in Online College Communities' (2019) Proceedings of the 10th ACM Conference on Web Science
22 Müller and Schwarz, 'Making America Hate Again?' (n 15), Karsten Müller and Carlo Schwarz, 'Fanning the Flames of Hate: Social Media and Hate Crime' (2020) <https://ssrn.com/abstract=3082972> accessed 3 October 2024
23 Lyn KL Tjon Soei Len and Anniek de Ruijter, 'Conceptualising the Tortuous Harms of Sexist and Racist Hate Speech' (2023) 2 European Law Open 23
24 Ronald Dworkin, 'A New Map of Censorship' (1994) Index on Censorship 10 <https://journals.sagepub.com/doi/pdf/10.1080/03064229408535633> accessed 1 September 2024
25 Dworkin (n 24) 12
26 Heinze, *Hate Speech and Democratic Citizenship* (n 4) 126–127

leaves some of us unsure about how to interpret and apply empirical research effectively. This is particularly evident in studies that, although valuable, may rely on data derived from observational studies rather than controlled experimental settings. Such an approach can make it difficult to establish a definitive correlation between hate speech and its reported impacts or prevalence, as other intervening factors may influence the results. Additionally, the use of artificial intelligence to identify hate speech requires careful oversight to account for context and linguistic nuances; otherwise, datasets may suffer from inaccuracies. While empirical limitations are beyond the focus of this book and my own expertise, the points raised earlier highlight the need for caution when engaging with such work. Even when scholars clearly outline methodological constraints, interpreting findings can remain a challenge for some of us. On this matter, I reference a significant body of work by researchers specialising in hate speech, offering valuable insights into the complexities of empirical research in this field.[27] In relation to the ECtHR, while it is absolutely crucial that the Court commence substantial use of scholarship, including empirical work, an idea could be that judicial assistants also have expertise or receive training on the handling of empirical work. This not only benefits case law on Article 10 but is also particularly important for this article, and specifically hate speech, due to the very contentious nature of hate speech on the one hand and the very fundamental nature of freedom of expression on the other, rendering empirical work vital for ascertaining harms.

Beyond the discussion on empirical findings, we turn to stereotypes, which are a particular strand of hate speech harms that has been identified by scholars and courts, including the ECtHR. It has been argued that stereotyping can have adverse effects on victims of hate speech, their groups and society at large. Greenwalt emphasises the enduring effects of hate speech, noting that 'epithets and slurs that reflect stereotypes about race, ethnic group, religion and gender may reinforce prejudices and feelings of inferiority in seriously harmful ways.'[28] In the landmark Canadian case of *R v Keegstra*, Dickson CJ held that 'hate propaganda' subverts the democratic process of a country because 'individuals are denied respect and dignity simply because of racial or religious characteristics.'[29] Stereotypes are characterised as 'social ideas and preconceptions that exist about a particular group,' and they create dichotomies, such as 'us versus them.'[30] Examples of stereotyping effects include, but are not limited to, the divisive and classificatory impact of such stereotypes. Bell highlights the unique dignitary harms inherent in racial

27 Christian Strippel and others (eds), 'Challenges and Perspectives of Hate Speech Research (Digital Communication Research 12)' <https://www.ssoar.info/ssoar/handle/document/86272> accessed 1 October 2024

28 Kent Greenawalt, *Speech, Crime and the Uses of Language* (1st edn, OUP 1989) Chapter 2

29 *R v Keegstra*, [1990] 3 S.C.R. 697 at 764

30 Alexandra Timmer, 'Toward an Anti-Stereotyping Approach for the European Court of Human Rights' (2011) 11 Human Rights Law Review 4

discrimination, stating that 'damage to the autonomy and freedom of action, the badges and incidents of citizenship, is the threshold damage which always occurs in a race discrimination case, and would merit compensation greater than it has generally received.'[31] Delgado believes that racial insults are an affront to human dignity.[32] Waldron asserts that hate speech undermines the 'social sense of assurance on which members of vulnerable minorities rely'[33] and erodes the collective commitment to human dignity and respect. He argues that hate speech should be prohibited because its detrimental effects extend beyond individuals, impacting entire groups and potentially destabilising social harmony. Furthermore, he argues that 'prejudicial speech initiates, perpetuates and aggravates socially accepted misrepresentations about outgroups.'[34] Timmer highlights the damaging consequences of these stereotypes, which include psychological distress and hindered achievement. Timmer has proposed an anti-stereotyping approach for the ECtHR, with a specific focus on gender discrimination. This approach requires the Court to critically assess the underlying assumptions in legal reasoning and public policy that contribute to systemic discrimination. In the case of *Vejdeland v Sweden* (2012),[35] where the ECtHR examined homophobic speech, the concurring opinions of Judges Spielmann (Luxembourg) and Nussberger (Germany) referenced a Committee of Ministers Resolution Against Croatia. This Resolution criticised statements similar to those in the Swedish case, declaring that 'these statements stigmatise homosexuals and are based upon negative, distorted, reprehensible and degrading stereotypes about the sexual behaviour of all homosexuals.'[36] The issue of stereotypes was not integrated in the more recent case on homophobic speech, namely, *Lenis v Greece* (2023). Stereotypes were also incorporated in the judgements of cases such as *Féret v Belgium* (2000)[37] and *Zemmour v France* (2022),[38] but interestingly, not in the similar case of *Le Pen v France* (2010). In the 2021 cases of *Behad and Gutman v Bulgaria* and *Chaprazov v Bulgaria*, the ECtHR addressed the harmful impact of extreme negative stereotyping in hate speech. Siderov, a far-right politician well-known for his harsh and xenophobic statements directed against the Jewish and Roma populations, was the object of accusations in both cases. Citing Siderov's right to free speech, domestic courts

31 Derrick Bell, *Race, Racism and American Law* (5th edn, Aspen Publishers 2004) 321
32 Richard Delgado, 'Words That Wound: A Tort Action for Racial Insults, Epithets, and Name-Calling' (1982) 17 Harvard Criminal Law Review 166
33 Waldron, *The Harm in Hate Speech* (n 1) 88
34 Tsesis, *Destructive Messages* (n 11) 138
35 *Vejdeland v Sweden* App no 1813/07 (ECHR, 9 February 2012)
36 Resolution CM/ResChS (2009) 7, Collective Complaint No 45/2007 by the *International Centre for the Protection of Human Rights (INTERIGHTS) v Croatia*, as cited in Concurring Opinion of Judge Spielman and Judge Nussberger in *Vejdeland* (n 35) para 6
37 *Féret v Belgium* App no 15615/07 (ECHR, 16 July 2009) para 76
38 *Zemmour v France* App no 63539/19 (ECHR, 20 December 2022) para 61

rejected the applicants' arguments that his remarks amounted to harassment and incitement to discriminate. The ECtHR highlighted the role of stereotypes in sustaining harm against vulnerable groups and concluded that domestic courts had not fulfilled their positive obligations under Article 8, on the right to private life, and Article 14, which prohibits discrimination.

As such, the positions on the harm caused by hate speech are diverse, reflecting a spectrum of perspectives on its impact and regulation. However, cognisant of the possibility, and evidence, that hate speech can lead to mass atrocities as well as hate crimes, psychological effects and stereotyping and marginalisation, it is imperative to treat it with due seriousness and adopt measures to address its effects. Furthermore, the different harms discussed earlier reflect different levels of severity. This is an important factor for consideration within the hate speech debate more broadly. Not all hate speech is equal, and therefore, not all responses, if any, should be equal. As an extreme comparison in order to illustrate this point, a pre-genocidal volatile context in which calls for extermination of a group are disseminated cannot be dealt with in the same framework as anti-immigrant stereotypes by a far-right party in a stable, non-violent democracy. Restrictive measures ought to be used only in situations when there is an incitement to or encouragement of actual violence, where the risks and repercussions warrant them.

1.2 Critical Race Theory: Current Developments

Given that several critical race theorists are discussed in this chapter when looking at the notion of a free marketplace of ideas as well as the effects of hate speech, this section will provide a short overview of the origins and basic idea at the heart of the theory, as well as recent developments in the United States in the framework of critical race theory, in order to illustrate further the role, impact and limitations of this lens on the effects of phenomena such as hate speech.

Critical race theory came about in the mid-1980s[39] after scholars, activists and lawyers identified the need for 'new theories and strategies . . . to combat the subtler forms of racism that were gaining ground.'[40] Instances of racism on university campuses in the United States triggered the writings of critical race theorists such as Matsuda, Lawrence and Delegado, 'who wrote the phrase

39 However, it can be traced back to the Black liberationist movement of the 1960s and the critical legal studies movement of the 1970s and the 1980s: Jeffrey Pyle, 'Race, Equality and the Rule of Law: Critical Race Theory's Attack on the Promises of Liberalism' (1999) 40(3) Boston College Law Review 798

40 Richard Delegado and Jean Stefancic, *Critical Race Theory: An Introduction* (1st edn, New York University Press 2006) 4

hate speech into the legal lexicon.'[41] The theory considers a variety of issues looked at through, for example, the civil rights lens but instead

> places them in a broader perspective that includes economics, history, context, group and self-interest, and even feelings and the unconscious . . . [and] questions the very foundations of the liberal order, including equality theory, legal reasoning, enlightenment rationalism, and neutral principles of constitutional law.[42]

For critical race theory, racism 'lies at the very heart of American and Western culture.'[43] Its central objective is to 'eliminat[e] racial oppression'[44] and to bring about 'fundamental social transformation.'[45] This theory offers a lens through which a wide range of issues, such as law, education and political science, can be examined.[46]

As might be expected, critical race theory is not without criticism. For example, it has been described as having a 'single-mindedly critical character,'[47] which involves extensive discussion, analysis and blame, without offering concrete solutions to the issues it identifies. Tushnet encapsulates this concern by stating that, within critical race theory, 'critique is all there is.'[48] Butler challenges the theory's assumption of a direct and inevitable connection between hate speech and the harm it purportedly causes.[49] Heinze argues that critical race theorists rely on 'wholly abstract, decontextualised and formalist readings of international norms,'[50] which leads to consequences such as a lack of engagement with international human rights law (IHRL). Theorists in this field emphasis bigotry and inequality, highlighting how hate speech stifles a fair discussion and erodes the marketplace of ideas. According to critical race theory, conversations about free speech regarding hate speech are distorted by institutional racism and the biases attached to particular groups. However, it appears that their theory avoids discussing IHRL, which is essential to their discussion. The theory's inability to provide specific answers to the problems it highlights is another point of contention. It is unclear whether this reality

41 Heinze, *Hate Speech and Democratic Citizenship* (n 4) 15
42 Delegado and Stefancic (n 40) 3
43 Angela Harris, 'Foreword, The Jurisprudence of Reconstruction' (1994) 82(4) California Law Review 749
44 Matsuda and others (n 1) 6–7
45 Matsuda and others (n 1)
46 Delegado and Stefancic (n 40)
47 Pyle (n 39) 816
48 Mark Tushnet, *Red, White and Blue: A Critical Analysis of Constitutional Law* (1st edn, University Press of Kansas 2015) 318
49 Judith Butler, *Excitable Speech. A Politics of the Performative* (1st edn, Routledge 1997) 16
50 Eric Heinze, 'Truth, Myth and Critical Theory' in Reza Banakar (ed), *Rights in Context: Law and Justice in Late Modern Society* (1st edn, Routledge 2010) 98

warrants the restriction of fundamental rights, such as freedom of expression, despite its important sociopolitical analysis of the inequalities underlying hate speech and its contention that such speech exacerbates the marginalisation of already-marginalised groups. Regretfully, within the scope of IHRL, there is a dearth of normative analysis addressing the validity of linking the need to eliminate institutional prejudice with limits on hate speech. Furthermore, it could be argued that critical race theory exposes the risks of content-based speech control even if it offers a useful critique of the harms created by hate speech. Critical race theory introduces subjective enforcement of laws and risks suppressing dissenting voices. By prioritising protection from harm over the open exchange of ideas, critical race theory's framework challenges the foundational belief that freedom of expression is essential to democracy and societal progress.

Interesting developments have been taking place in the USA *vis-à-vis* critical race theory. Initially a scholarly approach within critical legal studies, critical race theory has since influenced discussions on education, social justice and public policy. Legislative efforts to ban critical race theory have been particularly prominent in Republican-led states. Lawmakers in states such as Florida, Texas and Tennessee have introduced bills to prohibit the teaching of critical race theory in K–12 (primary and secondary) schools, arguing that critical race theory's concepts are not suitable for young pupils. For example, Florida's Stop WOKE Act, signed into law in 2022, bans any educational content that suggests an individual's moral character or worth is determined by their race. Florida governor Ron DeSantis argued that critical race theory 'teaches kids to hate their country or to hate each other.'[51] Similar laws have been passed or proposed in several other states, with proponents arguing that these measures protect students from what they see as ideologically driven, anti-American teachings. The 'Combating Racist Training in the Military Act of 2023,'[52] 'The Warrior Act,'[53] and 'Securing Our Schools Act of 2023'[54] are just a few of the measures that have been presented in Congress that aim to outlaw the teaching of critical race theory. The proposed policies either completely prohibit the teaching of critical race theory or stop providing federal financing to public universities that use it in their curricula. Bans on critical race theory are opposed on the grounds that they violate academic freedom and amount to censorship. They claim that prohibiting critical race theory prevents students from engaging with difficult social issues and stifles critical conversations about inequality, history and race. Critics, including educators, civil rights organisations and some scholars, argue that efforts to ban critical race theory are politically motivated attempts to whitewash American history

51 Ron DeSantis, 'Remarks on the Stop WOKE Act' (Governor's Press Conference 2022) <https://www.youtube.com/watch?v=kWUgjZrBkNY> accessed 15 November 2024
52 S. 556 (118th Cong.)
53 H.R. 2378 (118th Cong.)
54 S. 1082 (118th Cong.)

and avoid uncomfortable truths about racism's impact on society.[55] As the debate goes on, it brings to light how divisive conversations about race and education are in America, posing important queries about how the country deals with its history and persistent social injustices. Möschel notes that while critical race theory has its roots in American difficulties and reality, some of the major problems it tackles are also pertinent in Europe. However, the theory has 'received scant attention in European legal scholarship.'[56] Möschel situates his analysis within the context of continental Europe and attributes the limited application of critical race theory there to the absence of a conceptualisation of race. He argues that there is a 'fear . . . that by referring to race one might be implicitly and normatively recognising the existence of different human races from the scientific viewpoint.'[57] This apprehension could hinder the theory's broader application, as it necessitates grappling with the concept of race.

1.3 Is Restricting Speech the Right Response?

The contentious discussion about the negative effects of hate speech and whether these effects call for regulation reflects larger conflicts about the boundaries of free speech. There is disagreement about whether hate speech warrants legal action, even though some people believe it seriously harms both persons and communities. Others have doubted the real-life link between hate speech and harm, while methodological limitations hamper findings on hate speech harms. Proponents of hate speech regulation argue that the harm it causes is sufficiently severe to warrant legal restrictions. Waldron argues that hate speech targets the 'social sense of assurance on which members of vulnerable minorities rely'[58] and guarantees that all citizens adhere to principles of human dignity and respect. As such, he underlines that hate speech should be prohibited in that it is so damaging, not only on an individual level, but also on a group level, that such speech can almost affect social harmony.[59] Tsesis also highlights the broader social harms of hate speech. He argues that hate speech is not merely a personal attack but that 'the very purpose of intimidating hate speech is to perpetuate and augment existing inequalities.'[60] According to Tsesis, regulations can be extremely important in preserving the values of equality and shielding marginalised groups from deliberate mistreatment.[61]

55 See, for example, Kimberlé Williams Crenshaw, 'This is not a Drill: The War Against Antiracist Teaching in America' (2022) 68 UCLA Law Review 1702 <https://www.uclalawreview.org/wp-content/uploads/securepdfs/2022/06/Crenshaw-68-6.pdf> accessed 15 September 2024

56 Mattias Möschel, 'Race in Mainland European Legal Analysis: Towards a European Critical Race Theory' (2011) 34(10) Ethnic and Racial Studies 1649

57 Möschel (n 56) 1651

58 Waldron, *The Harm in Hate Speech* (n 1) 88

59 Waldron, *The Harm in Hate Speech* (n 1) 166–167

60 Alexander Tsesis, 'Dignity and Speech: The Regulation of Hate Speech in a Democracy' (2009) 44 Wake Forest Law Review 505

61 Tsesis, *Destructive Messages* (n 11) 131

Tsesis dismissed theories of free speech in the face of the violent realities that traditionally marginalised groups have experienced as a result of the systematic development of hate speech, which subsequently becomes part of accepted dialogue, pinpointing examples such as slavery to illustrate this point.[62] However, prohibiting hate speech by law can be controversial, since such legislation may impose on the freedom of expression, thereby leading to self-censoring and a diluted sphere of public debate. Heinze critiques European approaches to hate speech regulation for a variety of reasons, developed in this chapter, including the very fundamental reason that, for him, freedom of expression is one of the 'legitimising expressive conditions of democracy.'[63] Any restrictions thereto may, according to Heinze, undermine democracy and damage state legitimacy.[64] For Heinze, the right to freedom of expression is 'the most human right.'[65] Strossen contends that hate speech laws are more likely to be misapplied or abused than to protect vulnerable communities, warning that such laws often suppress the voices of the very people they are meant to protect, and that there is a 'predictable pattern now in which hate speech codes and laws are introduced, purporting to protect minorities, but end up censoring them.'[66] Strossen emphasises that combatting hate speech through counterspeech is more effective, as legal restrictions can create a chilling effect that stifles open debate.[67] Rauch emphasises the critical importance of safeguarding robust free speech protections, advocating for counterspeech as a more effective remedy than regulation. As he characteristically stated, 'bigoted ideas and hateful speech play an essential part in advancing minority rights. Even if we have every right to boycott *Ender's Game*, gays are better served by answering people like Card than by trying to squelch or punish them.'[68] As such, opponents of hate speech regulation argue that such laws may pose significant dangers for free speech, may target dissenting/minority voices and erode the very foundation of democratic discourse and its legitimacy. Hate speech regulation may also prevent counterspeech, which can be a means to address hate speech and discrimination through what can be described as 'the purifying effect of open public discourse.'[69]

62 Tsesis, *Destructive Messages* (n 11) 136
63 Heinze, *Hate Speech and Democratic Citizenship* (n 4) 95
64 Heinze, *Hate Speech and Democratic Citizenship* (n 4) 49
65 Eric Heinze, *The Most Human Right: Why Free Speech is Everything* (1st edn. MIT Press 2023)
66 Nadine Strossen, 'Minorities Suffer the Most for Hate-Speech Laws' *Spiked* (2018) <https://www.spiked-online.com/2018/12/14/minorities-suffer-the-most-from-hate-speech-laws/> accessed 10 September 2024
67 Strossen, 'Minorities Suffer the Most for Hate-Speech Laws' (n 66)
68 Jonathan Rauch, 'The Case for Hate Speech' *The Atlantic* (2013) <https://www.jonathanrauch.com/jrauch_articles/the-case-for-hate-speech/> accessed 1 September 2024
69 Audun Fladmoe and Marjan Nadim, 'Silenced by Hate? Hate Speech as a Social Boundary to Free Speech' in Arnfinn H Midtbøen, Kari Steen-Johnsen and Kjersti Thorbjørnsrud (eds), *Boundary Struggles: Contestations of Free Speech in the Norwegian Public Sphere* (Cappelen Damm Akademisk 2017) 46

Hate speech laws that selectively protect certain groups can cultivate what Volokh terms 'censorship envy' among those who feel marginalised by their exclusion from these safeguards. This dynamic arises when people start to wonder if these limitations are fair, posing the question, "If my neighbour is permitted to suppress speech they find offensive, why should I not have the same privilege?" These differences run the risk of widening social gaps and threatening the credibility of the laws, as well as the more general ideals of equality and free speech.[70] A selective approach to regulating hate speech based on viewpoints undermines the fundamental principle of free expression, and this approach risks perpetuating societal inequalities and fostering 'censorship envy' among groups that are not afforded equal protection. Additionally, the inconsistent positions taken by human rights organisations diminish both their credibility and the broader defence of free speech.

Feinberg argues that for speech to warrant prohibition, it must induce profound offence rather than mere nuisance. He delineates five characteristics that distinguish profound offence. Namely, they carry a particularly menacing tone; are unacceptable, even to those who do not directly witness them; are unacceptable regardless of whether they occur in private;[71] remain perceptible, despite attempts to ignore them; and are deemed morally objectionable.[72] Feinberg notes that racial insults, in particular, provoke profound outrage to the victim due to their moral reprehensibility and the sense of threat they create.[73]

However, repression of harmful speech, particularly within organised groups, may be counter-effective. For example, Ravndal argues that 'openness and dialogue might work better than public repression, stigmatisation or aggressive confrontation.'[74] He suggests that the surge in far-right extremism across Western Europe results from a combination of high immigration rates, limited electoral success for radical right-wing parties, and the 'extensive public repression of radical right actors and opinions.'[75] Although he acknowledges that such repression may deter some individuals from aligning with extreme groups, he finds that it may also drive others toward more violent trajectories and social unrest.[76]

Ultimately, the question of whether hate speech necessitates regulation remains contentious. Conscious of the psychological and physical effects of

70 Eugene Volokh, 'Censorship Envy' *The Volokh Conspiracy—Reason* (13 November 2023) <https://reason.com/volokh/2023/11/13/censorship-envy-2/>

71 Joel Feinberg, *Offence to Others—The Moral Limits of the Criminal Law* (1st edn, OUP 1985) 58

72 Feinberg (n 71) 59

73 Feinberg (n 71)

74 Jacob Aasland Ravndal, 'Explaining Right-Wing Terrorism and Violence in Western Europe: Grievances, Opportunities and Polarisation' (2017) 57 European Journal of Political Research 4

75 Ravndal (n 74)

76 Bjørnskov and Mchangama (n 7)

hate speech, and even if we assume that hate speech may result in real-life harm, the balance between protecting individuals and preserving the free exchange of ideas is not clear-cut. In short, even if we were to regulate hate speech, would that mean that hate speech would disappear? If one accepts the premise that hate speech can cause significant harm, the question arises as to how best to address it within a democratic society. Should it be prohibited even if it does not incite violence but instead causes psychological harm or perpetuates social exclusion? Or should it remain protected under the principle of free expression, unless it directly leads to violent acts?

Outlawing hate speech does not always guarantee a successful solution and could seriously jeopardise the right to free speech. Ironically, broadly interpreted bans on hate speech can be used as a weapon against the exact groups they are intended to protect and to silence opposing views.[77] Furthermore, will minority groups be better protected by a regulatory approach? I am still sceptical. Is it more likely that those who spread hate will seize the opportunity to portray themselves as victims? Almost certainly. While any form of hate speech is deplorable for victims and society more broadly, 'it does not necessarily follow that restriction on free speech is an effective remedy.'[78] As such, a response to hate speech must carefully balance the need to address alleged harms considering the context in which the harm is taking place and the type of harm in question.

Silencing dissent, restricting counterspeech, amplifying extreme propaganda and escalating social unrest are just a few of the unexpected consequences that can arise from suppressing hate speech, especially when done through unduly wide legislative prohibitions. However, it is impossible to overlook the facts of hate speech's effects, especially on marginalised communities and online. A measured, context-sensitive approach that considers proportionality, democratic principles and the evolving nature of hate speech is therefore essential. A core argument of this book is that what is emphatically lacking from ECtHR hate speech judgements is an in-depth analysis of the aforementioned questions, something that is necessary, *inter alia*, to justify the restriction of the fundamental right to freedom of expression. As discussed in Chapters 4 and 5, this has resulted in the development of broad assertions regarding the damage and consequences of hate speech in ECtHR law.

Frequently, though, these claims do not provide a comprehensive analysis of the existence, type and magnitude of harm in the particular instance being considered.

77 Jacob Mchangama and Nadine Strossen, 'Hate Speech Laws are no Friends of Minorities' *Spiked* (2020) <https://www.spiked-online.com/2020/06/02/hate-speech-laws-are-no-friend-of-minorities/> accessed 6 November 2024

78 Jacob Mchangama and Natalie Alkiviadou, 'Hate Speech and the European Court of Human Rights: Whatever Happened to the Right to Offend, Shock or Disturb?' (2021) 21 Human Rights Law Review 4

2 Hate Speech Restrictions

2.1 Analysis Through the Prism of Free Speech

Strossen and Lukianoff have emphasised the many reasons free speech is so important, such as fostering tolerance and human rights, individual autonomy, democratic self-governance, and peaceful conflict resolution.[79] Hate speech lies 'in a complex nexus with freedom of expression and group rights, as well as concepts of dignity, liberty and equality.'[80] The complex interplay between hate speech and free expression forms the cornerstone of debates surrounding its regulation. Even while hate speech's capacity to injure people on an individual, societal and systemic level is well acknowledged, there are still concerns about how best to restrict free speech in order to mitigate these effects. Through an analysis of the fundamental notions of free speech, such as the "marketplace of ideas," this section critically investigates these concerns. It also discusses recent criticisms that draw attention to the market's shortcomings in mitigating the effects of hate speech in the real world. By scrutinising these theoretical underpinnings, the section provides a framework for understanding the tension between protecting free expression and regulating harmful speech, a tension that the ECtHR must navigate in its jurisprudence, as explored in this book.

The 'marketplace of ideas' theory is a cornerstone of free speech jurisprudence, encapsulating the belief that the free exchange of ideas leads to the discovery of truth and the betterment of society. This theory's roots can be traced to the works of early libertarian philosophers, like John Stuart Mill and John Milton, whose theories established the fundamental framework for the contemporary idea of the marketplace of ideas. Milton, one of the most significant early proponents of free speech, spoke vehemently against pre-publication censorship in his landmark work *Areopagitica* (1644). The basic tenet of Milton's thesis was that the search for truth and the intellectual advancement of both people and society depend on the free flow of ideas. Mill placed importance on free expression as a fundamental element of societal development, arguing that a flourishing society needs individuals 'capable of being improved through free and equal discussion.'[81] Nevertheless, he

79 Greg Lukianoff and Nadine Strossen, 'Does Free Speech "Inevitably" Lead Towards Truth? Is the "Marketplace of Ideas" a Broken Metaphor?' *The Fire* <https://www.thefire.org/news/blogs/eternally-radical-idea/does-free-speech-inevitably-lead-towards-truth-marketplace-ideas> accessed 25 October 2024

80 Leandro Silva and others, 'Analyzing the Targets of Hate in Online Social Media' [2016] Proceedings of the Tenth International AAAI (Association for the Advancement of Artificial Intelligence) Conference on Web and Social Media 688

81 John Stuart Mill, 'On Liberty' in Mary Warnock (ed), *Utilitarianism and On Liberty: Including Mill's Essay on Bentham and Selections from the Writings of Jeremy Bentham and John Austin* (2nd edn, Blackwell 2012) (original version: 1859) 136

articulated a framework for regulating rights, famously known as the harm principle. Mill underlined that

> as soon as any part of a person's conduct affects prejudicially the interests of others, society has jurisdiction over it and the question whether the general welfare will or will not be promoted by interfering with it, becomes open to discussion.[82]

Notably, he argued that 'even opinions lose their immunity when the circumstances in which they are expressed are such as to constitute their expression a positive instigation to some mischievous act,'[83] highlighting a conceptual precursor to modern hate speech doctrines which address incitement to hatred or violence. While both advocated for a non-absolute version of freedom of expression, both Milton and Mill envisioned a society where debate and the exchange of conflicting ideas were essential to a vibrant democracy, in which truth emerges and effective solutions to societal issues are discovered through open discourse.[84] Their ideas laid the conceptual groundwork for the 'marketplace of ideas' theory, later articulated in *Abrams v United States* (1919), a case concerning anti-war activists. In his dissent, Justice Holmes (joined by Justice Brandeis) famously opined that 'the best test of truth is the power of thought to get itself accepted in the competition of the market.'[85] While the dissenting opinion does not directly refer to the marketplace of ideas, this term has been subsequently used in many Supreme Court majority decisions.

The problems with the marketplace of ideas have been examined by more modern academics. For instance, Post argues that free speech is crucial for citizens to participate in the deliberative processes required for democracy to work, and he defends the marketplace of ideas, especially in the context of democratic governance. Post underlines the importance of free speech in the ambit of enabling dialogue that reflects diversity as a precondition for legitimising democracy and maintaining public trust in it.[86] As he argues, 'persons prevented from expressing opposition to a statute are likely to regard the statute as unfairly enacted.'[87] In discussing the marketplace of ideas and the pursuit of truth, referencing Post and Weinstein, Volokh argues that the creation of knowledge relies on processes that consistently differentiate

82 Mill (n 81) 147
83 Mill (n 81) 131
84 John Milton, Areopagitica in Ernest Sirluck (ed), *Two Complete Prose Works of John Milton* (1st edn, Yale University Press 1959) (original version: 1644) 486
85 *Abraham v United States*, 250 US 616 (1919): The Court upheld the conviction of five anti-war protestors who had been charged with sedition for distributing anti-war pamphlets—at 630 (Holmes J., dissenting)
86 Robert Post, 'Participatory Democracy and Free Speech' (2011) 97(3) Virginia Law Review 22
87 Robert Post, 'Legitimacy and Hate Speech' (2017) 32 Constitutional Commentary 654

between truth and falsehood, as well as between what is superior and what is inferior. However, he stipulates that the marketplace of ideas must, in some way, be regulated. But this does not imply that the government should be responsible for imposing such regulations through coercive measures. He proposes alternative measures for regulatory pursuit, referring to academia, civil society and think tanks as those who are 'constantly engaging in a process through which truth and falsehood are separate.'[88] In this ambit, he argues that the government should leave those actors free to engage in this non-restrictive regulation of the marketplace.

Scholars like Smolla contend that hate speech contributes nothing to the positive development of society and does not fit within the framework of a healthy marketplace of ideas. Smolla posits that hate speech 'states no fact, offers no opinion, proposes no transaction, attempts no persuasion.'[89] Brink adds that 'hate speech can poison the well of mutual respect and discourage participation in the deliberative community,'[90] thus negating the marketplace framework as a basis for its permissibility. Vulnerable and marginalised groups, including those targeted by hate speech, often lack the resources, platforms or societal power to counter harmful narratives effectively.[91] A study of the harms of sexist and racist hate speech found that many victims of such speech are pressured into ceasing engagement with public discourse. One participant in the study said:

> My whole family wants me to stop. And even my mother is getting all kinds of comments when she walks through our city.[92]

As well as group visibility and participation in the marketplace, group interest is also centrifugal for a healthy marketplace, since 'a precondition for an enlightened democratic debate is that all group-based interests are represented in public discourse.'[93] Furthermore, the theory assumes that individuals are capable of discerning truth from falsehood through rational deliberation, a presumption that does not account for cognitive biases, misinformation or the emotional impact of hate speech.

Critical race theorists contend that the libertarian approach to free speech and hate speech does 'not acknowledge the imbalance of power that exists

88 Eugene Volokh, 'In Defense of the Marketplace Ideas/Search for Truth as a Theory of Fire Speech Protection' (2011) 97(3) Virginia Law Review 596
89 Rodney A. Smolla, *Free Speech in an Open Society* (1st edn, Alfred A. Knopf 1993) 166–167
90 David O. Brink, 'Millian Principles, Freedom of Expression and Hate Speech' (2001) 7(2) Legal Theory 140
91 Tsesis, *Destructive Messages* (n 11) 44–50, 98–105
92 Tjon Soei Len and de Ruijter (n 23) 24
93 Fladmoe and Nadim (n 69) 53

within American society.'[94] According to critical race theory, society is marked by profound inequality of arms due to an entrenched prejudice against marginalised groups, which results in these groups being unable to participate equally in discourse with those who espouse hateful views.

Matsuda defines *speech* as hateful in circumstances when the message is hateful, degrading and menacing; is founded on ideas of racial inferiority; and is directed at a traditionally marginalised group.[95] Given the emphasis of critical race theory on the unequal position historically experienced by marginalised groups, Matsuda argues that, when hate speech is directed at society's dominant group, the libertarian model of free speech should apply.[96] On one hand, this stance could be justified by the fact that the majority group is not impeded by systemic inequalities, prejudices and discrimination and can, thus, effectively respond to hate speech without any detriment to its societal position, which remains dominant. On the other hand, this approach could be difficult to reconcile with foundational legal principles, such as the equal application of the law. Lawrence argues that racism is embedded within both expression and conduct, asserting that racist speech by White supremacists curtails the freedom of their targets. He criticises free speech absolutists for their lack of understanding of the lived experiences of hate speech victims, as they 'fail to comprehend both the nature and extent of the injury inflicted by racist speech.'[97] Drawing on the libertarian concept of the free marketplace of ideas, Lawrence suggests that racist speech represents a failure of this marketplace, as its functioning is undermined by racial power structures that place certain groups in inferior positions. Lawrence discusses the silencing impact of hate speech on its target by noting that it triggers an instinctive, defensive psychological reaction, characterised by fear, rage, shock and a tendency to flee, all of which hinder a reasoned response. He adds that many victims may not find words to articulate their experience 'until well after the assault, when the cowardly assaulter has departed.'[98] Brink asserts that hate speech 'evokes visceral, rather than articulate responses,'[99] provoking violence or, more commonly, silencing individuals through insult or intimidation. According to Delgado and Stefancic, hate speech frequently plays on fear and prejudice, rather than rational discussion, influencing feelings and feeding negative preconceptions rather than promoting sincere dialogue.[100] These scholars essentially discover that there is a basic problem with using conventional reasoning to combat hate

94 Mark Slagle, 'An Ethical Exploration of Free Expression and the Problem of Hate Speech' (2009) 24(4) Journal of Mass Media Ethics 239
95 Matsuda and others (n 1) 36
96 Matsuda and others (n 1) 38
97 Lawrence (n 19) 457
98 Lawrence (n 19) 452–453
99 Brink (n 90) 139
100 Richard Delgado and Jean Stefancic, *Must We Defend Nazis?* (1st edn, New York University Press 2018)

speech: The intense impact it produces frequently prevents real communication between opposing viewpoints, thereby limiting the possibility of rational discourse and positive results. Barendt argues that hate speech 'silences the voice of members of the targeted group,'[101] as hate speech 'may reinforce prejudices and feelings of inferiority in a seriously harmful way,'[102] and that allowing such expression effectively restricts the ability of certain groups to exercise their own rights.[103] In this sense, hate speech has an effect that goes beyond direct injury, since it influences the willingness of people to participate in public discourse, frequently resulting in self-censorship and decreased visibility. As a result, the experience of hate speech, or even the mere expectation of it, can suppress the expression of individuals who are targeted, so eliminating their viewpoints from the marketplace of ideas and essentially silencing them. In this regard, hate speech functions as a 'social boundary for free speech,'[104] constraining the exercise of this fundamental right for those who are its targets.

These arguments position freedom of expression within societal realities, highlighting how hate speech deepens the marginalisation of its victims, who are excluded from a truly free marketplace of ideas. While critiques of the marketplace model are compelling, it remains uncertain whether regulating hate speech through legislation effectively addresses the issue. I contend that such regulation is fraught with limitations for reasons of the fundamentality of free speech, but also in terms of the repercussions which hate speech regulations can have on, *inter alia*, social cohesion and stability. Moreover, speech restrictions fail to tackle the systemic injustices that distort public discourse and marginalise underrepresented voices. Instead of addressing the power imbalances that enable hate speech, these policies risk exacerbating social divides and increasing state control over expression. The focus should shift towards dismantling structural inequalities that silence marginalised voices. The challenge lies in fostering an environment where all individuals, particularly those historically excluded, can participate fully and equitably in public discourse. However, I acknowledge that this is a long-term and perhaps overly ambitious goal, unlikely to be achieved in its entirety. This recognition does not, however, negate the importance of regulating speech that incites real-world violence, particularly in volatile contexts, where such speech poses an immediate threat to safety and stability. Striking a balance between long-term structural change and the need for immediate safeguards remains complex.

For the ECtHR, a crucial starting point is to engage with the diverse perspectives on the harms caused by hate speech and the challenges of its regulation. As highlighted, the severity of harm varies depending on factors such as

101 Delgado and Stefancic (n 100)
102 Eric Barendt, 'Hate Speech: Lecture Given at Hull' (November 21, 2013): <www2.hull.ac.uk/fass/pdf/Eric%20Barendt-HATE%20SPEECH.pdf> accessed 1 October 2024
103 Barendt (n 102)
104 Fladmoe and Nadim (n 69) 47

the type and context of speech, underscoring the need for regulatory measures that reflect these nuances rather than a uniform approach. Any coherent definitional framework must account for these variations to clearly delineate what should and should not be prohibited. Before asserting narratives that lack empirical or normative support, the Court must critically explore these different approaches to hate speech, its meaning, impact and harm. Doing so would not only ensure that its judgements substantially satisfy the test of necessity but also deepen its understanding of hate speech and its complex impacts. This, in turn, would aid the ECtHR in crafting a sound framework for assessing harm thresholds, enabling more informed and principled decisions in this challenging area of law.

2.2 *Theorising the Approach of the European Court of Human Rights*

Article 10 of the ECHR allows for restrictions to speech on grounds such as respecting the rights and reputation of others and maintaining public order. This set-up rings militant democracy bells, where democratic rights can be limited for purposes of protecting democracy itself. However, Article 17 of the ECHR, titled 'prohibition of abuse of rights,' prohibits any state, group or individual from using any of their Convention rights for purposes of destroying any of the other rights and freedoms set forth in the ECHR. This is the closest embodiment of the doctrine of militant democracy theory that we find in the ECHR and has been used in an array of hate speech cases. The underlying rationale for the ECtHR's stance is rooted in (a very broad) understanding of the concept of militant democracy, discussed in what follows. As such, and in order to better understand theoretical elements underlying the treatment of hate speech cases by the ECtHR, as discussed in Chapters 4 and 5, the following section will give an overview of the doctrine of militant democracy.

3 Militant Democracy

3.1 *History and Overview*

The doctrine of militant democracy is to protect itself from anti-democratic forces. As Joseph Goebbels infamously said, 'it will always remain one of the best jokes of democracy that it provides its own deadly enemies with the means with which it can be destroyed.'[105] Overcoming the core flaws in democratic institutions that anti-democratic forces could exploit is the aim of the militant democracy philosophy. Militant democracy, therefore, proposes pre-emptive restrictions on civil and political rights, particularly freedoms of expression, association and assembly, when such rights are used to threaten the democratic order itself. Militant democracy was first conceptualised by Karl Loewenstein

105 As quoted in *Nationalsozialistische Diktatur 1933–1945*: Eine Bilanz 16 (K. D. Bracher and others (eds), Droste 1983)

in his seminal 1937 articles, written after he fled Nazi Germany. Loewenstein argued that democracy must proactively defend itself against internal threats, particularly those exploiting democratic freedoms to subvert the system. He asserted that 'democracy and democratic tolerance have been used for their own destruction'[106] and warned that 'constitutions . . . have to be stiffened and hardened when confronted by movements intent upon their destruction.'[107] Loewenstein's arguments were shaped by the rise of the Nazi Party, which had exploited the democratic institutions of the Weimar Republic, highlighting the necessity for democracies to adopt defensive measures against anti-democratic actors.

In post-war Germany, the basic law adopted the use of militant democracy as a guarantee against a return to Nazi authority, and it became a fundamental doctrine. The German Constitution established a precedent as the first European model, and several post–World War II European constitutions adopted comparable safeguards against anti-democratic and extremist forces. Since then, this concept has been the focus of intense discussion in the legal, political and academic domains, as academics and decision-makers grapple with its ramifications.

Despite its foundational influence, militant democracy lacks a singular, universally accepted definition. Various scholars have articulated different interpretations, emphasising distinct aspects of the doctrine. Macklem defines it as 'a form of constitutional democracy authorised to protect civil and political freedom by pre-emptively restricting the exercise of such freedoms.'[108] Harvey describes *militant democracy* as a system 'capable of defending the constitution against anti-democratic actors who use the democratic process in order to subvert it.'[109] Pfersmann highlights both the political and legal functions of militant democracy, noting that it 'aims at preserving democracy against those who want to overturn it from within or those who openly want to destroy it from outside.'[110] The principle underlying militant democracy is that democracies must be vigilant and, at times, militant in their self-preservation. Pfersmann succinctly states that 'democracies are always more or less militant,'[111] reflecting the necessity of defensive measures to ensure their survival. Posner supports this view, arguing that liberal constitutions should

106 Karl Loewenstein, 'Militant Democracy and Fundamental Rights I' (1937) 31(3) The American Political Science Review 423

107 Loewenstein (n 106)

108 Patrick Macklem, 'Militant Democracy, Legal Pluralism, and the Paradox of Self-determination' (2005) 4(3) International Journal of Constitutional Law 488

109 Paul Harvey, 'Militant Democracy and the European Convention on Human Rights' (2004) 29(3) European Law Review 408

110 Otto Pfersmann, 'Shaping Militant Democracy: Legal Limits to Democratic Stability' in Andras Sajó (ed), *Militant Democracy* (1st edn, Eleven International Publishing 2004) 47

111 Pfersmann (n 110) 53

adopt self-defence measures[112] when faced with existential threats.[113] This perspective remains relevant today, particularly given the rise of far-right and neo-Nazi movements that give leverage to democratic freedoms to promote anti-democratic agendas.

3.2 Challenges and Criticisms

When evaluating militant democracy, it is crucial to consider the practical impact of the doctrine beyond its theoretical foundations. Karl Loewenstein warned against placing excessive faith in legal measures alone to counteract anti-democratic forces, cautioning that one must not 'overestimate the ultimate efficiency of legislative provisions against fascist emotional technique.'[114] His insight underscores the limitations of militant democracy in achieving its aims through legislation alone, highlighting the potential unintended consequences when dealing with ideologically driven movements.

This dynamic is exemplified by Germany's experience in the 1990s, where despite stringent measures against far-right groups, there was a notable rise in far-right violence, organised mobilisation and a radicalisation of their ideologies rather than their suppression. Minkenberg observed that despite the implementation of restrictive measures against far-right groups, the state experienced an increase in far-right violence, more cohesive mobilisation, and a radicalisation of the movement's ideology, rather than the eradication of the threat.[115] This underscores a paradox of militant democracy, where efforts to suppress extremist groups can unintentionally reinforce their determination and garner increased public sympathy. Critics warn that the doctrine's expansive reach risks transforming democracies into illiberal regimes overly focused on stability at the expense of freedom. Sajó cautions that 'a militant democracy can easily become an illiberal democracy, more concerned with its own stability than with political developments.'[116] Some, such as Macklem, note that 'the legality of militant democracy . . . is far from clear,'[117] with others, including Kelsen, taking a stricter approach, namely, that when a democracy attempts to safeguard itself from anti-democratic entities, it is no longer a democracy.[118] Loewenstein himself acknowledged the inherent

112 Richard A Posner, *Not a Suicide Pact: The Constitution in a Time of National Emergency* (1st edn, OUP 2006)

113 Posner (n 112)

114 Loewenstein (n 106) 658

115 Michael Minkenberg, 'Repression and Reaction: Militant Democracy and the Radical Right in Germany and France' (2006) 40(25) Patterns of Prejudice 43–44

116 John E Finn, *Constitutions in Crisis: Political Violence and the Rule of Law* (1st edn, OUP 1991) 217

117 Macklem (n 108) 488

118 Paul Cliteur and Bastiaan Rijpkema, 'The Foundations of Militant Democracy' in Afshin Ellian and Gelijn Molier (eds), *The State of Exception and Militant Democracy in a Time of Terror* (1st edn, Republic of Letters Publishing 2012) 243

contradiction in militant democracy, noting that 'democracy stands for fundamental rights, for fair play for all opinions, for free speech, assembly, press. How could it address itself to curtailing these without the very basis of its existence?'[119] Yet he justified these restrictions by arguing that democracies must protect themselves 'even at the risk and cost of violating fundamental principles' to guard against 'the opportunistic platitudes of fascism.'[120] This dilemma is echoed in Karl Popper's 'paradox of tolerance,'[121] which posits that 'unlimited tolerance must lead to the disappearance of tolerance,'[122] and that societies must 'reserve the right not to tolerate the intolerant'[123] to maintain an open society. Rosenblum argues that including anti-democratic actors within the democratic process could potentially compel them to adjust their tactics and align more closely with democratic norms, stating that their participation might force them to 'reformulate their objectives in ways that are consistent with democratic partisanship.'[124] Accetti and Zuckerman argue that the doctrine's application often involves an 'irreducible element of arbitrariness in whichever way the decision is taken as to what constitutes an enemy of democracy,'[125] raising the spectre of majoritarian tyranny or political opportunism. They caution that decisions regarding who may participate in the democratic process ultimately 'define the boundaries of the political community itself'[126] and are, thus, inherently undemocratic. Loewenstein and other scholars have warned against overestimating the effectiveness of militant democratic measures, particularly when confronting movements that employ subtle, non-violent tactics. Loewenstein noted, '[O]ne must not overestimate the ultimate efficiency of legislative provisions against fascist emotional technique.'[127] For example, despite the stringent measures in place in post-war Germany, far-right violence surged in the 1990s, demonstrating that militant democracy can sometimes exacerbate rather than eliminate extremist threats.[128]

119 Loewenstein (n 106) 656
120 Loewenstein (n 106) 432
121 As explained in Karl Popper, *The Open Society and Its Enemies* (published in two volumes: *The Spell of Plato* and *The High Tide of Prophecy: Hegel, Marx, and the Aftermath*) (1st edn, Routledge 1945) 546
122 Popper (n 121)
123 Popper (n 121)
124 Nancy Rosenblum, *On the Side of the Angels: An Appreciation of Parties and Partisanship* (1st edn, Princeton UP 2008)
125 Carlo Invernizzi Accetti and Ian Zuckerman, 'What's Wrong with Militant Democracy?' (2017) 65(1) Political Studies 183
126 Accetti and Zuckerman (n 125) 100
127 Loewenstein (n 106) 658
128 Michael Minkenberg, 'Repression and Reaction: Militant Democracy and the Radical Right in Germany and France' (2006) 40(1) Patterns of Prejudice 43–44

3.3 Militant Democracy and the European Court of Human Rights

The ECtHR has applied the doctrine of militant democracy in Article 10 (freedom of expression) and Article 11 (freedom of assembly and association) cases. The Court's application of militant democracy often centres on the 'prohibition of abuse of rights' clause found in Article 17. This provides that:

> Nothing in this Convention may be interpreted as implying for any State, group or person any right to engage in any activity or perform any act aimed at the destruction of any of the rights and freedoms set forth herein or at their limitation to a greater extent than is provided for in the Convention.

While militant democracy pre-emptively restricts rights for the protection of democracy itself, Article 17 prohibits the abuse of rights, which may destroy any of the other rights and freedoms set forth in the Convention. So the militancy in the ECtHR's democracy is manifested in its prohibition of abusing the rights found therein so as to prevent the destruction of ECHR rights (not referring, in the article, to democracy itself but, rather, to the rights set out therein). As such, it can be argued that Article 17's approach aligns with the aims of militant democracy, which are to prevent the abuse of rights by those who seek to subvert them. In older Commission hate speech cases, direct reference was made to the protection of democracy, thereby perfectly embodying the doctrine of militant democracy. For example, in *Kuhnen v Germany* (1988), the ECtHR examined the case of a neo-Nazi activist who was convicted for promoting Nazi ideology and inciting racial hatred through his speeches. The Court dismissed the application, invoking Article 17 to justify the restriction of Kuhnen's speech, which sought to revive National Socialism. The European Commission on Human Rights (EComHR/Commission) considered that the applicant's proposals 'ran counter to one of the basic values underlying the Convention, as expressed in its fifth preambular paragraph, namely, that the fundamental freedoms enshrined in the Convention are best maintained . . . by an effective political democracy.'[129] With some exceptions, such as *Garaudy v France* (2003), which involved a case of holocaust denial and in which the ECtHR held that this is 'incompatible with democracy and human rights,'[130] more recent Article 17 jurisprudence on hate speech does not directly refer to democracy. Article 17 cases emanate from speech being (1) contrary to the text and spirit of the Convention and (2) contrary to Convention values. Starting with the former, we have several examples which will be analysed later on in the book, but basic reference to the use and application of Article 17 with emphasis on the aspect of militant democracy is made

129 *Kühnen v Germany* App no 12194/86 (EComHR, 12 May 1998)
130 *Garaudy v France* App no 65931/01 (ECHR, 24 June 2003)

here. For example, in *Pastörs v Germany* (2019), the applicant, a politician affiliated with the National Democratic Party of Germany, made public statements the day after Holocaust Remembrance Day in which he denied the occurrence of the Holocaust. He was subsequently convicted for denying the systematic, racially motivated genocide of the Jewish people, specifically the mass exterminations carried out at Auschwitz during the Third Reich. The ECtHR deemed his application manifestly ill-founded and rejected it accordingly. In applying Article 17, the Court noted that 'the applicant sought to use his right to freedom of expression with the aim of promoting ideas contrary to the text and spirit of the Convention.'[131] This was also phrased as part of the government's submission. The Court did not extrapolate on what is meant by the spirit of the Convention, nor did the case of *Perinçek v Switzerland* (2015) cited provide any explanation of this term. In *M'Bala and M'Bala v France* (2015), the applicant, a comedian, performed a show in which he publicly honoured a well-known revisionist academic. The performance was characterised by overtly anti-Semitic content and was deemed by the Court to run counter to the text and spirit of the Convention[132] (without explanation of what this may mean). In *Witzsch v Germany* (2005), the applicant sent a (private) letter to a professor in response to an article the professor had published which discussed the culpability of the Nazi Party and Hitler's intent to murder the Jewish people. In his letter, the applicant asserted that these statements were false. He was subsequently convicted of disparaging the memory of the deceased and was sentenced to imprisonment. The ECtHR, relying on Article 17 of the Convention, held that his speech fell outside the scope of Convention protection as it was aimed at denying historical facts and promoting hate speech. The Court observed that 'the general purpose of Article 17 is to make it impossible for individuals to take advantage of a right with the aim of promoting ideas contrary to the text and spirit of the Convention.'[133] It found that the applicant's views regarding the culpability of the Nazi Party and Hitler ran counter to the aforementioned spirit but did not offer any explanation of what this may mean.

Some cases refer to the speech's compatibility with Convention values. More explanation has been put forth regarding this 'leg' of Article 17 explanation, although remaining insufficient. For example, in *Norwood v the United Kingdom* (2004), the applicant, a member of the far-right British National Party, displayed a poster depicting the Twin Towers in flames with the words "Islam Out of Britain—Protect the British People." The applicant challenged his conviction under Article 10. However, the ECtHR dismissed the application through Article 17 and held that 'such expressions are incompatible

131 *Pastörs v Germany* (2019) App no 55225/13 (ECHR, 3 October 2019) para 46
132 *M'Bala and M'Bala v France* (2015) App no 25239/13 (ECHR, 20 October 2015) paras 33, 41
133 *Witzsch v Germany* App no 41448/89 (ECHR, 20 April 1999)

with the values proclaimed and guaranteed by the Convention, notably tolerance, social peace, and non-discrimination.'[134] This line of reasoning was followed in *Pavel Ivanov v Russia* (2007), along with some form of extrapolation of what convention values mean. The case involved a newspaper publisher who produced a series of anti-Semitic articles accusing Jewish people of conspiring against Russia. Ivanov's conviction for inciting hatred was contested on the grounds of free speech. The ECtHR, applying Article 17, ruled that a 'general and vehement attack on one ethnic group is in contradiction with the Convention's underlying values, notably tolerance, social peace and non-discrimination.'

The 2023 case of *Lenis v Greece* involved a high-ranking church official who faced criminal conviction for public incitement to violence or hatred and abuse of ecclesiastical office. Some of the speech discussed in the case included a blog titled "The scum of society have reared their heads! Let's be honest spit on them!" In applying Article 17 on the grounds that the speech in question is contrary to Convention values, the Court noted that Article 17

> should only be resorted to if it is immediately clear that the disputed statements sought to deflect this Article from its real purpose by employing the right to freedom of expression for ends clearly contrary to the values of the Convention.

It proceeded to give a 'list' of cases that fall under the framework of Article 17 and, although it noted that this is non-exhaustive, referred to Holocaust denial, Islamophobia, anti-Semitism and inciting violence against all non-Muslims.[135]

3.4 *Criticisms of the ECtHR's Militant Democracy Approach*

The ECtHR's reliance on Article 17 in hate speech cases is critical to its application of militant democracy. By prohibiting the abuse of Convention rights, Article 17 ensures that the freedoms guaranteed under the ECHR cannot be used as tools to undermine democratic values. This approach reflects a core tenet of militant democracy: protecting the democratic order from those who seek to destabilise it from within. As the Court has stated, 'the general purpose of Article 17 is . . . to prevent totalitarian or extremist groups from exploiting in their own interests the principles enunciated by the Convention.'[136] However, as reflected earlier, its use has gone far beyond the doctrine of militant democracy to protect generic themes, such as 'values.' In fact, the ECtHR's broad application of Article 17 risks suppressing legitimate political expression, as will be further discussed later on in the book.

134 *Norwood v the United Kingdom* App no 23131/04 (ECHR, 16 November 2004)
135 *Lenis v Greece* App no 47833/20 (ECHR, 27 June 2023) para 52
136 See, for example, *Paksas v Lithuania* App no 34932/04 (ECHR, 6 January 2011) para 87

3.5 *Final Thoughts*

Militant democracy thus remains an issue of extensive debate due to the complex balance it seeks between protecting democratic order and limiting personal freedoms. Despite the theoretical justifications for limiting democracy to protect it, practical implementation poses numerous challenges, such as suppression of minority voices, restriction of the fundamental right of freedom of expression and several more that will be looked into later on. Defining the exact point at which restrictions should commence and determining how long they should last are contentious issues. As Macklem argues, 'the legality of militant democracy and its effectiveness will remain vague and open to abuse unless clear legal standards are established, including definitions of what constitutes a threat to democracy.'[137] This has not been the case with the ECtHR, which has applied a broad interpretation of Article 17 in hate speech cases.

Conclusion

The most profound consequences of hate speech are evident in its potential to incite mass violence. Historical instances, such as the Rwandan genocide and the atrocities against Rohingya Muslims in Myanmar, underline how hate speech, disseminated through media, such as radio and social platforms, escalates societal animosities to catastrophic levels. Empirical findings, such as Yanagizawa-Drott's study linking radio penetration to violence in Rwanda and the UN Fact-Finding Mission's conclusion on Myanmar, highlight this reality. Beyond violence, hate speech also operates as a mechanism of subordination, perpetuating systemic inequalities and psychological harm. Scholars like Matsuda, Waldron, and Delgado have underscored its role in degrading dignity, eroding democratic values and fostering societal divisions.

While hate speech can and does result in harm (the level of harm is disputed), the debate over its regulation remains fraught with tension between protecting free expression and mitigating harm. Proponents of regulation, such as Waldron, argue that it safeguards inclusiveness and equality, while critics like Strossen and Rauch warn of overreach, potential misuse and the stifling of dissent. In the digital age, challenges multiply, as regulations may inadvertently push harmful speech into unregulated spaces, creating echo chambers that reinforce extremist views. As Shaw aptly observes, cyberspace, and participating therein, makes perpetrators 'more likely to become entrenched in their hateful beliefs when given the legitimacy of a global audience.'[138] This is even more so when hate speech is removed from mainstream platforms, as this often drives perpetrators to less-regulated or underground spaces, where they create echo chambers insulated from broader public scrutiny. This insight is increasingly applicable to the digital age, where attempts to silence

137 Macklem (n 108) 495

138 Lashel Shaw, 'Hate Speech in Cyberspace: Bitterness without Boundaries' (2012) 25(1) Notre Dame Journal of Law, Ethics & Public Policy 282

hate speech may inadvertently amplify its impact and further radicalise those spreading it. Thus, any response to hate speech must carefully balance its harm with the unintended consequences of regulation, particularly in the complex and evolving digital environment. My position is that speech should only be restricted when it has the demonstrable potential to incite real-world violence, as determined by factors such as context, timing and typology. Regulation risks becoming overly expansive, leading to unintended consequences, such as the suppression of dissent, the amplification of extremist rhetoric and the erosion of public trust in the legitimacy of regulation. Rather than adopting a "plaster approach" that seeks to regulate speech indiscriminately, the focus should be on addressing the structural inequalities that underlie and perpetuate the marginalisation of vulnerable groups. These deeper systemic issues are the root cause of hate speech's most damaging effects and require long-term, transformative solutions that empower marginalised voices to participate fully and equitably in public discourse.

In light of the factors put forth in the chapter, my position is rooted in caution. By limiting regulation to speech that incites violence, an area where the risks and harms are most acute and demonstrable, it is possible to strike a balance between protecting vulnerable groups and preserving the fundamental right to freedom of expression. This approach also avoids the pitfalls of overreach and ensures that the focus remains on addressing the structural conditions that enable hate speech to thrive, rather than merely silencing it. However, I recognise that this threshold is unlikely to be adopted by the ECtHR, given its current jurisprudence, which restricts even offensive or insulting speech. Instead, the Court should begin by engaging more critically with the nuanced findings of empirical and theoretical scholarship. This would not only help its judgements meet the test of necessity but also foster a deeper understanding of hate speech's impacts, enabling the development of a more coherent framework for assessing harm. Ultimately, regulating hate speech involves navigating the severity of the speech and the possibility of harm, ascertained through socio-political and contextual nuances. Unfortunately, as subsequent chapters will reveal, the ECtHR has yet to grapple substantively with these complexities.

3 The Council of Europe

Introduction

The Council of Europe emerged from the devastation of the Second World War, with its founding members pledging to uphold human rights and fundamental freedoms. Membership of the Council of Europe is no longer confined to Western European nations. Since the dissolution of the Soviet Union and the conclusion of the Cold War, the geographic and cultural reach of the Convention has extended eastward, now incorporating all the former Soviet Eastern Bloc countries (except Russia). In March 2022, and after 26 years of membership, Russia was suspended from the Council of Europe as a consequence of the country's aggression against Ukraine.[1] It ceased to be a contracting party to the ECHR on 16 September 2022.[2] At the core of the commitment of the countries to the COE lies the ECHR and the related jurisprudence of the European Court of Human Rights (ECtHR/Court). All 46 Council of Europe member states are parties to this Convention. The European Convention on Human Rights (ECHR) has been hailed as the 'greatest monument to the Council,'[3] representing the 'most comprehensive and developed system for supranational human rights protection.'[4] Since its enactment, the ECHR has been a 'standard setting text for transition to peace and democracy throughout Europe.'[5] The ECHR was opened for signature on 4 November 1950 and entered into force on 3 September 1953. The contracting parties of the ECHR

1 Council of Europe, 'The Russian Federation is Excluded from the Council of Europe' (16 March 2022) <https://www.coe.int/en/web/portal/-/the-russian-federation-is-excluded-from-the-council-of-europe> accessed 28 July 2024

2 'Resolution of the European Court of Human Rights on the Consequences of the Cessation of Membership of the Russian Federation to the Council of Europe considering Article 58 of the European Convention on Human Rights' (22 March 2022) <https://www.echr.coe.int/documents/d/echr/Resolution_ECHR_cessation_membership_Russia_CoE_ENG> accessed 28 July 2024

3 Ivan Hare and James Weinstein, *Extreme Speech and Democracy* (2nd edn, OUP 2011) 63

4 Hare and Weinstein (n 3)

5 Joseph Zand, 'The Concept of Democracy and the European Convention on Human Rights' (2017) 5(2) University of Baltimore Journal of International Law 196

DOI: 10.4324/9781003560548-4

commit to securing the rights and freedoms outlined therein, and the ECHR provides a system of individual judicial redress through ECtHR judgements. Article 19 established the ECtHR for purposes of 'ensuring the observance of the engagements undertaken by the High Contracting Parties in the Convention and the Protocols thereto.' The European Commission on Human Rights (EComHR/Commission) functioned between 1953 and 1998 but ceased to exist following the restructuring of the ECtHR. It assisted the ECtHR by assessing the admissibility of cases. This jurisprudence, as explored throughout this book, demonstrates both the Court's potential and its limitations in addressing hate speech in a manner that upholds democratic values and the principles of freedom of expression. Reference to EComHR hate speech case law is integrated in the discussion where relevant. The case law reflects enduring tensions between combatting harmful rhetoric and safeguarding pluralistic debate, a theme critically explored in subsequent chapters. The Committee of Ministers of the Council of Europe is responsible for monitoring the execution of ECtHR judgements, doing so through communication with national authorities, civil societies and national human rights institutions. As well as its enforcement role, the Committee issues recommendations to member states of the Council of Europe, such as Recommendation 15 on Combatting Hate Speech, discussed in Chapter 1.

In addition to the ECHR and its implementing body, the ECtHR, the Council of Europe is home to the European Commission against Racism and Intolerance (ECRI). This is a human rights monitoring body which prepares reports and issues recommendations to member states of the Council of Europe on matters pertaining to its mandate. More specifically, it monitors action against racism; discrimination on grounds of racial, ethnic or national background; skin colour; citizenship; religion; language; sexual orientation, gender identity and sex characteristics; and intolerance in Europe.[6]

This chapter provides a foundational framework for the book's critical examination of the ECtHR's and the EComHR's jurisprudence on hate speech under the ECHR. Serving as a crucial precursor to the analyses in Chapters 4 and 5, it situates the ECtHR's adjudicative practices, elucidating the historical, theoretical and doctrinal tensions that underpin the regulation of hate speech. The chapter looks at Articles 10 and 17 of the ECHR, which collectively articulate the principles governing the protection of freedom of expression and its permissible limitations. By examining the substance of the aforementioned articles, the interpretative methodologies adopted by the ECtHR and former EComHR, along with practical application of the provisions, the chapter reveals how the ECtHR grapples with the intricate balance between safeguarding democratic freedoms and addressing the pernicious effects of hate speech. This discussion is extended to include the Additional Protocol to the Convention on Cybercrime, which addresses the criminalisation of racist and

6 'European Commission against Racism and Intolerance' <https://rm.coe.int/leaflet-ecri-2022/1680a969c9> accessed 28 July 2024

xenophobic acts in the digital domain, underscoring the evolving challenges posed by online platforms in the regulation of harmful expression. By critically engaging with the historical, textual and institutional dimensions of the Court's approach, the chapter not only contextualises the case law analyses that follow but also frames the book's broader critique of the inconsistencies and overreach that have characterised the ECtHR's hate speech rulings. In situating these issues within the Council of Europe's broader legal and philosophical ethos, this chapter elucidates the ways in which the ECtHR's jurisprudence both shapes and is shaped by the contested interplay between individual rights and collective societal values. This analysis is intended to provide readers with the tools necessary to critically engage with the thematic and jurisprudential explorations that underpin the book's argument for recalibrating the ECtHR's restrictive approach to hate speech adjudication.

1 The Council of Europe and the Freedom of Expression: An Overview

The freedom of expression is 'the great bulwark of liberty'[7] and a 'cornerstone upon which the very existence of a democratic society rests.'[8] It constitutes one of the 'basic conditions for [a democratic society's] progress, encapsulating ideas that may even 'offend, shock or disturb.'[9] Freedom of expression is intimately connected with democracy, freedom, human welfare and prosperity.[10]

Article 10 of the ECHR protects the right to freedom of expression. It is a qualified right which provides that:

> 1. Everyone has the right to freedom of expression. This right shall include freedom to hold opinions and to receive and impart information and ideas without interference by public authority and regardless of frontiers. This Article shall not prevent States from requiring the licensing of broadcasting, television or cinema enterprises.
> 2. The exercise of these freedoms, since it carries with it duties and responsibilities, may be subject to such formalities, conditions, restrictions or penalties as are prescribed by law and are necessary in a democratic society, in the interests of national security, territorial

7 John Trenchard and Thomas Gordon, 'Catos Letters' in Ronald Hamowy (ed) *Cato's Letters: Or Essays on Liberty, Civil and Religious, and Other Important Subjects* (Liberty Fund 1995)

8 Claudio Grossman, 'Challenges to Freedom of Expression within the Inter-American System: A Jurisprudential Analysis' (2012) 34(2) Human Rights Quarterly 361

9 *Handyside v the United Kingdom* App no 5493/72 (ECHR, 7 December 1976) para 49

10 See amongst others: John Gerring and others, 'Democracy and Human Development: Issues of Conceptualization and Measurement' (2021) 28(2) Democratization; Carl Henrik Knutsen, 'Why Democracies Outgrow Autocracies in the Long Run: Civil liberties, Information Flows and Technological Change' (2015) 68(3) Kyklos; Lasse Skjoldager Eskildsen and Christian Bjørnskov, 'Does Freedom of Expression Cause Less Terrorism?' (2020) 70 Political Studies 1 Simon Wigley and Arzu Akkoyunlu-Wigley, 'The Impact of Democracy and Media Freedom on Under-5 Mortality, 1961–2011' (2017) 190 Social Science & Medicine

> integrity or public safety, for the prevention of disorder or crime, for the protection of health or morals, for the protection of the reputation or rights of others, for preventing the disclosure of information received in confidence, or for maintaining the authority and impartiality of the judiciary.

The provision stipulates that 'everyone' has the right to freedom of expression. This includes natural and legal persons.[11] In addition to respecting the rights or reputations of others and protecting national security, public order, public health or morals, as provided for in the limitation grounds of Article 19, Article 10(2) of the ECHR permits legitimate formalities, conditions, restrictions or penalties for purposes such as territorial integrity, preventing disorder or crime, preventing the disclosure of confidential information and maintaining the authority and impartiality of the judiciary. However, it is crucial to note that these restrictions are limited by the requirement that they are necessary in a democratic society, rather than merely necessary to achieve one of the listed objectives, as stipulated in Article 19(3). Article 10 sets out all the different forms that interferences may take, rather than just referring to 'restrictions,' as is the case with Article 19.

Article 10, just like Article 19 of the ICCPR, of the International Covenant on Civil and Political Rights (ICCPR), has an additional qualification to other non-absolute rights. It holds that the exercise of the freedom of expression 'carries with it duties and responsibilities,' a feature absent in other articles of the Convention, reflecting the drafters' concerns regarding potential abuses or associated dangers linked to this right. Interestingly, no such additional qualification is associated to other similar rights, such as those of assembly and association, provided for in Article 11 of the ECHR.

Unlike the ECHR, the ICCPR contains Article 20(2), which is the closest we come to a hate speech clause in an international instrument that has an effect on Europe. Note that the regional equivalent of the Americas, namely, the American Convention on Human Rights, provides that

> any propaganda for war and any advocacy of national, racial or religious hatred that constitutes incitements to lawless violence or to any other similar action against any person or group of persons on any grounds including those of race, colour, religion, language or national origin shall be considered as offences punishable by law.[12]

11 Andrew Lester, David Pannick and Javan Herberg, *Human Rights Law and Practice* (3rd edn, LexisNexis 2009). For legal persons see cases such as *Sunday Times v the United Kingdom* App no 6538/74 (1979); *Delfi AS v Estonia* App no 64569/09 (2015)

12 Article 13(5) of the American Convention on Human Rights <https://www.cidh.oas.org/basicos/english/basic3.american%20convention.htm> accessed 28 July 2024

Notwithstanding the absence of an Article 20(2) equivalent in the ECHR, this has not hindered the ECtHR from ruling against applicants whose speech was considered to fall under the type of speech prohibited by Article 20(2). Also, it has not prevented the ECtHR or the former EComHR from deeming such cases inadmissible. In addition to the limitation clauses of Article 10 (freedom of expression), the 'prohibition of abuse of rights' clause found in Article 17 has also played a significant role in this context. When assessing hate speech cases under Council of Europe instruments, both in terms of the Court and the former Commission, the differentiation in approaches to hate speech and the varying use and application of Article 10 and Article 17 according to the type of hate speech are particularly interesting and will be assessed during the jurisprudential analysis.

According to long-standing jurisprudence of the ECtHR, the rights articulated in Article 10(1) are to be interpreted and applied broadly. The landmark case of *Handyside v the United Kingdom* (1976) dealt with the confiscation of a book. The applicant had purchased the rights to this book, which aimed to educate young people about sex. He was then convicted of possessing obscene material for gain under the Obscene Publications Act. In this case, the ECtHR famously highlighted:

> [F]reedom of expression constitutes one of the essential foundations of [a democratic society], one of the basic conditions for its progress and for the development of every man. . . . It is applicable not only to 'information' or 'ideas' that are favourably received or regarded as inoffensive or as a matter of indifference, but also to those that offend, shock or disturb the State or any sector of the population. Such are the demands of that pluralism, tolerance and broadmindedness without which there is no democratic society.[13]

However, the Court proceeded to find that the restriction to the applicant's Article 10 right fell within the state's margin of appreciation to ascertain what was necessary in a democratic society. In reaching this decision, the ECtHR referred to the lacking European consensus on the protection of public morals (particularly in relation to children), and that the publication was aimed at children between 12 and 18, and that, given the book's style, it was comprehendible even by the younger group of readers in that age group. Nevertheless, this case (one of the first freedom of expression cases before the ECtHR) is also considered to be one of the leading judgements on Article 10 due to references made to strict standards when limiting expression.

The Court has consistently emphasised the pivotal role of freedom of expression in a democratic and pluralist society, quoting the preceding paragraph in post-1976 cases on free speech. Whilst *Handyside* does emphasise the significance of freedom of expression in a democratic society, the ECtHR

13 *Handyside* (n 9) para 49

holds that a democracy should protect itself and its basic principles and must 'fight against abuses, committed in the exercise of freedom of speech, that openly target democratic values.'[14] In fact, the ECtHR has been rigorous in restricting speech it considers harmful to democracy and harmful to minority groups, building 'a substantial body of inconsistent case-law allowing restrictions on hate speech that severely questions the degree to which offensive, shocking and disturbing speech is truly protected.'[15] In relation to the preservation of democracy, and reflective of militant democracy principles, the Court has upheld the notion that a democracy must 'fight against abuses, committed in the exercise of freedom of speech, that openly target democratic values.'[16] This aligns with its self-preservation framework, which mirrors the objectives of militant democracy, emphasising that a democratic society is 'tolerant but not inert.'[17] The spirit of militant democracy is embodied in Article 17 of the Convention, which, particularly given the history of the Council of Europe and the reasons for its formation, could make sense. However, we have seen this article being used in cases where the threat to democracy is doubtful, with a recent example being the use of Article 17 to oust an application involving homophobic speech uttered by the applicant priest.[18] When it comes to minority protection, the Court has, through a doubtfully broad interpretation of Article 10 limitation grounds, prevented speech which is, *inter alia*, insulting,[19] offensive[20] and promoting stereotypes.[21] While this situation will be discussed in the analysis of hate speech case law, the note that is made at this point is that, despite the position of the Court in *Handyside* about the extensiveness of permissible speech, the jurisprudential reality paints a different picture, one of a weak protection of Article 10 in the face of controversial speech.

2 The Freedom of Expression and Its Abuse: A Short History

During the drafting of what would become Article 10 of the ECHR, several proposals were put forth for the content of the article. For example, Greece proposed 'special measures to deal with those who, under the pretext of

14 Jean-François Flauss, 'The European Court of Human Rights and the Freedom of Expression' (2009) 84(3) Indiana Law Journal 837

15 Jacob Mchangama and Natalie Alkiviadou, 'Hate Speech and the European Court of Human Rights: Whatever Happened to the Right to Offend, Shock or Disturb' (2021) 21(4) Human Rights Law Review 1009

16 Flauss (n 14)

17 Flauss (n 14)

18 *Lenis v Greece* App no 47833/20 (ECHR, 27 June 2023)

19 Examples include: *Féret v Belgium* App no 15615/07 (ECHR, 16 July 2009); *Vejdeland v Sweden* App no 1813/07 (ECHR, 5 September 2012); *Lilliendahl v Iceland* App no 29297/18 (ECHR, 11 June 2020)

20 *Lilliendahl* (n 19)

21 Examples include: *Vejdeland v Sweden* App no 1813/07 (ECHR, 5 September 2012)

expressing their opinion, have resorted to violence or else try to provoke it.'[22] The drafters considered that this situation was already tackled by the provision which would become today's Article 17.[23] Turkey suggested that freedom of expression should be permissible only to the extent consistent with the principles in the preamble to the Council of Europe's statute.[24] This proposal was driven by a Turkish law restricting extremist propaganda.[25] This proposal was rejected as overly restrictive.[26]

The most expansive provision within the ECHR for restricting various forms of expression, including hate speech, is Article 17, which allows for the absolute denial of certain expressions *ab initio*. The *Travaux préparatoires* illuminate the significant influence of Article 30 of the UDHR and Article 5 of the ICCPR (the 'prohibition of abuse of rights' clauses) on its formulation, as evidenced by numerous references to these texts during the consultations of the Council of Europe's consultative assembly.[27] In the initial discussions on Article 17, the Greek representative emphasised that 'human freedom, just because it is sacred, must not become an armoury in which the enemies of freedom can find weapons that they can later use unhindered to destroy this freedom.'[28] He suggested that the Convention be constructed in a way not only to prevent the tyrannical acts of those who misuse power but also against those who misuse freedom.[29] This sentiment was echoed by the French and Italian representatives, who also voiced concerns about preventing totalitarian ideologies from exploiting freedoms to undermine human rights.[30] Article 17 of the ECHR mirrors the rationale behind its counterpart in the ICCPR, specifically Article 5(1), which was designed to curb the rise of Nazi, fascist and other totalitarian ideologies. This legal framework embodies the concept of militant democracy, first articulated in 1937 by Karl Loewenstein, who argued that democracy should defend itself against those who would use its freedoms to undermine it, even if it means restricting fundamental principles,[31]

22 Statement of Mr. Callias, Eur. Consult. Ass. Deb. 1st Sess. 208 (September 1949) in Collected Edition of the Travaux *Preparatoires* of the European Convention on Human Rights (1975), as cited in Stephanie Farrior, 'Molding the Matrix: The Theoretical and Historical Foundations of International Law and Practice Concerning Hate Speech' (1996) 14(1) Berkley Journal of International Law 65

23 Farrior (n 22)

24 European Commission of Human Rights, Preparatory Work on Article 10 of the European Convention on Human Rights, Information document, Strasbourg 17 August 1956, 9

25 European Commission of Human Rights (n 24)

26 European Commission of Human Rights (n 24)

27 Council of Europe, Preparatory work on Article 17 of the European Convention of Human Rights, 23 April 1957

28 Comments made by Mr Maccas (Greece) during the First Session of the Consultative Assembly of the Council of Europe, 19 August 1949

29 Comments made by Mr. Maccas (n 28)

30 Comments made by Mr Benvenuti during the Assembly debate, 8 September 1949

31 Karl Loewenstein, 'Militant Democracy and Fundamental Rights I' (1937) 31(3) The American Political Science Review 423

as discussed in Chapter 2. The *Travaux* of the ECHR state that it was created to 'prevent rebirth of totalitarianism' and 'strengthen the resistance in all our countries against insidious attempts to undermine our way of life.'[32]

The drafters of Article 10, Article 17 and, to some extent, Article 11, on the freedom of association, envisioned restricting freedom of expression and association for movements and parties seeking to supplant democracy with totalitarian doctrines like Communism, Nazism and fascism. Nevertheless, there was less-explicit support for the blanket restriction of individuals expressing offensive, bigoted or racist views under the ECHR, despite many member states having enacted laws against incitement to hatred.[33] Thus, while the Travaux support the Court's reluctance to extend protection under the ECHR to genuine totalitarian movements and parties, much of the speech found to fall outside Convention protection by the Court does not fall within the spectre of totalitarianism. At the same time, the way Article 10 limitation grounds have been used is also difficult to reconcile with the Convention's history and the position of the Council of Europe states at that time to Article 20(2) of the ICCPR, discussed in Chapter 1. Specifically, the Court has restricted free speech in cases where expressions are insulting towards groups based on certain characteristics, including, amongst many others, *Féret v Belgium* (2009) and *Vejdeland v Sweden* (2012), discussed in Chapter 4. This stance is less aligned with the original intent of the Travaux, weakening protection for freedom of expression, particularly concerning the ill-defined concept of hate speech.

3 Article 10 and Types of Speech

From the jurisprudence of the ECtHR, a hierarchy of speech emerges, with political, artistic and commercial speech[34] being the main identifiable categories, in addition to freedom of the press[35] and whistleblowing.[36] Political speech is at the top of the speech league. As highlighted in *Lingens v Austria* (1986), the freedom to engage in political debate 'is at the very core of the concept of a democratic society.'[37] *Wingrove v the United Kingdom* (1990)

32 Council of Europe, Collected Edition of the Travaux Préparatoires of the European Convention on Human Rights, vol. 1, 30, 192; vol. 5, 332 (1975–1985)

33 Mchangama and Alkiviadou (n 15)

34 Ian Leigh, 'Damned If They Do, Damned If They Don't: The European Court of Human Rights and the Protection of Religion from Attack' (2011) 17(1) Res Publica 57

35 See, for example, *Jersild v Denmark* App no 15890/89 (ECHR, 23 September 1994)

36 Lucy Vickers, *Freedom of Speech and Employment* (1st edn, OUP 2002) 1; Council of Europe Parliamentary Assembly Resolution 1729 (2010) 'Protection of Whistle-Blowers'; *Heinisch v Germany* App no 28274/08 (ECHR, 21 October 2011) para 43

37 Case law includes, amongst others: *Lingens v Austria* App no 9815/82 (ECHR, 8 July 1986) para 42; *Özgürlük v Dayanişma Partisi (ÖDP v Turkey)* App no 7819/04 (ECHR, 10 May 2012) para 28; *Raëlien Suisse v Switzerland* App no 16354/06 (ECHR, 13 July 2012) para 46

emphasises that there is limited scope under Article 10(2) of the Convention to restrict political speech or matters of public interest.[38] In *Mouvement Raëlien Suisse v Switzerland* (2012), the ECtHR noted that the varying width of a state's margin of appreciation in interpreting and imposing restriction on expression depends on a range of issues, including the type of speech.[39] In this case, it held that 'there is little scope under Article 10(2) of the Convention for restrictions on political speech.'[40] In *Vereinigung Bildender Künstler v Austria* (2005), the Court held that a person's 'public standing as a politician' means that they must 'display a wider tolerance in respect of criticism.'[41] In addition to looking at the type and significance of speech, the ECtHR has also said that it evaluates the form, tone and content of expression.[42] The right to hyperbolic and provocative language and speech is considered a central part of political speech and, in this light, polemical,[43] sarcastic[44] and satirical[45] language is permitted. Moreover, a certain degree of exaggeration is broadly understood to be accepted, particularly in discussions on political issues.[46] In *Mariya Alekhina and Others v Russia* (2018), the Court was faced with the conviction of three members of the Pussy Riot band for incitement to religious hatred or enmity, the deeming of one of their performances as extremist and the banning of access to the performance's recording on the internet. Here, the ECtHR found that a protest performance in a cathedral constituted a 'mix of conduct and verbal expression and amounts to a form of artistic and political expression covered by Article 10.'[47]

Despite the primacy accorded to political speech, the Commission and the Court have underscored the responsibilities incumbent upon politicians in fostering peace and coexistence within a democratic society. For instance, in *Sener v Turkey* (2000), the Commission emphasised the duties and responsibilities associated with exercising freedom of expression in the political arena, noting that 'it is important for persons addressing the public on sensitive political issues to take care that they do not support unlawful political violence.'[48] Linked to this, and particularly pertinent to the domain of xenophobic speech by politicians and the significance attributed to such

38 *Wingrove v the United Kingdom* App no 17419/90 (ECHR, 25 November 1996) para 58; *Surek v Turkey* no 1 App no 26682/95 (ECHR, 8 July 1999) para 6; *Mouvement Raëlien Suisse v Switzerland* App no 16345/06 (ECHR, 13 July 2012) para 61

39 *Mouvement Raëlien Suisse* (n 38) para 61

40 *Mouvement Raëlien Suisse* (n 38)

41 *Vereinigung Bildender Künstler v Austria* (2005) App no 68354/01 (ECHR, 25 January 2007) para 34

42 *Fedchenko v Russia* App no 33333/04 (ECHR, 28 June 2010) para 38

43 *Lopes Gomes da Silva v Portugal* App no 37698/97 (ECHR, 28 September 2000) para 35

44 *Katrami v Greece* App no 19331/05 (ECHR, 6 December 2007)

45 *Eon v France* App no 26118/10 (ECHR, 14 June 2013) para 61

46 *Dabrowski v Poland* App no 18235/02 (ECHR, 19 December 2006) para 35

47 *Mariya Alekhina and others v Russia* App no 38004/12 (ECHR, 17 July 2018) para 206

48 *Şener v Turkey* App no 26680/95 (ECHR, 18 July 2000) para 79

political discourse, are the cases of *Féret v Belgium* (2009) and *Le Pen v France* (2010). In *Féret*, the leader of the National Front, a radical right political party, challenged his conviction for incitement to racism before the ECtHR. The case revolved around anti-immigrant statements and proposals made by Féret in leaflets distributed during an election campaign, such as "Stop the Islamization of Belgium" and "Save our people from the risk posed by Islam, the conqueror." The Court emphasised that 'political speech that stirred hatred based on religious, ethnic or cultural prejudices was a threat to social peace and political stability in democratic states.'[49] It further stressed the importance of politicians exercising caution in their public statements to avoid fostering intolerance, and that they should, rather, uphold democratic principles and underlying values.[50] Therefore, while acknowledging the role of political parties and that their representatives 'must enjoy broad freedom of expression to be able to attract voters,'[51] it did recognise that where racist or xenophobic comments were concerned, 'the electoral context helped to kindle hatred and intolerance and the impact of this type of speech grew worse and more harmful.'[52] The Court did not undertake further analysis to assess the potential harm or impact of such speech, nor did it engage in a balancing exercise between the significance of political speech, as delineated in *Wingrove*, and the allowance for speech that may 'shock, offend or disturb,'[53] as articulated in *Handyside*.

In *Le Pen*, the Court addressed a case brought by the leader of the radical right National Front, contesting the alleged violation of his Article 10 rights following his conviction for inciting hatred against Muslims during an interview with *Le Monde* newspaper. Among his statements, he remarked, "[W]hen I tell people that when we have 25 million Muslims in France we French will have to watch our step, they often reply, 'But, Le Pen, that is already the case now!'—and they are right." While the Court did not explicitly reference the specific responsibilities of politicians in promoting social cohesion and the broader obligations associated with political speech, as seen in *Féret*, this line of reasoning was implicitly apparent in the judgement. For instance, the Court acknowledged the importance of safeguarding free political expression while also emphasising the imperative to protect the rights of others and combat racial discrimination. The Court found this case to be manifestly ill-founded on the grounds that the applicant had promoted rejection and hostility against the Muslim community.[54]

49 *Féret* (n 19) para 73
50 *Féret* (n 19) para 75
51 *Féret* (n 19) para 75
52 *Féret* (n 19) para 76
53 *Handyside* (n 9) para 49
54 *Le Pen v France* App no 187788/09 (ECHR, 20 April 2010)

3.1 *Limiting Article 10 of the European Convention on Human Rights*

As noted by Buyse, 'few issues are as contested as the limits of freedom of expression.'[55] Whilst there is a plethora of positions across civil society and academia, and also amongst states themselves, on the limits of speech, both the former Commission and the ECtHR have systematically demonstrated a readiness to restrict what it identifies as hate speech. To determine these limits, the ECtHR has formulated a justification test derived from Article 10(2). As in the landmark case of *Sunday Times v the United Kingdom* (1979), the Court must ascertain whether the interference is necessary in a democratic society, whether there is a 'pressing social need' for the interference, whether it was proportionate to the legitimate aim pursued and whether its reasons are relevant and sufficient in light of the aims listed in Article 10(2). Moreover, the interference must be 'prescribed by law,' which means it must have a basis in domestic law, which is sufficiently accessible and foreseeable. In Chapters 4 and 5, emphasis is put on the issues of necessity and proportionality, unless issues arise under the other elements of Article 10(2), as these are the ones which are central to understanding how the ECtHR deals with hate speech.

3.1.1 *Prescribed by Law*

The ECtHR has established that the term 'law' should be interpreted in a manner that acknowledges and includes the various types of legal sources within the country concerned. In *Sunday Times*, the Court noted that 'law' encompasses both written statutes and the case law interpreting them. The Court identified two essential requirements arising from the 'prescribed by law' element. Firstly, the law must be readily accessible to citizens as 'the citizen must be able to have an indication that is adequate in the circumstances of the legal rules applicable to a given case.'[56] Secondly, the law must be 'formulated with sufficient precision to enable the citizen to regulate his conduct and to foresee, to a reasonable degree, the consequences which a given action may entail.'[57] However, the ECtHR acknowledged that striving for certainty and foreseeability might lead to excessively rigid laws that cannot adapt to changing circumstances. To this end, it noted that 'many laws are inevitably couched in terms which, to a greater or lesser extent, are vague and whose interpretation and application are questions of practice.'[58] In *Olsson v Sweden* (1988), the Court underlined that the phrase 'prescribed by law' pertains not only to the existence of the law itself but also to its quality, which must align

55 Antoine Buyse, 'Dangerous Expressions: The ECHR, Violence and Free Speech' (2014) 63(2) International and Comparative Law Quarterly 492
56 *Sunday Times* (n 11) para 47
57 *Sunday Times* (n 11)
58 *Sunday Times* (n 11)

with the rule of law.[59] The Court further recognised that the effort to maintain the organic nature of the law in a dynamic society can result in inherent vagueness. In *Sanoma Uitgevers BV v the Netherlands* (2010), the Court found that domestic law must 'afford a measure of legal protection against arbitrary interferences by public authorities with the rights safeguarded by the Convention.'[60]

3.1.2 Necessary in a Democratic Society

Article 10(2) of the ECHR stipulates that any interference must be 'necessary in a democratic society.' In order for the restriction to be in line with the freedom of expression, it must, amongst others, be necessary in a democratic society. The limitation ground which is usually relied on in hate speech cases is that of the protection of the rights and reputation of others. Under the ECHR, limitations to expression do not need to threaten the democratic order to be justified and legitimate. The 'necessary in a democratic society' prong of Article 10 must not be confused with the protection of democracy itself (the latter being more relevant to Article 17). Instead, restrictions must be necessary in a democratic society for purposes of ensuring one or more of the article's limitation grounds (such as the rights and reputation of others). To compare to the ICCPR, while Article 19 of the ICCPR overall sets a higher bar of free speech protection, it is interesting to note that the limitations under Article 19 make reference to the restriction being solely necessary rather than necessary in a democratic society.

In *United Communist Party of Turkey and Others v Turkey* (1998), the Court affirmed that 'democracy is the only political model contemplated by the Convention and, accordingly, the only one compatible with it.'[61] In *Ždanoka v Latvia* (2006), the Court highlighted that 'democracy constitutes a fundamental element of the European public order.'[62] Nevertheless, the substance and content of a democratic society test 'remains highly fluid and indeterminate.'[63] As noted, the phrase 'democratic society' is

> arguably one of the most important clauses in the entire Convention since, in principle it gives the Strasbourg organs the widest possible discretion in condoning or condemning interferences with rights which

59 *Olsson v Sweden* App no 10465/83 (ECHR, 24 March 1998) para 61(b)

60 *Sanoma Uitgevers B.V. v the Netherlands* App no 38224/03 (ECHR, 14 September 2010) para 82

61 *United Communist Party of Turkey and others v Turkey* App no 133/1996/752/951 (ECHR, 30 January 1998) para 45

62 *Ždanoka v Latvia* App no 58278/00 (ECHR, 16 March 2006) para 98

63 Conor A Gearty, 'The European Court of Human Rights and the Protection of Civil Liberties: An Overview' (1993) 52(1) The Cambridge Law Journal 96

> states seek to justify by reference to one or more of the legitimate purposes in the second paragraphs of Articles 8 to 11.[64]

However, what actually forms and characterises a democratic society, according to the ECHR and ECtHR, is not explicitly defined by the Court. Instead, the Court provides characteristics that define such a society. For instance, in *Handyside*, the Court emphasised the fundamental role of freedom of expression in a democratic society and described essential elements, such as 'pluralism, tolerance, and broadmindedness, without which there is no democratic society.'[65]

In *Young, James and Webster v the United Kingdom* (1982), the Court stated that this pluralism implies that

> democracy does not simply mean that the views of a majority must always prevail: a balance must be achieved which ensures the fair and proper treatment of minorities and avoids any abuse of a dominant position.[66]

The balancing test between the freedom of expression and hate speech is grounded on the premise that one must grant due consideration to 'the democratic importance of freedom of speech on the one hand and the harmful consequences of hate propaganda on the other hand.'[67]

In *Klass v Germany* (1978), the Court noted that 'some compromise between the requirements for defending democratic society and individual rights is inherent in the system of the Convention.'[68] In *Thomas v Luxembourg* (2001), it emphasised that restrictions on rights guaranteed by the Convention must be narrowly construed and enforced to serve the interests of public and social life as a whole, as well as those of the individuals constituting that society.[69] In *Ždanoka v Latvia*, the Court found that 'in order to guarantee the stability and effectiveness of a democratic system, the State may be required to take specific measures to protect itself.'[70] However, as highlighted in *United Communist Party of Turkey and Others v Turkey* (1998), the challenge lies in striking a balance between defending democracy and safeguarding individual rights and freedoms. To mitigate potential risks, this balancing must be

64 Steven Greer, 'The Exceptions to Articles 8 to 11 of the European Convention on Human Rights' (1997) Council of Europe Publishing—Human Rights Files no 15, p 14 <www.echr.coe.int/LibraryDocs/DG2/HRFILES/DG2-EN-HRFILES-15(1997).pdf> accessed 28 July 2024

65 *Handyside* (n 9) para 49

66 *Young, James and Webster v the United Kingdom* App nos. 7601/76, 7806/77 (ECHR, 13 August 1981) para 63; *Gorzelik v Poland* App no 44158/98 (ECHR, 10 November 2005) para 90; *Leyla Sahin v Turkey* App no 44774/98 (ECHR, 10 November 2005) para 108

67 *Stefan Sottiaux*, 'Bad Tendencies in the ECtHR's Hate Speech Jurisprudence' (2011) 7(1) European Constitutional Law Review 48

68 *Klass and others v Germany* App no 5029/71 (ECHR, 6 September 1978) para 59

69 *Thoma v Luxembourg* App no 38432/97 (ECHR, 29 March 2001) para 48

70 *Ždanoka v Latvia* App no 58278/00 (ECHR, 16 March 2006) para 100

conducted with meticulous care and thorough consideration of all involved actors and institutions. Despite some variation by the Court in interpreting the margin of appreciation, a state should indeed serve as the guiding force in balancing the different rights at stake, ensuring that individuals and groups do not exploit the legitimate aims of Article 10(1) for purposes contrary to the Convention. The Court tends to be overly zealous in restricting what it deems to be harmful speech in the name of a democratic society. A contributing factor to this is the lack of a robust theoretical analysis of the democratic society within which these restrictions are justified.

In *Sunday Times v the United Kingdom* (1979), the ECtHR determined that the term 'necessary' as incorporated in Article 10(2) 'is not synonymous with indispensable, nor does it possess the flexibility of terms like admissible, ordinary, useful, reasonable, or desirable; rather, it implies the existence of a pressing social need.' As noted in *Otto-Preminger-Institut v Austria* (1994), the Court considers whether the expressions under consideration are 'gratuitously offensive to others and, thus, an infringement of their rights and which, therefore, do not contribute to any form of public debate capable of furthering progress in human affairs.'[71] This is problematic, for several reasons. Firstly, in *Handyside*, the Court underlined that expression can extend to offensive ideas. Does the addition of the adjective 'gratuitously' alter that precedent? So if something is 'just' offensive, it should be accepted, but if something is 'gratuitously' so, then it should not? In *Otto-Preminger-Institut*, the Court gave the national authorities a broad margin of appreciation as they were considered better placed to assess what would be offensive. Is that not an overstep of state power? Determining whether or not (in this case a film) would be offensive to some? Surely, the people watching the film would choose whether or not to go and watch it. No one was forced to do so. Further, why should all forms of expression have to contribute to a public debate that furthers progress in human affairs? Why should the exercise of Article 10 rights lead to something specific, such as the progress mentioned? On the other hand, are not the existence and maintenance of a public space contributing factors to human progress? Further, how does the Court decide what human affairs entail?

3.1.3 Legitimate Aim

For interference with the freedom of expression to be deemed acceptable, it must pursue a legitimate aim. In assessing limitations on the freedom of expression, in *Otto-Preminger-Institut v Austria* (1994), the Court considered whether the expressions are 'gratuitously offensive to others and, thus, an infringement of their rights and which, therefore, do not contribute to any form of public debate capable of furthering progress in human affairs.'[72] The

71 *Otto-Preminger-Institut v Austria* App no 13470/87 (ECHR, 20 September 1994) para 49
72 *Otto-Preminger-Institut* (n 71)

legitimate aim of protecting the rights of others is one of the key limitation grounds featuring hate speech case law, sometimes in conjunction with other grounds, as can be seen in *Féret* in what follows. For example, in *Seurot v France* (2004), the ECtHR addressed the case of a teacher who was dismissed for writing an article in a school publication that referred to French citizens of North African descent as "Muslim hordes impossible to assimilate." The Court determined that the interference with this expression pursued at least one legitimate aim under the Convention, specifically the protection of the reputation or rights of others.[73] Similarly, in *Féret*, where no violation of Article 10 was found, the ECtHR recognised the necessity of a national restriction on racist and xenophobic expression to protect the rights of others and maintain public order.

In the aftermath of the devastating atrocities perpetrated by the Nazis during World War II, the treatment of revisionist speech has been pivotal in shaping the approach of the EComHR and ECtHR towards hate speech. These institutions have consistently adopted a firm stance against any forms of speech that seek to deny the Holocaust, often addressing such cases within the framework of protecting the rights of others. For instance, in *X v the Federal Republic of Germany* (1976), an individual displayed pamphlets on his garden fence asserting that the Holocaust was a "zionist swindle or lie." His conviction included civil prosecution for group defamation and criminal charges for incitement to hatred. The Commission affirmed that such interference was necessary in a democratic society and pursued a legitimate aim, specifically the protection of the rights of others. The Commission emphasised that democratic society 'rests on the principles of tolerance and broadmindedness, which the pamphlets in question clearly failed to observe.'[74] Similarly, in *Remer v Germany* (1995), the Commission determined that a conviction for incitement to racial hatred due to publishing information denying the gassing of Jews in Nazi Germany aligned with legitimate aims, including preventing disorder and crime, as well as protecting the rights of others.[75] However, shortly after *Remer*, in *Honsik v Austria* (1997), the Commission did not explicitly refer to the legitimate aims outlined in Article 10 of the ECHR in allowing restrictions on such expression. Instead, it stated that the restriction was necessary in a democratic society, as provided in Article 10, because permitting such expression would undermine the rights and freedoms safeguarded by the Convention. It underlined that 'the freedom of expression enshrined in Article 10 . . . may not be invoked in a sense contrary to Article 17.'[76] The approach in *Honsik* seems to blend aspects of Article 10 and Article 17, with the Court enforcing the former while essentially upholding the purpose of the latter,

73 *Seurot v France* App no 57383/00 (ECHR, 18 May 2004)
74 *X v Federal Republic of Germany* App no 9235/81 (EComHR, 1982) para 7.12
75 *Remer v Germany* App no 25096/95 (EComHR, 6 September 1995)
76 *Honsik v Austria* App no 25062/84 (ECHR, 18 October 1995)

an issue that will be explored further in subsequent discussion. This pattern continued into more recent hate speech case law, as will be discussed during the jurisprudential analysis of hate speech cases. Intertwined with the prohibition of revisionist/negationist speech, the Court and, previously, the Commission have consistently emphasised the advocacy of National Socialism as inconsistent with the fundamental objectives of the Convention. For instance, in the case of *B. H., M. W., H. P. and G. K v Austria* (1989), the Commission noted that the prohibition of activities involving the expression of National Socialist ideas was necessary in a democratic society to safeguard national security, territorial integrity and to prevent crime. Consequently, the interference was deemed compatible with Article 10(2) of the ECHR. Additionally, it highlighted that 'National Socialism is a totalitarian doctrine incompatible with democracy and human rights,' and that its proponents undoubtedly pursue objectives akin to those delineated in Article 17 of the ECHR. This case resulted in a finding of a violation of Article 10, concluding with a reference to Article 17. Thus, hate speech has been curtailed to protect the rights of others and, in specific circumstances, to uphold national security and territorial integrity and to prevent crime and disorder. The case of *Honsik* stands out as the only one among those mentioned that did not clearly align with one of the legitimate aims articulated in the relevant article.

3.1.4 Proportionality

The principle of proportionality holds significant weight in the assessment of restrictions on Article 10 of the ECHR, as it is a pivotal consideration in determining the reasonableness of an interference. As articulated in *Handyside*, 'every formality, condition, restriction or penalty imposed in this sphere must be proportionate to the legitimate aim pursued.'[77] In *Lehideux and Isorni v France* (1998), the principle of proportionality played a decisive role. The Court observed that opting for criminal proceedings rather than less severe measures through civil channels was 'disproportionate and, as such, unnecessary in a democratic society.'[78] Consequently, the Court found a violation of Article 10. Similarly, as emphasised in *Incal v Turkey* (1998) and reiterated in cases like *Balsytė-Lideikienė v Lithuania* (2008), governments should refrain from resorting to criminal sanctions where alternative measures could suffice. In this case, the Court acknowledged that governments may adopt measures, including options in the ambit of criminal law, provided they respond 'appropriately and without excess to such expressions.'[79] Moreover, the nature and severity of penalties imposed are crucial considerations in assessing the

77 *Handyside* (n 9) para 49
78 *Lehideux and Isorni v France* App no 24662/94 (ECHR, 23 September 1998) para 57
79 *Balsytė-Lideikienė v Lithuania* App no 72596/01 (ECHR, 4 February 2009) para 81

proportionality of an interference with Article 10.[80] Similarly, in finding no violation of Article 10 in *Féret*, the Court underlined that the Belgian courts used restraint in the use of the criminal route when other appropriate means are possible. Note that the applicant was sentenced to 250 hours of community work and 10 years of ineligibility to stand for elections.[81] Restraint in the use of criminal options as a factor to be considered in assessing the proportionality of the impugned measure was also noted in the older case of *Incal v Turkey*,[82] which the *Féret* court relied on in its analysis of proportionality.

3.1.5 *Margin of Appreciation*

The ECtHR has 'devised and applied its well-known margin of appreciation doctrine as an instrument to negotiate between conflicting interests in a multi-layered legal order.'[83] This doctrine has been developed by case law of the ECtHR and now constitutes a central doctrine taken into consideration in ensuing jurisprudence.

In *Handyside*, the Court stated that 'it is for the national authorities to make the initial assessment of the reality of the pressing social need implied by the notion of necessity in this context.'[84] This is because it is impossible to find a uniform conception of morals in all contracting parties, and anyhow, this conception varies according to the time and the place.[85] Also, as underlined in *Müller and Others v Switzerland*, state authorities are in a better position than international judges to rule on the necessity of a restriction, given the contextual and moral framework of their country.[86] Furthermore, as well as allowing states parties a margin of appreciation in determining whether there exists a pressing social need that would justify a restriction, the Court also provides them with leeway when deciphering other issues. For example, in *Rekvényi v Hungary*, the Court held that national authorities enjoy a certain margin of appreciation in determining whether the impugned interference is proportionate to the legitimate aim in question.[87]

The margin of appreciation is granted to the legislature, the judiciary and other relevant bodies.[88] It can be argued that when a state is permitted, through the margin of appreciation, to decide on whether or not a particular type of speech or form of association or assembly is offensive, and therefore a

80 *Sürek v Turkey* App no 26682/95 (ECHR, 8 July 1999) para 64
81 *Féret* (n 19) para 79
82 *Incal v Turkey* App no 22678/93 (ECHR, 9 June 1998) para 54
83 Janneke Gerards, 'Pluralism, Deference and the Margin of Appreciation Doctrine' (2011) 1(1) European Law Journal 81
84 *Handyside* (n 9) para 48
85 *Handyside* (n 9) para 48
86 *Müller and others v Switzerland* App no 10737/84 (ECHR, 24 May 1988) para 35
87 *Rekvényi v Hungary* App no 25390/94 (ECHR, 20 May 1999) para 42
88 *Handyside* (n 9) para 48

source of violation of other rights and freedoms, it is inevitably empowered with much subjectivity, given that the personal and/or structural approaches, attitudes and convictions of members of governing bodies may influence any such decisions. Relevant to this argument is the finding that the impact of viewpoints on what constitutes a risk varies dramatically amongst experts and that disagreements between such experts emanate from a different set of values and value choice.[89] This is based on the hypothesis that culture comes cognitively prior to facts in the sense that cultural values shape what individuals believe the consequences of such policies to be.[90]

The states parties to the ECHR do not enjoy an unmonitored margin of appreciation, given that the ECtHR has the last say in deciding whether an interference with the freedom of expression is in fact in line with Article 10. The 'domestic margin of appreciation goes hand in hand with a European supervision.'[91] In *Sunday Times*, the Court underlined that, in exercising its supervisory powers, its role is to determine whether an interference 'was proportionate to the legitimate aim pursued and whether the reasons given by the national authorities to justify it are relevant and sufficient.'[92] In *Özgür Gündem v Turkey* (2000), the Court noted that 'in exercising its supervisory judgement, the Court must look at interference in light of the case as a whole, including the content of the impugned statements and the context in which they were made.'[93]

The width of this margin very much depends on the type and subsequent significance of the right being considered. In the framework of expression, the Court has generally been particularly restrictive in its approach to the margin of appreciation but has been prepared to accept a wider margin in relation to issues likely to offend personal convictions in the religious or moral domain.[94] This was manifested in *Soulas and Others v France* (2008), where the Court held that states should be granted a wider margin of appreciation in cases where they limit hate speech or discriminatory speech because of the risks they pose to social relationships and the treatment of immigrants.[95] In relation to this case, Lester, Pannick and Herberg criticised the Court's decision to uphold a restriction on anti-immigrant and Islamophobic speech. More particularly, they held that, by applying the margin of appreciation, the Court did not recognise the significance of protecting and promoting plurality of

89 András Sajó, 'From Militant Democracy to the Preventive State' (2006) 22(5) Cardozo Law Review 2289

90 Paul Brest and Linda Hamilton Krieger, *Problem Solving, Decision Making, and Professional Judgment: A Guide for Lawyers and Policymakers* (1st edn, OUP 2010) 504

91 Brest and Krieger (n 90)

92 *Sunday Times* (n 11) para 62

93 *Gundem v Turkey* App no 23144/93 (ECHR, 16 March 2000) para 57

94 *Lehideux and Isorni v France* App no 24602/94 (ECHR, 23 September 1998) Joint Dissenting opinion of Judge Foighel, Loizou and Sir John Freeland

95 *Soulas and others v France* App no 15948/03 (ECHR, 10 July 2008) para 38

opinions.[96] The wide margin of appreciation is also granted to states if expressions 'incite to violence against an individual, a public official or a sector of the population.'[97] However, as noted by Buyse, the Court does not 'conclusively explain when this is the case.'[98]

In *Mouvement Raëlien Suisse*, the Court acknowledged that the varying value level and subsequent extent to which a state will enjoy a certain margin of appreciation in interpreting and imposing restriction on expression depend on a range of issues, including the type of speech.[99] In this case, it held that 'there is little scope under Article 10(2) of the Convention for restrictions on political speech.'[100]

4 Article 17: The 'Prohibition of Abuse of Rights' Clause

Article 17 of the Convention is titled 'prohibition of abuse of rights' and provides:

> Nothing in this Convention may be interpreted as implying for any State, group or person any right to engage in any activity or perform any act aimed at the destruction of any of the rights and freedoms set forth herein or at their limitation to a greater extent than is provided for in the Convention.

The incorporation of abuse clauses in post–World War II international human rights documents was first reflected in Article 30 of the Universal Declaration of Human Rights, which provides thus:

> Nothing in this Declaration may be interpreted as implying for any State, group or person any right to engage in any activity or to perform any act aimed at the destruction of any of the rights and freedoms set forth herein.

A few years later, and 'breaking with the darkest pages of European history,'[101] the Council of Europe incorporated Article 17 into the Convention. Interestingly, 'very little explanation accompanied the introduction of this

96 Lester and others (n 11)
97 *Ceylan v Turkey* App no 23556/94 (ECHR, 8 July 1999) para 34
98 Buyse (n 55)
99 *Mouvement Raëlien Suisse* (n 38) para 61
100 *Mouvement Raëlien Suisse* (n 38)
101 Sebastien Van Drooghenbroeck, 'L'Article 17 de la Convention Européenne des Droits de L'Homme: Incertain et Inutile?' in H. Dumont, P. Mandoux, A. Strowel and F Tulkens (eds), *Pas de liberté pour les ennemis de la liberté. Groupements liberticides et droit* (Bruylant 2000) 144

clause'[102] into the ECHR, with the only trace being some interventions at the Parliamentary Assembly, which referred to the need for protection against totalitarian regimes that had been present in Europe around that time and had caused mass destruction.[103] Article 17 constituted European democracies' tools against such regimes seeking to prevent history repeating itself.[104] The motivation for Article 17 is reflected in the first decision in which the article was enforced, namely, the *German Communist Party v Germany* (1957), in which the EComHR permitted the prohibition of the German Communist Party, whose declaration included reference to proletarian revolution and dictatorship. The EComHR enforced this article to 'protect the rights enshrined in the Convention by safeguarding the free functioning of democratic institutions.'[105] As such, in relation to the article's incorporation into the ECHR and its application in earlier jurisprudence, it was the fear of totalitarianism that was the guiding objective. As argued, 'it is not in the case of self-confessed totalitarian parties that the application of Article 17 has proved to be troublesome.'[106] The application of Article 17 to restrict speech, particularly revisionist speech and, more recently, speech that is racist, targets religion or is homophobic, remains a contentious issue in the protection of freedom of expression. A critical aspect of examining the ECtHR's current use of Article 17 is understanding the historical context of its inclusion in the Convention and how the Court has interpreted and applied the abuse clause in the decades following World War II. Article 17 was conceived in a specific historical milieu, the immediate post-war period, while the geopolitical landscape has transformed significantly over the past 70 years. While the approach to older revisionist and negationist cases can be historically justified within the post–World War II context, the application of Article 17 in more recent cases raises significant concerns. In fact, when it comes to hate speech, in 2020, the ECtHR differentiated between the use of Article 10 limitation grounds and the enforcement of Article 17 through a simple hierarchisation of hate speech as 'gravest' and 'less grave,' respectively.[107]

Furthermore, the historical context of Article 17 suggests an underlying commitment to the preservation of democracy, despite this not being explicitly

102 Hannes Cannie and Dirk Voorhoof, 'The Abuse Clause and Freedom of Expression in the European Human Rights Convention: An Added Value for Democracy and Human Rights Protection?' (2011) 29(1) Netherlands Quarterly of Human Rights 56

103 Cannie and Voorhoof (n 102)

104 See, for example, Karel Vasak, *La Convention Européenne des Droits de L'Homme* (1st edn, Pedon 1964) 71

105 *Communist Part of Germany v Germany* App no 250/57 (EComHR, 20 July 1957)

106 Majid Nikouei and Masoud Zamani, 'Jurisprudence of Tolerance: Hate Speech, Article 17 and Theory of Democracy in the European Convention on Human Rights' (2019) 8(1) International Human Rights Law Review 84

107 *Lilliendahl v Iceland* App no 29297/18 (ECtHR, 12 May 2020) paras 34, 35

included in the provision. The relationship between democracy and Convention rights, encompassing both the 'victim' and the 'perpetrator,' has been explored and elaborated upon in jurisprudence. For instance, in *Klass v Germany* (1978), the ECtHR underscored the inherent need for a compromise between the imperatives of defending democratic society and upholding individual rights within the Convention framework. In *Lehideux and Isorni*, the Court referred to the existence of a 'category of clearly established historical facts—such as the Holocaust—whose negation or revision would be removed from the protection of Article 10 by Article 17.' The concurring opinion of Judge Jambrek (Slovenia) attempted to set out the conditions for the application of Article 17. More particularly, it held that, for this article to be enforced, the aim of the offending actions must be

> to spread violence or hatred, to resort to illegal or undemocratic methods, to encourage the use of violence, to undermine the nation's democratic and pluralist political system, or to pursue objectives that are racist or likely to destroy the rights and freedoms of others.

In *Witzsch v Germany* (1999), the Court found that 'the general purpose of Article 17 is to make it impossible for individuals to take advantage of a right with the aim of promoting ideas contrary to the text and the spirit of the Convention.'[108] In *Thoma v Luxembourg* (2001), the ECtHR articulated that limitations on Convention rights must be narrowly construed, serving the interests of both public and social life as a whole and those of the individuals comprising society.[109] In *Ždanoka v Latvia* (2004), the Court underlined that 'no one should be authorised to rely on the Convention's provisions in order to weaken or destroy the ideals and values of a democratic society.'[110]

5 The Additional Protocol to the Convention on Cybercrime, Concerning the Criminalisation of Acts of a Racist and Xenophobic Nature Committed Through Computer Systems

The Council of Europe's 2001 Convention on Cybercrime[111] is the first multilateral treaty that aims at combatting crimes committed through computer systems and has, to date, been ratified by 75 countries. Eighteen countries have signed it or have been invited to accede to it.[112] The Convention was both signed and ratified by member states of the Council of Europe and countries outside it, including the United States. Despite not being a member of the Council, the United States holds observer status. Due to its First Amendment

108 *Witzsch v Germany* App no 7485/04 (ECHR, 13 December 2005) 7
109 *Thoma v Luxembourg* App no 384329/97 (ECHR, 29 March 2001) para 43
110 *Ždanoka v Latvia* App no 58278/00 (ECHR, 16 March 2006) para 99
111 Convention on Cybercrime 2001, European Treaty Series No 185
112 Convention on Cybercrime 2001 (n 111)

traditions, the United States only acceded to the Convention after the subject of online hate was excluded from the discussions.[113] The Council of Europe accommodated this demand and later incorporated the issue of online racism and xenophobia in the 2003 Additional Protocol Concerning the Criminalisation of Acts of a Racist and Xenophobic Nature.[114] This has been ratified by 29 countries, and a further 13 have signed it.[115] The Additional Protocol seeks to achieve a common set of standards for participating states and promote co-operation amongst them in the criminalisation of relevant acts. This document is seen as a supplement to the Cybercrime Convention, to ensure that the latter's procedural and substantive provisions encompass racism and xenophobia online. Thus, a series of the Convention's articles apply *mutatis mutandis* to the Protocol under consideration, including, amongst others, Article 13 on sanctions and measures and Article 22 on jurisdiction.

However, upon initial examination, this document reveals several significant limitations. As indicated by its title, this Protocol addresses only racist and xenophobic hate, entirely overlooking other forms of hate based on factors such as sexual orientation, gender identity and disability. Religion is considered a protected characteristic within the definitional framework established by Article 2 of the Additional Protocol. The Protocol's preamble states that the members of the Council of Europe and other states parties to the Cybercrime Convention are 'mindful of the need to ensure a proper balance between freedom of expression and an effective fight against acts of a racist and xenophobic nature.' The preamble also echoes *Handyside*, by recognising that freedom of expression constitutes 'one of the essential foundations of a democratic society and is one of the conditions for its progress and for the development of every human being.' Interestingly, it does not continue to quote the same paragraph of *Handyside* which mentions that ideas expressed must extend to those which shock, offend or disturb. The Protocol provides that each party adopt such legislative or other measures as may be necessary to criminalise (1) the dissemination of racist and xenophobic material through computer systems, (2) racist and xenophobia-motivated threat, (3) racist and xenophobia-motivated insult and (4) denial, gross minimisation, approval or justification of genocide or crimes against humanity. Apart from racist and xenophobia-motivated threat, states may opt not to apply, in whole or in part, the necessary provisions under the aforementioned headings. Article 4, which addresses racist and xenophobic threats, appears to receive the most comprehensive protection within the Protocol. Unlike other provisions, its reach

113 James Banks, 'Regulating Hate Speech Online' (2010) 24(3) International Review of Law, Computers & Technology 236

114 Additional Protocol to the Convention on Cybercrime, Concerning the Criminalisation of Acts of a Racist and Xenophobic Nature Committed Through Computer Systems (28 January 2003)

115 List of signatures and ratifications of the Cybercrime Convention <www.coe.int/en/web/conventions/full-list/-/conventions/treaty/189/signatures> accessed 28 July 2024

extends to both private and public communications and, as noted, does not allow for any opt-out possibility, thereby ensuring more robust enforcement. This is reasonable, considering the severity of a threat in comparison to, for example, a racist insult. However, questions arise in relation to enforcement and to terms and concepts. The Protocol notes that terms and expressions used in this Protocol shall be interpreted in the same manner as they are interpreted under the Convention. However, the fact of the matter is that the ECtHR has not adequately provided a succinct explanation of terms such as *discrimination* or *hatred* throughout its jurisdiction, with the definitional peak of hate speech having been reached in *Lilliendahl v Iceland* (2020), where the Court merely separated different types of hate speech based on their severity rather than offering a sound conceptualisation of notions. In short, what the Protocol is referring to are ambiguous concepts that can vary from place to place and from person to person and, within this framework, seeks the criminalisation of relevant acts. Whilst exclusion clauses are granted to most of these 'acts,' the Protocol nevertheless sets the default to be the criminalisation of even a racial insult, opening the doors of abuse by states that wish to do so, stifling public discourse, potentially turning haters into martyrs of the system and all the other issues that may arise when silencing speech on the grounds of hatred or discrimination, and as discussed in Chapter 2.

The issue of intent is crucial when evaluating the Protocol. It criminalises the dissemination of material, threats, insults and revisionist rhetoric, as well as aiding and abetting such offences, provided these acts or expressions are carried out intentionally. What happens with internet service providers (ISPs)? Are they criminally liable? According to the Explanatory Report to the Additional Protocol, an ISP, merely hosting the material, cannot be found guilty of any of the Protocol's offences if the required intent, as defined by domestic law, is absent. It also stipulates that an ISP is not required to monitor conduct to avoid criminal liability.[116] This is of particular interest taking into account the case of *Delfi v Estonia* (2015), in which the ECtHR, in finding no violation of Article 10, ruled that the measures Delfi (a large news portal) had implemented to remove comments which the Court considered to be hate speech and speech inciting violence were insufficient and led to the six-week delay of their removal. Whilst the proceedings taken against the company were of a civil nature, the parallel is interesting to make. As such, the Explanatory Report, in part, limits the liability of ISPs acting without knowledge but leaves the general conceptualisation of intent uncertain and subject to national interpretation. Also, it does not incorporate a general or specific monitoring obligation.

116 'Explanatory Report to the Additional Protocol to the Convention on Cybercrime, Concerning the Criminalisation of Acts of a Racist and Xenophobic Nature Committed through Computer Systems' (28 January 2003) <https://rm.coe.int/16800d37ae> accessed 28 July 2024

As well as some general weakness of the Protocol, as referred to earlier, it must be noted that, since February 2024, the European Union's Digital Services Act (DSA) has been in force. This places private companies such as social media platforms at the epicentre of regulating online hate speech. This paradigm is particularly dangerous as companies are private, not bound by IHRL; have a business model to follow; and wish to avoid hefty fines or other run-ins with the European Union and, thus, could over-remove content. While the DSA is complementary to any other document, such as the Protocol, it is becoming evident that, in the online world, the preceding paradigm is the one which the EU (and not only) is now following. Moreover, as of 2008, the EU has the Framework Decision on Combating Certain Forms and Expressions of Racism and Xenophobia by means of Criminal Law. It is not applicable to the online world in particular but does not exclude it. The Framework Decision prohibits several acts, such as publicly inciting violence or hatred against a group of people due to, amongst others, their race or religion, with fewer possibilities for reservations than the Protocol.

Conclusion

The system of human rights protection of the Council of Europe is pivotal to the enjoyment of human rights in the region. However, this is marred by limitations, such as non-enforcement of judgements by member states and by the procedural and financial hurdles which applicants must overcome to get to the ECtHR, predominantly the exhaustion of domestic avenues. In relation to the handling of hate speech, the history of the institution plays two separate roles. On the one hand, the resistance of post–World War II Council of Europe states towards the hate speech clause of the ICCPR and the rejection of proposals to incorporate the prohibition of extremist propaganda in the limitation grounds of Article 10 reflect some form of speech-protective approach to the role and limits of expression. Nevertheless, the deep trauma suffered as a result of World War II infiltrated into hate speech judgements that involved denial of the Holocaust or anti-Semitic speech, often relying on Article 17, which eliminates the Article 10(2) test and, if included as an interpretative aid, dilutes the role and impact of Article 10(2). The aim of this chapter was to set the scene of the history of the Convention, the functioning of the relevant institutions and the central tenets of the two important articles in any examination of hate speech, namely, Articles 10 and 17. This will hopefully allow readers to better understand the jurisprudential analysis that will follow. At the same time, and due to the book's general theme, the chapter has sought to provide an overview on the Additional Protocol to the Convention on Cybercrime, Concerning the Criminalization of Acts of a Racist and Xenophobic Nature Committed Through Computer Systems, a document separate from the ECHR which provides a set of provisions for countries to implement through their own legislation. For hate speech, these institutional dynamics highlight both the promise and shortcomings of the ECtHR's jurisprudence, a tension that resonates throughout this book. By critically examining these dynamics, the book seeks to unpack the Court's role in mediating the balance between democratic freedoms and the need to curb harmful rhetoric. This chapter has laid the groundwork for this analysis, contextualising the hate speech cases that will be dissected in detail in the chapters that follow.

4 Hate Speech Jurisprudence

Protecting Protected Characteristics Before the European Court of Human Rights

1 Background, Central Questions and Structure

The European Court of Human Rights (ECtHR) has stipulated that the right to freedom of expression extends to 'ideas that offend, shock or disturb the State or any sector of the population.'[1] This significant positioning by the regional human rights court of Europe was articulated in the landmark case of *Handyside v the United Kingdom* (1976) and has been reaffirmed time and again in cases which have followed. Despite the strong protection that freedom of expression is meant to enjoy under the *Handyside* precedent, the Court's hate speech jurisprudence draws another picture. A recent study reviewed 60 hate speech cases heard by the ECtHR and the obsolete European Commission on Human Rights (EComHR) from 1979 to 2020. It revealed that 62% of cases brought by speakers resulted in restrictions on speech being upheld. Only 38% of cases led to judgements favouring the applicants.[2] As such, free speech restrictions were upheld in about two-thirds of the cases. These outcomes highlight a judicial tendency to prioritise regulation of expression over free speech rights in hate speech cases. Against this backdrop, the next two chapters look at the consistency and rationale underpinning hate speech judgements, with the overarching aim of identifying patterns and shortcomings.

This chapter will focus on cases addressing hate speech targeting protected characteristics, such as race, religion, ethnicity, sexual orientation and gender identity. It analyses how the Court navigates the tension between freedom of expression under Article 10 of the ECHR and issues such as minority rights, social cohesion, the protection of democracy and other 'convention values.' Some of the questions that will be tackled in this chapter include how, if at all, the ECtHR defines *hate speech*, what thresholds it uses to determine whether speech merits protection, how the Court's balancing of individual expression and societal interests has evolved over time. In the ambit of these questions,

1 *Handyside v the United Kingdom* (1976) App no 5493/72 (ECHR, 7 December 1976) para 49
2 Future of Free Speech, Hate Speech Database <https://futurefreespeech.org/hate-speech-case-database/> accessed 24 October 2024

DOI: 10.4324/9781003560548-5

the chapter also looks at the margin of appreciation afforded to states in hate speech cases. While respecting states parties' cultural and social diversity, this doctrine has often allowed significant variations in the handling of similar issues. This chapter critiques how this discretion may enable the Court to avoid establishing clear, consistent standards for hate speech regulation, leading to an overly broad encroachment of Article 10. While recognising that it is not the ECtHR's position to interpret and apply domestic law, its role as European supervisor of Convention rights means that it has a duty to be thorough and substantive when assessing the necessity of free speech interferences, elements which are often lacking in the Court's hate speech cases. The chapter also explores how the digitalisation of speech is reshaping hate speech jurisprudence, with a discussion on the increased pressure put on intermediaries and public individuals for third-party speech in the online world. By holding online platforms and social media users increasingly responsible for third-party comments, the Court has set the foundation of a speech-restrictive paradigm to address the challenges posed by the digital age.

As such, the chapter assesses key aspects of the ECtHR's hate speech jurisprudence, starting with an analysis of how the Court has interpreted hate speech broadly to include expressions of insult, ridicule or defamation, even when there is no explicit or implicit element of incitement, as seen in cases like *Féret v Belgium* (2009) and *Vejdeland v Sweden* (2012). It then looks at cases which fall within the framework of incitement to ethnic, racial or religious hatred or violence, examining how context and societal sensitivities shape the threshold for permissible speech, as demonstrated in judgements like *Erbakan v Turkey* (2006) and *Balsytė-Lideikienė v Lithuania* (2008). Another area of focus is speech that fosters marginalisation or societal division, exploring cases such as *Smajić v Bosnia and Herzegovina* (2018) and *Le Pen v France* (2010). The chapter examines the application of Article 17 to hate speech cases outside the ambit of Holocaust denial, critiquing its use in judgements such as *Norwood v the United Kingdom* (2004) and *Lenis v Greece* (2023), highlighting inconsistencies in the Court's approach when defining the boundaries of acceptable speech. It proceeds to analyse how speech against religious figures, doctrines and institutions is dealt with by the Court, with the most recent hate speech case at the time of writing falling within this section, namely, *Sokolovskiy v Russia* (2024). The chapter also conducts a jurisprudential analysis of relevant cases pertaining to themes such as hate speech and journalistic freedom, the digitalisation of speech and the role of third parties, boycotting as hate speech and the positive obligations of states in the ambit of hate speech. This chapter ultimately argues that the ECtHR's approach to hate speech requires recalibration. The chapter recommends that the Court adopt a sound definitional framework of hate speech and set clearer thresholds of harm, with its *Handyside* principle constituting a starting point. It also urges for more consistency throughout case analysis and greater reliance on evidence-based reasoning. Such changes would contribute to the clarity and predictability of case law and ensure a more robust protection of Article 10 of the Convention.

The cases in each section are, for the most part, incorporated in a chronological manner. At times, for purposes of direct comparison of key elements, cases are assessed thematically. Also, to ease the reading of this chapter and its analysis and to maximise the reader's understanding of cases in their entirety, information on case facts and deliberations and outcomes on a domestic level that go beyond a brief overview are incorporated into the sections. It must be noted that the focus of this book is the ECtHR, but cases from the obsolete EComHR are also considered where relevant.

2 Hate Speech Jurisprudence: The Low-Threshold Hatred Paradigm

The ECtHR has long grappled with how to handle freedom of expression under Article 10 of the ECHR when confronted with hate speech cases. A pivotal development in this area has been the emergence of what I refer to as the low-threshold hatred paradigm. This paradigm is generally characterised by the Court's willingness to permit restrictions on speech that insults, ridicules, defames or prejudices individuals or groups, even in the absence of direct incitement to violence or the committal of other criminal acts. This represents a significant departure from earlier principles, such as those established in *Handyside v the United Kingdom* (1976), where the Court emphasised the importance of protecting speech that 'shocks, offends or disturbs.'[3] The defining case in this sphere is *Féret v Belgium* (2009), which involved leaflets disseminated by a far-right politician, and has been followed in a plethora of cases, including *Vejdeland v Sweden* (2012), where the applicants left homophobic leaflets in school lockers, and *Lilliendahl v Iceland* (2020), where the applicant made homophobic and transphobic comments under an online post. None of the cases amounted to incitement of any kind, and all involved the imposition of criminal penalties. The Court's broad interpretation of *harm* in such cases risks stifling legitimate public debate and disproportionately privileging state-sanctioned narratives, as highlighted in dissenting opinions, such as that of the Hungarian Judge Sajó in *Féret*, discussed later. Other issues include the difficulties in proving a direct causal link between the speech and societal harm. In this light, the following section delves into the ECtHR's application of the low-threshold hatred paradigm, scrutinising its impact on political discourse and the public space more broadly. Through detailed analysis of cases, it highlights the tensions between protecting marginalised groups and upholding the foundational right to freedom of expression. Its main argument is that, in the sphere of the low-threshold hatred paradigm, the content and meaning of Article 10 have been severely diluted.

3 *Handyside* (n 1) para 49

2.1 *The Féret* ***Paradigm: When Insult, Ridicule, Prejudice or Defamation Is Enough to Allow for Article 10 Restrictions***

In *Féret*, the applicant, a far-right party leader and member of parliament at that time, was convicted for his role as the author and publisher of the contested leaflets and the owner of the website used to disseminate hateful materials. The leaflets contained statements such as "Stop the Islamization of Belgium" and "Save our people from the risk posed by Islam, the conqueror" and allegations that a refugee centre "poisons the lives of residents." The court of appeal sentenced the applicant to 250 hours of community service, with a subsidiary sentence of ten months' imprisonment. Furthermore, the court imposed a ten-year ban on the applicant from standing for election and awarded provisional damages of EUR 1 to each civil party, deferring the decision on any additional compensation.

The ECtHR ruled, by a majority, that there was no violation of the applicant's right under Article 10. It found that Féret's statements were 'inevitably of such a nature as to arouse, particularly among the less informed members of the public, feelings of distrust, rejection or hatred towards foreigners.'[4] In relation to this point, the dissenting opinion by Judge Sajó (Hungary), joined by Judge Zagrebelsky (Italy) and Judge Tsotsoria (Georgia), argued that the Court majority treated people as 'nitwits . . . incapable of replying to arguments and counterarguments, due to the irresistible drive of their irrational emotions.'[5] The ECtHR also asserted that 'to recommend solutions to immigration-related problems by advocating racial discrimination was likely to cause social tension and undermine trust in democratic institutions.'[6] However, the precise link between the speech in question and the alleged severe effect of undermining trust in democratic institutions, whatever that may be or may entail, remains ambiguous. The Court provided no substantial clarification on how Féret's speech specifically threatened democratic structures, leaving the causal link between the speech and the asserted harms essentially unexplained. In fact, the Court did not delve into any substantial analysis of the specific meaning or extent of the harm caused by the speech in question, nor did it undertake a balancing analysis of the value of political speech, as established in *Wingrove v the United Kingdom* (1996), and the right to express ideas that may shock, offend, or disturb, as recognised in *Handyside*, both of which were discussed in the previous chapter. It did, however, emphasise the importance of politicians exercising caution in their public statements, aiming not to fuel intolerance but to uphold democracy and its foundational values.[7] This open-ended standard appears to privilege expressions that align with state-endorsed narratives, enabling a wider margin of appreciation for states

4 *Féret v Belgium* App no 15615/07 (ECHR, 16 July 2009) para 69
5 *Féret* (n 4) Dissenting Opinion by Judge Sajó joined by Judge Zagrebelsky and Judge Tsotsoria
6 *Féret* (n 4) para 77
7 *Féret* (n 4) para 75

to suppress speech they deem to be controversial. Pertinent to the preceding point is the fact that the Court attached particular importance to the medium used and the political context in which the statements were made. It notes:

> [I]f, in an electoral context, political parties must benefit from a broad freedom of expression in order to try to convince their voters, in the event of racist or xenophobic speech, such a context contributes to stir up hatred and intolerance. . . . The impact of racist and xenophobic discourse then becomes greater and more damaging.[8]

However, the decision does not clearly delineate when speech crosses the line from acceptable political discourse into unprotected hate speech, leaving the boundaries subject to interpretation and subjective state preferences. In their dissent, Judges Sajó, Zagrebelsky and Tsotsoria argued that the majority's approach disregards the 'paramount protection to be afforded to political discourse,'[9] essential in any democratic society. The dissent highlights the importance of protecting political speech, even if controversial, as foundational to democratic governance. The majority's ruling in *Féret*, therefore, reflects an assumption that there exists an underlying tension between preserving democratic freedoms and preventing speech that could contribute to social division and, essentially, make some people racist. The Court offers no explanation or elaboration of this alleged tension. In this ambit, the dissenting opinion also criticised the value-based approach to free speech, noting that judges, as humans, are influenced by their own viewpoints and predispositions on matters and, thus, should be particularly careful when it comes to free speech restrictions. Specifically, the opinion stated that

> content regulation and content-based restrictions on speech are based on the assumption that certain expressions go 'against the spirit' of the Convention. But 'spirits' do not offer clear standards and are open to abuse. Humans, including judges, are inclined to label positions with which they disagree as palpably unacceptable and therefore beyond the realm of protected expression. However, it is precisely where we face ideas that we abhor or despise that we have to be most careful in our judgment, as our personal convictions can influence our ideas about what is actually dangerous.[10]

This opinion highlights the challenges associated to regulating speech on the basis of viewpoints which present substantial risks to the protection of freedom of expression and the integrity of democratic discourse. The subjectivity of

8 *Féret* (n 4) para 76
9 *Féret* (n 4) Dissenting Opinion by Sajó and others, para 5
10 *Féret* (n 4)

viewpoint-based restrictions can lead to overreach, enabling governments or institutions to suppress dissent or unpopular opinions under the guise of combatting harm. This creates a chilling effect, discouraging legitimate speech and hindering public debate, whilst controlling public narratives as a result of state viewpoints which can erode trust in the state itself.[11] Historical examples highlight the danger of labelling progressive movements as harmful, potentially stifling social progress. An important example is the civil rights movement in the United States, which was often vilified as subversive or dangerous during its early years.[12] Further, when democratic states implement viewpoint-based restrictions to combat hate speech or misinformation, they risk creating a dangerous precedent that authoritarian regimes can exploit to legitimise repression. For instance, countries like Russia, Venezuela and Belarus have cited Western regulatory frameworks to justify crackdowns on dissent.[13] Such practices not only stifle cross-border activism but also weaken the credibility of democratic states in advocating for human rights, as their restrictive measures diminish moral authority and erode solidarity against repression.

Further, a particularly significant aspect of the Court's reasoning in *Féret* is its expansive view of what may constitute hate speech:

> The Court considered that incitement to hatred did not necessarily require the calling of a specific act of violence or another criminal act. Attacks on persons committed through insults, ridicule or defamation aimed at specific population groups or incitement to discrimination, as in this case, sufficed for the authorities to give priority to fighting hate speech when confronted by the irresponsible use of freedom of expression which undermined people's dignity, or even their safety.[14]

This standard diverges from the *Handyside* judgement discussed in detail in the previous chapter, which upheld the right to shock, offend or disturb. Essentially, *Féret* built on the Court's stance on hate speech in *Gündüz v Turkey*

11 See, amongst others, Kristian Skagen Ekeli, 'Democratic Legitimacy, Political Speech and Viewpoint Neutrality' (2023) 47 Philosophy and Social Criticism (2020); James Weinstein, 'Viewpoint Discrimination, Hate Speech, And Political Legitimacy: A Reply' (2017) 23 Constitutional Commentary <https://constitutionalcommentary.lib.umn.edu/article/viewpoint-discrimination-hate-speech-and-political-legitimacy-a-reply/?utm_> accessed 12 November 2024

12 Peniel E Joseph, 'America's Nonviolent Civil Rights Movement was Considered Uncivil by Critics at the Time' *Washington Post* (2018) <https://www.washingtonpost.com/news/post-nation/wp/2018/07/04/the-civil-rights-movement-might-have-been-nonviolent-but-to-critics-it-was-considered-uncivil/> accessed 14 November 2024

13 Jacob Mchangama and Natalie Alkiviadou, 'The Digital Berlin Wall—How Germany (Accidentally) Created a Prototype for Global Online Censorship—Act Two' *Justitia* (2020) <https://futurefreespeech.org/the-digital-berlin-wall-how-germany-accidentally-created-a-prototype-for-global-online-censorship-act-two/>

14 *Féret* (n 4) para 73

(2004), where it held that 'there can be no doubt that concrete expressions constituting hate speech, which may be insulting to particular individuals or groups, are not protected by Article 10 of the Convention.'[15] In *Gündüz*, the applicant argued that his pro-Sharia statements should not have been deemed 'hate speech' by domestic courts. Crucially, however, the ECtHR found that his right to free expression had, indeed, been violated, determining that support for Sharia did not qualify as hate speech in the absence of any incitement to violence.[16] *Féret* subsequently expanded upon the 'insult' criterion, extending *prohibited speech* to speech which defames and ridicules, and clearly stipulated that hate speech does not have to entail a call for violence for it to fall outside the spectrum of Article 10. Interestingly, while incitement to discrimination is incorporated into the Court's conceptualisation of what counts as permissible speech, and while direct reference to the term 'hate speech' is made in the Court's judgement, there is no reference in the preceding paragraph to incitement to hatred, as could be expected in light of the theme of the case, but also considering the standards set out by Article 20(2) of the ICCPR, IHRL's hate speech clause.

However, the Court did note, elsewhere in the judgement,

> tolerance and respect for the equal dignity of all human beings constitute the foundation of a democratic and pluralistic society. It follows that in principle it may be considered necessary in a democratic society to punish, or even prevent, all forms of expression which propagate, encourage, promote or justify hatred based on intolerance (including religious intolerance).[17]

While the threshold incorporated in the preceding paragraph incorporates incitement to hatred, *Féret* also developed the low-threshold hatred paradigm, where insults, ridicules or defamatory speech is sufficient for finding no violation of Article 10. *Féret* significantly narrows the protections for public discourse, including, in this case, political speech. This occurred due to the broadening of the scope of what constitutes hate speech, to include expressions that ridicule or defame in addition to *Gündüz*'s insult. It also stated that incitement is not a necessary prerequisite for prohibition.

In the 2010 case of *Le Pen v France*, the ECtHR addressed a case involving Jean-Marie Le Pen, former leader of the far-right National Front, who had been convicted by French courts for incitement to discrimination, hatred and violence towards a group of people because of their origin or their membership or non-membership of a specific ethnic group, nation, race or religion. This conviction emanated from statements he had made against Muslims in

15 *Gűndűz v Turkey* App no 35071/97 (ECHR, 4 December 2003) para 41
16 *Gűndűz* (n 15) para 51
17 *Gűndűz* (n 15) para 64

France. Specifically, during an interview with *Le Monde*, Le Pen said, amongst other things:

> [T]he day there are no longer 5 million but 25 million Muslims in France, they will be in charge.

He was fined EUR 10,000 for that comment, and an additional EUR 10,000 for his subsequent commentary on the initial fine in the weekly *Rivarol*, in which he said: "When I tell people that when we have 25 million Muslims in France we French will have to watch our step, they often reply: 'But Mr Le Pen, that is already the case now!'—and they are right."

The applicant had lodged an appeal with the court of cassation, which was rejected. While the ECtHR did not explicitly mention the specific duties of politicians to promote social cohesion or the particular responsibilities tied to political speech, as it had in *Féret*, this reasoning was implicitly present in its judgement. The Court acknowledged the importance of safeguarding free political speech but also emphasised the need to protect the rights of others and the crucial role of combatting racial discrimination.[18] The Court found that the applicant's comments were 'certainly capable of giving a negative, and even worrying, image of the "Muslim community" as a whole,'[19] and that they were 'likely to arouse a feeling of rejection and hostility towards the targeted community.'[20] The ECtHR unanimously held the application manifestly ill-founded. A particularly interesting element of this case is that, despite the similarity of the applicant's profile, mandate and statements, and even though a speech-restrictive approach was taken in this case, *Féret* was not cited in *Le Pen*. In fact, as in *Féret*, the contested statements in *Le Pen* did not amount to incitement to violence or unlawful acts. However, while the Belgian case led to a finding of no violation, *Le Pen* was dismissed as manifestly ill-founded; therefore, it did not undergo a complete review under Article 10. The reasons for this divergence remain unexplained.

Zemmour v France (2022) involved an application by Eric Zemmour, a controversial journalist and far-right politician who was convicted for inciting discrimination and hatred against Muslims in France. The statements in question were made during a 2016 interview:

1. He answered "No" when asked if "there are Muslims in France who live in peace, who don't take the Koran literally and are fully integrated."
2. He stated that "those who wage jihad are seen by all Muslims, whether they say so or not, as good Muslims—they are warriors, soldiers of Islam."

18 *Le Pen v France* App no 187788/09 (ECHR, 20 April 2010)
19 *Le Pen* (n 18)
20 *Le Pen* (n 18)

3. He responded to the interviewer's statement that "terrorism is apocalyptic" by saying, "No, it's not terrorism, it's jihadism. So it's Islam." And then he said that jihadism and Islam are "the same to [him]."
4. He stated, "For 30 years we've been experiencing an invasion, a colonisation, which is bringing about a conflagration," and "[I]n countless neighbourhoods, on the outskirts of French cities, where many young women are veiled—that's also Islam, that's also jihad, that's also the fight to Islamise a territory which is not, which is in the ordinary course a non-Islamised land, a land of infidels. It's the same thing, it's territorial occupation."
5. He stated, "I think they [Muslims who live in France] need to be given a choice between Islam and France," and "So, if they're French, they have to—and this is hard because Islam doesn't lend itself to this—they have to let go of what their religion is."

After the applicant's interview, the advocacy group Coalition for Just Peace in the Near East initiated legal proceedings against him at the criminal court, citing the statements outlined earlier. The criminal court found the applicant guilty, convicting him of inciting discrimination and religious hatred against the Muslim community and sentencing him to pay EUR 5,000 as a fine. He appealed to the court of appeal, which partly reversed the decision, holding that only two of the five statements (the last two referred to earlier) incited discrimination and religious hatred, reducing his fine to EUR 3,000. The applicant appealed to the court of cassation, which dismissed the appeal.

In its judgement, the ECtHR first considered whether the application should be dismissed on Article 17 grounds but noted that this article can only be applied in 'exceptional circumstances.'[21] It found that there was no evidence that the applicant sought to destroy the rights and freedoms set out in the Convention and so decided not to apply Article 17.[22] The Court proceeded to underline that the applicant's remarks related to a matter of public interest.[23] It noted that the statements were made during a televised interview as a journalist and commentator discussing his recent book, which addressed Islam's role in French society. Given the applicant's prominence, the interview's timing amid recent terrorist attacks and the public nature of the broadcast, the Court deemed the subject to be of legitimate public concern.[24] Even though the application of Article 17 was rejected, in reaching its decision, the Court noted that the statements in question were not protected speech under Article 10 'in light of Article 17.'[25] The ECtHR determined that these statements contained

21 *Zemmour v France* App no 64549/19 (ECHR, 20 December 2012) para 26
22 *Zemmour* (n 21) paras 28, 29
23 *Zemmour* (n 21) para 58
24 *Zemmour* (n 21)
25 *Zemmour* (n 21) para 61

assertions of a 'negative and discriminatory nature'[26] which, according to the Court, risked deepening societal divisions between French citizens and the Muslim community.[27] It agreed with the domestic view that the applicant's statements were not merely criticisms of Islam but aimed at inciting viewers to reject and marginalise the Muslim community, which threatened social cohesion.[28] The ECtHR recycled the *Féret* paradigm for ascertaining the threshold of what is prohibitable speech, noting:

> [I]ncitement to hatred does not necessarily require a call for acts of violence or other unlawful acts. Attacks on individuals through insults, ridicule or defamation targeting certain segments of the population may suffice for authorities to prioritise combating racist speech over the freedom of expression when exercised irresponsibly.

The Court also noted that the applicant's statements were widely accessible due to their prime-time broadcast on live television, a medium that remains influential in France. It highlighted that, as a journalist, the applicant should have recognised the likely impact of his words and exercised professional caution, even though he was speaking as an author.[29]

In conclusion, the Court found that the national courts' reasoning justified restricting the applicant's freedom of expression under Article 10. Considering that the sentence imposed was a fine of EUR 3,000, well below the statutory maximum, the Court deemed the restriction proportionate. In light of the preceding point, the Court unanimously held that this interference was necessary in a democratic society and did not infringe on the applicant's Article 10 rights.

Zemmour demonstrates the reality that, more than a decade after *Féret* and *Le Pen*, the Court has continued to apply the same restrictive standard for free speech, particularly regarding political expression, without further justification or assessment of the impact of this approach or without considering that, despite restrictive approaches to even prejudicial speech, the phenomenon of hate speech in Europe has been on the rise, as has the rise of far-right groups in France and Europe more generally.[30] Further, the low-threshold hatred paradigm persists in cases involving politicians even though the Court has acknowledged that political speech is fundamental to democratic society and should only be subject to narrow restrictions under Article 10(2).[31] Similarly,

26 *Zemmour* (n 21)
27 *Zemmour* (n 21)
28 *Zemmour* (n 21)
29 *Zemmour* (n 21) para 62
30 See, *inter alia*, Andrea LP Pirro, 'The Contemporary Far Right from *Contra* to Control' (2024) 41 Political Communication 6
31 See, for example, *Lingens v Austria* App no 9815/82 (ECHR, July 1986) para 42 and *Wingrove v the United Kingdom* App no 17419/90 (ECHR, 25 November 1996) para 58

its professed strong protection of freedom of expression for politicians appears difficult to align with its rulings in *Féret*, *Le Pen* and *Zemmour*.

While the *Féret* paradigm has significantly influenced ECtHR jurisprudence concerning speech that may not directly incite hatred or violence by articulating a paradigm that encompasses even insults, this does not mean that the Court was previously tolerant of hate speech. Comparable remarks to those made in *Le Pen* and *Zemmour* were addressed in *Seurot v France* (2004), though in a school setting. In this case, the applicant, a secondary school history and geography teacher, authored an article published in the school's internal newspaper, which was distributed to pupils and their parents. The applicant was convicted of incitement to racial hatred, leading to the termination of his teaching contract. The teacher's statements included thus:

> The illusionists had not foreseen that in exchange for the desperate flight of these cursed French from North Africa, unassimilable Muslim hordes would land and invade the most remote of our cantons.
>
> There are five million of them today, building mosques everywhere and when they talk about setting sail . . . don't rejoice too much, it's only for their dirty arrogant kids!

At the domestic level, two anti-racism organisations filed a legal complaint against the applicant and the college director, accusing them of incitement to discrimination and racial hatred. Following a judicial investigation, the school principal and the applicant were indicted and referred to the criminal court. However, the criminal court acquitted them, ruling that the charges did not fit the legal classification established at the outset of the prosecution. On appeal, the court reconsidered the case, focusing solely on the offence of incitement to racial hatred. The defendants were found guilty, and the applicant was fined 5,000 francs.

In its judgement, the ECtHR, citing cases such as *Handyside*, reiterated the significance of freedom of expression. It also noted that 'it is of utmost importance to combat racial discrimination in all its forms and manifestations.'[32] Since this case involved an application made by a civil servant, especially a teacher, the Court found that the duties and responsibilities set out in Article 10(2) 'take on a special meaning' which granted the authorities of the respondent state a degree of discretion in assessing whether the interference in question was proportionate to the stated aim. The Court noted that teachers are 'a symbol of authority for their pupils in the field of education, the special duties and responsibilities incumbent upon them also apply to a certain extent to their activities outside school.' The Court found that Article 17 was not applicable given the 'general tone of the text in dispute.' However, it found that the content of the statements was 'undeniably racist' and so 'incompatible

32 *Seurot v France* App no 57383/00 (ECHR, 18 May 2005)

with the applicant's particular duties and responsibilities.' It held that, even if the applicant wanted to write something humorous, as he alleged was his intention, he should have taken more care due to his status as a history teacher and the risk of the text's dissemination. As such, the ECtHR balanced the applicant's right to freedom of expression against the need to combat racism and uphold the responsibilities associated with his role as a teacher. Given the racist nature of the statements and the potential harm caused by their dissemination, the interference with his speech was deemed necessary and proportionate in a democratic society.

In *Vejdeland and Others v Sweden* (2012), the applicants visited a secondary school and distributed around 100 leaflets by placing them in students' lockers. The leaflets were produced by a far-right organisation known as National Youth and included, among others, the following statements:

> In the course of a few decades society has swung from rejection of homosexuality and other sexual deviances to embracing this deviant sexual proclivity. Your anti-Swedish teachers know very well that homosexuality has a morally destructive effect on the substance of society and will willingly try to put it forward as something normal and good.
>
> Tell them that HIV and AIDS appeared early with the homosexuals and that their promiscuous lifestyle was one of the main reasons for this modern-day plague gaining a foothold.
>
> Tell them that homosexual lobby organisations are also trying to play down (*avdramatisera*) paedophilia and ask if this sexual deviation should be legalised.

The applicants were charged with agitation against a national or ethnic group. The district court found the applicants guilty, noting that their intention was to express contempt for homosexuals. The first and second applicants received a prison sentence of two months, the third applicant received a suspended sentence and a fine and the fourth applicant received a community service order. The applicants appealed, asking the Court to reject the charges or lower the sentences, while the prosecutor also appealed, requesting the Court to consider the criminal acts to be aggravated or for the punishment to be increased. The court of appeal rejected the charges on freedom of expression grounds. The prosecutor-general appealed to the Supreme Court, which convicted the applicants of agitation against a national or ethnic group. The first three applicants received suspended sentences and fines ranging between EUR 200 and 2000, and the fourth applicant was sentenced to probation.

Vejdeland was the first opportunity the Court had to rule on a case of homophobic speech. The Court underlined that 'discrimination based on sexual orientation is as serious as discrimination based on race, origin or colour.'[33]

33 *Vejdeland v Sweden* App no 1813/07 (ECHR, 9 February 2012) para 55

This interpretation rightly expanded the scope of hate speech beyond its traditional focus on race and ethnicity, affirming that discrimination based on sexual orientation is equally serious. In the concurring opinion by Ukrainian judge Yudkivska joined by Swiss judge Villiger, it was argued that the Court missed a valuable opportunity to 'consolidate an approach to hate speech'[34] against homosexuals. According to their view, this was because the majority found that statements lacking a direct recommendation for individuals to commit hateful acts constituted 'serious and prejudicial allegations' rather than incitement to violence.[35] However, it must be highlighted that no prior cases had led to a consolidated approach to hate speech, even when it comes to racist speech which both the EComHR and the ECtHR had been dealing with for years. Also, the Court simply followed the *Féret* paradigm by finding that it is not required for speech 'to directly recommend individuals to commit hateful acts,'[36] as attacks on individuals can also occur through 'insulting, holding up to ridicule, or slandering specific groups of the population.'[37] Furthermore, the Court noted that speech employed irresponsibly may fall outside the framework of Article 10 protection.[38] In this ambit, the Court noted that 'although these statements did not directly recommend individuals to commit hateful acts, they are serious and prejudicial allegations.'[39] In reaching this position, it followed *Féret* in its assessment of incitement, noting:

> [T]he Court reiterates that inciting to hatred does not necessarily entail a call for an act of violence, or other criminal acts. Attacks on persons committed by insulting, holding up to ridicule or slandering specific groups of the population can be sufficient for the authorities to favour combating racist speech in the face of freedom of expression exercised in an irresponsible manner. In this regard, the Court stresses that discrimination based on sexual orientation is as serious as discrimination based on 'race, origin or colour.'[40]

In *Vejdeland*, the Court added the element of prejudice and replaced the word *defamation* (*la diffamation*) with *slander*, which is legally erroneous, considering that the speech was written rather than oral. The same comments also apply to *Lilliendahl*, discussed later.

Furthermore, the Court also considered the audience targeted by the speech and the medium through which the speech was disseminated. It noted that the contested statements were distributed through leaflets placed in the lockers of young individuals who were at an impressionable and vulnerable age, with no

34 *Vejdeland* (n 33) Concurring Opinion of Judge Yudkivska joined by Judge Villiger, para 5
35 *Vejdeland* (n 33) Concurring Opinion of Yudkivska and Villiger, para 5
36 *Vejdeland* (n 33) para 54
37 *Vejdeland* (n 33) para 55
38 *Vejdeland* (n 33)
39 *Vejdeland* (n 33) para 54
40 *Vejdeland* (n 33) para 55

opportunity to refuse or avoid receiving them.[41] Here it should be recognised that the Court employs an interchangeable approach in its consideration of the medium used to disseminate speech and the resulting scope of its reach. For instance, in *Lilliendahl*, discussed later, the Court acknowledged that the speech in question had limited visibility. Nevertheless, it concluded that the speech fell outside the protections of Article 10.

It is interesting to note that the concurring opinion of Judge Spielman (Luxembourg) joined by Judge Nussberger (Germany) in *Vejdeland* referred to *Alekseyev v Russia* (2010), an Article 11 case which involved the systematic banning of marches, which aimed to draw public attention to homophobic discrimination in Russia and promote tolerance and respect for human rights. That case noted that:

> [T]here is no scientific evidence or sociological data at the Court's disposal suggesting that the mere mention of homosexuality, or open public debate about sexual minorities' social status, would adversely affect children or "vulnerable adults." On the contrary, it is only through fair and public debate that society may address such complex issues as the one raised in the present case. Such debate, backed up by academic research, would benefit social cohesion by ensuring that representatives of all views are heard, including the individuals concerned.[42]

Another concurring opinion of that case also referred to scholarship, specifically to Alexander Bickel's paper on domesticated civil disobedience. One of the most extensive uses of scholarship is found in the dissenting opinion of Judge Sajó (Hungary), joined by Judge Tsotsoria (Georgia), in *Delfi*, which looked at papers by, *inter alia*, Jack M. Balkin and a selection of authors in privacy rights.[43]

As noted in the introduction, in the sphere of hate speech case law, reliance on scholarship including empirical data appears seldomly and only in individual opinions, as also reflected earlier. This practice should also occur for the articulation of themes and issues in the core of the Court's judgement. In brief, the Court's analysis needs to be engaging, with a broad range of available normative and empirical research for purposes of answering questions before repeating narratives in relation to issues such as harm and the impact of hate speech.

Vejdeland is a positive development insofar as it ensures that sexual orientation is also considered a protected characteristic in the sphere of hate speech, thereby ensuring equal treatment of targeted groups by maintaining the *Féret* paradigm and allowing for criminal penalties in a case of prejudice ('serious

41 *Vejdeland* (n 33) para 56
42 *Vejdeland* (n 33) Concurring Opinion of Judge Spielman joined by Judge Nussberger, para 4
43 *Delfi AS v Estonia* App no 64569/09 (ECHR, 16 June 2015) Joint Dissenting Opinion of Judges Sajó and Tsotsoria

and prejudicial allegations'). This continues to be particularly troubling, given the fundamental nature of free speech, but also for an array of reasons set out in Chapter 2 on how hate speech restrictions may, essentially, backfire and cause more harm than good for society and the groups that are targets of such speech. This is so particularly when dealing with low-threshold hatred. This approach underscores a significant debate within European human rights law over the boundaries of freedom of expression and the degree to which it can be limited in cases of harmful, but non-violent, speech. Interestingly, the opinion of Ukrainian judge Yudkivska, joined by Swiss judge Villiger, made the comparison with the USA, noting that hate speech is protected until it threatens to lead to imminent violence, and noted that 'this is a very high threshold, and for many well-known political and historical reasons today's Europe cannot afford the luxury of such a vision of the paramount value of free speech.'[44] In his concurring opinion, Slovenian judge Zupančič articulated reservations about the majority's reasoning but ultimately concurred due to the case's specific circumstances. He referred to the US case of *Snyder v Phelps* (2011), which involved the picketing of a soldier's funeral with homophobic signage. He noted that the American Supreme Court has set a higher standard for the law to be 'facially constitutional' in that it avoids content discrimination and viewpoint-based restriction. To this end, he spoke of sensitivities, noting that the First Amendment approach could be considered as 'insensitive' and the Swedish approach could demonstrate an 'oversensitivity in collision with free speech postulates.'[45] He attributed this difference to a 'culturally predetermined debate.'[46] Concluding his reflections, he suggested that the Court might '[have gone] too far in the present case . . . in limiting freedom of speech by over-estimating the importance of what is being said.'[47]

In *Lilliendahl v Iceland* (2020), an Icelandic municipal council approved a proposal aimed at enhancing education and counselling in schools on matters concerning individuals who identify as lesbian, gay, bisexual or transgender. This decision garnered significant public attention, being widely reported in the news and discussed on the call-in program of the radio station 'ÚS.' In response to an online news article about the proposal, the applicant posted comments containing terms such as "sexual deviation" and "disgusting." Subsequently, the applicant was charged with making public statements that constituted threats, mockery, defamation and denigration of a group of individuals based on their sexual orientation and gender identity. The district court acquitted the applicant, citing the protection of free speech and concluding that the comments did not meet the requisite legal threshold under

44 *Vejdeland* (n 33) Concurring Opinion of Yudkivska and Villiger, para 6
45 *Vejdeland* (n 33) para 6
46 *Vejdeland* (n 33)
47 *Vejdeland* (n 33) para 12

the applicable law. However, the Supreme Court of Iceland overturned this decision and imposed a fine of approximately EUR 800 on the applicant.

This case is significant when examining the evolution of the Court's jurisprudence on homophobic and/or transphobic speech, as well as its broader approach to defining hate speech.

As noted in Chapter 3, *Lilliendahl* marked the first time in its jurisprudence on hate speech when the Court posed the following question:

> *Did the applicant's comments amount to 'hate speech' within the meaning of the Court's case-law?*[48]

Rather than extrapolating on the meaning of *hate speech* under its case law, the Court simply applied a hierarchical classification of the two types of hate speech which are not protected by the ECHR.[49] According to the Court in *Lilliendahl*, the first category of hate speech consists of what the Court described as the 'gravest forms of hate speech,'[50] which are entirely excluded from protection under Article 17. The second category encompasses 'less grave forms of hate speech'[51] which, while not automatically excluded from Article 10, 'may be restricted by Contracting States.' In this category, the Court included not only calls for violence or other criminal acts but also insults, ridicule and slander aimed at countering 'prejudicial speech within the bounds of permissible restrictions on freedom of expression.'[52] However, the Court did not specify what constitutes or could constitute such permissible restriction, reflecting its habit of putting forth keywords and phrases without further substantiation. While such substantiation must undoubtedly give leeway to national courts, guidance is needed for the purposes of ensuring proper protection of Convention articles. The Court noted that in cases where hate speech falls into the second category and does not call for violence or other criminal acts, the assessment of the content and manner of the speech's delivery is also taken into consideration when assessing if it qualifies as hate speech.[53]

The ECtHR agreed with the Supreme Court of Iceland that the comments were 'serious, severely hurtful and prejudicial.'[54] The ECtHR noted the nature of the comments in addition to the applicant's apparent disgust. Specifically, it held thus:

> As reasoned by the Supreme Court, the use of the terms *kynvilla* (sexual deviation) and *kynvillingar* (sexual deviants) to describe homosexual

48 *Lilliendahl v Iceland* App no 29297/18 (ECHR, 12 May 2020) para 32
49 *Lilliendahl* (n 48) para 33
50 *Lilliendahl* (n 48) para 34
51 *Lilliendahl* (n 48) para 35
52 *Lilliendahl* (n 48) para 36
53 *Lilliendahl* (n 48)
54 *Lilliendahl* (n 48) para 45

> persons, especially when coupled with the clear expression of disgust, render the applicant's comments ones which promote intolerance and detestation of homosexual persons.[55]

In terms of whether the speech constituted hate speech, the Court adopted the *Féret* paradigm and found that the applicant's conviction did not amount to a violation of Article 10. With respect to Article 17, the Court held that the statements in question did not reach the high threshold required for an application of Article 17, since the speech was 'highly prejudicial,'[56] although it was not immediately clear that it aimed at inciting violence or hatred or destroying Convention rights.[57] When assessing the impact of the speech in question, the ECtHR noted that the limited potential reach of the comments to a broader audience was irrelevant to its assessment.[58] Interesting comparators to this point are two other hate speech cases, specifically *Soulas and Others v France* (2008) *and Karataş v Turkey* (1999). In *Soulas*, the ECtHR emphasised that the book titled *The Colonization of Europe: True Speech on Immigration and Islam* was written in an accessible style and was aimed at a broad audience, thereby amplifying its potential to cause harm, one of the reasons which contributed to the ECtHR finding no violation of Article 10.[59] In *Karataş*, the ECtHR observed that the applicant addressed the Kurdish issue through poetry, a medium of artistic expression that, despite containing some aggressive passages, typically appeals to a relatively small audience.[60] This was one of the contributing factors for finding a violation of Article 10. Thus, in both *Soulas* and *Karataş*, the extent of the material's dissemination and the size of its readership played a significant role in the Court's assessment, something that played no role in *Lilliendahl*. In fact, the Court was specific in recognising the small reach of *Lilliendahl*'s speech, although concluding that there was no Article 10 violation. Moreover, in *Vejdeland*, the ECtHR took into account the fact that the leaflets were disseminated to schoolchildren in their lockers, thereby rendering their contact with the speech unavoidable, and this, theoretically, contributed to the finding of no violation.

In relation to the proportionality of punishment, the Court observed that, although the offence for which Lilliendahl was convicted could carry a sentence of up to two years' imprisonment, he was not given a custodial sentence. Instead, he was fined approximately EUR 800, which the Court deemed proportionate under the circumstances, given that a prison sentence was available under the law but, instead, the applicant received a fine.[61] However, this

55 *Lilliendahl* (n 48) para 38
56 *Lilliendahl* (n 48) para 26
57 *Lilliendahl* (n 48)
58 *Lilliendahl* (n 48) para 39
59 *Soulas and others v France* App no 15948/03 (ECHR, 10 July 2008) para 39
60 *Karataş v Turkey* App no 23168/94 (ECHR, 8 July 1999) para 52
61 *Lilliendahl* (n 48) para 46

assessment of proportionality is problematic since it employs a comparative approach to what exists on a domestic level. The fact that a prison term existed for a speech 'crime' should not be the benchmark against which the proportionality of punishment is assessed by the ECtHR, particularly when faced with speech that, albeit prejudicial, does not incite violence.

In *Atamanchuk v Russia* (2020), the applicant, an entrepreneur, politician, founder of a newspaper and freelance journalist, had written an article for the local newspaper explaining his decision not to vote in the upcoming elections. The piece was headlined "Why I will not vote in these elections." Relevant parts of the passage included, amongst others:

> In fifteen years of 'new style' democracy no Russian person [русский человек] has seen anything good. He has been pushed down to the level of a simpleton who is to serve various small ethnic groupings that call themselves 'republics', within Russia or elsewhere.
>
> Just look around and you will see crowds of them staring at you greedily at every corner.
>
> They will speak Russian later, when they have totally paralysed our will. That is when they will start to burn, slaughter, rape, rob and enslave, in line with their barbaric ideas, as it was in Chechnya.
>
> They participate in the destruction of the country. . . . Various processes of destruction dominate our society today. That is why I will not take part in the election.

The same piece was reprinted in another newspaper, with the heading related to the applicant's criminal prosecution. Both newspapers were distributed for free in the Sochi area. The applicant was convicted of inciting hatred and enmity, debasing the human dignity of a person or group of people on account of their ethnicity, language, origin and religious beliefs. For each instance of the article's publication, the applicant received a fine of EUR 5,086 and was prohibited from engaging in any journalistic or publishing work for two years. The applicant appealed this decision, but the regional court upheld the previous judgement.

The government requested that the complaint be dismissed under Article 17. To this, the Court noted that this request and Article 10 considerations were closely linked to the merits of the complaint and should therefore be connected, demonstrating a blended Articles 17–10 approach. In some cases, Article 17 is applied directly, 'categorically excluding certain expressions from the protection of Article 10.'[62] However, there is also the approach of indirect application, where Article 17 acts as an 'interpretative aid'[63] when assessing

62 Hannes Cannie and Dirk Voorhoof, 'The Abuse Clause and Freedom of Expression in the European Human Rights Convention: An Added Value for Democracy and Human Rights Protection?' (2011) 29(1) Netherlands Quarterly of Human Rights 58

63 Cannie and Voorhoof (n 62)

the limitation grounds of Article 10(2). It could be argued that the indirect application of Article 17 can reduce risks by allowing for a more nuanced and flexible approach to balancing free speech with limitations, potentially avoiding the overreach of directly excluding certain expressions. On the other hand, it could also be argued that both direct and indirect applications ultimately lead to similar outcomes in hate speech cases, namely, the restriction of certain speech. However, given the severity of the issues that relate to the use of Article 17, I would hold that the Court should simply keep that article for extreme cases, as originally envisaged in the article's drafting, rather than blending it in its interpretative exercise of free speech.

The ECtHR made reference to the fact that ideas and opinions include those which offend, shock or disturb. It proceeded to note that offensive language may fall outside Article 10 protection if it amounts to 'wanton denigration.'[64] The Court did not find that the applicant's speech fell within such denigration. It proceeded to consider whether the speech was violent, finding that the publication did not directly call for violence, but nevertheless, its majority found no violation of the applicant's right under Article 10. In doing so, it underlined that incitement to hatred does not always require an explicit call for violence[65] and noted that the Court has been 'particularly sensitive towards sweeping statements attacking or casting in a negative light entire ethnic, religious or other group.'[66]

The ECtHR, once again, followed the *Féret* example, underlining that:

> Inciting hatred does not necessarily involve an explicit call for an act of violence, or other criminal acts. Attacks on persons committed by insulting, holding up to ridicule or slandering specific groups of the population can be sufficient for the authorities to favour combating xenophobic or otherwise discriminatory speech in the face of freedom of expression exercised in an irresponsible manner.[67]

In relation to the national courts' decision to suspend the applicant's journalistic activities for two years, the ECtHR noted that such sentencing can occur only in exceptional circumstances, which must be carefully scrutinised.[68] The ECtHR considered that the sentencing was justified for the following reasons. Firstly, it noted that the charges against the applicant were grounded on the protection of non-Russians. Interestingly, the Court referred to a state's positive obligation to protect the rights of others and regulate free speech if such speech would affect their rights. In doing so, it made reference to

64 *Atamanchuk v Russia* App no 4493/11 (ECHR, 11 February 2020) para 47
65 *Atamanchuk* (n 64)
66 *Atamanchuk* (n 64) para 51
67 *Atamanchuk* (n 64) para 52
68 *Atamanchuk* (n 64) para 67

Article 8 of the ECHR on the right to private and family life.[69] To support the domestic sentencing further, the ECtHR expressed doubts about whether the article genuinely aimed to contribute to the public debate.[70] The Court considered, rather arbitrarily, that since the applicant's main profession was that of an entrepreneur, the prohibition of his journalistic activities would not have any significant practical consequences.[71] Considering that the speech did not directly incite violence but remained within the spectrum of insulting and/or discriminatory speech, it is doubtful whether the Court did, in fact, live up to its strict scrutiny standards when assessing the legitimacy of the applicant's journalistic ban.

The flaws in this decision were reflected in the dissenting opinion of Cypriot judge Serghides, who held that the judgement was 'not a fully-fledged one, but rather a statement of opinion.' He held that, while the Court referred to the importance of strict scrutiny when it comes to speech restrictions, it did not apply it in practice to the present case. He argued that the penalties imposed were disproportionate, and that the interference was not justifiable.

Outside the direct spectrum of the *Féret* paradigm, but important for the understanding of the Court's conceptualisation of hate speech and viewpoint-based restrictions, are the cases of *Ottan v France* (2018) and *National Youth Council of Moldova v Republic of Moldova* (2024).

In *Ottan*, the ECtHR found a violation of Article 10 in a case concerning the conviction of a lawyer for his allegedly racist remarks made about the verdict in a case he was dealing with. The case arose from the 2009 acquittal of a gendarme who fatally shot a young man from an immigrant community residing in a working-class neighbourhood during a car chase in 2003. Shortly after the verdict, in response to a journalist's question, the applicant, who was representing the victim's father, remarked that the acquittal was unsurprising due to the jury's ethnic make-up, which was entirely composed of Whites:

> A white jury, exclusively white, where the communities are not all represented with, it may well be said, an extremely soft accusation, debates conducted in an extremely biased manner, the road to acquittal was a royally open road, this is no surprise.

The process before domestic institutions was complex. The attorney general initiated disciplinary action against the applicant for controversial comments following a case verdict. Although the president of the Bar Association did not find the remarks outrageous, the disciplinary process moved forward. During the hearing, the applicant argued that his comments defended his client's interests and were protected by Article 10 of the Convention. The Disciplinary

69 *Atamanchuk* (n 64) para 70
70 *Atamanchuk* (n 64) para 70
71 *Atamanchuk* (n 64) para 71

Board acquitted him, recognising the remarks as a broader commentary on the verdict within the scope of freedom of expression. However, the public prosecutor appealed, seeking a temporary ban on his practice. Before the court of appeal, the applicant clarified that his remarks targeted jury diversity rather than integrity. However, the court of appeal found that he cast suspicion of racial prejudice amongst jurors and discredited the court and proceeded to issue a warning. The applicant appealed to the court of cassation, which upheld the previous decision.

In unanimously finding a violation of Article 10, the ECtHR highlighted that the disputed remarks were made within a debate of general interest on the functioning of the criminal justice system in the context of media coverage of the case.[72] It noted that the case had had a significant effect on a local and national scale.[73] In this setting, the Court did not view the comments as either insulting or racially motivated. When assessing the applicant's reference to "white, exclusively white" in relation to the jury composition, the Court grappled with concepts such as unconscious bias and history to explain that the applicant's comments were not inherently racist.[74] While agreeing with the court of appeal and the court of cassation that the comments applied to the entire court which heard the case in question and could potentially discredit the institution as a whole, the ECtHR found that the facts of this case did not violate the authority and impartiality of the judiciary and that, as a result, the warning issued to the applicant violated Article 10.[75]

In *National Youth Council of Moldova v Republic of Moldova* (2024), the ECtHR dealt with an application by an association which was part of a coalition combatting discrimination. It sought permission from Chişinău City Hall to display a billboard promoting an anti-discrimination helpline. The advertisement featured caricatures of various marginalised individuals, including two men holding hands, a Black man, an elderly woman, a pregnant woman, a person in a wheelchair and a couple representing Roma people. The text which accompanied the image read: "Are you discriminated against? Call the anti-discrimination hotline free of charge and confidentially at 0-8003-8003." The advertisement sparked objections from local Roma and disability organisations, who criticised the depictions as offensive and unrepresentative. The City Hall refused to allow the advertisement, citing violations of fairness and decency under advertising laws. Efforts to overturn the decision through domestic courts failed, with rulings favouring the City Hall's stance and dismissing the association's arguments under freedom of expression laws. The applicant subsequently brought the case before the ECtHR, alleging a violation of their right to freedom of expression under Article 10 of the

72 *Ottan v France* App no 41841/12 (ECHR, 19 April 2018) para 61
73 *Ottan* (n 72) para 58
74 *Ottan* (n 72) para 64
75 *Ottan* (n 72) paras 70–72

Convention. The Court unanimously concluded that the interference with the applicant's freedom of expression was unjustified. While recognising that the poster could potentially offend some viewers, the Court found no evidence that it would incite discrimination or hostility.76 The Court recognised that the poster was part of a broader anti-discrimination campaign addressing a significant public interest issue in Moldova. Rather than being a commercial advertisement, it was classified as a social advertisement aimed at raising awareness about discrimination.77 The Court emphasised that the caricatures were intended to highlight and challenge existing stereotypes, not to reinforce or incite hatred.78 Additionally, the failure of the domestic courts to conduct a thorough review reinforced the finding that the restriction was not necessary in a democratic society. The Court, therefore, held that there had been a violation of Article 10 of the Convention.79

The ECtHR's approach in *Ottan* and *National Youth Council of Moldova* underscores its nuanced stance on free speech, particularly when it comes to speech addressing significant societal concerns. In *Ottan*, the Court found no violation of Article 10 despite remarks that critiqued jury composition based on racial homogeneity. By framing the applicant's comments as part of a broader discourse on unconscious bias, the Court protected his right to free expression without endorsing the potentially divisive nature of his remarks. Similarly, in *National Youth Council of Moldova*, the Court found no violation in a case involving caricatures intended to raise awareness about discrimination, recognising the speech's social utility despite its capacity to offend some viewers. These rulings demonstrate the Court's willingness to tolerate controversial or unsettling speech which matches its own viewpoints, namely, the existence of racial discrimination and unconscious bias and the prohibition of discrimination, respectively. While this is laudable in itself, as is the fight against all forms of discrimination, the Court's approach in the preceding cases demonstrates how subjective determinations of acceptability can jeopardise the robust protection of free expression.

2.2 Final Comments

In *Vejdeland*, the Court equated homophobic speech with racist speech, recognising that discrimination based on sexual orientation is equally as serious. This principle was reiterated in *Lilliendahl*, which dealt with both homophobic and transphobic speech. By broadening the scope of protected characteristics, the ECtHR has demonstrated its commitment to addressing forms of

76 *National Youth Council of Moldova v Republic of Moldova* App no 15379/13 (ECHR, 25 June 2006) para 77
77 *National Youth Council of Moldova* (n 76) para 73
78 *National Youth Council of Moldova* (n 76) para 70
79 *National Youth Council of Moldova* (n 76) paras 81, 82

discrimination beyond the sphere of race and religion. This is especially significant, given that international and European human rights instruments, such as Article 20(2) of the ICCPR, the European Union's Framework Decision on Racism and Xenophobia and the Council of Europe's Additional Protocol to the Convention on Cybercrime, fail to provide equal protection to victims of homophobic and transphobic speech and/or crimes when compared to the sphere of racism and xenophobia.

Beyond this positive finding, there are several criticisms that can be drawn from the preceding analysis. *Féret* represents a defining moment in ECtHR's articulation of hate speech. It signalled a shift towards a more expansive interpretation of what constitutes hate speech, encompassing expressions of insult, ridicule, defamation and prejudice without the need of incitement to violence or criminal acts. Essentially, *Féret* built on the Court's stance on hate speech in *Gündüz*, where it held that 'there can be no doubt that concrete expressions constituting hate speech, which may be insulting to particular individuals or groups, are not protected by Article 10 of the Convention.'[80] *Féret* added to the 'insult' criterion by extending the scope of prohibited speech to include expressions that defame or ridicule. It also clarified that hate speech does not need to incite violence to fall outside the protections of Article 10. This case has been the go-to case for many hate speech cases which do not reach higher thresholds of severity, such as inciting violence. However, its expansive approach has raised critical questions about the adequacy of evidentiary standards, the proportionality of restrictions and the broader implications for political discourse in democratic societies. *Féret* is significant for its explicit articulation that hate speech need not involve a direct call to violence, or even hatred, to warrant restriction under Article 10. This principle was reiterated in *Vejdeland*, where the applicants were convicted for distributing homophobic leaflets which, while not advocating violence, were considered by the ECtHR to have expressed serious and prejudicial views about homosexuals. The *Féret* precedent demonstrates the Court's increasing willingness to prioritise societal interests, such as social cohesion and protecting the feelings of targeted groups, over the fundamental right to freedom of expression, even in cases involving political speech. Yet this approach diverges from earlier decisions, such as *Handyside*, discussed in the previous chapter, where the Court underscored the right to express ideas that shock, offend or disturb as a cornerstone of democratic discourse. The tension between these principles has become increasingly pronounced in the ECtHR's hate speech jurisprudence.

Furthermore, this section reflects the unique responsibilities placed on politicians in democratic societies. The Court emphasised that, given their influence, politicians must exercise caution in their statements to avoid exacerbating societal tensions. In *Le Pen*, the ECtHR dismissed the application of a prominent politician whose statements painted an alarmist and discriminatory

80 *Gűndűz* (n 15) para 41

picture of Muslims in France, holding that such remarks could foster rejection and hostility. Similarly, in *Zemmour*, the Court echoed this reasoning, finding no violation of Article 10, where a politician's televised statements incited discrimination against Muslims by portraying them as a homogeneous and threatening group. These cases highlight the ECtHR's view that the impact of politicians' statements is magnified by their influence on public opinion, particularly in electoral contexts. However, dissenting opinions in cases like *Féret* have raised concerns about the Court's broad interpretation of hate speech. In *Féret*, Hungarian judge Sajó, joined by Judges Zagrebelsky (Italy) and Tsotsoria (Georgia), cautioned against treating the public as incapable of rational engagement with provocative speech. This paternalistic approach, they argued, risks stifling democratic debate by privileging state-determined standards of acceptability.[81] Essentially, the Court's reasoning in such cases risks conflating offensive political discourse with hate speech, thereby chilling legitimate democratic expression.

In addition, a recurring critique of the ECtHR's hate speech jurisprudence is its lack of rigorous standards for assessing the harm caused by contested speech. In *Féret*, the Court did not clearly articulate how the applicant's statements undermined democratic institutions or caused tangible harm, leaving the causal link between speech and societal harm broadly defined. The *Féret* paradigm further complicates this balancing act by allowing restrictions on speech based on its potential to incite negative emotions rather than concrete actions. This principle was applied in *Zemmour*, where the Court relied on the speech's divisive potential rather than specific evidence of its harmful effects. As things stand, the ECtHR's commitment to upholding the right to offend, shock or disturb is challenging to reconcile with its generally permissive stance towards hate speech legislation. Similarly, its professed robust protection of freedom of expression for politicians appears difficult to align with its rulings in *Féret*, Le Pen and Zemmour. This reveals the risks of privileging state-endorsed narratives at the expense of democratic pluralism. The dissenting opinions in *Féret* and *Atamanchuk* caution against the dangers of subjective content regulation, which can suppress dissenting voices.[82] The recent case of *National Youth Council of Moldova* demonstrates the Court's recognition of the importance of non-discrimination in shaping its Article 10 jurisprudence. In this case, the Court protected the applicant's freedom of expression by overturning a municipal refusal to display an anti-discrimination advertisement. The Court acknowledged the intention behind the speech as central to

81 *Féret* (n 4) Dissenting Opinion by Sajó and others

82 Stefan Sottiaux recommends the creation of a new category of unprotected speech, namely, intentional intimidation or harassment to combat the abuse of the Court's approach by governments which seek to silence political dissent. See Stefan Sottiaux, 'Conflicting Conceptions of Hate Speech in the ECtHR's Case Law' (2022) 23 German Law Review 9. Sottiaux has long been criticising the Court's approach in hate speech cases in previous work too. See, for example, Stefan Sottiaux, 'Bad Tendencies in the ECtHR's Hate Speech Jurisprudence' (2011) 7(1) European Constitutional Law Review

its decision, recognising the poster's role as part of a broader public campaign to raise awareness about discrimination. By rejecting the domestic authorities' reliance on subjective notions of offence and emphasising that the caricatures were intended to challenge stereotypes rather than incite hatred, the Court underscored its commitment to upholding expressive rights when addressing public interest issues. However, this decision also highlights potential tensions within the ECtHR's approach, as reliance on subjective perceptions of harm risks opening the door to viewpoint-based restrictions on speech, particularly when comparing to other cases, such as those mentioned earlier. This is also the major concern with *Ottan*.

Varying approaches to the medium used for the dissemination of speech and the impact of the alleged harm also marks the case law. For example, in *Lilliendahl*, the applicant's homophobic and transphobic comments under an online news article were deemed sufficiently harmful to warrant a criminal penalty, despite their limited audience and impact, even though, in *Karatas*, the fact that poetry had limited readership played a role in the Court's final decision of finding an Article 10 violation.

Added to the jurisprudential critique is the lacking nuance in ECtHR decisions. Specifically, the ease with which the Court restricts even insulting speech or speech which is prejudicial is problematic for a host of reasons, not least because of the fundamental nature of the freedom of expression. Also, as discussed in Chapter 2, empirical evidence suggests that silencing offensive views can exacerbate tensions, transform speakers into martyrs and drive harmful speech underground. As such, it is possible that the Court's restrictive approach may inadvertently undermine its stated objective of fostering social cohesion. However, the Court continues to demonstrate reluctance in grappling with the broad range of substantial issues on the matter, which would allow for a better-informed approach, particularly when dealing with contentious areas of speech, such as cases which fall within the low-threshold hatred paradigm. Here, it is important to reiterate that it is not within the Court's remit to determine what specific evidence national law requires to establish the constituent elements of the offence for which applicants have been prosecuted. The interpretation and application of domestic law primarily fall within the jurisdiction of national authorities, particularly the courts. Nevertheless, the ECtHR is tasked with ensuring coherent European supervision within the margin of appreciation.[83] In summary, there is scope for the Court to adopt a more critical stance toward national authorities, as it has occasionally done in a minority of cases, such as *Ibragimov*, *Ottan* and *National Youth Council of Moldova*. Additionally, the Court could engage more substantively with broader issues, including the implications of hate speech laws on freedom of expression and their broader consequences when ascertaining the necessity of restrictions, as explored in Chapter 2.

83 *Lehideux and Isorni v France* App no 24662/94 (ECHR, 23 September 1998) para 51

In light of the above, *Féret* encapsulates the ECtHR's expansive interpretation of harm. It raises significant questions about the threshold, consistency and proportionality of speech restrictions. As the challenges posed by hate speech, particularly in the online sphere, continue to grow, the ECtHR must refine its jurisprudence to ensure that Article 10 remains a robust safeguard for democratic expression. Clearer standards and definitions and a more rigorous analysis of harm, and a renewed commitment to the principles established in *Handyside*, are essential to preserving the delicate balance between freedom and regulation in a pluralistic society. As things stand, the ECtHR's commitment to upholding the right to offend, shock and disturb is challenging to reconcile with its generally permissive stance towards restrictions of what it has very broadly conceptualised as hate speech.

3 Beyond Offence: Inciting Hatred or Violence

This section critically examines the ECtHR's jurisprudence on cases involving incitement to ethnic, racial or religious hatred or violence. The section begins with *Erbakan v Turkey* (2006), a case highlighting the importance of imminence and proportionality when restricting speech. It then moves to *Balsytė-Lideikienė v Lithuania* (2009) and *Soulas and Others v France* (2008), which illustrate the impact of historical and societal sensitivities on the Court's reasoning. Other cases, such as *Tagiyev and Huseynov v Azerbaijan* (2019) and *Sokolovskiy v Russia* (2024), focus on the reliance on expert opinions and the adequacy of assessments of contested speech by domestic courts. Finally, the section explores *Smajić v Bosnia and Herzegovina* (2018), which raises significant questions about the proportionality of criminal sanctions for hypothetical speech in post-conflict societies. Through this analysis, the section critiques the ECtHR's consistency in defining hate speech, its application of harm and imminence principles and the implications of its approach for the right to freedom of expression in Europe within the sphere of hate speech which allegedly incites hatred or violence.

3.1 Cases of Incitement to Ethnic/Racial or Religious Hatred, Animosity and/or Violence

In *Erbakan v Turkey* (2006), the applicant was a prominent politician who had served as the prime minister of Turkey between 1996 and 1997. At the material time, he was the chairman of Refah Partisi (the Welfare Party), which was dissolved in 1998 for conducting activities deemed contrary to the principles of secularism. In 1994, during a local election campaign, the applicant delivered a public speech. No official recording of the speech was made. Over four years later, criminal proceedings were initiated against him for allegedly inciting hatred or hostility through remarks in the 1994 speech that allegedly made distinctions between religions, races and regions. Some of the impugned speech included remarks describing all parties, except his own, as parties of the unjust, lovers of the infidel. Defending a system purportedly based on self-interest, the applicant had advocated the view that "those parties had declared war, according to the Koran, against Allah." He was convicted for inciting hatred due to his remarks during the speech and was, as a result, imprisoned for one year and received a fine of around EUR 6,000.

The ECtHR started off, as is often the case in hate speech cases, by emphasising the importance of free speech and the *Handyside* principle.[84] It also underlined the importance of combatting all forms of intolerance as a cornerstone of human rights protection.[85] It noted that 'there is no doubt that concrete expressions constituting hate speech . . . which may be insulting to individuals or groups, do not enjoy the protection of Article 10 of the Convention.'[86] Nevertheless, it underscored the vital interest of a democratic society in safeguarding freedom of political debate.[87] In its assessment of the particular facts, the Court observed that the authorities had waited four years since the rally to investigate the speech in question. This delay undermined the case against the applicant, as the authorities relied solely on a video recording of disputed authenticity, without establishing the content of the speech at the time of the rally.[88] The Court also found it particularly challenging to hold the applicant accountable for all the statements attributed to him in the indictment, particularly since the authenticity of the video recording was in dispute. Importantly, it noted that, at the time of prosecution, it had not been demonstrated that the speech had caused, or was likely to cause, a 'present risk'[89] or 'imminent danger.'[90] For the Court, the long time period (over four years) between the speech and the prosecution diluted such risks and dangers. Moreover, the Court took into account the extraordinarily harsh sentence imposed on a prominent politician, stressing the 'chilling effect'[91] that imprisonment for speech could have on political expression. As a result of the preceding, the ECtHR held, by a majority, that there had been a violation of Article 10. Interestingly, in 2001, the ECtHR found that the dissolution of *Refah Partisi* did not violate Article 11 on the right to association and assembly.[92]

In Judge Steiner's (Austria) partly dissenting opinion, she noted that the applicant's speech constituted 'hate speech, an apology for violence or

84 *Erbakan v Turkey* App no 59405/00 (ECHR, 6 July 2006) para 55
85 *Erbakan* (n 84) para 64
86 *Erbakan* (n 84) para 57
87 *Erbakan* (n 84) para 55
88 *Erbakan* (n 84) para 70
89 *Erbakan* (n 84) para 68
90 *Erbakan* (n 84) para 68
91 *Erbakan* (n 84) para 58
92 *Refah Partisi (The Welfare Party) and others v Turkey* App nos. 41340/98, 41342/98 and 41344/98 (ECHR, 31 July 2021)

incitement to violence,' and, as a result. was not protected speech.[93] Connected to this is the possibility that the Court's stance might have differed had the prosecution been initiated more promptly following the speech and had the sentence been less severe. One of the important elements of this case when looking at the broader ambit of hate speech cases is that the judgement underscores the fact that, despite the Court's role as a supervisory body, it retains the discretion to assess the risks, harms, and dangers associated with speech within a specific context in a manner distinct from that employed by national authorities. While it is generally the case that the Court defers to the contextual knowledge and assessments of national authorities, this is not always the case. As demonstrated in *Erbakan*, the Court possesses the latitude to engage in assessing issues pertaining to context beyond the narrative provided for by states.

In *Balsytė-Lideikienė v Lithuania* (2009), the applicant owned a publishing company responsible for producing the *Lithuanian Calendar*, which became the subject of a complaint that its content incited hatred towards individuals of Polish, Russian and Jewish descent. The calendar reportedly contained statements deemed to provoke ethnic and national animosity, leading to the applicant being issued an administrative fine and the calendar being confiscated. The back cover of the calendar contained a map of the Republic of Lithuania. The neighbouring territories of the Republic of Poland, the Russian Federation and the Republic of Belarus were marked as "ethnic Lithuanian lands under temporary occupation." Statements in the calendar included the following:

- 17 March: "The new Lithuanian government . . . puts on trial the Lithuanian nation for the extermination of the Jews . . . but is not interested in the genocide of the Lithuanians and dances Jewish foxtrots to the music of the Wiesenthals and Zurroffs."
- 15 June: "The soviet occupying power, with the help of the communist collaborators, among whom, in particular, were many Jews, for half a century ferociously carried out the genocide and colonisation of the Lithuanian nation."
- 23 June: "In 1944 in Dubingiai and its surrounding area the Polish Krajova Army brutally killed more than a hundred Lithuanians . . . among whom were women, little children, even babies and old people. This was the way the Poles, in war conditions, carried out ethnic cleansing."

In its Article 10 analysis, the ECtHR referred to the *Handyside* principle[94] and noted that any limitations to expression must be strictly construed.[95] It took

93 *Erbakan* (n.84) Partially Dissenting Opinion of Judge Steiner, para 1
94 *Balsytė-Lideikienė v Lithuania* (2009) App no 72596/01 (ECHR, 4 November 2008) para 74
95 *Balsytė-Lideikienė* (n 94) para 75

note of the government's position that issues pertaining to territorial integrity and national minorities continued to be sensitive in post-independent Lithuania.[96] The Court found that

> the impugned passages contained statements inciting hatred against the Poles and the Jews. The Court considers that these statements were capable of giving the Lithuanian authorities cause for serious concern.[97]

In its judgement, the ECtHR relied very much on the national court's use of expert opinions. Specifically, the district court appointed experts who had opined on the seriousness and the dangers they carry. The domestic court requested four experts from the fields of history, psychology, political science and library science to provide their opinion. The history and political science professors found that the calendar could be characterised as

> promoting the radical ideology of nationalism, which rejected the idea of the integration of civil society, incited ethnocentrism, contained xenophobic and offensive statements, in particular with regard to the Jewish and Polish populations, and promoted territorial claims and national superiority *vis-à-vis* other ethnic groups. The experts nonetheless noted that the calendar did not directly incite violence against the Jewish population, nor did it advocate implementing discriminatory policy against this ethnic group.[98]

The psychology expert took a different view, namely, that the calendar

> did not contain expressions of hatred against the Polish population, the superiority of the Lithuanians over other nationals was not emphasised, and the negative statements about the Jewish population were not to be seen as anti-Semitic.[99]

However, the domestic courts and the ECtHR adopted the position of the reports issued by the professors in history and political science regarding the alleged harm caused by the calendar, noting that, despite the position of the psychologist, this did not retract from the other evidence put forth.[100] The Court did not provide any explanation as to why it endorsed the position of the domestic courts, other than the fact that, in such instances, they were granted a wide margin of appreciation and that they had received expert opinion on the nature and impact of statements. The Court did not deconstruct

96 *Balsytė-Lideikienė* (n 94) para 78
97 *Balsytė-Lideikienė* (n 94) para 79
98 *Balsytė-Lideikienė* (n 94) para 16
99 *Balsytė-Lideikienė* (n 94) para 29
100 *Balsytė-Lideikienė* (n 94)

or assess those opinions or offer an explanation or conceptualisation of what was included in the expert opinions, such as the hindrance of civil society,[101] as a reason for the restriction. Moreover, it did not further consider the differing view presented by the expert in psychology and the ramifications on Article 10 if that expert had been followed, for example, that the statements were not anti-Semitic and did not contain expressions of hatred against the Polish population. They disregarded it in the same manner as did the national courts. Despite the wide margin of appreciation for national authorities and the heightened contextual knowledge held by each of such authority for its specific country in comparison to the ECtHR, delving further into all expert opinions would better fit with the Court's supervisory function. As is often the case, the Court did not clarify the connection between the statements found in the calendar and the possibility of actual harm, danger or other form of impact serious enough to restrict the fundamental right to freedom of expression. Neither did it assess the post-independence context and its impact on harm. This context was put forth by the government and was also referred to in its own analysis of the issues, but without any further extrapolation. Within these loopholes and gaps in substantive analysis, the ECtHR unanimously decided that there was no violation of Article 10, endorsing the position of the domestic courts that the statements included in the calendar incited ethnic and national hatred.

Judge Myjer, from the Netherlands, issued a partly dissenting opinion. He contended that expert opinions on the matter held little relevance, as the issue ultimately required a legal, not scientific, determination by a judge. While he acknowledged the value of expert opinions for complex technical or medical subjects, he maintained that, in this case, such opinions were secondary to judicial interpretation in determining whether the calendar contained material that incited national, racial or religious hatred.[102] This dissenting opinion reflects the position taken by the Court in a 2019 case against Azerbaijan and a 2024 case against Russia, in which the Court disagreed with the overreliance on expert opinions. Specifically, *Tagiyev and Huseynov v Azerbaijan* (2019) involved an application by persons who were imprisoned for publishing an article, titled "Europe and Us," which argued that Europe does not accept Islam or the Prophet Muhammad. The ECtHR observed that certain statements in the article could be considered offensive, particularly the description of the Prophet Muhammad as a "frightful creature" in contrast to Jesus Christ and could potentially be seen as an 'abusive attack.'[103] The ECtHR found a violation of Article 10. Specifically, the ECtHR held that

> the domestic courts failed to examine the report and merely endorsed its conclusions. The relevant assessment clearly went far beyond resolving

101 *Balsytė-Lideikienė* (n 94) para 80
102 *Balsytė-Lideikienė* (n 94)
103 *Tagiyev and Huseynov v Azerbaijan* (2019) App no 13274/08 (ECHR, 5 December 2019) para 46

> mere language and religious issues, such as, for instance, defining the meaning of particular words and expressions or their religious importance, and provided, in essence, a legal characterization of the impugned remarks.[104]

Sokolovskiy v Russia (2024) involved an application made by a popular blogger with approximately 470,000 YouTube subscribers. The case is discussed in what follows. One of the central elements in the ECtHR's finding of an Article 10 violation was that domestic courts relied heavily on expert conclusions without considering their immediate context and without the necessary legal analysis.[105]

Moving now to *Soulas and Others v France* (2008), the three applicants were associated with the publication of a book titled *The Colonization of Europe*, subtitled *True Speech on Immigration and Islam*. The three applicants were involved in publishing the aforementioned book, which was distributed in bookshops, aiming, according to the author, "to underline particularly what he believes to be the incompatibility of European civilization with Islamic civilization in a given geographical area."

The book included the following:

- "It is only if an ethnic civil war breaks out that the solution can be found."
- "The foreseeable amplification of delinquency and the territorial guerrillas carried out by the ethnic bands."
- Claims that young Muslims were engaged in "ritual rape" of young White girls.
- Claims that delinquency among Afro-Maghrebian individuals was a strategy for "territorial conquest."
- Argument for the "gradual seizure of political power by Islam in Europe," and description of an "ethnic civil war" as a necessary solution.

Following the publication, the public prosecutor charged the three applicants with inciting discrimination, hatred or violence against individuals or groups based on their origin, race, nationality, ethnicity or religion. The International League Against Racism and Anti-Semitism (LICRA) and the Movement Against Racism and for Friendship between Peoples (MRAP) joined the legal proceedings. The court of appeal found the applicants guilty of provoking hatred and violence against a specific group. Each was fined EUR 7,500, and the Court awarded symbolic damages of EUR 1 to LICRA and EUR 0.15 to MRAP. All subsequent appeals were dismissed.

The ECtHR commenced its analysis by looking at the margin of appreciation and its role in determining the necessity of the interference. It noted that, although contracting states have a margin of appreciation in determining this necessity, the Court retains the authority to exercise European oversight of

104 *Tagiyev and Huseynov* (n 103) para 47
105 *Tagiyev and Huseynov* (n 103) para 105

both the legal framework and its application, even when the decisions originate from an independent judiciary.[106] Later on, the Court noted that states have a wide margin of appreciation in determining measures implemented to deal with challenges resulting from immigration and integration policies.[107] The Court also made its classic reference to *Handyside* and tits subsequent case law, which, at least theoretically, denote the importance of freedom of expression.[108]

The ECtHR acknowledged that the book discussed the topic of immigrant integration, which it deemed a matter of ongoing debate within European societies.[109] The Court held that the book was written in an accessible style and aimed at a broad audience, thus increasing the risk of impact/harm.[110] It outlined the author's views on what he perceived as the harmful effects of immigration, particularly by non-Europeans and Muslims.[111] In talking of the book's style and accessibility, the Court's judgement could have benefitted from considering that, as noted in a dissenting opinion in the 2005 case of *I.A. v Turkey* (2005), discussed further in the coming paragraphs, 'nobody is ever obliged to buy or read a novel.'[112] The Court argued that these effects were portrayed in a highly negative manner, depicting immigration as a dangerous influence on society[113] and potentially causing a 'sense of rejection and antagonism in the reader, heightened by the use of military language, toward the targeted communities, which were identified as the main enemy.'[114] Specifically, the ECtHR found that phrases such as 'it is only if an ethnic civil war breaks out that the solution can be found' could potentially incite aggression against a particular group[115] and is, thus, unacceptable speech under Article 10, although it was not deemed serious enough to fall within the framework of Article 17.[116] Nevertheless, the purported link between the expression and the alleged incitement to aggression remained unproven. The Court also referred to the severity of the penalties, noting that, while the amounts imposed on the applicants may seem substantial given the circumstances, it is important to note that they initially faced the possibility of prison sentences.[117] As with other cases examined in this chapter, where criminal law has been employed to penalise speech, such an approach does not align with the prevailing principle under international law that criminal sanctions should be applied to speech only as a measure of last resort. The fact that prison sentences existed but

106 *Soulas and others* (n 59) para 32
107 *Soulas and others* (n 59) para 38
108 *Soulas and others* (n 59) paras 34, 35
109 *Soulas and others* (n 59) para 40
110 *Soulas and others* (n 59) para 39
111 *Soulas and others* (n 59) para 40
112 *I.A v Turkey* App no 42571/98 (ECHR, 13 September 2005) para 43
113 *Soulas and others* (n 59) para 41
114 *Soulas and others* (n 59) para 43
115 *Soulas and others* (n 59)
116 *Soulas and others* (n 59) para 48
117 *Soulas and others* (n 59) para 46

were not applied constituted the benchmark for concluding that the penalty was lenient but is not an objective way to assess the issue of proportionality. Adopting a country-specific benchmark to determine the legally objective test of proportionality does not bode well with the requirements attached to the overall questions of the legitimacy of the restriction. In light of these points, and while finding that the Article 17 threshold had not been met, without extrapolations of the reasons,[118] the ECtHR unanimously concluded that there was no violation of Article 10.

In *Smajić v Bosnia and Herzegovina* (2018), the applicant, a Bosnian lawyer, had posted statements across various online forums calling for military action against Serb villages and neighbourhoods. Using a pseudonym, the applicant made a number of posts on an online forum about what should be done by Bosniac citizens of the district he inhabited in the event of a war and the secession of one of the two constituents of Bosnia and Herzegovina, specifically, the Republika Srpska.

His statements included the following, amongst others:

> [I]f we organise ourselves they stand no chance of taking over Brčko. . . . Ilićka settlement—which has around 3,500 to 5,000 Serbs—is problematic. . . . Ilićka and Grčica should be struck at first, as these are two key Serb settlements.
>
> . . . Serbs who came from different shitholes live there; there is [only a very small native] population. . . . Ilićka is a settlement [which consists mostly] of radical-thinking Serbs who would be the first to concoct [a fight] with Bosniacs from Brčko and which, in the event of any scenarios [involving secession] from [Republika Srpska] should be attacked and neutralised first.

He was found guilty of inciting national, racial and religious hatred, discord or intolerance. The applicant did not deny making those statements. He was sentenced to one year in prison, suspended for three years, ordered to pay approximately EUR 50 and had his laptop and computer seized. The applicant appealed the decision. He contended that the elements of the alleged criminal offence had not been satisfied, asserting that a 'closed forum' on the internet could not qualify as a 'public place.' He further argued that his statements did not incite hatred but merely reflected his personal opinion in relation to a hypothetical scenario which, he claimed, was relevant to 'real-world' events, specifically frequent secessionist rhetoric by leading political figures in the Republika Srpska. Additionally, the applicant noted that media coverage of the case only arose after the prosecutor publicised it. The appellate court agreed with the lower court's decision. In dealing with the question of whether or not the forum was 'open' or 'closed,' the appellate court concluded that the forum

118 *Smajić v Bosnia and Herzegovina* App no 48657/16 (ECHR, 16 January 2018) para 48

was 'closed' only insofar as active participation on the forum was involved. For this purpose, registration was necessary. However, access to content was open for anyone, regardless of whether they had registered or not. The applicant lodged an appeal to the constitutional court, which rejected his claim.

The ECtHR concurred with the national courts, concluding that the applicant's statements were harmful to inter-ethnic relations in the region. In assessing the applicant's complaint for an Article 10 violation, the Court habitually commenced with the *Handyside* reference about the extent and plurality of ideas and information. It then underlined that the applicant's statements, 'even if written in a hypothetical form, had touched upon the very sensitive matter of the ethnic relations in post-conflict Bosnian society.'[119] On this premise, satisfied with the national courts' examination of the case, and in light of what the court considered to be a proportionate penalty, the ECtHR proceeded to find the case manifestly ill-founded. It must be noted that the imposition of criminal penalties for hypothetical speech raises profound questions regarding the proportionality of such measures. From a legal and normative perspective, this approach appears to encroach upon the fundamental principles of freedom of expression, as well as the broader framework of legitimacy underpinning the imposition of criminal sanctions. While the sensitivities of post-conflict or transitional contexts may indeed necessitate heightened vigilance, such contexts should not serve as a *carte blanche* to curtail rights disproportionately. Context-focused responses have also been seen in other cases, such as *Balsytė-Lideikienė*, where the Court placed significant weight on the government's assertion that matters concerning territorial integrity and national minorities remained acutely sensitive in the post-independence period. The reliance on contextual justifications, whether rooted in post-conflict reconciliation, concerns over social cohesion or other sociopolitical concerns, while imperative for the case analysis, often become a pretext for undermining core democratic principles. These considerations underscore the need for a rigorous application of the test under Article 10(2), ensuring that any restrictions to speech remain narrowly tailored.

Further, a notable omission in the ECtHR's analysis in *Smajić* was its failure to engage with the question of whether the forum in question was open, closed, semi-public or semi-private. This distinction is particularly significant in the digital age, where the boundaries between public and private speech forums are increasingly blurred. The Court's lack of discussion on this point undermines the clarity and rigour of its necessity analysis. The nature of the forum, whether it permits open access to the public or is restricted to a specific group, directly impacts the scope of permissible restrictions on speech. In this case, while the appellate court characterised the forum as 'closed' for active participation due to the registration requirement, it acknowledged that the content was accessible to the public at large. This hybrid nature of the forum

119 *Smajić* (n 118) para 39

warranted a deeper examination by the Court, particularly given the critical implications for freedom of expression in online spaces. By not addressing this issue, the Court missed an opportunity to provide clear guidelines on how the digitalisation of speech affects the interpretation of public and private spheres in freedom of expression cases.

3.2 *Final Comments*

In *Erbakan*, the disproportionately high penalty imposed on a political figure for speech that lacked a clear and imminent threat underscored the risks of a chilling effect on political discourse. By recognising that even provocative and unsettling speech often warrants protection, the Court reaffirmed the democratic necessity of a healthy public sphere, albeit with boundaries to prevent incitement to violence or hatred. Conversely, such a robust approach was not taken in the other cases discussed in the section. *Balsytė-Lideikienė* demonstrated the ECtHR's willingness to endorse national courts' findings and reliance on expert views rather than an in-depth legal analysis. In *Smajić*, the Court acknowledged the sensitivity of post-conflict ethnic relations in Bosnia and took it so seriously into account that it supported the imposition of criminal penalties for the utterance of hypothetical discussions about violent action, setting a dangerous precedent in terms of the necessity test and potential of actual harm. This case also serves as a cautionary tale about the complexities of adjudicating speech in the digital age, with the ECtHR omitting to discuss the reach of the forum in terms of its public or private nature.

The ECtHR's jurisprudence, discussed in this section, also reflects the role of the margin of appreciation in respecting member states' cultural, historical and social contexts. This doctrine allows states some latitude in addressing speech that may threaten social cohesion, provided their actions remain consistent with the Convention's principles. For instance, in *Soulas and Others*, the Court's deference to the French authorities' characterisation of a publication as inciting racial hatred acknowledged the sensitivities surrounding immigration and societal integration in France. However, as seen in *Balsytė-Lideikienė*, the reliance on expert opinions without thorough scrutiny by the ECtHR raises concerns about the potential overreach of national authorities. Such deference risks eroding the Court's role as a supranational safeguard against arbitrariness, especially when domestic courts fail to substantiate the causal link between contested speech and tangible harm. The Court took another position in the cases against Azerbaijan (*Tagiyev and Huseynov*) and Russia (*Sokolovskiy*), with judgements in those two underscoring the tensions emanating from undue reliance on expert conclusions, which led to violations of Article 10.

As such, a recurrent critique of the ECtHR's approach is the lack of a consistently articulated standard for assessing the imminence and severity of harm posed by contested speech. While the Court usually references the *Handyside* principle, its application in many cases appears fickle or non-existent. Several of the judgements discussed in the chapter could have benefitted from a deeper examination of the causal nexus between the expression in question and the alleged harm. The principle of imminence, central to the Court's analysis in *Erbakan*, ought to serve as a universal benchmark for determining whether restrictions on speech inciting hatred or violence are justified. Yet as seen in *Smajić* and *Soulas*, the Court has sometimes prioritised contextual sensitivities over a rigorous imminence analysis. This inconsistency risks creating ambiguity about the threshold for restricting speech and undermining the ECtHR's role as a protector of free expression.

4 Article 17: Islamophobia and Homophobia

Article 17, the 'prohibition of abuse of rights' clause, has traditionally been associated with cases involving Holocaust denial, as established in foundational decisions of the EComHR. In these early cases, the EComHR laid the groundwork for the principle that expressions directly contradicting the values of the Convention are excluded from its protection. This approach reflected the specific historical and social imperatives of post-war Europe, prioritising the prevention of racial hatred and totalitarian ideologies.

In recent decades, the application of Article 17 has expanded beyond its original context, addressing cases involving Islamophobia, anti-Semitism and homophobia. Notable examples include *Norwood v the United Kingdom* (2004), where the provision was invoked to address Islamophobic speech; *Ivanov v Russia* (2007), concerning anti-Semitic publications; and *Lenis v Greece* (2023), the first case to apply Article 17 to homophobic hate speech. These cases mark a significant evolution in the ECtHR's jurisprudence, reflecting a broader interpretation of Article 17 to combat expressions deemed incompatible with the Convention's underlying values of tolerance, non-discrimination and social peace.

This section examines the development and application of Article 17 outside the Holocaust denial framework, tracing its evolution from *Glimmerveen and Hagenbeek* through to more contemporary cases. It explores how the ECtHR has employed Article 17 to address hate speech targeting protected characteristics, highlighting the relationship between Article 17 and Article 10. The analysis will consider the thresholds established for invoking Article 17, the reasoning behind its application in specific cases and its broader implications within the ECtHR's hate speech jurisprudence. By examining key cases like *Norwood*, *Ivanov* and *Lenis*, this section aims to provide a comprehensive understanding of how Article 17 has been adapted to meet contemporary challenges in regulating harmful speech.

4.1 *The Use of Article 17 Outside the Framework of Holocaust Denial*

The application of Article 17 to restrict hate speech is a significant matter that profoundly impacts freedom of expression by excluding such speech from an evaluation under Article 10 and the accompanying balancing process.

As will be demonstrated in the next chapter, historically, the now-obsolete EComHR and the ECtHR have primarily invoked Article 17 in cases involving content that includes revisionist or negationist speech.[120] It was also used in old EComHR cases, such as *Glimmerveen and Hagenbeek v the Netherlands* (1979), involving racist speech, discussed later. When it comes to speech related to the Holocaust and National Socialism, the application of Article 17 has not been limited solely to cases concerning revisionism or negationism but has also been applied to instances of anti-Semitism that do not seek to challenge historical tragedies. For instance, in *Ivanov v Russia* (2007), discussed later, the Court adjudicated on a case involving a newspaper editor convicted for publishing articles advocating the exclusion of Jews from social life. These publications alleged a causal link between social, economic and political issues and Jewish activities, depicting Jews as a malign ethnic group. In its decision, the Court relied explicitly on Article 17 to address this matter.[121] This article provision emerged in response to the historical context marked by the atrocities of World War II, aiming to equip democratic societies with necessary legal tools to prevent the grave abuses committed by past totalitarian regimes. This foundational rationale is evident in the 1957 case of *Communist Party of Germany v Germany*, where the now-defunct EComHR upheld the prohibition of the German Communist Party. Regarding 'hate speech,' Article 17 has subsequently been invoked in cases involving negationist and revisionist speech concerning the Holocaust (though not the Armenian genocide) and instances of anti-Semitic speech. Interestingly, it has also been applied sporadically, including in a case involving Islamophobia. Recently, the Court extended its application to homophobic speech in the case of *Lenis v Greece* (2003). Prior to *Lenis*, the ECtHR had addressed instances of homophobic speech in cases such as *Vejdeland v Sweden* in 2012 and *Lilliendahl v Iceland* in 2020.

In *Glimmerveen and Hagenbeek* (1979), the EComHR established the position that hate speech is not entitled to Convention protection. This was the first case involving racist speech in which Article 17 was enforced. The applicants were president and vice president of the far-right Dutch People's Union. The first applicant faced legal consequences for possessing leaflets advocating the expulsion of foreign workers from the Netherlands, with the intent to distribute them. Additionally, both the first and second applicants challenged the authorities' decision to bar them from standing as candidates on an electoral list representing the far-right Dutch People's Union. The applicant received a two-week prison sentence for possessing racist leaflets intended for distribution. The leaflets contained statements such as:

> As soon as the Nederlandse Volks Unie will have gained political power in our country, it will put order into business and, to begin with will

120 See, amongst others, Cannie and Voorhoof (n 62) 60

121 *Pavel Ivanov v Russia* App no 35222/04 (ECHR, 20 February 2007) para 53

> remove all Surinamers, Turks and other so-called guest workers from the Netherlands . . .

The Commission held that this policy contained elements of racial discrimination and that 'the expression of the political ideas of the applicants clearly constitutes an activity within the meaning of Article 17 of the Convention.'[122] When discussing Article 17 in this case, the Commission noted that, in allowing the applicants to promote their belief system with no restriction, the Dutch authorities would, in fact, be encouraging discrimination, which is prohibited by Article 14 of the ECHR and the ICCPR, thereby implying a positive obligation emanating from the article in question. Interestingly, framing an Article 10 case within the prism of positive obligation is not something we see often in more recent cases, with a few exceptions discussed in the next chapter. This is so unless claims have been brought by the 'victims' of impugned speech who have raised applications under, for example, Article 8, on the right to respect of private and family life. The Commission noted that the policy promoted by the applicants contained elements of racial discrimination and, thus, held the view that 'the expression of the political ideas of the applicants clearly constitutes an activity within the meaning of Article 17 of the Convention.'[123]

Moving to more recent cases, in *Norwood v UK* (2004), the applicant served as a regional organiser for the far-right British National Party (BNP). He displayed a large poster in the window of his first-floor flat. The poster, provided by the BNP, featured an image of the Twin Towers engulfed in flames, accompanied by the text "Islam out of Britain—Protect the British People" and a crescent-and-star symbol crossed out in a prohibition sign. Following a public complaint, the police removed the poster. The applicant was subsequently charged with the offence of causing alarm or distress, aggravated by hostility towards members of a racial or religious group based on their membership of that group. The applicant was fined GBP 300 by the magistrate's court. He appealed to the High Court, which dismissed his appeal.

Without providing substantial explanation as to its reasoning, the ECtHR agreed with domestic courts that the poster in question amounted to a public expression of attack on all Muslims in the UK and that 'such a general, vehement attack against a religious group, linking the group as a whole with a grave act of terrorism, is incompatible with the values proclaimed and guaranteed by the Convention, notably tolerance, social peace and non-discrimination.'[124] The ECtHR applied Article 17 to the case, which appears somewhat arbitrary. Why, for example, was Article 17 invoked in *Norwood* but not, for example, in *Féret*? Was characterising Islam as the 'conqueror' that Belgian people needed

122 *Glimmerveen and Hagenbeek v the Netherlands* App nos. 8348/78 and 8406/78 (EComHR, 11 October 1979)
123 *Glimmerveen and Hagenbeek* (n 122)
124 *Norwood v the United Kingdom* App no 23131/03 (ECtHR, 16 November 2004)

to be saved from and stopping the Islamisation of Belgium not a general vehement attack linking the entire group to the conquering of Belgium posing Islam as a threat to the Belgian people? If not, why not? The Court provides no rationale for this disparity and offers no clarification regarding the criteria governing the applicability of these provisions in such cases. It does not explain what it understands by a general vehement attack, and as such, its use and application to cases cannot be ascertained. For example, in *De Becker v Belgium* (1962), the EComHR emphasised that Article 17 is applicable solely to individuals who pose a threat to the democratic system of the contracting parties, and even then only to the extent strictly proportionate to the gravity and duration of that threat.[125] This threshold was notably absent in the assessment of Norwood's poster. The Court did not examine whether Norwood was acting in his official capacity as a BNP member or on behalf of the party, nor did it evaluate whether the BNP could be classified as a totalitarian organisation. Instead, Article 17 was applied with apparent ease, not to safeguard democracy *per se*, but to uphold the values enshrined in the Convention.

In *Ivanov v Russia* (2007), the applicant was the founder, owner and editor of a newspaper in Russia. He faced charges of publicly inciting ethnic, racial and religious hatred through mass media. The prosecution argued that, through a series of articles in his newspaper, the applicant called for the exclusion of Jewish people from social life; claimed a causal link between social, economic and political challenges and Jewish activities; and portrayed people of Jewish origin as harmful. At first instance, the applicant was acquitted on the grounds that it was not proven that he was the author of the publication. This was later quashed at the regional level, and the case was remitted to the first instance court. The town court subsequently found him guilty and prohibited him from engaging in journalism for three years. The applicant lodged an appeal, which was dismissed. However, his penalty was changed from the cessation of journalistic activities to a monetary fine of approximately 300 Euros.

In assessing the applicant's complaint under Article 10, the Court employed Article 17, ousting the case from consideration under Article 10. The reasons it provided were that his publication had a 'markedly anti-Semitic tenor' and, following *Norwood*, noted that 'such a general and vehement attack on one ethnic group is in contradiction with the Convention's underlying values, namely tolerance, social peace and non-discrimination.'[126] The Court reasoned that such hostile attacks on an ethnic group conflict with core ECHR values, including tolerance, social peace and non-discrimination, thus excluding his actions from Article 10's protection. Given that this case involved anti-Semitism and can thus be correlated to phenomena such as Nazism and Holocaust denial, categories that the Court has consistently excluded from Convention protection under Article 17, the judgement therein aligns more

125 See, for example *De Becker v Belgium* App no 214/56 (EComHR, 8 January 1960) para 279
126 *Pavel Ivanov* (n 121) para 1

coherently with the Court's established jurisprudence. While the case raises potential concerns regarding freedom of expression, the application of Article 17 is more justifiable in this context compared to its use in *Norwood* and *Lenis*, as discussed later.

In *Lenis v Greece* (2023), the applicant, a senior church official, authored a blog post at a time when the Hellenic Parliament was nearing a debate on proposed legislation to establish civil unions for same-sex couples. His post, titled "The scum of society have reared their heads! Let's be honest, spit on them," included a range of statements directed at both homosexual individuals and politicians, such as:

> Greece is governed by some such petty people! Of course they are a small minority of the total of the Hellenic Parliament, nevertheless, they exist! They are some of the scum of society marginal people, defective, humiliated people of the dark who now with the rising of the left have reared their heads! I give you advice. Do not go near them! Do not listen to them! Do not trust them! They are the damned of Society! It is their right of course, to live secretly—privately—the way they want! But disgraced people cannot defend the passions of their souls in public! Our Greece is now governed by atheists. . . . So, these disgraced people, spit on them, Condemn them! Blacken them out!

The applicant's article was widely republished, often under derogatory headlines, such as "The Rantings of Amvrosios" and "The Unbelievable Raving of Amvrosios Against Homosexuals." In response to the controversy, he released a second article, titled "Let's Get Things Clear—Love the Sinner but Deal with the Sin." In it, he clarified that his original post was intended as criticism of a specific politician who had shown support for civil unions between same-sex couples at the funeral of a gay actor and of those with similar beliefs. He claimed that his call to "spit on them" was directed at these politicians and their ideology, and that the phrase was meant metaphorically, implying "despise them."

He was convicted of public incitement to violence or hatred based on sexual orientation and for abusing his ecclesiastical office. Although he appealed, the judgement was upheld, with his prison sentence reduced from seven to five months, suspended.

By a majority ruling, the ECtHR applied Article 17 to this case. The Court commenced its analysis of the issues in question with its customary affirmation of the significance of freedom of expression as one of the 'essential foundations of a democratic society,'[127] referencing the *Handyside* principle on speech that may shock, offend or disturb. The Court reiterated that any restrictions

127 *Lenis v Greece* App no 47833/20 (ECtHR, 27 June 2023) para 36

on Article 10 'must be convincingly established'[128] and emphasised its duty to assess such restrictions in the context of the case as a whole, examining their proportionality, legitimacy and necessity.

The Court then turned to the purpose of Article 17, stating that its role is

> to make it impossible for [groups and individuals] to derive from the Convention a right to engage in any activity or perform any act aimed at destroying any of the rights and freedoms set forth in the Convention.[129]

In its examination of Article 17, the Court noted that it agreed with the courts that the applicant's statements were capable of stirring up violence against homosexual people and causing them fear.[130] It noted that consideration must be made for the 'words used and the context in which they were published' in order to determine whether the comments constituted incitement to violence.[131] The Court found that the applicant's speech amounted to hate speech, agreeing with the national court that he 'used harsh expressions which went so far as to deny homosexual people their human nature.'[132] Examples included phrases such as "They are not humans!" and "They are the scum of society . . . defective, humiliated, people of the dark . . .," which the Court held fall outside the protections of freedom of expression. The Court identified multiple examples of incitement in the article, refuting the applicant's claim that the phrase "spit on them" was metaphorical. Instead, it determined that this phrase, in combination with others like "Condemn them," "Blacken them out" and "Do not go near them," was intended literally.[133] However, the Court did not clarify how it reached this conclusion. Interestingly, although the judgement was about homophobic phrases, in its analysis and conclusions, the Court considered phrases like "Condemn them" and "Blacken them out," despite having agreed with the domestic courts that these targeted politicians rather than homosexual individuals. The Court held that these phrases, prefaced with "Do not hesitate," could induce 'stress, anguish and terror'[134] in any homosexual person and, together with the article's hate speech, were 'capable of stirring up violence against them.'[135] The ECtHR also noted that the applicant's article was widely republished, making it broadly accessible,[136]

128 *Lenis* (n 127)
129 *Lenis* (n 127) para 37
130 *Lenis* (n 127) para 46
131 *Lenis* (n 127) para 47
132 *Lenis* (n 127)
133 *Lenis* (n 127) para 48
134 *Lenis* (n 127)
135 *Lenis* (n 127) para 46
136 *Lenis* (n 127) para 50

and that it targeted a group requiring 'enhanced protection.'[137] Nonetheless, this analysis did not account for the fact that media outlets largely framed the applicant's comments as a rant, prompting his follow-up article to clarify his stance. Nor did it address the fact that many of the article headlines it referenced, published by other outlets, were actually forms of counterspeech critical of the applicant's statements, to the extent that he felt compelled to issue a follow-up article. Furthermore, the Court referred to low levels of social acceptance toward the LGBTQ community, citing statistics and findings from various reports. While these statistics were credible, the Court's reasoning might also have benefitted from considering the ongoing civil union discussions and media reactions that opposed the applicant's views. The Court ultimately concluded that 'it was immediately clear that the statements sought to deflect Article 10 from its real purpose . . . for ends clearly contrary to the values of the Convention.'[138] It acknowledged that criticism of certain lifestyles on religious or moral grounds does not automatically fall outside the protections of Article 10. However, 'denying LGBTI people their human nature as in the present case'[139] and inciting violence necessitated invoking Article 17.[140] Nevertheless, it did not ascertain how the speech in question resulted in these harms. The Court further highlighted that the applicant, as a senior church official, wielded significant influence over his congregation, and potentially a substantial portion of the Greek Orthodox community, which represents the majority of the population. However, it did not take into account that the alleged widespread adherence to the Greek Orthodox faith does not necessarily imply endorsement of the applicant's views.

In view of these, the Court held that, considering Article 17, the complaint could not be protected under Article 10. As such, 2023 marked the first time that the Court applied Article 17 to address homophobic hate speech, thereby extending its use to cover this category of expression. Prior to *Lenis*, the ECtHR had dealt with cases involving homophobic speech under Article 10, as seen in *Vejdeland and Lilliendahl*. On this point, the Court observed that *Lenis* was 'distinguishable from Lilliendahl,'[141] holding that, in the latter case, it was not immediately apparent that the comments in question were intended to incite violence or undermine the Convention's freedoms. In *Lilliendahl*, the applicant's speech was classified as hate speech, but not of the 'gravest form,' and the applicant, being an ordinary member of the public, had limited capacity to reach a large audience. By contrast, in *Lenis*, the Court highlighted the applicant's influential role, the 'violent' undertones in the statements, and

137 *Lenis* (n 127) para 51
138 *Lenis* (n 127) para 53
139 *Lenis* (n 127) para 54
140 *Lenis* (n 127)
141 *Lenis* (n 127) para 56

the article's widespread dissemination, all of which warranted the application of Article 17. However, considering the serious nature of cases warranting the application of Article 17, the Court should have undertaken an in-depth assessment of the theme of violence and the interpretation of the statements in question and the hyperbolic nature of the language used, including hyperbolic and symbolic speech, as well as colloquialisms. As it stands, the connection of the statements to inciting violence remains insufficiently substantiated and falls short of the immediate clarity required when applying Article 17. In fact, *Lenis* illustrates just how far the application of Article 17 has shifted from its original purpose, which was to protect democracy from destructive forces.[142] While the Convention is indeed a living instrument, the Court must exercise caution and critically reassess its current approach to this Article. In fact, the broad application of Article 17 in *Lenis* risks undermining democratic principles, threatens freedom of speech and may negatively impact social cohesion and other social ills, as discussed in Chapter 2.

4.2 Article 17 and Protected Characteristics

Article 17 was designed as a safeguard to prevent the Convention's protections from being misused to destroy the rights and freedoms it guarantees. This provision directly aligns with the doctrine of militant democracy, which justifies restrictions on rights to protect democratic systems from anti-democratic forces. Employing Article 17 to prohibit hate speech necessitates careful consideration. Its use significantly impacts the exercise of freedom of expression by exempting the speech in question from an Article 10 evaluation and, thus, the accompanying process of balancing conflicting interests. As such, one of the inherent problems with the use of Article 17 in speech cases is the 'frightening possibility of a democracy becoming too intolerant and, therefore, self-destructive.'[143] A broad interpretation of Article 17 risks inadvertently undermining the very democratic principles it aims to protect against erosion. While the existence of Article 17 'conforms to historical common sense,'[144] its application may detract from the functioning of a liberal democracy, contrary to its original purpose. The recent use of Article 17 departs from this foundational principle. In the previously discussed cases, the Court invoked Article 17 not to protect democracy *per se* but to uphold Convention values. In *Norwood*, the application of Article 17 was justified on the basis of the poster's broad and vehement attack on a religious group, equating all Muslims with terrorism. The values referred to included tolerance, social peace and

142 *De Becker* (n 125)

143 Majid Nikouei and Masoud Zamani, 'Jurisprudence of Tolerance: Hate Speech, Article 17 and Theory of Democracy in the European Convention on Human Rights' (2019) 8 International Human Rights Law Review 85

144 Nikouei and Zamani (n 143) 69

non-discrimination.[145] Similarly, *Ivanov* involved anti-Semitic rhetoric that sought to exclude an ethnic group from social and political life, thereby in contradiction with the same Convention values mentioned in *Norwood* and *Ivanov*. In *Lenis*, the Court extended Article 17 to homophobic hate speech, marking the first instance where such speech was categorically excluded from Article 10 protection.

This shift broadens the scope of Article 17, raising concerns about overreach and the potential erosion of freedom of expression. In fact, the expansive application of Article 17 risks undermining the democratic principles it seeks to protect. By excluding certain forms of speech from Article 10 protection, the Court bypasses the test that needs to be conducted under Article 10(2) that lies at the heart of the Convention's framework for balancing rights. On the one hand, this approach creates a chilling effect on free speech, particularly for controversial or unpopular expressions that are essential to democratic discourse. However, as demonstrated in previous analyses and case law such as *Féret* and *Vejdeland*, the threshold for deeming speech unprotected, even within the Article 10 framework, is notably low. As such, this book emphasises the significant human rights risks posed by the use of Article 17 while acknowledging the restrictive approach to speech that the ECtHR often adopts, even when applying Article 10 in hate speech cases. Moreover, the Court's failure to adopt a high threshold of severity for speech that falls outside the spectrum of Article 10 protection exacerbates this chilling effect. In *Lenis*, for example, the Court conflated metaphorical expressions with literal incitement to violence, thereby lowering the threshold for applying Article 17. This not only risks silencing legitimate criticism but also shifts legitimacy and necessity burdens from those seeking to restrict speech, contrary to established principles of freedom of expression.

Furthermore, the application of Article 17 of the ECHR beyond the context of Holocaust denial illustrates a pivotal shift in the ECtHR's approach to hate speech, reflecting a significant expansion of Article 17's scope. While the use of Article 17, mainly for Holocaust denial cases, is not without its challenges and risks, as will be discussed in the next chapter, the further expansion of the Article's use is alarming for the protection of Article 10. Despite all forms of hate speech being reprehensible to victims and society at large, and irrespective of the author's objection to any hierarchical categorisation of hate speech types or targets, the expansive nature which Article 17 has taken over time is of utmost concern to democracy and free speech. As the Convention evolves as a living instrument, the Court must exercise caution in re-evaluating its application of this article. At the same time, even when Article 10 and the proper test to its limitation is carried out as with most hate speech cases, the protection of the right to freedom of expression has not been adequate. Here, it is important to note that several of the cases involving hate speech discussed

145 *Lenis* (n 127) para 39; *Norwood* (n 124)

in the book were declared 'manifestly ill-founded' under Article 35(3)(a) of the ECHR and, thus, not dealt with by the Court. This route is taken when Article 17 is applied, and the application is found to involve the abuse of Convention rights. However, the jurisprudential analysis will reveal that Article 35(3)(a) is also applied in cases where elements of Article 10 are considered, albeit only partially. For instance, in *Le Pen,* the ECtHR briefly engaged with aspects of Article 10, such as necessity and proportionality. However, this analysis was not conducted in depth, as the Court determined that the impugned speech fell outside the scope of protection afforded by the right to freedom of expression. Article 35(3)(a) is also applied in cases where Article 10 is applied in combination with Article 17, with the latter acting as an 'aid in the interpretation of Article 10.[146]

5 Religious Hatred and Extremism

This section examines the ECtHR approach to cases involving speech targeting religious figures, doctrines and institutions, as well as the Court's treatment of religious extremism. These areas of jurisprudence reveal the Court's attempts to reconcile the fundamental right to freedom of expression under Article 10 with the protection of religious beliefs under Article 9 of the ECHR. By analysing landmark cases such as *IA v Turkey* (2005), *ES v Austria* (2006), *Belkacem v Belgium* (2017) and *Ibragimov and Others v Russia* (2018), the section highlights the interplay between offensive speech, incitement to hatred and the challenges posed by extremism in multicultural and pluralistic societies. The analysis is organised into three parts. The first part explores the ECtHR's jurisprudence on offensive and abusive speech, focusing on its attempts to distinguish permissible critique from gratuitous or inciteful attacks, as reflected in cases like *IA* and *ES*. The second part evaluates the Court's inconsistent application of contextual factors and the margin of appreciation, drawing comparisons between cases such as *Giniewski v France* (2006) and *Tagiyev and Huseynov v Azerbaijan* (2019). The third part addresses the Court's treatment of religious extremism, highlighting its nuanced approach in *Ibragimov and Others v Russia* (2018), which upheld protections for non-violent religious texts, and *Belkacem v Belgium* (2017), where Article 17 was invoked to exclude violent, hate-filled rhetoric from the scope of Convention protections. Through this structured analysis, the section seeks to identify recurring themes and inconsistencies in the ECtHR's jurisprudence, including the risks of overreliance on domestic courts, the ambiguous thresholds for incitement and gratuitous offence and the chilling effect of criminal sanctions. The section critically evaluates the ECtHR's capacity to balance religious sensitivities with the imperative of safeguarding pluralism, tolerance and democratic principles within the broader, fundamental spectrum of free speech.

146 *Williamson v Germany* App no 64496/17 (ECHR, 8 January 2019); *Pastörs v Germany* App no 55225.14 (ECHR, 3 October 2019)

5.1 *Speech 'Against' Religious Figures, Doctrines and Institutions*

In *IA v Turkey*,[147] the applicant, a resident of France, was the owner and director of a publishing house. His publishing house released a novel titled *The Forbidden Phrases*. The book, written in a novelistic style, expressed the author's views on philosophical and theological topics. Examples of some of the novel's text depicted, amongst others, the Prophet breaking his fast by having sexual intercourse with Aisha after dinner and before prayer and that he did not forbid sexual intercourse with a dead person or a live animal. The applicant was charged for committing blasphemy against "God, the Religion, the Prophet, and the Holy Book" through the book's publication. The charges were based on an expert report prepared at the request of the public prosecutor. The report noted, *inter alia*:

> [A]lthough these passages may be regarded as a polemic in support of the author's philosophical views, it may be observed that they also contain statements that imply a certain element of humiliation, scorn and discredit *vis-à-vis* religion, the Prophet and belief in God according to Islam.[148]

The court of first instance convicted the applicant to two years in prison and a fine. The Court commuted the prison sentence to a fine, so the applicant was ordered to pay 16 USD at that time. The applicant appealed to the court of cassation, which upheld the judgement.

The ECtHR, by a majority, found no violation of Article 10. It started off with the classic *Handyside* reference but argued that the speech in question constituted more than mere offensiveness, amounting to an abusive attack on the Prophet Muhammad, and noted that:

> Notwithstanding the fact that there is a certain tolerance of criticism of religious doctrine within Turkish society, which is deeply attached to the principle of secularity, believers may legitimately feel themselves to be the object of unwarranted and offensive attacks.[149]

The ECtHR's distinction between offence and the alleged 'abusive attack' remains unclear, as the Court failed to substantiate this differentiation or provide supporting evidence. This ambiguity is further compounded by another statement, in which the Court asserted that believers in Turkey could reasonably perceive the book as 'an abusive attack on the Prophet of Islam'[150] and noted that domestic measures were intended to 'provide protection against

147 *I.A* (n 112)
148 *I.A* (n 112) para 7
149 *I.A* (n 112) para 9
150 *I.A* (n 112) para 29

offensive attacks on matters regarded as sacred by Muslims.'[151] This comment further blurred the line between mere offence and a more substantial attack, making the Court's reasoning even more problematic. The Court also referred to the fact that 'members of a religious majority or a minority, cannot reasonably expect to be exempt from all criticism. They must tolerate and accept the denial by others of their religious beliefs and even the propagation by others of doctrine hostile to their faith.'[152] This has been cited in several cases involving hate speech related to religion, including *IA*. However, this position is inherently unstable. Even when the Court acknowledges the principle of religious toleration by believers in cases such as *IA*, it nonetheless found no violation of Article 10 when assessing the impugned speech. Moreover, there are instances where restrictions are imposed on religious speech even if they do not fall within a broad, direct or indirect sphere of hate speech. *Murphy v Ireland* (2003), although outside the scope of hate speech, is noteworthy for comparative purposes regarding the exemption from criticism. In *Murphy*, the applicant, a pastor, sought to broadcast an advertisement inviting listeners to attend Easter meetings at his church on the resurrection of Christ. The Irish authorities prohibited the advertisement under legislation banning any broadcast with a religious purpose. In finding no violation of Article 10, the Court emphasised contextual factors and concurred with the domestic courts' view on the need for caution regarding religious advertising sensitivities in Ireland. It underscored the significance of protecting against the potential offence arising from such advertisements, given the cultural and historical dynamics at play. The ECtHR endorsed the findings of domestic courts that Irish religious believers

> tended to belong to a particular church so that religious advertising from a different church might be considered offensive and open to the interpretation of proselytism.[153]

In light of the comparison with *Murphy*, the following can be discerned. Hate speech cases involving religious matters often exhibit superficial narratives, such as the claim that religious adherents must tolerate criticism or denial of their beliefs. This was evident in *IA v Turkey*, where, despite the emphasis on religious tolerance and the deeply embedded principle of secularism, the ECtHR found no violation of Article 10, noting that the impugned text was offensive to believers. The case law is also marred by inconsistencies. For example, the ECtHR found a violation of Article 10 in *Ibragimov and Others v Russia* (2018), which concerned the prohibition of allegedly extremist religious texts. On the other hand, a seemingly innocuous radio broadcast, as

151 *I.A* (n 112) para 30
152 *I.A* (n 112) para 28
153 *Murphy v Ireland* App no 44179/98 (ECHR, 10 July 2003) para 73

in *Murphy*, where an invitation was made for listeners to attend church, was deemed unprotected speech due to the specific national context.

Moreover, in *IA*, the ECtHR noted that the prison sentence was commuted, that the fine was modest and that the books were not seized. Consequently, the Court's majority concluded that there was no violation of Article 10. Judges Costa (France), Cabral Barreto (Portugal) and Jungwiert (Czech Republic) issued a dissenting opinion. It noted that the aforementioned statements are deeply insulting but that they should not be taken in isolation, that no one is obliged to read the novel and that the approach taken by the domestic courts could have a chilling effect and lead to self-censorship. By upholding the fine, the Court risked allowing the subjective feelings of religious believers to dictate the boundaries of permissible discourse, even when that discourse does not incite violence or hatred. Such a low threshold for offence can lead to the suppression of critical thought and artistic expression, as individuals may be deterred from engaging in controversial or provocative topics for fear of legal repercussions. This approach can have a chilling effect on free expression, fostering self-censorship and undermining the essential role of free speech in a democratic society. The dissenting opinion correctly highlights that no one is obliged to read the novel, and that its restriction could set a dangerous precedent for future cases.

In *Giniewski v France* (2006), the applicant, a journalist/historian/sociologist, authored a newspaper article addressing the role of the "fulfilment" of the Old Covenant in the New Covenant, arguing that it contributed to anti-Semitism and laid the foundation for the Holocaust.

Some of the applicant's writings included thus:

> The Catholic Church sets itself up as the sole keeper of divine truth. . . . It strongly proclaims the fulfilment of the Old Covenant in the New, and the superiority of the latter. . . . Many Christians have acknowledged that scriptural anti-Judaism and the doctrine of the "fulfilment" [accomplissement] of the Old Covenant in the New led to anti-Semitism and prepared the ground in which the idea and implementation [accomplissement] of Auschwitz took seed.

The applicant was convicted and fined for publicly defaming a group of persons on the ground of membership of a religion, in this case the Christian community. The association General Alliance Against Racism and for Respect for the French and Christian Identity (AGRIF) initiated legal proceedings against the publishing director of the newspaper, the applicant and the newspaper itself. AGRIF claimed that the article included racially defamatory remarks targeting the Christian community, in violation of the Freedom of the Press Act of 1881. The criminal court found the publishing director and applicant guilty of publicly defaming Christians, and each was fined 6,000 French francs and ordered to pay AGRIF 7,000 French francs in damages. The court also ordered that the judgement be published in a national newspaper with related costs payable by the defendants (up to 10,000 French francs). The applicant appealed to the court of appeal, which ruled in favour of the applicant. AGRIF appealed to the court of cassation which ruled in its favour.

The ECtHR determined that the applicant was analysing potential factors behind the extermination of Jewish people rather than criticising or attacking Christians.[154] It unanimously found a violation of Article 10. The Court underlined the *Handyside* principle and noted that Article 10 comes with special duties and responsibilities, which include avoiding offence, particularly regarding religious opinions and beliefs.[155] The Court noted that the applicant's critique was directed at a particular doctrine of the Christian religion and not to Christianity as a whole,[156] and that it aimed to contribute to an ongoing public discussion regarding the Holocaust.[157] It underlined the significance of free speech in looking for historical truth[158] and considered that the statements were not gratuitously offensive or revisionist in nature.[159] In relation to the issue of proportionality, the ECtHR noted that requiring the publication of the ruling in a national newspaper and the payment of minimal damages may not, in itself, amount to an excessive restriction on freedom of expression. However, it found that labelling the matter as a criminal offence of defamation had an alarming effect, and the penalty imposed was disproportionate, considering the significance and public interest of the debate.[160] The Court's acknowledgment of the criminal aspect of the state's response aligns with the principle that criminal law should serve as a last resort in addressing hate speech. This position, which recognises the broader tension between criminal sanctions and the protection of freedom of expression, is a welcome development. It reflects the understanding that the use of criminal law to regulate speech is inherently fraught and should be approached with caution to avoid unnecessary interferences with fundamental rights. In a plethora of hate speech cases, the Court fails adequately to address the inherent chilling effect that arises when speech is subjected to criminal penalties, as demonstrated in this chapter and the next. Instead of engaging with the broader implications of using criminal law to regulate expression, the Court often dismisses these concerns by focusing narrowly on proportionality, arguing that the penalty imposed was modest or less severe than the maximum possible sentence. This approach disregards the fundamental issue that the very use of criminal sanctions for hate speech poses a significant threat to freedom of expression. Moreover, the Court's reasoning appears selective and tailored to fit its conclusions, as it emphasises proportionality in some cases while entirely overlooking it in others. The Court's observations on the use of criminal law for

154 *Giniewski v France* (2006) App no 64016/00 (ECHR, 31 January 2008) para 28
155 *Giniewski* (n 154) para 43
156 *Giniewski* (n 154) para 49
157 *Giniewski* (n 154) para 50
158 *Giniewski* (n 154) para 51
159 *Giniewski* (n 154) para 52
160 *Giniewski* (n 154) paras 54, 55

'speech crimes' were poignant. However, by avoiding adopting a consistent and principled stance on the criminalisation of speech, the Court allows for inconsistencies and arbitrary applications of its jurisprudence.

In *ES v Austria* (2019), the applicant, a public speaker, conducted seminars titled "Basic Information on Islam" at the Freedom Party Education Institute, a right-wing organisation. These seminars, promoted as 'top seminars' in a 'free education package' by the party leader, were publicly advertised and open to the public. The applicant had no role in selecting participants. The regional criminal court acquitted the applicant of inciting hatred but convicted her of disparaging religious doctrines by publicly disparaging the Prophet Muhammad, considered an object of veneration of a domestic church or religious society. She was fined EUR 480 and ordered to cover the costs of the proceedings. Her appeal, arguing that her statements were factual rather than value judgements, was dismissed by the court of appeal. A request to reopen the case was also rejected by the Supreme Court.

Some of the controversial statements, exposed by an undercover journalist, included the following:

> One of the biggest problems we are facing today is that Muhammad is seen as the ideal man, the perfect human, the perfect Muslim. That means that the highest commandment for a male Muslim is to imitate Muhammad, to live his life. This does not happen according to our social standards and laws. Because he was a warlord, he had many women, to put it like this, and liked to do it with children. And according to our standards he was not a perfect human. We have huge problems with that today, that Muslims get into conflict with democracy and our value system. . . .
>
> The most important of all Hadith collections recognised by all legal schools: The most important is the Sahih Al-Bukhari. If a Hadith was quoted after Bukhari, one can be sure that all Muslims would recognise it. And, unfortunately, in Al-Bukhari the thing with Aisha and child sex is written.

In finding no violation of Article 10, the ECtHR commenced its assessment of whether the restriction was necessary in a democratic society by doing what it habitually does, underlying the importance of freedom of expression and that this extends to opinions and ideas that may shock, offend or disturb, citing *Handyside* and subsequent case law. However, it recognised that, in the context of religious beliefs, that is

> the general requirement to ensure the peaceful enjoyment of the rights guaranteed under Article 9 to the holders of such beliefs including a duty to avoid as far as possible an expression that is, in regard to objects of veneration, gratuitously offensive to others and profane.[161]

161 *E.S v Austria* App no 38450/12 (ECHR, 25 October 2018) para 43

It proceeded to underline the 'absence of a uniform conception of the requirements of the protection of the rights of others in relation to attacks on their religious convictions.'[162]

Based on this premise, the ECtHR gives states a wide margin of appreciation to assess what constitutes a religious attack, but also a positive obligation to ensure the peaceful co-existence of all religions by ensuring mutual tolerance.[163] It does not extrapolate on how a state can actually ensure such a difficult objective. It noted that ascertaining whether a statement constitutes a fact rather than a value judgement (the applicant noted that her statements were a fact) lies within the margin of appreciation of the state.[164] It then proceeded to note that the issue before the Court was to balance what it called the 'conflicting interests' between the exercise of Article 9 and Article 10.[165] It noted that the statements in question were of a 'particularly sensitive nature,'[166] but that it was the duty of the domestic authorities to find whether or not they could disturb the religious peace of the country.[167] The Court did not consider relevant that only 30 people participated in the seminars, but it did find that the title of the seminar was deceiving, since 'Basic Information on Islam' could give the impression that it would include objective information on Islam. It also found that anyone could enrol, and not just members of the Freedom Party, who may share the same views on Islam, but also others who could have been offended by the applicant's statements.[168] This finding seems rather superficial; it would be reasonable to assume that people who sign up for the course also know or read up on the organisers, and by doing so in this case, the far-right direction of the courses would be clear.

After weighing up Articles 9 and 10 rights, the Court concluded that the applicant's remarks were unsubstantiated generalisations that exceeded the acceptable boundaries of objective debate. The statements were deemed an attack on the Prophet Muhammad, with the potential of 'stirring up prejudice and putting religious peace at risk.'[169] The Court made no mention in its conclusion of whether the speech in question did, in fact, lead to the incitement to hatred or intolerance, which was noted as a threshold in the main body of its judgement. So even though the Court referred to *Handyside* and noted that religious groups must tolerate denial/propagation of their doctrine by others,

162 *E.S* (n 161) para 44
163 *E.S* (n 161)
164 *E.S* (n 161) para 47
165 *E.S* (n 161) para 46
166 *E.S* (n 161) para 50
167 *E.S* (n 161)
168 *E.S* (n 161) para 51
169 *E.S* (n 161) para 57

as long as they do not incite to hatred or religious intolerance, the ECtHR Court found no violation of Article 10.[170]

In light of these, I argue that the Court granted an overly broad margin of appreciation to the state, allowing it to classify the applicant's statements as factual or offensive without rigorous scrutiny, weakening Article 10 protections. It failed to substantiate how the remarks posed a genuine threat to religious peace rather than merely offending sensibilities, particularly given the small number of participants. Its focus on the seminar's title and open participation diverted attention from the absence of evidence showing incitement to hatred or intolerance, a threshold highlighted in its own reasoning. By equating unsubstantiated generalisations with harmful speech, the Court risks conflating offence with actual harm, setting a troubling precedent for freedom of expression.

Tagiyev and Huseynov v Azerbaijan (2019) involved an application by a columnist and editor-in-chief who were sentenced to three and four years' imprisonment, respectively, for publishing an article titled "Europe and Us" in a newspaper. This piece argued that Europe does not accept Islam or the Prophet Muhammad. Specifically, they were found guilty of inciting religious hatred and hostility for remarks made in the preceding publication, which included:

> In comparison with Jesus Christ, the father of war fatwas the Prophet Muhammad is simply a frightful creature.
>
> At best, Islam would advance in Europe with tiny demographic steps. And maybe there would be a country in which Islam would be represented by a few individuals or terrorists living incognito.

The district court ordered the applicants' pre-trial detention, and they were subsequently found guilty of incitement to ethnic, racial, social or religious hatred and hostility, committed publicly or by use of mass media. The applicants appealed to the court of appeal and to the Supreme Court, which both upheld the judgements. All courts relied on a forensic report issued on the matter.

The ECtHR observed that certain statements in the article could be considered offensive, particularly the description of the Prophet Muhammad as a "frightful creature" in contrast to Jesus Christ, and that this could potentially be seen as 'an abusive attack on the Prophet of Islam and Muslims living in Europe, capable of causing religious hatred.'[171] Nevertheless, it underlined the importance of free speech and political speech or speech on issues pertaining to public interest, but also that tolerance and respect are centrifugal to a democratic society.[172] Particularly problematic for the ECtHR was the fact that domestic courts

170 *E.S* (n 161) para 52
171 *Tagiyev and Huseynov* (n 103) para 46
172 *Tagiyev and Huseynov* (n 103) paras 36–38

relied on expert reports without substantive reasoning to demonstrate how the specific remarks amounted to incitement to religious hatred.[173]

It noted that, despite the potentially insulting or offensive nature of the statements, it is for the national authorities

> to carry out a comprehensive assessment of the impugned remarks, putting forward relevant and sufficient reasons for justifying the interference and carefully balancing the applicants' right to freedom of expression with the protection of the right of religious people not to be insulted on the grounds of their beliefs.[174]

The Court held that the domestic courts solely reiterated the findings of the expert report without conducting a legal analysis to explain how and why the remarks constituted incitement to religious hatred. Specifically:

> the domestic courts failed to examine the report and merely endorsed its conclusions. The relevant assessment clearly went far beyond resolving mere language and religious issues, such as, for instance, defining the meaning of particular words and expressions or their religious importance, and provided, in essence, a legal characterization of the impugned remarks.[175]

Given this lack of judicial analysis and the harshness of the penalties imposed, the majority of the ECtHR concluded that there had been a violation of Article 10. It is positive that the Court, in this case, set a benchmark by highlighting that restrictions on freedom of expression cannot rely solely on expert reports. However, this approach underscores the broader inconsistency in the Court's hate speech case law. In *Balsytė-Lideikienė*, for example, the issue of overreliance on expert reports was raised in a dissenting opinion, yet the majority found no violation of Article 10 and thus had no issue with the domestic overreliance on expert reports. While that case included a less severe penalty, this selective scrutiny of issues pertaining to the Article 10 test undermines the need for a consistent and principled approach across cases. The Court should prioritise analytical consistency rather than allowing isolated factors to dictate the level of judicial scrutiny. All elements of Article 10's test must be looked at individually, but also in conjunction with each other, but clear indicators for the analysis of each have yet to be developed and applied in an evidence-based and definitionally sound framework where unacceptable thresholds of harm are clearly set out.

173 *Tagiyev and Huseynov* (n 103) para 47
174 *Tagiyev and Huseynov* (n 103) para 46
175 *Tagiyev and Huseynov* (n 103) para 47

In *Yefimov and Youth Human Rights Group v Russia* (2021), the first applicant, who founded and directed the applicant association, wrote the following on the second applicant's website. The piece was titled "Karelia is fed up with priests" and read as follows:

> Anti-church attitudes are on the rise in the Karelian capital. Nothing surprising about that. Thinking members of society have realised that the church is also a party in power. The Russian Orthodox Church, just like the [ruling] United Russia party, is fooling people with fairy tales about our good life while raking in money. Total corruption, oligarchy, and the absolute power of security services are the reasons for a revival of the Russian Orthodox Church (ROC). Churches in Karelia are being built with public funds while there is no money for basic needs; ROC gets day nurseries for use at a time when childcare facilities are desperately lacking. Bearded men in fancy robes—modern-day ideology instructors—have filled the television screens. They give their opinion on everything, from canalisation to modernisation. All of this makes normal people puke; unable to do anything about the clerical stranglehold, they express their attitude to the ROC's provincial officials by tagging walls in places where the Orthodox scum hangs out. "Pay and pray," "Christ is dead" [is written] on the walls of the Orthodox Centre in Petrozavodsk . . . which once was a day nursery.

The first applicant was charged with degrading the dignity of a person or group of persons on account of their attitude to the religion, while the second applicant, an organisation, was dissolved on the grounds that the first applicant, as a founding member, was suspected of involvement in an extremist offence. Additionally, the first applicant was added to the list of terrorists and extremists and the town court also authorised his placement in a psychiatric facility to conduct a 'granular analysis of his personality traits.' However, the first applicant left Russia and evaded this order.

The ECtHR unanimously found a violation of Article 10 concerning the first applicant and a violation of Article 11, interpreted in conjunction with Article 10, concerning both applicants. The ECtHR relied on *Handyside* and other case law to underline the importance of freedom of expression and, citing *Ibragimov*, noted that

> merely because a remark may be perceived as offensive or insulting by particular individuals or groups of individuals does not mean that it constitutes hate speech. Whilst such sentiments are understandable, they alone cannot set the limits of freedom of expression.[176]

176 *Yefimov and Youth Human Rights Group v Russia* (2021) para 44

It also underlined that discussion about the place of religion in society is an issue of public concern[177] and that the applicant did not criticise individuals but, rather, religious organisations.[178]

The ECtHR noted that in cases restricting free speech, factors including the following are taken into account:

> [T]he existence of a tense political or social context, the presence of calls for or justification of violence, hatred, or intolerance, the manner in which the statements were made, and their potential to cause harmful consequences.[179]

In this ambit, it underlined that the government had not put forth evidence that there was a context which justified restrictions on grounds of national security or for preventing disorder. Importantly, citing *Vajnai v Hungary*, it noted that 'the containment of a mere speculative danger, as a preventative measure for the protection of democracy, cannot be seen as pursuing a pressing social need.'[180] The way the Court appraised the speculative danger of harm in this case did not extend to the speculative *form* of speech in *Smajić v Bosnia and Herzegovina*, where the ECtHR noted that, even though the impugned speech was written in 'hypothetical form,'[181] it had touched on a sensitive topic in a sensitive context, and this contributed to a finding that the applicant's free speech was not violated.[182]

In this case, the ECtHR was not satisfied with the legal analysis conducted by the government when deciding to commence criminal proceedings against the applicants. The Court noted that the government did not identify which parts of the publication were against the law and, instead of conducting the relevant legal analysis, merely relied on an unnamed expert in linguistics and referred to provisions of criminal law.[183] The Court's dissatisfaction with the reliance on expert reports was reflected in cases such as *Tagiyev and Huseynov*, whereas in *Balsytė-Lideikienė*, the dissenting opinion argued that the Court did exactly that, overrely on expert reports, following the example of the domestic courts. In terms of the harsh punishment, the ECtHR noted that the threat of imprisonment should not apply to non-violent speech, with the threat itself possibly having a chilling effect on speech.[184]

The ECtHR's judgement in *Yefimov and Youth Human Rights Group* highlights significant issues in the regulation of freedom of expression, particularly

177 *Yefimov* (n 176) para 45
178 *Yefimov* (n 176)
179 *Yefimov* (n 176) para 43
180 *Yefimov* (n 176) para 46
181 *Smajić* (n 118) para 39
182 *Smajić* (n 118)
183 *Yefimov* (n 176) para 42
184 *Yefimov* (n 176) para 47

in the context of hate speech and extreme penalties. The finding of a violation of Article 10 for the first applicant, and of Article 11 in conjunction with Article 10 for both applicants, is a positive outcome. The Court rightly emphasised that offensive or insulting remarks alone do not constitute hate speech, reaffirming that limitations on expression require a higher threshold, including the presence of violence, hatred or intolerance. However, as with other cases involving harsh penalties, the finding of a violation appears strongly tied to the disproportionate nature of the punishment.

Mariya Alekhina and Others v Russia (2018) is also an interesting case, which does not have extensive legal reasoning beyond the two significant points raised in what follows, particularly because the domestic analysis was essentially lacking and because the trial was conducted without the participation of the applicants. In this case, the three applicants were members of the Russian feminist punk band Pussy Riot, known for impromptu performances featuring lyrics critical of the political process in Russia. In 2012, five band members, including the applicants, attempted to perform their song "Punk Prayer—Virgin Mary, Drive Putin Away" at the altar of Moscow's Christ the Saviour Cathedral. Although no service was in progress, several people were present in the cathedral. The band invited journalists and media to publicise the event. The performance lasted just over a minute before cathedral guards intervened and removed them. A video of the incident was later uploaded to YouTube. The applicants were subsequently convicted by the district court of hooliganism motivated by religious hatred and enmity and for reasons of hatred towards a particular social group and sentenced to two years' imprisonment. Additionally, a court deemed videos of the band's performances which were hosted on their website to be extremist, ordering the restriction of access via a filter on the website's IP address. All appeals were rejected. This case included applications on grounds of the violation of several Convention grounds. In relation to Article 10, the first two applicants complained that the domestic courts had violated their right to freedom of expression by declaring them as extremist and banning their online videos. The Court commenced its necessity test by citing cases such as *Wingrove*, noting that there is little scope for restrictions on political speech or questions of public interest if such speech does not incite violence.[185] The Court then noted the overreliance on expert reports which had substituted the implementation of proper legal analysis on a domestic level.[186] This observation has been reiterated in cases such as *Tagiyev and Huseynov*, discussed earlier, and *Sokolovskiy v Russia* (2024), discussed later. As already noted, the Court itself was criticised in a dissenting opinion for overreliance on national expert reports in *Balsytė-Lideikienė*. The ECtHR noted that the domestic court did not analyse the video itself, nor did it underline

185 *Mariya Alekhina and others v Russia* (2018) App no 38004/12 (ECHR, 17 July 2018) para 260

186 *Alekhina and others* (n 185) para 262

the problematic elements of the video. As a result, 'the virtual absence of reasoning by the domestic court makes it impossible for the Court to grasp the rationale behind the interference.'[187] The fact that the applicants were not given the opportunity to participate in the criminal proceedings against them was also noted by the Court.[188] The Court, by a majority, found a violation of Article 10.

Sokolovskiy v Russia (2024) involved an application by a popular blogger with approximately 470,000 YouTube subscribers who was prosecuted for videos criticising religion and religious institutions, including remarks about the Russian Orthodox Church, the existence of religious figures and playing Pokémon Go in a church. The Russian courts convicted him for public actions insulting religious beliefs and inciting hatred, viewing the content as extremist and aimed at provoking hostility towards specific social, ethnic or religious groups. He received a suspended sentence of three and a half years, with two years of probation, and it was ordered that the videos be removed from the Internet. The ECtHR unanimously concluded that the sanctions imposed by Russian authorities violated Article 10, as the interference was neither necessary nor adequately justified by the domestic courts.

The ECtHR considered Russia's request for an application of Article 17 to the case but underlined that this article can only be used in extreme and exceptional cases, where the speech in question aims to misuse freedom of expression and go against the core values of the ECHR.[189] The Court found that Sokolovskiy's comments, while offensive to some, were not severe enough to justify applying Article 17.[190] In relation to the issue of offence, the Court adopted its position in *Ibragim Ibragimov and Others* in that offence, in itself, is not sufficient to allow for a free speech restriction. Specifically, it stated thus:

> [T]he mere fact a remark may be perceived as offensive or insulting by certain individuals or groups does not mean it constitutes 'hate speech.' While such feelings may be understandable, they alone cannot determine the boundaries of freedom of expression (*Ibragim Ibragimov and Others*. . .).[191]

It proceeded to note that offensive speech may not be protected 'if it amounts to gratuitous denigration,' but that the 'use of vulgar expressions alone is not decisive in assessing offensive language, as such expressions may well serve purely stylistic purposes.'[192] The Court found that the domestic authori-

187 *Alekhina and others* (n 185) para 263
188 *Alekhina and others* (n 185) para 267
189 *Sokolovskiy v Russia* (2024) App no 618/18 (ECHR, 4 June 2024) para 76
190 *Sokolovskiy* (n 189) paras 76, 77
191 *Sokolovskiy* (n 189) para 101
192 *Sokolovskiy* (n 189)

ties had not assessed whether the statements were gratuitously offensive to religious beliefs or incited disrespect or hatred toward the Orthodox Church. By raising this issue, the judgement leaves open the possibility that, had such elements been examined and substantiated, the restrictions might have been deemed permissible.

It also underlined the need for a proper examination of the context in which the statements were made.[193] The ECtHR argued that the domestic courts failed to evaluate the statements within the broader context of the videos' content. Instead, the domestic courts merely cited isolated phrases from the videos, relying heavily on expert conclusions without considering their immediate context.[194] Moreover, the ECtHR held that they made no effort to determine whether the statements, despite their harsh or vulgar tone, were part of a discussion on matters of public interest or could be justified as a stylistic choice aligned with the applicant's role as a blogger targeting a young audience.[195] The ECtHR also noted that the speech in question did not make any calls for violence, nor were there any mentions of contextual sensitivities at that time, such as interreligious tensions, which could have meant that the statements could have provoked violence or serious conflict.[196]

The ECtHR's reasoning in this case stands out for its robust protection of freedom of expression, yet such careful analysis remains a rarity in its hate speech jurisprudence. The Court emphasised the necessity for contextual examination, criticising the domestic courts for isolating phrases from the videos rather than assessing them within their broader context. This approach contrasts starkly with cases like *Féret*, where the ECtHR upheld restrictions on political speech without providing a detailed contextual analysis, merely deeming the statements likely to provoke feelings of rejection or hatred. Similarly, in *Vejdeland*, the Court accepted the classification of prejudicial statements as hate speech despite the absence of incitement to violence, relying heavily on the vulnerable nature of the audience rather than a substantive contextual assessment. By comparison, the present case went further, noting that the contested speech, while harsh or vulgar, did not incite violence or exploit societal tensions, such as interreligious discord. Additionally, the ECtHR considered whether the statements were part of a broader public debate or reflected stylistic choices aligned with the speaker's role and audience, a nuanced approach often absent in cases like *Lilliendahl*, where speech deemed 'seriously prejudicial' was penalised without including the limited reach of the comments as a mitigating factor. The present judgement demonstrates how a principled, context-sensitive analysis should serve as a model

193 *Sokolovskiy* (n 189)
194 *Sokolovskiy* (n 189) para 105
195 *Sokolovskiy* (n 189) para 106
196 *Sokolovskiy* (n 189) para 111

for the ECtHR in reconciling free speech protections with the need to combat hate speech. The target in this case was an institution, the Orthodox Church, and not protected characteristics, the protection of which is more pronounced. As noted previously by the Court, 'it is particularly sensitive towards sweeping statements attacking or casting in a negative light entire ethnic, religious or other group.'[197] This could account for the differences between the treatment of free speech in *Sokolovskiy* and the group of cases which follow *Féret*. Nevertheless, the manner in which issues are deconstructed in the former, as described earlier, could constitute an analytical starting point for the Court to assess free speech, notwithstanding the particular sensitivities the Court has professed to having when it comes to speech targeting protected characteristics.

5.2 *Religious Extremism*

The case of *Ibragimov and Others v Russia* (2018) dealt with religious books which were prohibited on the grounds that they were extremist. This case is important for purposes of distinguishing between cases involving religious speech that may be deemed offensive to believers, because of depictions or statements made about religious figures, and cases involving religious speech and extremism. *Ibragimov* is of particular importance, as it demonstrates how the handling of offence varies in cases involving generic religious texts which do not disparage figures or doctrines but, rather, fall within the general discussion of extremism and moderation.

Ibragimov concerned the prohibition of the publication and distribution of Said Nursi's book on the grounds that it constituted extremist literature. The first applicant was the founder and chief executive officer of the second applicant, a non-profit organisation. The second applicant serves as the publisher of the *Risale-i Nur Collection*, a commentary on the Quran authored by the Muslim Turkish scholar Said Nursi in the early 20th century. In 2005, the prosecutor of the Tatarstan Republic initiated criminal proceedings against members of the Nurculuk religious movement, charging them with incitement to hatred or discord and abasement of human dignity for distributing books from the *Risale-i Nur Collection*. The prosecutor petitioned the district court to declare the books as extremist and to impose a ban on their dissemination. The district court ruled that Said Nursi's books constituted extremist material. This decision was upheld by the city court.

The Court rejected Russia's request to apply Article 17, reiterating that this provision is used only on an 'exceptional basis and in extreme cases.'[198] The ECtHR started its analysis with the conventional reference to *Handyside*

197 *Atamanchuk* (n 64) para 51

198 *Ibragimov and others v Russia* (2018) App nos. 1413/08 & 28621/11) (ECHR, 28 August 2018) para 62

and other subsequent cases on the importance of freedom of expression.[199] It proceeded to note that the rights and responsibilities under Article 10 include

> a duty to avoid as far as possible expressions that are gratuitously offensive to others and thus an infringement of their rights, and which therefore do not contribute to any form of public debate capable of furthering progress in human affairs.[200]

This raises complex and highly subjective questions of interpretation. For example, who determines whether an expression is *gratuitously offensive*? Is this not inherently linked to individual and societal viewpoints, which are susceptible to inconsistent application or even mismanagement by adjudicating bodies? Moreover, the Court's implied ***additional*** criterion, that expression must add value to public debate to warrant protection, complicates matters further as it introduces a public interest threshold that speech must satisfy, effectively narrowing the protective ambit of Article 10. Such scenarios raise the following question: Does the absence of contribution alone render expression unworthy of protection? This balancing exercise between the potential offensiveness of speech, the subjective perspectives of adjudicators and the ambiguous notion of contribution reveals a tension that remains at the heart of Article 10 jurisprudence. The inherent risks of arbitrariness in this assessment demand rigorous scrutiny, lest freedom of expression be curtailed in a manner inconsistent with the pluralism and tolerance the Convention seeks to safeguard.

The ECtHR also highlighted that states have a certain margin of appreciation in regulating freedom of expression when it comes to religious freedom, noting that there is 'no uniform European conception of the requirements of the protection of others in relation to attacks on religious convictions.'[201] It did highlight, however, that this margin of appreciation 'is not unlimited.'[202] In exercising its 'European supervision,' the Court found that the national courts failed to adhere to the principles enshrined in Article 10 of the ECHR. Instead of conducting a thorough and independent assessment, they relied solely on expert evidence[203] and denied the applicants the opportunity to present evidence in their defence, thereby breaching the doctrine of 'equality of arms.'[204] The ECtHR noted that Said Nursi's teachings promoted a moderate and non-violent interpretation of Islam[205] and highlighted that his books, which were widely available in numerous countries, including Russia, had not

199 *Ibragimov and others* (n 198) para 91
200 *Ibragimov and others* (n 198) para 92
201 *Ibragimov and others* (n 198) para 95
202 *Ibragimov and others* (n 198) para 96
203 *Ibragimov and others* (n 198) para 107
204 *Ibragimov and others* (n 198) para 108
205 *Ibragimov and others* (n 198) para 101

been linked to any harmful consequences.[206] The ECtHR unanimously found a violation of Article 10. This kind of substantial examination of core issues at stake is not only welcome but also fundamental for a proper assessment of Article 10 in hate speech cases. Unfortunately, as we have seen in cases such as *Féret*, *Vejdeland*, and *Lilliendahl*, to name but a few, the Court has not functioned in an analytical framework similar to the one in *Ibragimov* but has instead followed the lead of domestic authorities in their approach to the speech and its alleged consequences without in-depth assessment, usually under the guise of the wide margin of appreciation when it comes to certain kinds of speech, situations and contexts, such as racist speech during elections.

An important element of this case which is demonstrative of the preceding jurisprudential discrepancy is the handling of the issues of offence and insults, particularly when compared to other cases. Here, the ECtHR noted that

> merely because a remark may be perceived as offensive or insulting by particular individuals or groups does not mean that it constitutes 'hate speech.' Whilst such sentiments are understandable, they alone cannot set the limits of freedom of expression. The key issue in the present case is thus whether the statements in question, when read as a whole and in their context, could be seen as promoting violence, hatred or intolerance.[207]

This reading of Article 10 and hate speech is in line with the Court's own jurisprudence, specifically *Handyside*, but also international norms, such as Article 20(2) of the ICCPR, which prohibits advocacy of national, racial or religious hatred that constitutes incitement to discrimination, hostility or violence. In itself, the preceding overview of offensive and insulting speech falls within the threshold one would assume to come with Article 10, not only because of its fundamental nature, but also because of the Court's own judgement in *Handyside*. However, this approach has not been consistently applied in other cases. A reminder of this conflicting approach is the position in *Atamanchuk*, discussed earlier, involving alleged hate speech against non-Russians, in which the ECtHR noted:

> [I]nciting hatred does not necessarily involve an explicit call for an act of violence, or other criminal acts. Attacks on persons committed by insulting, holding up to ridicule or slandering specific groups of the population can be sufficient for the authorities to favour combating xenophobic or otherwise discriminatory speech in the face of freedom of expression exercised in an irresponsible manner.[208]

206 *Ibragimov and others* (n 198) para 102
207 *Ibragimov and others* (n 198) para 55
208 *Atamanchuk* (n 64) para 52

As such, in *Ibragimov*, the Court held that mere insult, without anything more, was insufficient to justify restricting speech. In contrast, taking *Atamanchuk* as an example, the ECtHR treated insult as part of the broader context of incitement to hatred, even though the Court did not clearly establish a connection between the insult and the incitement of hatred. The key differentiating factor between the two cases was that, in *Atamanchuk*, the speech targeted a specific group defined by a particular characteristic, such as ethnicity. On the other hand, *Ibragimov* involved the banning of a religious text on extremism grounds. This distinction highlights an important trend. As illustrated by the earlier comparison and further explored throughout this book, the Court tends to adopt a more permissive approach to restrictions on speech when it is directed against identifiable groups with distinct characteristics, as it is 'particularly sensitive towards sweeping statements attacking or casting in a negative light entire ethnic, religious or other group.'[209] This approach effectively lowers the threshold for limiting speech in such contexts, prioritising the protection of vulnerable groups over broader speech rights. Moreover, this prioritisation emanates from a binary which is unfounded and which does not result from any substantial conceptualisation by the Court of the harm of insulting speech and the benefits that restricting it may bring to marginalised or vulnerable groups, social cohesion or Convention values, neither does it take into account the fundamentality of freedom of expression.

In *Belkacem v Belgium* (2017), the applicant, who served as the leader and spokesperson for the organisation "Sharia4Belgium," dissolved in 2012, was prosecuted for inciting discrimination, hatred and violence through remarks made in YouTube videos about non-Muslim groups and Sharia. The ECtHR applied Article 17 to this case on the grounds that his statements advocated hatred and violence against non-Muslims and, as such, were not protected under the Convention.

Through his videos, the applicant urged viewers to dominate non-Muslims, punish them and fight against them. Statements included:

> Muslims are here to dominate, Allah is the one who proclaimed his message with the truth and the true religion is here to dominate the world to rule over all systems.
>
> I am not calling on Muslims to fight but it will still be the consequences. . . . We are not Christians, we do not turn our other cheek when someone hits us. We seek confrontation. Belgium is warned. Our honour is worth more than our life.

The criminal court sentenced him to a two-year prison sentence and a EUR 550 fine for a violation of various offences under the anti-discrimination law, such as publicly inciting to discrimination, violence and hatred. The sentence

209 *Atamanchuk* (n 64) para 51

was suspended for five years. The applicant appealed to the Antwerp Court of Appeal, which sentenced him to a prison term of one year and six months and a EUR 550 fine. The court of cassation dismissed the applicant's subsequent appeal.

The ECtHR underlined the importance of freedom of expression, citing case law such as *Handyside*. It found, however, that the aforementioned content fell outside the scope of Convention protection, noting that:

> The Court has no doubt as to the strongly hateful content of the applicant's opinions and endorses the conclusion of the domestic courts that the applicant sought, through his recordings, to hate, discriminate against and be violent against non-Muslims. In the Court's opinion, such a general and vehement attack is in contradiction with the values of tolerance, social peace and non-discrimination which underlie the Convention.[210]

In this light, it enforced Article 17, finding the application to be manifestly ill-founded, in line with the original intentions of Article 17, namely, protecting the Convention and democracy from destructive forces. The destructive nature of the speech in question emanates from its violent tone towards non-Muslims.

By applying Article 17 in *Belkacem*, the Court reaffirmed that expressions inciting hatred, violence or discrimination, such as those promoted by the applicant, fall outside the protective scope of Article 10. This decision aligns with the Convention's purpose of protecting democratic values and social peace from destructive ideologies. Ultimately, the judgement reiterates the role of Article 17 as a safeguard against the misuse of rights enshrined in the Convention for purposes that contradict its foundational principles.

5.3 Conclusions: Religious Hatred and Extremism

The ECtHR's treatment of speech targeting religious figures, doctrines and institutions reveals an intricate balancing act between safeguarding freedom of expression under Article 10 of the ECHR and protecting the rights and sensitivities of religious communities under Article 9. The cases examined illustrate the Court's struggle to articulate consistent standards for when offensive or critical speech about religion crosses the threshold of permissible expression. These decisions expose critical themes that shape the jurisprudence in this area, shedding light on both the strengths and the challenges of the ECtHR's approach.

The ECtHR consistently affirms the centrality of freedom of expression, including its capacity to shock, offend or disturb, as established in *Handyside*. Yet in cases involving religion, the Court often leans on the principle

210 *Belkacem v Belgium* (2017) App no 34367/15 (27 June 2017) para 33

that free expression entails responsibilities, especially in the context of sensitive religious beliefs. This is evident in *IA* and *ES*, where the Court upheld restrictions on speech deemed an 'abusive attack' on the Prophet Muhammad.[211] These judgements underscore the ECtHR's recognition of the social tensions that can arise from provocative or offensive remarks about religious beliefs, coupled with its deference to national authorities under the margin of appreciation doctrine. However, this balancing act creates significant challenges. The Court's reliance on the concept of 'gratuitous offensiveness' remains underexplored, leaving unclear criteria for distinguishing permissible critique or satire from impermissible denigration. As well as diluting the efficacy of the Article 10(2) test, this ambiguity risks undermining the foreseeability of restrictions on speech, as seen in the divergent outcomes of *ES* and *Tagiyev and Huseynov*, despite both involving offensive statements about religious figures.

The ECtHR's insistence on substantive analysis is pivotal, yet its application remains inconsistent, revealing significant uncertainty in its hate speech jurisprudence. For example, in *Giniewski*, the Court carefully distinguished between academic critique and defamatory attacks, finding the applicant's article contributed meaningfully to public discourse on historical responsibility. In stark contrast, *ES* saw the Court deem unsubstantiated generalisations as likely to stir prejudice, upholding Austria's restrictions on speech without critically examining whether these remarks incited harm. Similarly, in *Sokolovskiy*, the Court criticised domestic authorities for failing to assess the broader context of the applicant's videos and for overly relying on isolated statements, yet in *Tagiyev and Huseynov*, it faulted Azerbaijani courts for uncritically endorsing expert reports without properly situating the impugned remarks within their societal and communicative context. While these cases underline the ECtHR's requirement for national courts to perform contextual evaluations, the reality remains fragmented, with inconsistency in the Court's application of this principle.

A concern in some of the ECtHR's jurisprudence is the potential chilling effect of criminal penalties for speech about religion. In *Giniewski*, the Court explicitly recognised that labelling the applicant's critique as criminal defamation risked suppressing legitimate public debate. Similarly, in *Yefimov*, the Court condemned the extreme measures taken against the applicant, including his committal to a psychiatric institution and his inclusion on a list of terrorists and extremists, as disproportionate and indicative of overreach. By contrast, in cases like *IA* and *ES*, the Court appeared less sensitive to the deterrent effects of criminal penalties. Although it acknowledged the modesty of the sanctions, it did not adequately address how such measures could discourage others from engaging in controversial or provocative discussions about religion. This inconsistency weakens the ECtHR's role as a guardian

211 *IA* (n 112) para 29; *ES* (n 161) para 57

of freedom of expression, particularly in cases involving speech on matters of public interest.

When it comes to the sphere of religious extremism, *Ibragimov* set an important precedent by emphasising that religious texts perceived as offensive or extreme must be evaluated within their broader context and impact. The Court's insistence on a substantive, independent assessment, rather than blind deference to domestic findings, signals its recognition of the dangers inherent in arbitrary restrictions on speech. The rejection of Article 17 in this case, coupled with the acknowledgment that mere insult is insufficient for censorship, reinforces a high threshold for interference under Article 10. This approach promotes a commitment to protecting moderate, non-violent expressions within the broader framework of freedom of religion and expression. In *Belkacem*, the Court's application of Article 17 reflects the outer limits of protected speech, explicitly excluding expressions that advocate violence and promote hatred against specific groups. This judgement underscores the ECtHR's role in safeguarding democratic principles and social peace by excluding manifestly harmful speech from the Convention's protection. Therefore, while *Ibragimov* demonstrates the Court's capacity for rigorous scrutiny and nuanced judgement, *Belkacem* underscores its readiness categorically to exclude destructive speech from Article 10 protections.

6 Hate Speech and Journalistic Freedom

In the landmark case of *Jersild v Denmark* (1994), the majority of the ECtHR's Grand Chamber found that punishing a journalist for conducting interviews with members of the racist group known as the 'Greenjackets' violated his right to freedom of expression under Article 10 of the ECHR. The case arose from a documentary produced by the *Sunday News Magazine*, a programme of 'Danmarks Radio,' where the applicant, a journalist, interviewed three members of the "Greenjackets," a racist youth group. The segment also included the input of a local social worker. During the interview, members of the "Greenjackets" made abusive and derogatory remarks about immigrants and ethnic groups in Denmark. These remarks were subsequently broadcast as part of the documentary. Following the televised broadcast, a church official lodged a complaint with the minister of justice. This led the public prosecutor to initiate criminal proceedings against the three interviewees in the city court, resulting in their conviction for disseminating threatening, insulting or degrading statements based on race, colour, national or ethnic origin or belief. The applicant was charged with aiding and abetting the three youths for the aforementioned crime; the same charge was brought against the head of the news section of "Danmarks Radio." The city court found them guilty. They appealed to the High Court and Supreme Court, which both dismissed their appeal.

The specific remarks at issue included:

> [T]he Northern States wanted that the niggers should be free human beings, man, they are not human beings, they are animals.
>
> Just take a picture of a gorilla, man, and then look at a nigger, it's the same body structure and everything, man, flat forehead and all kinds of things.
>
> A nigger is not a human being, it's an animal, that goes for all the other foreign workers as well, Turks, Yugoslavs and whatever they are called.
>
> It's drugs they are selling, man, half of the prison population in "Vestre" are in there because of drugs. . . . [T]hey are the people who are serving time for dealing drugs.

The ECtHR found that the applicant's Article 10 rights had been violated since he was conducting his role as a journalist seeking to inform the public about the problem of racism in Denmark without ever sharing those views. The ECtHR recognised that the applicant started the programme by referring to a recent public discussion on racism in Denmark, thereby framing the programme within that context, and then proceeded to underline that the objective of the programme was to address the problem by identifying racist individuals and setting out their mentality and social background.[212] Importantly, the Court noted that it is not for the judiciary to decipher what method of reporting is to be adopted by journalists, recalling that 'Article 10 protects not only the substance of the ideas and information expressed, but also the form in which they are conveyed.'[213] The Court noted that this was part of a 'serious Danish news programme and was intended for a well-informed audience.'[214] This sweeping allegation of the level of information and understanding of a group of the population is arbitrary and rather condescending, to say the least, although the Court considered the viewers of that particular show contrasted with some of the potential recipients of the impugned material in *Féret*, whom the Court said could be 'less-informed' members of the public.[215] It also held that

> the punishment of a journalist for assisting in the dissemination of statements made by another person in an interview would seriously hamper the contribution of the press to discussion of matters of public interest and should not be envisaged unless there are particularly strong reasons for doing so.[216]

212 *Jersild v Denmark* (1994) App no 15890/89, (ECHR, 23 September 1994) para 33
213 *Jersild* (n 212) para 31
214 *Jersild* (n 212) para 34
215 *Féret* (n 4) para 69
216 *Jersild* (n 212) para 35

In light of the aforementioned, the *Jersild v Denmark* decision is a pivotal ruling that reflects one of the occasions in which the ECtHR adopts a nuanced approach to balancing freedom of expression with protection against racial discrimination. In this case, the ECtHR underlined its commitment to safeguarding journalistic freedom, even when it involves the dissemination of highly offensive and harmful views, provided that the journalist's intention aligns with public interest and responsible reporting. It cannot be deduced that such commitment extends to protecting freedom of expression in the ambit of offensive speech *per se*, as was anyhow demonstrated in case law that followed and included applications by the utterers of offensive speech. However, *Jersild* does reflect the Court's placing of significant weight on the role of public interest journalism on sensitive social issues, such as racism. Recognising the programme's role in contributing to a public debate on racism in Denmark, the Court established that journalism has a duty to expose and critically analyse social issues, even if this entails airing repugnant views. The Court's reasoning also highlights its insistence on protecting the form of expression, not just its content, as integral to Article 10. Here, the ECtHR emphasised that journalists must have the autonomy to decide how best to communicate sensitive or controversial information. The Court thus discouraged judicial interference with editorial choices, underscoring that effective public discourse requires diverse and sometimes provocative journalistic methods. This approach suggests a high threshold for justifying state interference with media activities, recognising that even inflammatory or distasteful material can play a valuable role in fostering informed debate. Moreover, the decision stressed the necessity for 'particularly strong reasons'[217] for imposing penalties on journalists merely for interviewing individuals who express discriminatory views. This sets a high bar for state interference in journalism and limits the scope of liability for journalists under Article 10 when reporting on sensitive topics. The ECtHR's stance in this regard delineates a protective boundary for the press, cautioning against punitive measures that could create a chilling effect, stifling critical reporting on contentious societal issues. Yet the judgement also reflects the Court's recognition of competing rights and interests under the ECHR, particularly in the context of anti-discrimination obligations.

Dink v Turkey (2010) involved the murder of a journalist and an examination of Article 10 in addition to Article 2, on the right to life, and Article 13, on the right to an effective remedy. The ECtHR found that authorities failed to protect journalist Dink, resulting in his murder. Dink was an outspoken member of the Armenian minority in Turkey and was murdered for his writings. The discussion of the case will only focus on the Article 10 element.

Dink served as publication director and editor-in-chief of *Agos*, a bilingual Turkish Armenian weekly newspaper based in Istanbul in circulation since 1996. Between November 2003 and February 2004, he published eight

217 *Jersild* (n 212)

articles in *Agos* in which he expressed his thoughts on the identity of Turkish citizens of Armenian heritage. He argued that "Armenians' obsession with having their status as victims of genocide recognised had become their raison d'être," noting that "this need on their part was treated with indifference by Turkish people," which he believed explained the enduring nature of Armenian trauma. He described the Turkish aspect of Armenian identity as "both a poison and an antidote." He published another article referencing the Armenian heritage of Atatürk's adopted daughter, which sparked intense backlash from extreme nationalist groups, including demonstrations, threatening letters and a criminal complaint against the applicant. A criminal court convicted the journalist of denigrating 'Turkishness' and imposed a suspended prison sentence. This conviction was upheld by the court of cassation.

Regarding the alleged violation of freedom of expression, the Court initially assessed whether the interference was prescribed by law. Although it acknowledged that the applicant's prosecution and conviction had a legal basis, namely, the offence of denigrating 'Turkishness' under the Turkish Penal Code, the Court raised concerns that the judiciary's broad and different interpretation of 'Turkishness' might compromise the accessibility and foreseeability of this provision.[218]

In unanimously finding a violation of Article 10, the ECtHR held that the national court had failed to conduct an adequate analysis of the journalist's articles. According to the ECtHR, the journalist's use of the term "poison" had not referred to "Turkish blood," as the court of cassation had interpreted, but rather to the "perception of Turkish people" by Armenians and the intense drive within the Armenian diaspora to secure Turkish recognition of the 1915 events as genocide. Article 10 did not justify restrictions on freedom of expression within the realm of political debate and matters of public interest.[219] As such, the Court found that 'contrary to the Government's position, these statements were in no way aimed at "the Turks" and could not amount to hate speech.'[220] It also noted that the articles, taken as a whole, did not incite violence, resistance or revolt.[221]

In terms of the use of criminal law, the Court noted that 'the dominant position which the Government occupies makes it necessary for it to display restraint in resorting to criminal proceedings, particularly where other means are available for replying to the unjustified attacks and criticisms of its adversaries or the media.'[222]

This observation is astute, particularly when compared to the Court's approach in numerous cases discussed earlier. The proportionality element

218 *Dink v Turkey* App nos. 2668/07, 6102/08, 30079/08, 7072/09 et 7124/09, para 116
219 *Dink* (n 218) para 133
220 *Dink* (n 218) para 128
221 *Dink* (n 218) para 134
222 *Dink* (n 218) para 133

in hate speech cases is frequently assessed in relation to the range of penalties prescribed under the relevant legal framework. For instance, where higher penalties are available but a lower sanction is imposed, the Court often deems this proportional without engaging in a deeper inquiry into whether criminal law itself is an appropriate mechanism for regulating speech. This tendency reflects a broader oversight into its jurisprudence. While proportionality is a cornerstone of the Court's analysis, its application sometimes lacks a critical examination of whether the use of criminal sanctions aligns with the principles of necessity and minimal interference inherent in a democratic society. Such a consideration is essential to ensure that speech-related offences are not unduly criminalised, thereby preserving the delicate balance between freedom of expression and the legitimate aims pursued by restrictions.

The Court also looked at the issue of positive obligations in relation to the right to freedom of expression, which requires that the state create

> an enabling environment by allowing for everyone to take part in public debate and express their thoughts and opinions free from fear even if such thoughts and opinions are contrary to those held by official authorities or a significant segment of the public and even if such opinions shock or disturb the public.[223]

Dink underscores the ECtHR's recognition of states' positive obligations to protect freedom of expression by fostering an enabling environment for public debate. The Court's critical stance on Turkey's failure to adequately analyse the journalist's articles and its rejection of overly broad interpretations of criminal provisions are significant. However, the heightened protection afforded in this case likely stems from the tragic context of Dink's murder, which underscored the severe consequences of failing to safeguard speech.

7 Speech Spoken by Others: Liability and Third-Party Speech in an Era of Digitalisation

Delfi AS v Estonia (2015) involved the liability of an internet news portal for offensive comments posted by readers beneath one of its online news articles. The applicant (the portal) argued that holding it liable for readers' comments infringed upon its right to freedom of expression. Delfi, one of the country's largest online news platforms, published an article in January 2006 about a ferry company's decision to change its ferry routes to certain islands. This route change caused ice to break in areas where ice roads, offering a more affordable and quicker alternative to ferry services, could have been formed in

223 *Dink* (n 218) para 137

the coming weeks. As a result, the opening of these ice roads was delayed by several weeks. Users were able to post comments under the article, and numerous readers left remarks that were allegedly offensive or threatening towards the ferry company and its owner. In April 2006, the owner of the ferry company (L) initiated legal proceedings against Delfi. The process was tumultuous. The county court dismissed L's claim on the grounds that the applicant's liability was excluded on a national law based on Directive 2000/31/EC/. The court considered that the comments section was to be distinguished from the journalistic section. The Tallinn Court of Appeal allowed an appeal by L, finding that the county court was wrong to find that Delfi had no liability under the aforementioned directive. The Supreme Court declined to hear an appeal by Delfi, and in 2008, the county court re-examined the case and found it in favour of L. It found that the comments were defamatory and held Delfi liable for their publication, awarding the ferry company's owner around 320 euros in damages. Delfi's appeal was subsequently dismissed by the Supreme Court of Estonia in June 2009.

The comments included statements such as:

> Fucking shitheads. . . .
>
> They bathe in money anyways thanks to that monopoly and State subsidies and now started to fear that cars may drive to the islands for a couple of days without anything filling their purses. burn in your own ship, sick Jew!
>
> Good that [L's] initiative has not broken down the lines of the web flamers. Go ahead, guys, [L.] into oven!

The court held by a majority that Delfi's liability constituted a justified and proportionate restriction of Article 10. This determination was based on several factors, namely, that the comments in question were highly offensive, the portal had failed to prevent their publication, it profited from hosting the comments, it allowed the commenters to remain anonymous and the fine imposed by the Estonian courts was deemed reasonable and not excessive. The Court found that the measures Delfi had implemented to remove comments which, in the Court's view, amounted to 'hate speech and speech inciting violence'[224] were insufficient and led to the six weeks' delay before removal. The ECtHR underlined that although the 'automatic word-based filter may have been useful in some instances, the facts of the present case demonstrate that it was insufficient for detecting comments whose content did not constitute protected speech under Article 10 of the Convention.'[225] The Court reiterated that the comments were of an 'extreme nature'[226] and also took into account

224 *Delfi AS v Estonia* App no 6459/09, (ECHR, 16 June 2015) para 162
225 *Delfi AS* (n 224) para 156
226 *Delfi AS* (n 224) para 162

that Delfi was a professionally managed new portal which runs on a commercial basis.[227] Although the Court did not delve deeply into the link between Delfi's status as a news portal and its duty to remove certain content, it can be inferred that Delfi's responsibilities to address hate speech promptly arose from its nature as (1) a professional news provider and (2) a profit-oriented business. The court's acknowledgment of Delfi's position as a major news outlet underpinned its distinction between unlawful censorship and the legitimate legal obligation to manage hate speech on its platform. The Court concluded that

> a large news portal's obligation to take effective measures to limit the dissemination of hate speech and speech inciting violence—the issue in the present case—can by no means be equated to 'private censorship.[228]

The Court also noted that the sanction imposed by the national court was 'moderate,'[229] recognising the importance of the internet as a tool for information dissemination and underscoring that it is 'mindful of the risk of harm posed by content and communications on the Internet.'[230]

In conclusion, the ECtHR held that Delfi, as a prominent, profit-driven professional news portal, had a legal obligation promptly to remove user-generated comments containing hate speech. A delay of six weeks in fulfilling this duty was deemed unjustifiable. The judgement has been characterised as 'unexpected,'[231] 'controversial'[232] and a restriction of the freedom of expression.[233] European Digital Rights[234] argued that this decision limits the rights of internet users, as it is 'not obvious why the Court appears to have given almost absolute priority to third-party rights ahead of the free speech rights of commentators.'[235] *Delfi* has important implications for the effectiveness of control systems in managing online hate speech, as it places a strict duty on news portals actively to monitor and promptly remove such content. In line with this reasoning, a notice-and-take-down procedure on social media

227 *Delfi AS* (n 224) para 162
228 *Delfi AS* (n 224) para 157
229 *Delfi AS* (n 224) para 162
230 *Delfi AS* (n 224) para 157
231 Tatiani Synodinou, 'Intermediaries' Liability for Online Copyright Infringement in the EU: Evolutions and Confusions' (2015) 31(1) Computer Law & Security Review 63
232 Hugh McCarthy, 'Is the Writing on the Wall for Online Service Providers? Liability for Hosting Defamatory User-Generated Content Under European and Irish Law' [2015] Hibernian Law Journal 39
233 McCarthy (n 232)
234 European Digital Rights <https://edri.org/>
235 European Digital Rights, 'Human Rights Violations Online' (2014) <https://edri.org/files/EDRI_CoE.pdf> accessed 1 September 2024

is not only required to be in place but must also operate swiftly to minimise harm to the targeted individual or group.

In the 2016 case of *Magyar Tartalomszolgáltatók Egyesülete and Index.hu Zrt v Hungary*, the ECtHR issued another judgement concerning intermediary liability on the internet. The applicants were two Hungarian websites; MTE, a self-regulatory body for Hungarian internet content providers, and INDEX, a major Hungarian news portal. Both sites allowed user-generated comments. In 2010, MTE published an opinion regarding two real estate management websites, which INDEX later republished. Users subsequently posted comments critical of the real estate companies on both MTE's website and INDEX's portal. However, in this instance, the Court unanimously found a violation of Article 10, distinguishing it from *Delfi* by observing that the comments in the case against Hungary were 'notably devoid of the pivotal element of hate speech,'[236] whilst MTE was a regulatory rather than a commercial body, and its professional nature 'was unlikely to provoke heated discussions on the Internet.'[237] The Court placed significant emphasis on the presence of hate speech in the comments as a key factor in determining there was no violation of Article 10. Additionally, in both cases, the applicants had a notice-and-take-down system in place. However, in *Delfi*, this system was deemed inadequate because it allowed the offensive material to remain publicly accessible for the six weeks, resulting in harm to the individual targeted.[238] In *MTE*, the Court concluded that a notice-and-take-down system was an effective means of balancing competing rights and indicated that a lower standard of responsiveness could be acceptable when the comments did not contain hate speech.[239]

Almost a decade later, the obligation for profit-making entities to monitor third-party comments set out in *Delfi* was extended to a public individual. In 2023, the ECtHR addressed this issue in *Sanchez v France*, a pivotal case that reshaped the contours of online responsibility. In this case, the applicant, a politician, was not convicted for his own statements but, rather, for his failure to promptly remove hateful comments posted by others on his Facebook page. At the relevant time, the applicant was the Mayor of Beaucaire and parliamentary candidate for the far-right Front National (Rassemblement National post-2018). He faced a criminal conviction and was fined for incitement to hatred or violence against individuals or groups based on their religion. This conviction stemmed from his failure to remove user comments beneath one of his Facebook posts. Agreeing with the findings of the Fifth Section of the

236 *Magyar Tartalomszolgáltatók Egyesülete and Index.hu ZRT v Hungary* App no 22947/13 (ECHR, 2 May 2016) para 70
237 *Magyar Tartalomszolgáltatók Egyesülete and Index.hu ZRT* (n 236) para 73
238 *Magyar Tartalomszolgáltatók Egyesülete and Index.hu ZRT* (n 236) para 152
239 *Magyar Tartalomszolgáltatók Egyesülete and Index.hu ZRT* (n 236) para 91

Court, the majority of the ECtHR's Grand Chamber found no violation of Article 10.

Sanchez had posted a comment regarding the website of his political opponent, FP, a member of the European Parliament. In response, a user, SB, commented that FP had

> transformed Nîmes into Algiers, there is not a street without a kebab shop and mosque; drug dealers and prostitutes reign supreme, no surprise he chose Brussels, capital of the new world order of sharia. . . . Thanks [F.] and kisses to Leila ([L.T]). . . . Finally, a blog that changes our life . . ."

Another user, LR, added three other comments directed at Muslims, such as allegations that Muslims sell their drugs without police intervention and that they throw rocks at cars belonging to "Whites."

The next day, LT confronted SB (whom she knew personally). He deleted his comment immediately after this confrontation.

LT wrote to the Nîmes public prosecutor to lodge a criminal complaint against Sanchez and the users who posted the offending comments. A day later, Sanchez posted a message on the wall of his Facebook account inviting users to "monitor the content of [their] comments" but did not remove already posted comments.

LT filed a criminal complaint against Sanchez and the two Facebook users responsible for the racist remarks. Following this complaint, Sanchez posted a new message, urging readers to be mindful of their comments' content; however, he did not moderate or delete the previous comments. The French public prosecutor subsequently initiated an investigation and supported LT's complaint. In response, Sanchez explained that he could not monitor the large number of comments posted each week on his Facebook wall. He was convicted for incitement to hatred and discrimination and summoned before the criminal court. Sanchez's criminal liability was established in his role as the producer of a publicly accessible website, as he failed promptly to remove the offensive comments once he became aware of them. The applicant, SB and LR, were ordered to pay a fine of EUR 4,000 each. SB and the applicant were ordered to jointly pay LT EUR 1,000 in compensation. The applicant did not receive any electoral disqualification. Sanchez appealed to the court of appeal, which upheld the first instance decision but reduced the applicant's fine to EUR 3,000 and ordered him to pay LT EUR 1000 for costs for the appeal proceedings. He then appealed to the French court of cassation, which dismissed his appeal.

In examining whether there was a violation of Sanchez's Article 10 rights, the ECtHR found the comments to be 'clearly unlawful.'[240] The Court, at

240 *Sanchez v France* App no 45581/15 (ECHR, 15 May 2023) para 86

chamber level and then before the Grand Chamber, adopted the *Féret* paradigm that incitement to hatred

> did not necessarily require the calling of a specific act of violence or another criminal act. Attacks on persons committed through insults, ridicule or defamation aimed at specific population groups or incitation to discrimination, as in this case, sufficed for the authorities to give priority to fighting hate speech when confronted by the irresponsible use of freedom of expression which undermined people's dignity, or even their safety.[241]

The ECtHR observed that by keeping his Facebook wall public, Sanchez assumed responsibility for the comments posted there.[242] Notably, Sanchez did post a message urging users to be mindful of their comments' content. The ECtHR applied its principles from *Delfi*, which concerned a news portal's responsibility for content moderation, to *Sanchez*, extending similar obligations to him as an individual politician. Although the Grand Chamber acknowledged that Sanchez, as an individual, differed from a news portal and that his 'situation cannot be compared to that of an Internet news portal,'[243] it nonetheless found 'no reason to hold otherwise in the present case.'[244] The Court elaborated that Article 10's 'duties and responsibilities' clause extends to politicians using social media for political purposes, stressing that 'the applicant was not merely a private individual.'[245] In reaching its decision, it also looked at the impact of online hate speech, noting that it can be quickly disseminated and that imposing liability for such speech is a good avenue through which a balance between Article 10 and Article 8 on the rights to private and family life can be struck.[246] The Court made statements on the impacts of online hate speech in a rather emphatic manner but did not accompany that with any empirical findings or other research on the matter. Given the criminal nature of the penalty, the fundamental nature of expression and the fact that the speech in question was not his, further analysis into online hate speech and its impact would have been expected.

Slovenian judge Bošnjak dissented, finding it inappropriate to prosecute Sanchez as a producer when the authors of the comments had already been convicted. Additionally, Judges Wojtyczek, from Poland, and Zünd, from Switzerland, issued a joint dissent, contending that the French government's interference with Mr Sanchez's freedom of expression did not meet the standard of foreseeability. Judge Ravarani from Luxembourg expressed partial agreement

241 *Sanchez* (n 240) para 155
242 *Sanchez* (n 240) para 155
243 *Sanchez* (n 240) para 122
244 *Sanchez* (n 240)
245 *Sanchez* (n 240) para 180
246 *Sanchez* (n 240) para 160

with the Court's reasoning but, ultimately, could not support the judgement's outcome. He concurred that the interference with the applicant's freedom of expression was lawful, and that the domestic courts had not violated Article 10 of the Convention concerning comments on the applicant's Facebook wall. However, Judge Ravarani opposed holding the applicant liable for a comment by user SB that had been deleted by the user just a day after posting. He argued that it was unreasonable to fault the applicant for not removing a comment that was self-deleted within 24 hours. Emphasising the principle of strict interpretation in criminal law, he criticised the majority's reasoning as 'an unacceptable extension of a criminal incrimination by an international court which constantly repeats that it is not a court of fourth instance.'[247]

As such, in *Sanchez*, the ECtHR permitted the criminalisation of expression not made by the applicant himself but by users commenting on his post, due to his failure to remove these comments even after he urged users to moderate their remarks and even after one of the comments was removed by the user. In this case, the ECtHR applied principles from *Delfi* to a (public) individual user, specifically assigning *Delfi* responsibilities to the applicant due to his political status. In the framework of this status, the Court reasoned that, although political parties generally enjoy broad freedom of expression in electoral contexts, this latitude does not encompass racist or xenophobic speech. Politicians, it held, bear a heightened duty to prevent hate speech, as has been reaffirmed in various cases. For instance, the *Sanchez* court referred to *Féret*, where the ECtHR stressed that 'political speeches that stir up hatred based on religious, ethnic or cultural prejudices represent a threat to social peace and political stability in democratic states.'[248] The Court further highlighted that politicians must exercise caution in their public statements to avoid inciting intolerance. However, the critical distinction between *Féret* and *Sanchez* lies in the nature of the speech at issue: in *Féret*, the applicant was directly responsible for the offensive statements, while here the applicant was held accountable for failing to regulate the statements of others.

8 Applicants Who Are the Victims of Hate Speech and the Role of Positive Obligations

Unlike instruments such as Article 4 of the International Convention on the Elimination of All Forms of Racial Discrimination (ICERD) or Article 20 of the ICCPR, the ECHR does not explicitly require the prohibition of certain forms of expression. Article 10 of the ECHR guarantees the right to freedom of expression for all individuals. However, this right is subject to limitations, including the protection of the rights and reputations of others. While Article 10 permits states to impose restrictions on freedom of expression under

247 *Sanchez* (n 240), Dissenting Opinion of Judge Ravarani para 5
248 *Sanchez* (n 240) para 155

specific conditions, it does not explicitly mandate them to do so. Nevertheless, cases such as *Aksu v Turkey* (2012) and *Beizaras and Levickas v Lithuania* (2020), as well as the almost-identical cases of *Gutman v Bulgaria* (2012) and *Budinova and Chaprazov v Bulgaria* (2012), as will be discussed later, suggest a shift in this approach.

In *Aksu v Turkey* (2012), the applicant, who was of Roma origin, argued that government-funded publications, including a book and two dictionaries, contained anti-Roma expressions which he believed, attacked his identity. He claimed these statements violated his rights under Article 8, on private and family life, in conjunction with the prohibition of discrimination under Article 14 of the ECHR and sought compensation for non-pecuniary damages. He also requested the confiscation, ban on publication and distribution of the book. The ECtHR, however, dismissed his application.

In a book funded by the Ministry of Education with the title *The Gypsies of Turkey*, a professor described the customs and lifestyle of the Roma minority in Turkey. Passages included, amongst others, characterising Roma persons as being involved in "illegal activities," referring to them as "thieves, pickpockets, swindlers, robbers, usurers, beggars, drug dealers, prostitutes and brothel keepers," and as "polygamist and aggressive." The applicant argued that such statements insulted the ethnic group he belonged to. He also filed a complaint against definitions in the *Turkish dictionary for pupils* and the *Turkish Dictionary*, which he found had negative, discriminatory and prejudiced connotations and requested their removal. Some of the entries regarding the word "Gypsy" included:

> "Gypsy" (*Çingene*): 1. an ethnic group or person belonging to an ethnic group originating from India, whose members lead a nomadic way of life and are widely dispersed in the world. 2. (metaphorically) miserly.
>
> "Gypsy tent" (*Çingene çergesi*) (metaphorically): a dirty and poor place.
>
> "Gypsy wedding" (*Çingene düğünü*): a crowded and noisy meeting.
>
> "Gypsy fight" (*Çingene kavgası*): a verbal fight in which vulgar language is used.

While the Ministry of Education and the Turkish Language Society amended their dictionaries at his request, the Language Association did not. He proceeded with the use of the court system, but his attempts at a domestic level failed.

In assessing the application, the ECtHR weighed the applicant's Article 8 right against Article 10 considerations. Within this framework, it determined that the book stemmed from academic research and lacked any intent to insult the Roma community.[249] Moreover, the Court noted that the book explicitly sought to illuminate the largely misunderstood Roma community in Turkey,

249 *Aksu v Turkey* App nos. 4149/04 & 41029/04 (15 March 2012) para 32

a group often subject to prejudice. In relation to the dictionaries, the Court found that labels denoting that expressions were 'pejorative' or 'insulting' would have been preferred, but that the nature of the expression was not sufficient for the Court to take a different stance than the national courts.

The Court recognised that negative stereotyping of a group can impact that group's sense of identity and, by extension, their right to private and family life.[250] Furthermore, it noted that Article 8 imposes a positive obligation on states to ensure the effective respect of private and family life, including the adoption of measures, even when it comes to relations of individuals between themselves. While not finding a violation of Article 8 in this case, the Court did emphasise the need for states, in appropriate contexts, to adopt positive measures to counteract harmful stereotyping, opening the way for this to happen in hate speech cases some years later, specifically *Beizaras and Levickas v Lithuania* (2020), *Behar and Gutman v Bulgaria* (2021) and *Budinova and Chaprazov v Bulgaria* (2022).

Beizaras and Levickas v Lithuania (2020) involved a case in which two men shared a public photograph of themselves kissing on Facebook, which quickly went viral. The first applicant shared a photograph on his Facebook page showing a same-sex kiss between himself and the second applicant. The image was publicly accessible, visible not only to his Facebook friends but also to the wider public. According to the applicants, the photo went viral, with more than 2,400 likes and more than 800 comments. Examples of the comments included thus:

- "These faggots fucked up my lunch; if I was allowed to, I would shoot every single one of them."
- "Scum!!!!!! Into the gas chamber with the pair of them."
- "Hey fags—I'll buy you a free honeymoon trip to the crematorium."
- "Oh for fuck's sake—get the fuck out of Lithuania and don't shame us, you fucking capon; we should put your head under a car and into the noose, you fucking faggot."

The applicants submitted a written request to an NGO working on LBGT rights, the LGL Association, of which they were members, asking it to inform the Prosecutor General's Office of the hateful comments posted under the photograph shared on the first applicant's Facebook page. They requested that this be done in the association's name, arguing that the comments were not only degrading and harmful to their dignity but also 'incited violence and physically violent treatment' and were, thus, frightening for them and homosexual people in general. The Prosecutor's Office decided not to initiate a pre-trial investigation. The LGL Association appealed this decision at the district court, which rejected the case, agreeing with the decision of the

250 *Aksu* (n 249) para 58

prosecutor that the authors of the contested comments had 'chosen improper words' to express their opposition to homosexual people. The LGL Association lodged a further appeal with the regional court, which also dismissed the case and emphasised that the first applicant had shared the photograph publicly rather than limiting its visibility to friends or 'like-minded people,' an option available on the Facebook platform. This action, the court suggested, could be seen as 'an attempt to deliberately provoke or shock individuals with different views, or to encourage negative comments.'

The ECtHR unanimously found that the applicant's experience with the state's reaction to the hateful speech constituted a violation of Article 8 in conjunction with Article 14. In its judgement, the ECtHR noted that the comments 'affected the applicant's psychological well-being and dignity,'[251] and that the comments included 'undisguised calls for violence'[252] against the applicants and the homosexual community. It continued to underline that those calls emanated from the

> very same discriminatory state of mind [that] was at the core of the failure on the part of the relevant public authorities to discharge their positive obligation to investigate in an effective manner.[253]

The ECtHR argued that the authorities failed to acknowledge the bias involved and that without a strict approach to this,

> prejudice-motivated crimes would unavoidably be treated on an equal footing with ordinary cases without such overtones, and the resultant indifference would be tantamount to official acquiescence or even connivance in hate crimes.[254]

The ECtHR found the comments to constitute 'hate speech and incitement to violence,' and that this 'may in principle require the State to take certain positive measures.'[255]

In 2021, the ECtHR decided on two almost-identical cases on the same day, namely, *Behar and Gutman v Bulgaria* and *Budinova and Chaprazov v Bulgaria*. The applicants Behar and Gutman, who are Jewish, and Budinova and Chaprazov, who are Roma, brought legal action against Siderov, a xenophobic politician, for his extremist propaganda targeting their communities. Siderov, the founding leader of the far-right nationalist Ataka Party and

251 *Beizaras and Levickas v Lithuania* (2020) App no 41288/15 (ECHR, 14 January 2020) para 117
252 *Beizaras and Levickas* (n 251) para 129
253 *Beizaras and Levickas* (n 251)
254 *Beizaras and Levickas* (n 251) para 155
255 *Beizaras and Levickas* (n 251) para 125

a former journalist, entered Parliament in 2005 and used various platforms to promote radical anti-minority rhetoric. In civil discrimination proceedings, the applicants claimed that Siderov's actions amounted to harassment and incitement to discrimination against their communities, seeking an apology and an injunction requiring him to abstain from such conduct. However, the courts dismissed their claims on the grounds of Siderov's right to freedom of expression.

Adopting essentially identical reasoning in both cases, the Court found a violation of Article 8 in conjunction with Article 14, the non-discrimination clause, concluding that the domestic courts had failed to fulfil their positive obligation to provide redress for the discriminatory public statements made by the politician. To evaluate the severity of such statements and determine their applicability under Articles 8 and 14, the Court looked at the groups targeted by the speech and the content and impact of the speech. To do so, it looked at several factors, with no single factor deemed determinative. These included the size, homogeneity and vulnerability of the group and status; the content of the statements, in particular, 'the degree to which they could convey a negative statement about the group as a whole, and the specific content of that stereotype';[256] the form and context in which the statements were made; the extent of their reach; the status of the speaker; the potential impact on the core identity and dignity of the group; and the broader socio-political context.[257] In light of the preceding test, the Court determined that the statements in *Behar* specifically targeted Jews as a group, recognising them as a vulnerable minority. It found that the statements constituted 'extreme negative stereotyping meant to vilify Jews and to stir up prejudice and hatred towards them'[258] The statements were described as 'virulently anti-Semitic,'[259] involving 'timeworn anti-Semitic narratives,'[260] including 'denying the Holocaust and casting it as a story contrived as [a] means for financial gain.'[261] Similarly, in *Budinova*, the Court found that the statements targeted Roma, a group 'long acknowledged as disadvantaged and vulnerable, and in need of special protection.'[262] The statements were 'deliberately couched in inflammatory terms,' portraying Roma as 'exceptionally prone to crime and depravity.' The Court noted that the statements depicted the Roma as 'immoral social parasites' who exploited their rights, 'lived off the back of the Bulgarian majority,' engaged in systematic violence and crime and 'aimed to take over the country.' These statements were considered by the Court to constitute 'extreme negative stereotyping

256 *Behar and Gutman v Bulgaria* App no 29335/13 (ECHR, 16 February 2021) para 67; *Budinova and Chaprazov v Bulgaria* App no 12567/13 (ECHR, 16 February 2021) para 63
257 *Behar* (n 256) para 60; *Budinova and Chaprazov* (n 256) para 56
258 *Behar* (n 256) para 71
259 *Behar* (n 256) para 69
260 *Behar* (n 256)
261 *Behar* (n 256) para 70
262 *Budinova and Chaprazov* (n 256) para 64

meant to vilify Roma . . . and to stir up prejudice and hatred.'[263] Given the speaker's position as a rising parliamentary party leader with significant media presence, the Court found that his statements had a substantial impact on the identity and self-worth of Jewish and Roma individuals.[264] In the preceding context, the ECtHR found that the domestic courts were obligated to balance the applicants' right to seek redress for the statements against the speaker's right to freedom of expression.[265] It considered that the domestic courts placed significant emphasis on protecting the freedom of expression and failed to perform the necessary balancing exercise between freedom of expression and the right to private and family life. Specifically, the court noted that

> by in effect ascribing considerable weight to Mr Siderov's right to freedom of expression in relation to the statements impugned by the applicants, and by playing down the effect of those statements on the applicants as ethnic Jews/ethnic Roma living in Bulgaria . . . the Bulgarian courts failed to carry out the requisite balancing exercise in line with the criteria laid down in the Court's case-law.[266]

Interestingly, and related to the aforementioned, the ECtHR noted that with regards to the anti-Semitic speech, the 'specific historical context in respect of Bulgaria, as opposed to that in respect of other European States, matters little in that regard,'[267] demonstrating the Court's intolerance of anti-Semitic speech in a context without a substantial history of anti-Semitism compared to other countries.

Thus, the development of the ECtHR's jurisprudence on positive obligations in hate speech cases finds its roots in *Aksu v Turkey*, where the Grand Chamber established a pivotal precedent under Article 8. In this case, the Court recognised that negative stereotyping of Roma individuals could harm their identity and dignity and, therefore, their rights related to their private and family life. Although it ultimately found no violation, emphasising the academic nature of the impugned publications and the absence of intent to insult, the case laid the foundation for a framework of positive obligations requiring states to counteract harmful stereotypes. Building on *Aksu*, the Court's reasoning evolved in *Beizaras and Levickas*. Here, the focus shifted to homophobic hate speech targeting two identifiable individuals whose photograph of a kiss posted on Facebook provoked hateful and violent comments. The Lithuanian authorities' refusal to investigate these comments led the Court to conclude a violation of Articles 8, 13, and 14. The Court found that the

263 *Budinova and Chaprazov* (n 256) para 65
264 *Behar* (n 256) para 72; *Budinova and Chaprazov* (n 256) paras 67–68
265 *Behar* (n 256) para 100; *Budinova and Chaprazov* (n 256) para 89
266 *Behar* (n 256) para 105; *Budinova and Chaprazov* (n 256) para 94
267 *Behar* (n 256) para 105

state's inaction amounted to acquiescence in discriminatory hate speech and emphasised the obligation to take proactive measures to protect vulnerable individuals from such harm. This case marked a critical step in extending positive obligations to hate speech involving identifiable victims. By 2021, the Court further advanced this framework in the Bulgarian cases, where hate speech targeted vulnerable groups, namely, Jews and Roma, without identifiable victims. Unlike earlier cases, the Court in *Behar and Gutman v Bulgaria* and *Budinova and Chaprazov v Bulgaria* focused on the broader impact of generalised stereotyping on community members. In the Bulgarian cases, the ECtHR found a violation of Article 8 in conjunction with Article 14, even in the absence of direct victims. The progression from *Aksu* to the Bulgarian cases highlights the ECtHR's growing recognition of the harmful effects of hate speech and stereotypes on vulnerable groups. By extending the scope of positive obligations from individual victims to entire communities, the Court has underscored states' responsibilities to combat harmful expression proactively.

In the Bulgarian cases, the ECtHR articulated a rather coherent methodical framework to evaluate the impact of stereotypes on targeted communities, considering factors such as the vulnerability of the targeted groups, the content and context of the statements, the speaker's influence and the potential of the speech to harm the dignity and identity of group members. Such a detailed test has not yet been seen in the context of Article 10 cases with snippets of similar elements articulated within certain cases. However, this could be a welcome development to assist with the improvement of jurisprudential explanation and consistency. By refining its methodology, the Court can better navigate the delicate balance between safeguarding freedom of expression and addressing the harm caused by hate speech, reinforcing its commitment to the foundational principles of the ECHR.

The aforementioned jurisprudence highlights a progressive expansion of the ECtHR's framework for positive obligations. By recognising the harmful impact of stereotyping and hate speech on vulnerable groups, the Court has paved the way for states to take proactive measures to combat such expression. However, this evolution also raises questions about the limits of state responsibility and the potential encroachment on freedom of expression. While the Court's intention to protect vulnerable groups is commendable, the previous approach can inadvertently empower states proactively to suppress dissenting or unpopular viewpoints under the guise of combatting harm. For example, the broad discretion afforded to states in defining what constitutes harmful expression risks embedding state-endorsed narratives within hate speech regulation. Imposing positive obligation on states in the field of protecting people from hate speech creates a fertile ground for state viewpoints to dominate the discourse on hate speech, allowing governments to shield their actions under the rhetoric of protecting vulnerable groups. In such instances, the risk of conflating genuine harm with state preferences becomes acute, as seen in *Féret*, where inflammatory political speech, critical of immigration policies was curtailed on the basis of potential societal division, despite limited evidence of actual harm. This trend raises concerns about the erosion of the ECtHR's supervisory role in ensuring that restrictions are proportionate and grounded in clear evidence rather than subjective interpretations of harm. Moreover, enhanced state obligations can affect Article 19 rights if states become increasingly concerned of future adjudication against them for not fulfilling such obligations, making them hypervigilant and potentially overrestrictive when it comes to speech.

9 Any Other Business: The Right to Boycott and the Issue of Speech?

In *Willem v France* (2009), the applicant, the mayor of Seclin at the material time, called for a boycott of Israeli products in his town as a response to the policies of Israel's prime minister. He was fined 1,000 euros for inciting discrimination. In this case, the first instance court acquitted the applicant on the grounds that his call for boycott targeted products rather than individuals and that his call for boycott was an exercise of his freedom of expression. The court of appeal overturned this decision, finding that the call to boycott products from a specific origin impeded the economic operations of producers by targeting them on the basis of their national affiliation. The court of appeal underlined that 'the applicant's motive, to protest against the Israeli Prime Minister's policy, was irrelevant.' The court of cassation affirmed this line of reasoning, determining that the case did not constitute an expression of opinion but rather amounted to 'an incitement to discrimination.' The ECtHR held, by a majority, that there was no violation of Article 10. The Court reasoned that the speech in question constituted incitement to discrimination.

In its Article 10 analysis, the ECtHR started by underlining that the freedom of expression is of particular importance for elected representatives, and that any interference thereof must undergo strict scrutiny,[268] while political debate should not be restricted without compelling reasons.[269] Nevertheless, the ECtHR separated this case from regular political debate, noting that the applicant 'was not convicted for his political opinions but for the incitement to a discriminatory act.'[270] Also, the fact that the boycott was announced by the applicant rather than put to a vote meant, for the ECtHR, that the applicant could not have supported free discussion on a matter of general interest.[271] The ECtHR highlighted that the mayor announced the boycott at a council meeting and disseminated the call on the municipality's website, with the latter further intensifying the discriminatory nature of the applicant's speech.[272]

268 *Willem v France* App no 10883/05 (ECHR, 16 July 2009) para 32
269 *Willem* (n 268) para 33
270 *Willem* (n 268) para 35
271 *Willem* (n 268) para 38
272 *Willem* (n 268) para 36

Moreover, it held that the mayor should be neutral and not discriminate, stating specifically:

> [A]s mayor, the applicant had duties and responsibilities. He must, in particular, maintain a certain neutrality and have a duty of reservation in his actions when these engage the local authority that he represents as a whole. In this regard, a mayor manages the public funds of the municipality and must not encourage members to spend them according to a discriminatory logic.

In his dissenting opinion, Czech judge Jungwiert noted that the applicant's call for boycott fell within the framework of public debate, which can include exaggeration and even provocation. The opinion proceeded to expand on the lack of contextualisation by French courts, noting that they considered neither the applicant's intent nor the fact that the statements were made within the broader context of escalating violence in the Israel–Palestine conflict.[273]

While the Court emphasised the heightened responsibilities of elected officials to promote neutrality and avoid discriminatory conduct, its reasoning reveals potential vulnerabilities in prioritising state-defined narratives over contextual analysis. The ECtHR's framing of the boycott as incitement to discrimination, without engaging with the broader political and historical context of the Israel–Palestine conflict, as noted by the dissenting opinion, illustrates the risks of overly narrow assessments. This approach leaves little room for nuanced consideration of the intent and impact of the speech, thereby risking a chilling effect on legitimate public debate. As the dissenting opinion cautions, a failure to contextualise speech and assess intent risks legitimising restrictive measures that may suppress unpopular but legitimate discourse.

Baldassi and Others v France (2020) involved 11 members of the 'Palestine 68 Collective,' a French organisation supporting the Boycott, Divestment, Sanctions (BDS) movement, advocating, among other things, for the boycott of Israeli products, who were penalised for incitement to discrimination and fined. The ECtHR unanimously held that the restrictions imposed by France were not necessary in a democratic society and consequently found a violation of Article 10.

On two occasions, the applicants participated in a demonstration inside a supermarket, during which they placed products they believed to be of Israeli origin into shopping trolleys and called for a boycott. They were subsequently fined, as their actions were deemed to constitute incitement to discrimination.

The ECtHR determined that a *boycott* constitutes a form of expressing political opinions. While it acknowledged that France's actions aimed to protect the commercial rights of producers and suppliers of goods from Israel, a legitimate objective, such a restriction was deemed unnecessary in a democratic society.

273 *Willem* (n 268) Dissenting Opinion of Judge Jungwiert

Consequently, the measures France imposed on the activists violated Article 10. The Court differentiated this case from *Willem*, where the applicant, a mayor, had called for a boycott of Israeli goods. Due to his official status, he held a specific duty to remain neutral.

The ECtHR looked at issues such as the role of boycotts, the unacceptability of anti-Semitism in whatever form, underlining that 'it is well established and worth repeating that forms of expression which serve as a screen or call for anti-Semitism do not fall within the protection guaranteed by the Convention.'[274] It also underlined the importance of public discussion on subjects of general interest, such as respect for public international law by Israel.[275]

In terms of boycotting as a form of expression, the ECtHR held that it

> constitutes a particular method of exercising freedom of expression in that it combines the expression of a protesting opinion and the incitement to differential treatment so that, depending on the circumstances which characterize it, it is likely to constitute a call to the discrimination of others. However, the call to discriminate is part of the call to intolerance, which, along with the call to violence and the call to hatred, is one of the limits that should not be exceeded under any circumstances in the context of the exercise of freedom of expression. . . . However inciting to treat differently does not necessarily amount to inciting discrimination.[276]

As such, the ECtHR's finding in the case underscores the importance of distinguishing between political expression through boycott and actual incitement to discrimination. By recognising the boycott as a legitimate means of expressing political opinions, the Court reaffirmed the broad scope of Article 10 in protecting freedom of expression, even when that expression includes calls for differential treatment. In *Baldassi*, while acknowledging France's interest in safeguarding commercial rights, the Court found that such restrictions were not necessary in a democratic society and, therefore, constituted a violation of Article 10. Additionally, by contrasting this case with *Willem*, where the applicant held public office, the ECtHR highlighted that private individuals do not share the same duty of neutrality. To do so, it equated the boycotting of Israeli products.

Conclusion

The ECtHR's approach to hate speech involving protected characteristics reflects an ongoing struggle to balance freedom of expression with the imperatives of Convention values. Cases like *Féret* and *Vejdeland* demonstrate the

274 *Baldassi and others v France* (2020) App no 15271/16 and 6 others, para 41
275 *Baldassi and others* (n 274) para 78
276 *Baldassi and others* (n 274) para 64

Court's readiness to restrict speech that fosters distrust or prejudice toward vulnerable groups, even when no direct incitement to harm is present. Yet this broad approach risks eroding the fundamental protections of Article 10. The Court's preventative rationale, restricting speech based on speculative harm rather than proven consequences, has led to worrying trends even when the impact is minimal, as seen in *Lilliendahl,* where a limited-audience comment resulted in a criminal penalty. Nevertheless, inconsistency marks the approach in *Karatas,* too, where the smaller reach of poetic expression contributed to a finding of an Article 10 violation. These inconsistencies highlight the need for clearer standards and a more rigorous harm analysis in hate speech cases.

In *Féret,* the Court ruled that expressions involving insult, ridicule or prejudice could be restricted if they foster distrust or hatred toward protected groups. This marked a significant broadening of what kind of hate speech can be prohibited, as reaffirmed in cases such as *Vejdeland.* Likewise, in *Lilliendahl,* derogatory online comments about LGBTQ+ individuals led the Court to uphold criminal penalties, despite the limited reach of these remarks. These cases illustrate the ECtHR's readiness to combat prejudicial or insulting speech with minimal consideration for Article 10. Specifically, these rulings have permitted restrictions on speech based on potential harm rather than actual incitement. This author's position is that the Court's threshold for limiting speech has fallen too low, enabling restrictions on expressions far removed from calls to violence or direct hatred. This expansive approach risks undermining freedom of expression, particularly when applied without consistent legal standards or a clear evidentiary basis. In cases that fall in the low-hatred threshold paradigm, offensive speech alone has been sufficient to justify restrictions under Article 10. However, in some, but not all, cases involving criticism of religious doctrines or beliefs, such as *Ibragim Ibragimov and Others,* the ECtHR has adopted a different stance. The Court emphasised that

> the mere fact a remark may be perceived as offensive or insulting by certain individuals or groups does not mean it constitutes hate speech. While such feelings may be understandable, they alone cannot determine the boundaries of freedom of expression.

However, as discussed earlier, the Court highlighted that it has been 'particularly sensitive towards sweeping statements attacking or casting in a negative light an entire ethnic, religious or other group.'[277] The approach in *Norwood* challenges the idea that criticism of institutions is treated more leniently if the court can find a connection with unprotected characteristics. In that case, Article 17 was invoked to exclude protection for a poster stating, "Islam out of Britain," which was classified as a 'general vehement attack' against all Muslims

277 *Atamanchuk* (n 64) para 51

in the United Kingdom. To complicate matters further, it is unclear why Article 17 was used in *Norwood* but not in *Féret*. Did calling Islam "the conqueror" and advocating for Belgium to purge itself of Islam for self-protection not amount to a vehement general attack? The Court in *Norwood* did not provide what elements are necessary for the finding of such an attack. The jurisprudence is also marked by contradictory rulings. For example, Article 17, the 'prohibition of abuse of rights' clause, was applied in *Norwood*, but not in *Féret*, despite similarly provocative statements. Nevertheless, despite the major shortfalls associated with the application of Article 17 to some of the cases discussed earlier, section 1 of this chapter regrettably underscores that, even when addressing such issues through Article 10, the Court has fallen short in safeguarding free speech in cases involving alleged hate speech.

The treatment of political speech has also varied significantly. In *Erbakan*, the Court found a violation of Article 10, despite inflammatory religious and political rhetoric, contrasting sharply with its restrictive stance in *Féret* and *Le Pen*. Without substantively explaining these variations, the anti-government speech compared to speech targeting protected characteristics is assumingly the reason. Rather than being led by sensitivities, the ECtHR's assessments should be anchored in rigorous and clearly established legal principles, rather than appearing discretionary or unpredictable. The absence of consistent legal criteria allows states a wide margin of appreciation, risking selective enforcement of hate speech laws based on political or societal pressures.

The ECtHR's preventative rationale, that being restricting speech based on its potential harm rather than proven consequences, also raises concerns. In *Smajić*, for example, online comments about ethnic conflict prompted severe legal sanctions, even though the applicant's statements did not directly incite violence. This preventative approach prioritises social cohesion but risks suppressing legitimate public debate and dissent. Additionally, criminal sanctions should be reserved for speech that poses a clear and imminent danger, not for speculative risks or offensive remarks. Applying legal penalties to offensive but non-violent speech risks chilling public discourse, as seen in *Zemmour*, where the Court failed to consider the broader consequences of silencing a politically significant figure. Despite acknowledging the importance of political speech, the Court has not adequately addressed the chilling effect its rulings may have on democratic debate and public discourse more broadly.

The Court's reluctance to engage with empirical jurisprudential evidence on the effectiveness of hate speech laws further compounds the previously described *status quo*. Studies discussed in Chapter 2 suggest that silencing offensive views can exacerbate social tensions, transform speakers into martyrs and prevent counterspeech. Despite these realities, the ECtHR has shown little interest in considering such broader societal impacts when determining the necessity and proportionality of restrictions. Ultimately, the ECtHR's approach reflects an assumed but unexamined tension between protecting Convention values, social cohesion, vulnerable groups and preserving freedom of expression. The Court's efforts to combat hate speech have led to a fragmented jurisprudence, where legal standards remain ambiguous, and rulings often lack clear, evidence-based justifications. This creates legal uncertainty and raises concerns about the necessity and the proportionality of speech restrictions. To reconcile its commitment to equality and dignity with its duty to uphold freedom of expression, the Court must adopt a sound definitional framework of hate speech, clearer thresholds and research-informed findings applied equally across the board, with context framed responsibly in order to avoid the lack of clarity amongst cases and their outcomes, as seen in several cases earlier. Strengthening these standards is crucial for ensuring that Article 10 continues to serve as a robust safeguard for democratic expression in an increasingly pluralistic and digital world. This chapter ultimately argues that the ECtHR's approach to hate speech requires recalibration.

5 Hate Speech Jurisprudence

Dealing with Totalitarianism, Genocide Denial and Violence Before the European Court of Human Rights

Introduction

This chapter addresses cases involving totalitarianism, genocide denial and violence. The cases involving violence do not, for the most part, target protected characteristics but are included because the Court has, rather oddly, referred to hate speech in several of them. However, this classification is arguably incorrect, as *hate speech*, by definition, targets protected characteristics, whether through racism or relevant phenomena discussed in Chapter 1; Holocaust denial, which the Court equates to a form of anti-Semitism, or totalitarian speech, which targets the victims of such regimes. The jurisprudence examined in this chapter reveals strengths and weaknesses, but also inconsistencies in the ECtHR's approach to the freedom of expression. While the Court has been resolute in excluding Nazi propaganda and Holocaust denial, its treatment of Communist symbols, genocide denial beyond the Holocaust and politically charged (and sometimes violent) speech is less predictable. The selective application of Article 17 for Holocaust denial and Nazi-related speech, with only a few exceptions to this rule, leads to implicit hierarchies of historical recognition. Such disparities not only raise concerns about the uniformity of Convention protections but may also erode the Court's role as a neutral arbiter of human rights. By exploring relevant cases, this chapter provides a comprehensive analysis of the ECtHR's evolving standards on hate speech as well as older cases heard before the obsolete European Commission on Human Rights (EComHR/Commission). It highlights the challenges of balancing historical memory, democratic stability and individual freedoms, while striving for legal consistency and justice in a multicultural and politically diverse Europe.

1 Totalitarianism

The ECtHR and the EComHR have dealt with balancing cases which involve freedom of expression under Article 10 of the European Convention on Human Rights (ECHR/Convention) against the need to combat totalitarian ideologies. Central to this effort is Article 17 of the ECHR, the 'prohibition of abuse of rights' clause, which prohibits the destruction of the rights

DOI: 10.4324/9781003560548-6

and freedoms set out in the Convention. This provision has been invoked most consistently in cases involving expressions linked to Nazism. This section examines how the ECtHR's differential treatment of symbols and expressions tied to various totalitarian ideologies reflects deeper jurisprudential tensions, highlighting inconsistencies in the balancing of historical sensitivity, democratic values and freedom of expression.

1.1 Totalitarian Organisations

In *Kühnen v Germany* (1988), the applicant held a leadership role within ANS/NA, an organisation reportedly aiming to revive the banned National Socialist Party (NSDAP) in Germany. In this capacity, he produced and distributed several publications promoting extremist ideologies. One such document, titled "Frankfurt Appeal," called for the establishment of an independent, socialist "Greater Germany." Another pamphlet declared: "We are called 'Neo-Nazis'! So what! . . . We are against: bigwigs, bolshevists, Zionists, crooks, cheats and parasites. We are against: capitalism, communism, Zionism, estrangement by means of masses of foreign workers, destruction of the environment." As a result, the applicant was convicted of creating and distributing propaganda linked to an unconstitutional organisation and received a prison sentence of three years and four months. The EComHR held that the applicant's speech was fundamentally incompatible with the values enshrined in the Convention. It determined that, by invoking his right to freedom of expression, the applicant was effectively seeking to undermine the very rights and freedoms the Convention aims to protect and that the rights enshrined in the Convention 'are best maintained . . . by an effective political democracy. The Commission considered that the applicant's policy clearly contains elements of racial and religious discrimination.'[1] The Commission enforced Article 17 and found the application to be manifestly ill-founded. The same strategy was followed in *BH, MW, HP and GK v Austria* (1989), which involved National Socialism. The applicants were convicted of engaging in activities motivated by National Socialist ideology, including the production and dissemination of pamphlets denying the Nazi genocide of six million Jews. As members and leaders of the Aktion Neue Rechte party, they advocated for the reintroduction of traditional Nazi songs and titles within the organisation. They were sentenced to conditional terms of imprisonment under the National Socialism Prohibition Act, receiving sentences of 9, 3, 18 and 12 months, respectively. The EComHR found that, considering Austria's historical context and the underlying purpose of the Convention, the corresponding penalties imposed on the applicants were justified. It determined that Austria's measures were consistent with the limitations outlined in Article 10(2), interpreting all relevant provisions through the lens of Article 17. It noted that 'in view of the

1 *Kühnen v Germany* (1988) App no 12194/86 (EComHR, 12 May 1988)

historical past forming the immediate background of the Convention itself,' the restrictions to the applicants' activities were justified in the interest of national security, for territorial integrity and for the prevention of crime.[2] The same approach to Nazi-related activities has been followed by the ECtHR. In *Schimanek v Austria* (2000), the applicant was sentenced to a prison term of no less than 8 years for engaging in activities in violation of the National Socialism Prohibition Act. Specifically, the applicant was arrested on suspicion of engaging in activities driven by National Socialist ideology. These activities included recruiting new members, organising paramilitary training camps and disseminating National Socialist propaganda. The applicant appealed, but the Supreme Court upheld the conviction, albeit reducing the sentence from 15 to 8 years' imprisonment. He submitted an application to the ECtHR, arguing that his Article 10 right had been violated. The ECtHR noted that 'National Socialism is a totalitarian doctrine incompatible with democracy and human rights and its adherents undoubtedly pursue aims of the kind referred to in Article 17 of the Convention.'[3] The ECtHR invoked Article 17, concluding that the application was manifestly ill-founded.

1.2 Totalitarian Symbols

The cases of *Vajnai v Hungary* (2008) and *Fáber v Hungary* (2012) reflect a robust protection of freedom of expression that should be followed in hate speech jurisprudence. More broadly, both judgements demonstrate the ECtHR's insistence that speech must incite violence or pose a genuine threat to public order before it can be restricted, even if such expression causes discomfort amongst victims of totalitarian regimes or their relatives. These cases also highlight several other issues, including the differential treatment between Communism, Nazism and national offshoots of fascist regimes.

In *Vajnai v Hungary* (2008), the applicant was addressing a lawful demonstration in central Budapest held at the former site of a Karl Marx statue which had been removed by the authorities. During the demonstration, the applicant wore a five-pointed red star on his jacket, representing the International Workers' Movement. A police patrol present at the scene instructed the applicant to remove the star, which he did. Despite this, criminal proceedings were initiated against him, and the district court found him guilty of using a totalitarian symbol. However, the district court refrained from imposing any sanction, instead placing the applicant under probation for one year. The applicant appealed the decision to the regional court. Interestingly, the regional court decided to refer the case to the Court of Justice of the European Union (CJEU) for a preliminary ruling. The regional court's question was whether the principle of non-discrimination implementing equal treatment precludes the relevant

2 *B.H, M.W, H.P. and G.K. v Austria* (1989) App no 12774/87 (EComHR, 12 October 1989)
3 *Schimanek v Austria* App no 32307/96 (ECtHR, 1 February 2000)

domestic national law, which imposes criminal sanctions on the public use of the symbol in question. The CJEU ruled that it had no jurisdiction on the matter. The regional court upheld the applicant's conviction.

The applicant submitted before the ECtHR that his conviction for wearing a symbol associated with the International Workers' Movement constituted an unjustified interference with his right to freedom of expression under Article 10 of the ECHR. The ECtHR unanimously found a violation of Article 10. In assessing whether the restriction was necessary in a democratic society, the Court first underlined that the state has a certain margin of appreciation and that the Court has a supervisory function.[4] It proceeded to note the significance of freedom of expression, as set out by *Handyside v the United Kingdom* (1976), although not directly citing it,[5] and also reiterated that there is little scope to limit political expression.[6] The Court determined that Hungary's restriction on the red star was unjustified, while at the same time acknowledging the historical scars left by the 'systematic terror applied to consolidate communist rule in several countries including Hungary.'[7] However, it noted that Hungary is a member of the European Union and has integrated into the value system of the Council of Europe and the ECHR. As a result, it determined that there was no evidence to indicate a genuine or imminent threat of a political movement or party re-establishing the Communist dictatorship.[8] The Court underlined that Hungary did not point to any 'instance where an actual or even remote danger of disorder triggered by the public display of the red star had arisen in Hungary.'[9] The Court argued that Hungary failed to demonstrate a genuine or imminent threat of the re-establishment of Communist rule, relying instead on a 'mere speculative danger'[10] that did not constitute a pressing social need. By rejecting speculative risks and emphasising the contextual absence of danger, the *Vajnai* judgement reinforced the foundational protections for political expression under Article 10.

In relation to Communism, the ECtHR recognised that the

> systematic terror applied to consolidate communist rule in several countries, including Hungary, remains a serious scar in the mind and heart of Europe. It accepts that the display of a symbol which was ubiquitous during the reign of those regimes may create uneasiness among past victims and their relatives, who may rightly find such displays disrespectful.[11]

4 *Vajnai v Hungary* App no 33629/06 (ECtHR, 8 July 2008) para 43
5 *Vajnai* (n 4) para 46
6 *Vajnai* (n 4) para 47
7 *Vajnai* (n 4) para 49
8 *Vajnai* (n 4) para 55
9 *Vajnai* (n 4)
10 *Vajnai* (n 4)
11 *Vajnai* (n 4) para 57

While recognising the destructiveness of totalitarian Communism, it noted that 'such sentiments, however understandable, cannot alone set the legal limits of freedom of expression.'[12] Despite the devastating impact of Communist dictatorships, which claimed over 20 million victims in Europe alone, the Court evaluated the contextual risk of restoring such regimes. However, it has not engaged in similar contextual assessments in cases concerning National Socialism, as reflected later on in the chapter.

In *Fáber v Hungary* (2012), the applicant objected to being fined for displaying the striped Árpád flag within 100 meters of an anti-racism and anti-hatred demonstration organised by the Hungarian Socialist Party and close to a counterdemonstration by the far-right group Jobbik. The flag traces its origins back over 800 years to a medieval dynasty. Although not an illegal symbol at the material time, it had contentious historical association in Hungary as it was appropriated by the Hungarian Arrow Cross Party, a Nazi-installed puppet regime responsible for the mass murder of thousands of Jews in late 1944. During the demonstration, police asked the applicant to remove the flag or leave, but he refused, arguing it was a historical symbol and not illegal. He was detained for six hours and fined approximately EUR 200 for disobeying police orders. His complaint to the district court was rejected. On appeal, the court upheld the fine. The majority of the ECtHR found that the applicant's penalisation constituted a violation of Article 10 of the ECHR.

In its analysis, the ECtHR referred to cases of the US Supreme Court, such as *Virginia v Black* (2003), which involved cross-burning by the Ku Klux Klan, as well as a German case involving the restriction of a planned far-right rally for purposes of demonstrating starkly contrasting approaches that may be taken to the issues at stake. In looking at whether the restriction was necessary in a democratic society, the Court reiterated that states have a certain margin of appreciation in determining this need, but that that goes along with European supervision.[13] It also reiterated the *Handyside* principle but did not make reference to that particular case, instead referring to *Oberschlick v Austria* (1991).[14] It highlighted the importance of political speech through the use of symbols[15] and, in relation to the facts and context of the specific case, found that the flag in question had multiple meanings, both as a historical symbol and also as a symbol reminiscent of the Arrow Cross Regime.[16] The Court emphasised the need for 'a careful examination of the context'[17] to distinguish between shocking or offensive expression protected under Article 10 and expression that incites violence or intimidation. While recognising the

12 *Vajnai* (n 4) para 57
13 *Fáber v Hungary* App no 40721/08 (ECHR, 24 July 2018) para 32
14 *Fáber* (n 13) para 34
15 *Fáber* (n 13) para 36
16 *Fáber* (n 13) para 54
17 *Fáber* (n 13) para 36

provocative nature of the flag and its potential to upset victims or their relatives, the Court upheld a high standard for restricting political speech, even when it involves symbols with troubling historical associations. It observed that, although provocative, the flag was displayed and there was no evidence that it materially disrupted the anti-racism demonstration, even if it made participants uncomfortable. The Court determined that, in the absence of any violent or abusive behaviour or a threat to public order, the applicant should not have been penalised solely for displaying the Árpád flag. It highlighted that 'ill feelings or even outrage, in the absence of intimidation,'[18] could not justify restrictions on expression. The ECtHR did acknowledge that when an applicant demonstrates contempt for the victims of totalitarian regimes, Article 17 may be applicable. However, it concluded that 'no such abusive element can be identified'[19] in the present case. Regrettably, the Court did not provide a detailed rationale for this conclusion, nor did it clarify why a symbol associated with the Arrow Cross Regime, which had an ideology similar to Nazism and which was responsible for the mass murder of Jews in Hungary, was treated differently from cases involving Nazism. Furthermore, considering the applicant's passive behaviour, his distance from the demonstration and the lack of any proven risk to security or order, the Court found the national authorities' justification for interfering with his rights to be neither relevant nor sufficient.[20] This was so despite the applicant's presence at the steps leading to the Danube embankment, a site of mass extermination of Jews during the Arrow Cross regime in 1944–1945. It recognised that the display of a 'contextually ambiguous flag'[21] at the site of mass murders on Remembrance Day could be offensive to the memory of those killed by the totalitarian regime and could even amount to a violation of Article 17, but that this was not the case in *Fáber*. It did not provide any extrapolation as to why it reached this conclusion. Alluding to Article 17, it merely stated that 'no such abusive element can be identified.'[22] The act of standing at this historically significant location while holding a flag could be interpreted as a denial of democratic values.[23] In her dissenting opinion, Judge Keller (Switzerland) highlighted that, in previous cases addressing Holocaust denial and related issues, both the Court and the Commission consistently concluded that such expressions should not receive protection under the Convention.[24]

18 *Fáber* (n 13) para 56
19 *Fáber* (n 13) 58
20 *Fáber* (n 13) paras 44, 47
21 *Fáber* (n 13) para 57
22 *Fáber* (n 13) para 58
23 Jacob Mchangama and Natalie Alkiviadou, 'Hate Speech and the European Court of Human Rights: Whatever Happened to the Right to Offend, Shock or Disturb?' (2021) 21(4) Humam Rights Law Review 1036
24 *Fáber* (n 13) Dissenting Opinion of Judge Keller

The judgements in *Vajnai* and *Fáber* demonstrate the ECtHR's adoption of a risk-based approach, focusing on the actual danger posed by expression rather than its symbolic associations and accompanying narrative that we often see mark the Court's hate speech case law. However, these cases also expose inconsistencies in the Court's treatment of symbols linked to various regimes. In *Vajnai*, the Court acknowledged the 'scar' left by Communist regimes in countries like Hungary but concluded that these sentiments alone were insufficient to justify restrictions under Article 10. Also, for the Court, the red star's dual meaning, as a symbol of both a totalitarian regime and the International Workers' Movement, meant it could not be universally interpreted as incitement. This judgement could, on the one hand, suggest that Communism is not viewed with the same level of severity as Nazism within the ECtHR's jurisprudence, where symbols or speech related to Nazi Germany are not protected by the ECtHR. This differentiation is demonstrated by the fact that the preceding reasoning was not applied to Nazi symbols in *Nix v Germany* (2018). Instead, in this case, the Court noted, due to their history, states which have experienced the horrors of Nazism 'may be regarded as having a special moral responsibility to distance themselves from the mass atrocities perpetrated by the Nazis.'[25] Through this, the Court goes beyond a permissibility of bans to a potential obligation of such bans. The Court's discussion in *Vajnai* regarding the temporal distance from the Communist regime, particularly noting that 20 years had elapsed since its fall, has no parallel in cases concerning Nazism. While this distinction does not imply a quantitative or qualitative comparison of totalitarian regimes, similar temporal analyses should be applied consistently across relevant cases in order to uphold a foundational commitment to freedom of expression. It is noteworthy that, in 1959, the EComHR invoked Article 17 to exclude the Communist Party of Germany from Convention protection,[26] whereas by 2008, in *Vajnai*, the Court offered a more nuanced perspective when addressing legislation banning totalitarian symbols. Of course, no direct parallel can be drawn before the reinstatement of an actual party and the use of symbols, but the nuance of the following reasoning is interesting:

> Hungary has become a member State of the European Union, after its full integration into the value system of the Council of Europe and the Convention. Moreover, there is no evidence to suggest that there is a real and present danger of any political movement or party restoring the communist dictatorship.[27]

25 *Nix v Germany* App no 35285/16 (ECHR, 13 March 2018) para 47
26 *Communist Party of Germany v the Federal Republic of Germany* App no 250/57 (EComHR, 20 July 1957)
27 *Vajnai* (n 4) para 49

Does this indirectly imply that the threat of Nazism is real in a democratic Germany, also a member of the European Union and the Council of Europe? Probably not. This difference illustrates a potential inconsistency in the Court's reasoning, specifically while Hungary's Communist past is assessed within a historical time frame, the legacy of Nazism is treated as a constant threat, regardless of time elapsed or Germany's current democratic stability. The Communism/Nazism divide in regard to acceptable speech is not rigid, though, with *Fáber* complicating this distinction. While the Árpád flag is linked to the fascist Arrow Cross Regime, which committed mass atrocities against Hungarian Jews, the Court found a violation of Article 10 when the applicant was penalised for displaying it. As it did in *Vajnai*, the Court emphasised that offensive or provocative expression, even when associated with a historical regime of persecution, cannot be restricted solely on the basis of its potential to upset victims or their relatives if it does not incite violence or constitute intimidation. The case law of totalitarian symbols/speech is rendered even more complex in *Šimunić v Croatia* (2019), discussed later. In this case, the ECtHR found inadmissible the application of a footballer who had chanted a slogan with a dual meaning, one of which was fascist in nature. The Court's reasoning was significantly influenced by the applicant's professional role and the amplified impact of his actions as a public figure.

The *Vajnai* and *Fáber* judgements highlight the ECtHR's principled approach to safeguarding freedom of expression. They reflect something significant which is lacking in other hate speech cases to the extent that we see it in *Fáber* and in *Vajnai*, namely, that a careful examination of the context is needed to decipher between shocking and offensive expression, protected by Article 10, and expression that is not. The Court emphasised that restrictions must be grounded in evidence of genuine harm or intimidation, rather than speculative risks or the subjective feelings of spectators. This focus on objective criteria and their application to the context in question as seen in these cases resonates with the concurring opinion of Slovenian Judge Zupančič in *Vejdeland v Sweden* (2012), discussed in Chapter 4. In his opinion, Judge Zupančič contrasted the 'insensitivity' of the US Supreme Court's position in *Snyder v Phelps*, which involved the picketing of the funeral of a US soldier with the 'oversensitivity' of the Swedish Supreme Court when confronted with the homophobic leaflets in the lockers of high school students, which, he argued, 'demonstrates an oversensitivity in collision with free speech postulates.'[28] The ECtHR's handling of *Vajnai* and *Fáber* avoids both extremes, offering a balanced, fact- and context-based approach that is neither dismissive nor overly reactive to the complexities of the cases at hand. This method demonstrates a robust commitment to upholding democratic discourse while addressing the concerns associated with provocative or offensive expression. Moreover, the two decisions highlight the importance

28 *Vejdeland and others v Sweden* (2012) App no 1813/07 (ECHR, 9 February 2012) para 6

of rejecting speculative dangers in safeguarding democratic discourse. However, the inconsistent treatment of symbols linked to Communism, Nazism and other regimes raises questions about the coherence of the Court's jurisprudence. Oversensitivity to societal reactions risks undermining free expression. To ensure a principled and equitable approach, the Court must apply its risk-based framework developed in the preceding cases consistently across cases involving symbols of totalitarian regimes and to hate speech more generally.

In *Nix v Germany* (2018), the applicant used his blog to document his German Nepalese daughter's experience with a state employment office. Through his posts, he aimed to contribute to a public debate about the challenges faced by children from migrant backgrounds and families receiving social welfare, particularly regarding discrimination in schools and employment offices, an issue already under public discussion. In one of his posts, he included an image of Himmler wearing a swastika. Specifically, the speech in question involved the publication of a statement over a page long on his blog. Under the heading "[Name of the staff member] offers 'customized' integration into the low-wage [economy]," he included a photograph of former SS chief Heinrich Himmler in full SS uniform, featuring a Nazi Party badge with a swastika on his front pocket and a swastika armband. Alongside the image, the applicant included a quote from Himmler about the education of children in Eastern Europe under Nazi occupation, stating that parents wishing to provide their children with a proper education had to submit a request to the SS and police leadership. The applicant also cited the sources for both the image and the quotation. The applicant was charged with using symbols of unconstitutional organisations in the aforementioned blog post. The district court convicted the applicant and sentenced him to four months' imprisonment. The sentence was suspended. The regional court dismissed the appeal but changed the sentence to 120-day fines of EUR 10 each. The applicant lodged an appeal, but the appeal was dismissed. The court of appeal rejected a further appeal, and the applicant lodged a constitutional complaint at the federal constitutional court, which refused to admit the complaint.

Nix claimed a violation of his Article 10 right to freedom of expression. However, the ECtHR unanimously determined that his application was manifestly ill-founded. In its analysis, the ECtHR proceeded to produce its classical references to the importance of freedom of expression, which extends to ideas that shock, offend or disturb, without a direct quote to *Handyside*,[29] noting the particular importance of political speech or debates of public interest,[30] but that it has been 'sensitive to the historical context'[31] of countries when reviewing the existence of a pressing social need. In relation to the historical context,

29 *Nix* (n 25) para 45
30 *Nix* (n 25) para 46
31 *Nix* (n 25)

the ECtHR highlighted that states with a history of Nazi atrocities, like Germany, bear a unique moral responsibility to distance themselves from such horrors. To uphold this, the Court underlined that German law criminalises the use of Nazi symbols, to preserve political peace, prevent Nazism's revival and align with historical accountability.[32] In this ambit, the ECtHR noted that the symbol in question, a photograph of Heinrich Himmler in SS uniform prominently displaying a swastika armband, 'cannot be considered to have any other meaning than that of Nazi ideology'[33] and contrasted this with cases like *Vajnai*, where the red star has dual meanings.[34] However, the ECtHR noted that the applicant, by including an image of Heinrich Himmler in SS uniform with a swastika armband in his blog post, did not aim to propagate totalitarian ideology, incite violence or engage in hate speech, nor did his actions result in any intimidation.[35] The Court also noted that various media reports highlighted allegations of discrimination against children of individuals receiving social welfare and those with migrant backgrounds in schools and employment offices. In this context, the Court recognised that the applicant's series of six blog posts could be reasonably interpreted as an effort to engage in and contribute to a wider public discourse on matters of significant societal interest.[36] It proceeded to state that the key question was whether the domestic courts were obliged to consider the blog post which led to the applicant's conviction in conjunction with his other posts addressing the interactions between the employment office and his daughter for purposes of ascertaining the public interest element of his blog more broadly. On this, the ECtHR found no fault with the domestic courts for focusing solely on the specific blog post that led to the applicant's conviction, as it contained no reference to his earlier posts or clear indication that it was part of a series intended to contribute to public debate. The post addressed to an employment office staff member criticised the handling of his daughter's case but made no mention of her foreign origin, alleged discrimination or social welfare status. Furthermore, the post drew no parallels between the staff member's actions and Nazi policies, nor did it reference racism or discrimination. The courts concluded that the use of Nazi imagery served merely as an 'eye-catching device' and lacked substantive connection to the post's content. To this end, the ECtHR concluded that Nix's use of the SS symbols, figures and uniform constituted a 'gratuitous use of symbols,'[37] which the national law sought to prohibit. The Court reiterated

32 *Nix* (n 25) para 48
33 *Nix* (n 25) 49
34 *Nix* (n 25)
35 *Vajnai* (n 4) para 52
36 *Nix* (n 25) para 51
37 *Nix* (n 25) para 45

the historical context of Germany and proceeded to declare the application inadmissible.[38]

When comparing the use of a Nazi symbol to the Árpád flag or symbols of Communist regimes, it appears that the ECtHR affords notably less free speech protection in the former case. Although the two Hungarian symbols both possessed dual meanings, the use of the Árpád flag at a site of mass extermination of Jews effectively limits the interpretation of how this flag was used in the case in question to one single interpretation. The Court's differing approach becomes particularly perplexing when considering the context in which Nix used Nazi symbols, especially in contrast to their use in *Fáber*. Nix employed his blog to document his daughter's experiences with the employment office, aiming to engage in a public interest debate. Under these circumstances, Germany's application of the relevant legislation effectively functioned as a form of sedition law, criminalising exaggerated criticism of government officials. Furthermore, the way in which the Court addressed contextual considerations raises significant concerns. In *Vajnai*, the Court acknowledged the 'terror' and 'scars' inflicted by Communist regimes in countries like Hungary but determined that these emotional legacies alone were insufficient to justify restrictions on Article 10 rights. However, this reasoning was not applied to the emotional impact of Nazism in *Nix*. In that case, the Court emphasised Germany's right and even went as far as mentioning a duty to impose a blanket prohibition on all symbols associated with the Nazi regime, citing the nation's unique historical responsibility due to the atrocities committed during that period.

A case affiliated to fascism in the former Yugoslavia is *Šimunić v Croatia* (2019). Here, the ECtHR found, by a majority, the application of a Croatian football player following his conviction for hate speech to be inadmissible. The player had been fined by domestic courts for using the phrase "For Home—Ready" after a match, a slogan linked to Croatia's WWII-era fascist regime. Although expert opinion on the matter before the domestic courts noted that the phrase had historical and poetic origins, the courts maintained that it symbolised ethnic and religious hatred in the modern context.

The applicant, a football player, was convicted of addressing messages to spectators of a football match that incited hatred based on race, nationality and religion. The incident occurred at a stadium in Zagreb after a match between Croatia and Iceland. After the game, the player took the microphone, walked to the centre of the pitch and shouted "For Home!" toward the crowd. The spectators responded with the phrase "Ready!"—a chant associated with the totalitarian regime of the Independent State of Croatia, which the national court underlined symbolises racial hatred, religious intolerance and the trivialisation of crimes against humanity. Despite hearing the crowd's response, the

38 *Nix* (n 25) paras 56, 57

player repeated the chant three more times with a raised hand. The national court found that, given the setting and nature of the interaction, the applicant's conduct had incited hatred on racial, national and religious grounds. Professor JJ provided expert opinion on the phrase and noted, amongst others, that the phrase "For Home" is a traditional Croatian greeting with a dual interpretation. One view, detached from historical context, simply signifies loyalty to one's homeland, embodying a protective sentiment without racial or social aggressiveness. From this perspective, it is connected solely to the concept of "home" and has no hostile historical connotation. "For Home" has appeared across Croatian society, from literature and art to politics, and served as a rallying cry during Croatia's defensive efforts in the Croatian War of Independence. Expert JJ noted that although totalitarian regimes, like the Independent State of Croatia, co-opted traditional symbols and slogans, including "For Home," for their purposes, Croatia itself has historically engaged in defensive wars only. Consequently, he argued, "For Home" is fundamentally a traditional Croatian greeting used defensively rather than offensively. The national court nevertheless found that, in this case, the circumstances surrounding the use of the chant "For Home," including the location, the way the accused addressed the crowd and his interaction with spectators, who responded "Ready!" to his initial call, indicate that his actions were intentional. The first instance court found that the footballer's exchange with the crowd demonstrated that he was deliberately inciting the crowd to respond in a manner associated with the official greeting of the totalitarian regime of the Independent State of Croatia. He was fined approximately EUR 650. The applicant filed an appeal against the first instance judgement, contending that the lower court had failed to consider the opinion of expert JJ and arguing that his actions had neither incited hatred nor discriminated against anyone. His conviction was upheld, and his fine was increased to approximately EUR 3,000. In its decision, the second court noted that the expert opinion was not binding and that the term was complex in nature, but that it is undisputedly a fascist salute. The applicant filed a subsequent appeal with the constitutional court, which rejected the appeal.

In its judgement, the ECtHR started off in its usual manner, noting that freedom of expression extends to information or ideas that shock, offend or disturb.[39] The Court emphasised the imperative of combatting racism within the realm of sport and found no grounds to warrant protection under Article 10. The Court noted that the applicant chanted the phrase used by a totalitarian regime at a football match in front of a large audience which replied to the chant and which the applicant repeated four times. Regarding the applicant's profession as a football player and thus a role model for fans, the Court noted that he 'should have been aware of the possible negative impact of provocative chanting on spectators' behaviour and should have abstained from

39 *Šimunić v Croatia* (2019) App no 20373/17 (ECHR, 22 January 2019) para 36

such conduct.'[40] In conducting a balancing exercise, the ECtHR highlighted that the respondent state struck a balance between the applicant's freedom of expression and the promotion of tolerance and mutual respect at sports events and combatting non-discrimination.[41] However, it did not refer to any of the named limitation grounds set out in Article 10 but did mention that the fine was low, thereby hinting at the proportionality of the measures taken. Interestingly, the ECtHR conducted a normative discussion of Article 17 and its application, citing some cases and concluding that it does not find it necessary to apply Article 17 since the complaint was anyhow deemed inadmissible, since the interference is justified under Article 10(2).[42] Opting not to invoke Article 17 despite engaging in a normative discussion of its scope was particularly striking, given that the Croatian government did not even advance an Article 17 argument.

Reversing the totalitarian perspective raises an intriguing question: What legal consequences arise if someone is labelled a Nazi? In *Pihl v Sweden* (2017), an anonymous post on a small blog run by a non-profit association accused the applicant of being affiliated with the Nazi Party, with the comment saying, "[T]hat guy Pihl is also a real hash-junkie according to several people I have spoken to." Nine days later, following a complaint by Pihl, the association removed the blog post and comment and issued a public apology. Pihl initiated defamation proceedings against the association, contending that it bore responsibility for both the post and the comment. Regarding the comment, he argued that the association's liability stemmed from its failure to remove it immediately. However, the national courts dismissed his claim. The ECtHR deemed his application manifestly ill-founded. Specifically, the ECtHR considered the balance between Articles 8 and 10. Taking into account the blog's prompt removal of the comment one day after being notified by the applicant, its publication of an apology, the blog's limited reach and the fact that the comment did not constitute hate speech or incitement to violence, the ECtHR concluded that the domestic courts had achieved a fair balance between the rights protected under Articles 8 and 10.[43] Interestingly, when a similar case was brought to the ECtHR by the utterer of the speech rather than the victim, as is the case in *Pihl*, the ECtHR found that there had been no violation of Article 10. Specifically, in *Hoffer and Annen v Germany* (2011), the applicants were anti-abortion activists who distributed pamphlets outside a medical centre in Nuremberg. These pamphlets compared abortions to the Holocaust, featuring statements such as "Then: Holocaust/Today: Babycaust," and specifically identified Dr F, a doctor at the clinic, by name. Initially, the district court acquitted the applicants, reasoning that their actions were protected

40 *Šimunić* (n 39) para 45
41 *Šimunić* (n 39) para 48
42 *Šimunić* (n 39) para 39
43 *Pihl v Sweden* (2017) App no 74742/14 (ECHR, 7 February 2017) para 37

under their right to freedom of expression, which outweighed the reputation interests of Dr F and the medical centre. However, this decision was overturned on appeal by the regional court. The appellate court determined that the statement "Then: Holocaust/Today: Babycaust" equated Dr F's lawful medical practice with the atrocities of the Holocaust, effectively accusing him of being a mass murderer. This was deemed an abusive insult, leading to the applicants' conviction for defamation and the imposition of fines. The federal constitutional court considered that the statements were not abusive insult but contained a serious interference with the doctor's personality rights. The first applicant received 15 daily fines of EUR 10, and the second applicant received ten daily fines of EUR 10.

The ECtHR noted the importance of expressing opinions on matters of public interest and that the domestic courts had acknowledged the applicants' right to engage in public debate on matters of political and societal interest, even through exaggerated and polemic criticism.[44] However, the specific statement "Then: Holocaust/Today: Babycaust" was deemed unacceptable as it constituted a severe violation of the doctor's personality rights, particularly given the historical and social context of Germany's past.[45] The domestic courts determined that the comparison of abortion to Holocaust atrocities was excessively detrimental to the doctor's honour, and the federal constitutional court agreed that all plausible interpretations of the statement amounted to a significant infringement of personality rights.[46] Ultimately, the ECtHR upheld the domestic courts' decision, finding no violation of Article 10 of the Convention.

As such, while *Pihl* highlights leniency towards publishers who mitigate harm, *Hoffer and Annen* underscores stricter scrutiny of speech directly targeting individuals with highly provocative comparisons.

1.3 Totalitarianism: Concluding Comments

The jurisprudence on totalitarian expression reveals a complex and evolving struggle to reconcile freedom of expression with the need to combat ideologies fundamentally opposed to democratic values. Cases such as *Kühnen*, *BH, MW, HP and GK* and *Schimanek* demonstrate the Court's unwavering stance against Nazi ideology, consistently applying Article 17 to bar any protection for speech promoting Nazism. This strict approach aligns with the historical context of the ECHR's creation, reflecting Europe's collective memory of World War II and its commitment to preventing a resurgence of fascist ideologies. However, the Court's treatment of Communist symbols and other contested

44 *Hoffer and Annen v Germany* App nos. 397/07 & 2322/07 (ECtHR, 13 January 2011) para 45
45 *Hoffer and Annen* (n 44) para 48
46 *Hoffer and Annen* (n 44)

expressions has been markedly different. In relation to Communism, it must be underlined that, in 1957, the EComHR upheld the decision of the German Federal Constitutional Court to dissolve the German Communist Party (KPD).[47] However, when it comes to symbols of Communism (and not only) presented in more recent years, the ECtHR has adopted a different approach. Specifically, in *Vajnai*, *Fáber*, and *Nix*, the Court displayed fluctuating levels of tolerance. There is no binary that the Court accepts Communist symbols but does not accept Nazi symbols, since it did find a violation in the case of the flag associated with the Arrow Cross Regime. These cases illustrate that while the Court recognises the potential for ideological harm in both Communist and fascist symbols, its scrutiny has been consistent in cases involving Nazi-related content. Similarly, in *Šimunić*, the Court upheld restrictions on a fascist-era slogan used at a sports event, framing the issue within the broader context of combatting racism and promoting tolerance. The contrasting approaches discussed in the preceding sections raise fundamental questions about the consistency of the Court's interpretive framework. While historical responsibility and democratic stability provide some justification for differential treatment, the absence of a clear and principled standard weakens the coherence of its hate speech jurisprudence.

2 Genocide Denial

In the broader framework of hate speech, and apart from some exceptions, such as *Lenis* and *Norwood*, discussed in the previous chapter, Article 17 is most frequently applied in cases involving Holocaust denial or revisionism. Specifically, in such cases, numerous applications have been dismissed as manifestly ill-founded. To comprehend the handling of such cases, it is essential to set out Article 17 of the ECHR. This provision, titled 'prohibition of abuse of rights,' states:

> Nothing in this Convention may be interpreted as implying for any State, group or person any right to engage in any activity or perform any act aimed at the destruction of any of the rights and freedoms set forth herein or at their limitation to a greater extent than is provided for in the Convention.

2.1 Genocide Denial: Cases of the European Commission on Human Rights

During the 1990s, the EComHR consistently relied on Article 17 to exclude applications related to denialism or revisionism of the Holocaust. For example, in *Remer v Germany* (1995), the applicant, an editor of the publication

47 *Communist Party* (n 26)

Remer Depeschen, oversaw the dissemination of articles denying the historical reality of the gas chambers, condemning Germany's policies toward Israel and alleging preferential treatment of asylum seekers, Romani individuals and drug traffickers over German nationals. The publication also warned of Germany's supposed destruction due to immigration. He was convicted of incitement to hatred, sentenced to one year and ten months' imprisonment, and had several of his publications confiscated. In dismissing his application as manifestly ill-founded, the EComHR invoked Article 17 of the ECHR. In doing so, the EComHR emphasised the function of Article 17, noting that speech promoting National Socialist ideology falls outside the protection of Article 10. In reaching its decision, the EComHR held that the speech contravened basic principles of the Convention, 'namely justice and peace and further reflected racial and religious discrimination.'[48] However, the precise application of Article 17 in this context remains somewhat unclear, since the Commission also referred to Article 10, noting that the speech was restricted on the grounds of preventing crime and disorder due to the incitement to hatred against Jews and the protection of rights and reputations of others. This may have been one of the cases which started the blended Article 17–10 approach extrapolated on further later.

In *Honsik v Austria* (1995), the applicant authored articles in a periodical denying the existence of gas chambers and the mass extermination of Holocaust victims. He was charged with denying the systematic mass extermination of Jews by Nazis in gas chambers of concentration camps and had presented them as false propaganda. The court of appeal rejected his appeal, and the court of assizes sentenced him to an additional term of imprisonment of one year, six months, and ten days. The Supreme Court rejected his plea for nullity. The EComHR held that promoting National Socialist ideologies falls outside the protection of Article 10. It highlighted the relevance of Article 17 and dismissed the application as manifestly ill-founded. As with *Remer*, the precise distinction between the application of these two provisions was not clearly defined in this case. The EComHR referred to the fact that prohibition of Nazi ideas is not only lawful in Austria but, also, given the historical past of the Convention, can be justified in the interest of national security, territorial integrity and the prevention of crime. According to the EComHR, the ideas were expressed in a 'biased and polemical manner far from any scientific objectivity,'[49] and that statements of this kind were in contravention with the basic ideas of the Convention, specifically justice and peace, and that they also reflect racial and religious discrimination.

In *Marais v France* (1996), the applicant authored an article questioning the existence of gas chambers at the Struthof-Natzweiler concentration camp. The criminal court sentenced the applicant to a fine of 10,000 French

48 *Remer v Germany* (1995) App no 25096/94 (EComHR, 6 September 1995)
49 *Honsik v Austria* App no 25062/94 (EComHR, 18 October 1995)

francs and ordered him to pay damages to the associations which had joined the proceedings as civil parties, including the League Against Racism and Anti-Semitism. He was charged and convicted of complicity in the denial of crimes against humanity. The court of appeal and the court of cassation rejected his appeals. The EComHR dismissed his application as manifestly ill-founded. The EComHR determined that the article's true intent, disguised as a scientific discussion, was to deny the use of gas chambers for genocide. It concluded that allowing the applicant to exercise his freedom of expression in this context would undermine the rights and freedoms protected by the Convention.[50]

In *Nachtmann v Austria* (1998), the applicant was the head of the editorial staff of the periodical *Aula, Das freiheitliche Magazin*. He was held responsible for publishing an article titled "Natural laws apply to Nazis and anti-fascists." The impugned statements downplayed and denied Nazi atrocities. The applicant was convicted of engaging in National Socialist activities and sentenced to a fine of 240,000 Austrian Schillings (AS) and ten months' imprisonment, suspended on probation by the regional criminal court. The court determined that the article grossly denied and minimised National Socialist genocide and related crimes. Its detailed analysis concluded that the statements suggested the number of victims, particularly Jews killed by poisonous gas and cremation, was "highly exaggerated and technically impossible." The applicant filed a plea of nullity to the Supreme Court, as well as an appeal against his sentence. The plea of nullity was rejected, but the appeal on the sentence was accepted, with the Supreme Court lowering his sentence to AS 193,000 and nine months' imprisonment on probation. The EComHR determined that the views expressed in the publication were incompatible with the values of the Convention. It held that restricting National Socialist ideologies fell within the scope of Article 10(2) and also acknowledged the applicability of Article 17. Ultimately, it dismissed the application as manifestly ill-founded. In this case, the distinction between the application of Articles 10(2) and 17 was not clearly delineated. It noted that, 'in view of the historical past forming the immediate background of the Convention itself,' prohibiting the expression of Nazi ideas is justified and necessary in a democratic society. It highlighted that 'National Socialism is a totalitarian doctrine incompatible with democracy and human rights and that its adherents undoubtedly pursue aims of the kind referred to in Article 17.' It noted that restricting such speech can be done in the interests of national security and territorial integrity as well as for the prevention of crime and is thus covered by Article 10(2). This case demonstrates a clear Article 17–10 blend in its analysis.[51]

50 *Marais v France* App no 31159/96 (EComHR, 24 June 1996)
51 *Nachtmann v Austria* (1998) App no 36773/97 (ECHR, 9 September 1998)

2.2 *Genocide Denial, the European Court of Human Rights, the Holocaust and Other Genocides*

The exclusionary approach to denying the Holocaust has been carried on by the ECtHR. *Lehideux and Isorni* (1998) involved a publication in Le Monde defending the memory of Marshal Pétain. The first applicant, the president of the Association for the Defence of the Memory of Marshal Pétain, and the second applicant, Pétain's former lawyer, were convicted of publicly defending collaborationist crimes. The case arose from an advertisement in Le Monde titled "People of France, you have short memories," referencing Pétain and inviting readers to contact the association. The second applicant authored the text. The case began before the criminal court, where the applicants were charged with publicly defending collaborationist crimes. The court acquitted them, finding that the text did not justify Nazi collaboration but reflected a campaign to rehabilitate Marshal Pétain. The court of appeal overturned the acquittals, concluding that the text glorified Pétain's policies and implicitly justified crimes of collaboration. It convicted the applicants, awarded symbolic damages to the civil parties, and ordered the publication of excerpts from its judgement in Le Monde. On appeal, the applicants argued that their conviction violated Article 10 of the ECHR. The court of cassation rejected their claim, ruling that the text effectively praised Pétain and justified his crimes. Ultimately, the penalty was purely symbolic, requiring Lehideux and Isorni to pay each civil party association one franc in damages and to cover the cost of publishing the judgement in Le Monde.

The (majority) of the ECtHR found a violation of Article 10, observing that the publication did not endorse Nazi atrocities. In relation to revisionism/negationism, the Court highlighted that justifying a pro-Nazi policy is clearly incompatible with the Convention's values and cannot be protected under Article 10.[52] However, it found that the applicants explicitly condemned "Nazi atrocities and persecutions" as well as "German omnipotence and barbarism." Their focus was not on praising a policy but on defending Pétain, aiming to secure a revision of his conviction, a purpose the court of appeal acknowledged as pertinent and legitimate, even if the methods used were contested. As the statements were not revisionist/negationist in its view, the ECtHR found that the case 'does not belong to the category of clearly established historical facts—such as the Holocaust—whose negation or revision would be removed from the protection of Article 10 by Article 17.'[53]

In *Lehideux and Isorni*, Judge Jambrek's (Slovenia) concurring opinion sought to clarify the criteria for applying Article 17. Specifically, he asserted that for the article to be invoked, the offending actions must aim to spread

52 *Lehideux and Isorni* (1998) App no 24662/94 (ECHR, 23 September 1998) para 53
53 *Lehideux and Isorni* (n 52) para 47

violence or hatred, to resort to illegal or undemocratic methods, to encourage the use of violence, to undermine the nation's democratic and pluralist political system or to pursue objectives that are racist or likely to destroy the rights and freedoms of others.[54]

In this case, the principle of proportionality was one of the most, if not the most, central issues that contributed to the outcome of the case. Specifically, the ECtHR concluded that resorting to criminal proceedings, rather than pursuing civil remedies, was 'disproportionate and, as such, unnecessary in a democratic society.' As such, *Lehideux* is one of the cases which demonstrate that the severity and nature of penalties are critical in assessing whether interference with Article 10 is proportionate. This was also highlighted in, for example, *Incal v Turkey* (1998), where the ECtHR argued that governments should prioritise non-criminal measures where feasible.[55] Nonetheless, in *Balsytė-Lideikienė v Lithuania* (2015), the Court acknowledged that states may adopt measures, including criminal ones, to address harmful speech, provided these responses are 'appropriate and without excess to such remarks.'[56] This is not consistently the case, as evidenced by numerous other judgements discussed in this chapter and Chapter 4. These cases illustrate that the ECtHR has often ruled in favour of state practice even where criminal measures have been employed against hate speech in cases where the harm threshold is low.

Before proceeding with other cases involving genocide denial, a reference will be made to a case of structurally similar focus to *Lehideux* in terms of the documentary nature of the speech in question. *Orban and Others v France* (2009) involved an application by the chairman and managing director of the applicant company (Editions Plon). In 2001, the applicant company published *Special Services: Algeria 1955–1957*, in which the author, a former special services operative, recounted acts of torture and summary executions during the Algerian War. The inside cover described him as "a Free French veteran" sent by General de Gaulle on "the most delicate secret operations" and "a living legend" within the special services. The applicant's chairman and managing director were convicted of publicly defending war crimes and aiding and abetting that offence. The ECtHR unanimously found that this violated Article 10.

The ECtHR underlined that France had a limited margin of appreciation regarding the press's role in conveying matters of public interest. It viewed the book as an eyewitness account, with the author's lack of remorse reflecting his stated mission. Criticising the publishers for not distancing

54 *Lehideux and Isorni v France* App no 24662/94 (ECHR, 23 September 1998), Concurring Opinion of Judge Jambrek, para 2

55 *Incal v Turkey* App no 22678/93 (ECHR, 9 June 1998) para 54

56 *Balsytė-Lideikienė v Lithuania* App no 72596/01 (ECHR, 4 February 2009) para 81

themselves from his account was deemed unjustified. The Court reaffirmed that Article 10 protects ideas that may shock, offend or disturb. Importantly, it stated:

> By publishing this work, the applicants have simply delivered this testimony to the public. . . . However, the publication of a testimony of this type—which, according to the publisher, 'contributes . . . to understanding the terrible complexity of an era which continues to inhabit our present'—was undoubtedly part of a debate of general interest of singular importance for collective memory. . . . [I]t confirms one of the theses present and defended by the latter, namely that not only did such practices take place, but that they did so with the approval of the French authorities.[57]

Witzsch v Germany (1999) was a case in which the applicant sent a private letter to a professor in response to an article discussing the Nazi Party's culpability and Hitler's intent to murder the Jews. Specifically, in an article published in a German weekly review, a well-known historian made the following commentary:

> Hitler wanted the murder of the Jews. He ordered it and certainly knew about it. Although he had not given a written order, there is evidence that he had given oral orders on several occasions. The murder of the Jews was wanted and organised from above and by NS-activists from the bottom.

A few months later, the applicant wrote to Professor Wolffson in reply to this article, stating, *inter alia*:

> Your statements which are false and historically unsustainable shall not stand unanswered. It is actually established that there is no indication in party programs of the National Socialist German Workers' Party, the NSDAP (*Nationalsozialistische Deutsche Arbeiterpartei*), that the NSDAP and Hitler intended to murder the Jews.

The professor gave the letter to the police. The district court convicted him of disparaging the dignity of the deceased, sentencing him to four months' imprisonment, suspended on probation. The court of appeal confirmed this. The federal constitutional court decided not to admit the applicant's constitutional complaint.

The ECtHR, relying on Article 17, unanimously held that such speech fell outside the scope of protection under the Convention. The Court started off

57 *Orban and others v France* (2009) App no 20985/05 (ECHR, 15 January 2009) para 49

by stating the provisions of Article 10, noting that states have a margin of appreciation and that the Court exercises European supervision to this end.[58] Citing *Lehideux and Isorni*, the Court noted that the 'negation or revision of clearly established historical facts—such as the Holocaust—would be removed from the protection of Article 10 by Article 17.' The Court found that the need to prevent crime and protect the interests of Holocaust victims outweighed the applicant's freedom to deny the existence of gas chambers and related mass murders. According to the ECtHR, these provided relevant and sufficient grounds for his conviction, making the interference necessary in a democratic society. Without extrapolating on the link between crime prevention and the statements and without conducting a substantive exercise showing why crime prevention and the protection of the interests of Holocaust survivors superseded the applicant's Article 10 right, the Court considered the application to be manifestly ill-founded.

This case could be deemed particularly concerning in the ambit of free speech and the *Handyside* principle since it concerned statements made in a private letter rather than in the public sphere. This expression was uttered as a personal and private assertion rather than as part of the propaganda activities of a totalitarian movement, which was the primary concern during the drafting of Article 17. So it is unreasonable that a private letter, particularly considering its scope and reach, could fall into the exceptional cases which are covered by Article 17. However, without providing any justification, the ECtHR dismissed as 'irrelevant' the fact that the comments were confined to a private letter. The ECtHR noted that while the applicant did not deny the Holocaust or the existence of gas chambers, he rejected the established fact that Hitler and the NSDAP planned and organised the mass killing of Jews. He characterised such claims as wartime and post-war atrocity propaganda, effectively denying their responsibility for the extermination of Jews, which 'showed the applicant's disdain towards the victims of the Holocaust.'

Garaudy v France (2003) concerned a book authored by the applicant titled *The Founding Myths of Israeli Politics*, which included statements such as "[T] he myth of six million exterminated Jews that has become a dogma justifying and lending sanctity (as indicated by the very word Holocaust) to every act of violence." The author was convicted of denying crimes against humanity, racial defamation and incitement to racial hatred and received suspended sentences of imprisonment, the longest being for six months, and fines in excess of EUR 25,900 and compensation of more than EUR 33,500 for the civil parties, which included the National Union of Associations of Deported and Interned Members of the Resistance.

The ECtHR unanimously rejected his application by employing Article 17. In its analysis, the ECtHR reiterated the importance of freedom of expression, citing cases such as *Handyside*. It then looked at Article 17, citing older

58 *Witzsch v Germany* App no 7485/03 (ECHR, 13 December 2005)

EComHR cases, such as *Glimmerveen and Hagenbeek*, and newer ECtHR cases, such as *Lehideux and Isorni*. The ECtHR proceeded to set out reasons for which revisionist speech is to be considered hateful, arguing that

> denying crimes against humanity is therefore one of the most serious forms of racial defamation of Jews and of incitement to hatred of them. The denial or rewriting of this type of historical fact undermines the values on which the fight against racism and anti-Semitism are based and constitutes a serious threat to public order. Such acts are incompatible with democracy and human rights because they infringe the rights of others.[59]

In this case, the ECtHR applied Article 17, emphasising that the promotion of pro-Nazi policies cannot benefit from the protections afforded by Article 10. It underscored that there is a 'category of clearly established historical facts—such as the Holocaust—whose negation or revision would be removed from the protection of Article 10 by Article 17.' The Court determined that the revisionist content of the book was fundamentally incompatible with the Convention's objectives, which include the pursuit of justice and peace, and posed a serious threat to public order. Consequently, it unanimously ruled that the applicant's claim of a violation of Article 10 was incompatible with the provisions of the Convention under Article 35(3). In *Witzsch*, mentioned earlier, the Court similarly observed that 'the general purpose of Article 17 is to make it impossible for individuals to take advantage of a right with the aim of promoting ideas contrary to the text and the spirit of the Convention.'

In *M'Bala M'Bala v France* (2015), the applicant, a comedian, staged a performance, during which he invited an academic, previously convicted in France for negationist and revisionist views, to join him onstage. During the performance, an actor wearing striped pyjamas adorned with a yellow star bearing the word "Jew" appeared to present the academic with a "prize for unfrequentability and insolence." The applicant was subsequently charged with committing public insult against a person of Jewish origin or faith. The court of first instance found him guilty and ordered him to pay a fine of EUR 10,000. The court of appeal upheld the judgement, and the court of cassation dismissed the appeal.

In its analysis, the ECtHR underlined the importance of freedom of expression, quoting cases such as *Handyside*, and noted that Article 10 extends to satire, which, it underlined, is a 'form of artistic expression and social commentary which, by virtue of its characteristic exaggeration and distortion of reality, is naturally intended to provoke and agitate.'[60] It proceeded to note, citing *Lehideux and Isorni*, that 'a statement directed against the value

59 *Garaudy v France* App no 65831/01 (ECHR, 25 June 2003)
60 *M'Bala M'Bala v France* App no 25239/13 (ECHR, 20 October 2015) para 31

underlying the Convention' is excluded by Article 17 from the protection of Article 10.[61] It then referred to the findings in *Garaudy*, as well as older cases, such as *Marais*, heard by the EComHR. It further noted that while Article 17 applies to 'explicit and direct statements which do not require any interpretation, it is convinced that a clearly hateful and anti-Semitic position, disguised under the guise of an artistic production, is as dangerous as a frontal and abrupt attack.'[62]

In relation to the artistic element of this case, the ECtHR noted:

> The applicant cannot claim, in the particular circumstances of the case and with regard to its context, as having acted as an artist with the right to express himself through satire, humor and provocation. Indeed, within the guise of a humorous representation, he invited one of the best known French Holocaust deniers, convicted a year ago for denying crimes against humanity, to honour him and give him the floor.[63]

In light of the above, and by finding that the applicant sought to use his Article 10 rights for purposes contrary to the Convention, the majority of the ECtHR applied Article 17, finding the application manifestly ill-founded. As with other Holocaust denial cases specifically, but also in relation to hate speech cases more broadly, apart from cases such as *Vajnai* and *Fáber*, discussed earlier, there was no thorough assessment of the alleged harm caused by the expression, or consideration of factors such as its impact on the audience or the likelihood that viewers had deliberately chosen to watch the comedian in question.

In the recent cases of *Williamson v Germany* (2019) and *Pastörs v Germany* (2020), the applicants denied the Holocaust during an interview and a political speech, respectively. Both applications were deemed manifestly ill-founded, with the latter extrapolating on when the blended approach of Articles 10–17 can be used.

Williamson v Germany (2019) involved an application brought by a bishop. He had given an interview to a Swedish television programme in which he claimed that six million Jews were not gassed and denied the existence of gas chambers. *Der Spiegel* later published an article quoting his statements verbatim. Specifically, a journalist from Swedish television conducted an interview with the applicant for the programme *Uppdrag granskning* ('Mission: Investigate'), which specialises in investigative journalism. The interview took place in Germany, where the applicant was temporarily present to consecrate a Swedish pastor as a deacon. At that time, the applicant did not reside in Germany. The interview was initially intended to focus exclusively on religious

61 *M'Bala M'Bala* (n 60) para 33
62 *M'Bala M'Bala* (n 60) para 50
63 *M'Bala M'Bala* (n 60) para 39

matters, as agreed upon beforehand by the journalist and the applicant. For approximately 45 minutes, the discussion remained confined to religious topics. However, the journalist later shifted the focus of the interview, leading to the following excerpts of dialogue:

Journalist:	Bishop Williamson, are these your words: "There was not one Jew killed by the gas chambers. It was all lies, lies, lies." Are these your words?
Applicant, pauses:	There, you are quoting from Canada, I believe, yes, of many years ago. I believe that the historical evidence, historical evidence is strongly, is hugely against six million Jews having been deliberately gassed in gas chambers as a deliberate policy of Adolf Hitler.
Journalist:	But you say not one Jew was killed.
Applicant:	In gas chambers. I think.
Journalist:	So there [were] no gas chambers?
Applicant:	I believe there were no gas chambers, yes. I think as far as I have studied the evidence—I am not going by emotion, I am going by—as far as I have understood the evidence, I think for instance, people who are against what is very widely believed today about "the Holocaust" I think that people, those people, conclude—the revisionists as they are called—I think the most serious conclude that between two and three hundred thousand Jews perished in Nazi concentration camps, but not one of them by gassing in a gas chamber. You may have heard of the Leuchter report? Fred Leuchter was an expert in gas chambers.

Der Spiegel published an article quoting the applicant's statements denying the existence of gas chambers during the Nazi regime. These remarks were subsequently covered by major German newspapers, television and radio outlets. The district court issued a penal order finding the applicant guilty of incitement to hatred and sentencing him to 100-day fines of EUR 65 each. Following the applicant's appeal, a main hearing was held, after which the court reduced the sentence to 90-day fines of EUR 20 each. All further appeals to the regional court, court of appeal and federal constitutional court were dismissed.

The ECtHR concurred with the regional court's evaluation of the applicant's minimisation of genocide, emphasising its own sensitivity to certain historical contexts.[64] Within this framework, coupled with the leniency of the imposed sentence, the Court found the application to be manifestly

64 *Williamson v Germany* App no 64496/17 (ECHR, 8 January 2019) para 27

ill-founded. In terms of the sensitivity the Court shows to the Holocaust and Germany's past, it stated that it

> sees no reason to depart from that assessment and reiterates that it has always been sensitive to the historical context of the High Contracting Party concerned when reviewing whether there exists a pressing social need for interference with rights under the Convention and that, in the light of their historical role and experience, States which have experienced the Nazi horrors may be regarded as having a special moral responsibility to distance themselves from the mass atrocities perpetrated by the Nazis.[65]

In addition to the particular sensitivity demonstrated by the Court to revisionist or negationist speech when it comes to the Holocaust and the hint at positive obligations in the preceding paragraph, the Court concurred with the domestic assessment that the applicant had downplayed genocide.[66] It then turned to ascertaining whether the penalty was necessary in a democratic society and, in doing so, agreed with the domestic assessment that the applicant explicitly denied and downplayed the genocide of Jews under the Nazi regime, disparaging the dignity of Jewish victims and potentially disturbing public peace in Germany.[67] The applicant claimed that he had not intended the statements to be broadcast in Germany. Here, the ECtHR emphasised, referring to *M'Bala M'Bala*, that interpreting and applying domestic law is primarily the responsibility of national authorities, particularly courts. Its role under Article 10 is limited to reviewing whether those decisions were based on an acceptable assessment of the relevant facts.[68] The ECtHR found that the applicant agreed to the interview in Germany, knowing his statements were subject to criminal liability there, and did not take sufficient steps to prevent its broadcast in Germany.[69] It noted that previous cases heard by the former EComHR and current ECtHR which involved the denial of the Holocaust and other such positions on Nazi crimes were inadmissible.[70] The ECtHR saw no reason to disagree, noting that the applicant neither distanced himself from the statements nor contested their assessment. Instead, he sought to prevent the interview's broadcast to avoid liability, leading the Court to conclude that his expression aimed to promote ideas contrary to the Convention.

In *Pastörs v Germany* (2019), the applicant, a politician and member of parliament affiliated with the National Democratic Party of Germany, delivered

65 *Williamson* (n 64)
66 *Williamson* (n 64) para 26
67 *Williamson* (n 64)
68 *Williamson* (n 64) para 23
69 *Williamson* (n 64) para 24
70 *Williamson* (n 64) para 20

Holocaust-denying remarks during a parliamentary session the day following Holocaust Remembrance Day. His speech included claims that "the so-called Holocaust is being used for political and commercial purposes." He further referenced a "barrage of criticism and propagandistic lies" and "Auschwitz projections." The district court convicted the applicant of violating the memory of the dead and defamation and sentenced him to eight months' imprisonment, suspended on probation. The regional court and court of appeal dismissed the appeals. The federal constitutional court declined to accept the applicant's complaint.

The ECtHR started off with a reference to Article 10 of the ECHR and looked at the government's submission regarding Article 17. It then proceeded to consider previous cases under Articles 10 and/or 17 in the framework of Holocaust denial, referring to cases such as *Williamson*, which was an Articles 10–17 blend. It reiterated that Article 17 is 'only applied on an exceptional basis and in extreme cases,'[71] and that it should be employed if the impugned speech sought to go against the values of the Convention. In this case, the Court extrapolated on when and how an Articles 10–17 blend can be used and underscored that, in cases concerning Holocaust denial, the decision to apply Article 17 directly and declare a complaint inadmissible, or to assess the matter under Article 10 and invoke Article 17 during the necessity analysis of the alleged interference, is determined on a case-by-case basis.[72] The Court's clarification is valuable as it provides insight into the application of Article 17, explaining when Article 17 is invoked as a stand-alone basis for inadmissibility versus when it is employed as an interpretative aid within the framework of Article 10. This distinction is critical for understanding the Court's blended approach, wherein Article 17 may shape the necessity assessment under Article 10(2) rather than being applied outrightly. By articulating the factors contributing to the way the articles are applied, the Court offers conceptual clarity regarding the interplay between these provisions, an area that has often been opaque in earlier case law. As welcome as clarifications are, this extrapolation may appear to be the Court's signalling that Article 17's application depends on a nuanced evaluation of the context, intent, and potential harm caused by the contested speech. However, this approach limits the automatic exclusion of controversial speech from protection and underscores the need for a detailed merits analysis when balancing freedom of expression against, *inter alia*, the rights and freedoms of others.

The Court highlighted the significance of political speech and that states 'have very limited latitude in regulating the content of Parliamentary speech. However, some regulation may be considered necessary in order to prevent forms of expression such as direct or indirect calls for violence.'[73] It proceeded

71 *Pastörs v Germany* (2019) App no 55225/14 (ECHR, 3 October 2019) para 37
72 *Pastörs* (n 71)
73 *Pastörs* (n 71) para 38

to recognise the importance of parliamentary immunity but highlighted that the Court may intervene in cases of speech by parliamentarians, although this is rare, even more so when it comes to members of the opposition.[74] In evaluating the case, the Court weighed the applicant's statements, which demonstrated contempt for Holocaust victims and thus conflicted with the core values of the Convention, against the context in which they were made during a parliamentary session by a sitting member of parliament. This setting could warrant enhanced protection and careful judicial scrutiny.[75]

Finding the case inadmissible, the ECtHR placed significant emphasis on the applicant's deliberate planning and careful selection of words to convey his message through obfuscation. It considered his speech to amount to a qualified form of Holocaust denial, expressing contempt for Holocaust victims and contradicting well-established historical facts.[76] He further alleged that representatives of the "so-called" democratic parties were exploiting the Holocaust to suppress and manipulate the German people. It was this element that led the Court to emphasise the critical significance of Article 17 of the Convention.[77] It determined that the applicant had clearly attempted to misuse his right to freedom of expression to advance ideas fundamentally at odds with the Convention's principles. This factor played a decisive role in assessing the necessity of the interference.[78] Further, the Court noted that the applicant 'intentionally stated untruths in order to defame the Jews and the persecution that they had suffered,'[79] reiterated that the court has 'always been sensitive to the historical context of the high contracting party when reviewing whether there exists a pressing social need for interference,'[80] and that 'states that have experienced the Nazi horrors may be regarded as having a special moral responsibility to distance themselves from the mass atrocities perpetrated by the Nazis.'[81] To this end, the speech 'affected the dignity of the Jews to the point that they justified a criminal law response.'[82] It did recognise that the penalty was not insignificant but found it to be proportional.

One may be tempted to make sense of decisions in Holocaust denial cases as a well-meaning yet paternalistic attempt by the Court to protect the memory of victims and the plight of the survivors of the Holocaust. While this does not automatically render legitimacy to the EComHR's and ECtHR's judgement in relation to free speech issues, the issue I would like to emphasise at the moment is the differential treatment of genocides. A stark contrast to the

74 *Pastörs* (n 71) para 38
75 *Pastörs* (n 71) para 35
76 *Pastörs* (n 71) para 46
77 *Pastörs* (n 71)
78 *Pastörs* (n 71)
79 *Pastörs* (n 71) para 48
80 *Pastörs* (n 71)
81 *Pastörs* (n 71)
82 *Pastörs* (n 71)

preceding is the ECtHR's treatment of the Armenian genocide. *Perinçek v Switzerland* (2015) concerned the applicant's criminal conviction for publicly disputing the occurrence of the Armenian genocide, referring to it as an "international lie" during several conferences in Switzerland. The ECtHR held that the applicant's statements did not constitute an abuse of rights under Article 17 of the Convention but did conclude that his conviction did not violate his right to freedom of expression under Article 10.

Perinçek, the chairman of the Turkish Workers' Party, made several public statements in Switzerland regarding the occurrence of the Armenian genocide. During a press conference, he referred to the genocide as "an international lie." In July, at a Treaty of Lausanne commemoration, he claimed the Armenian issue "did not exist," and in September, he asserted at a rally that there was "no genocide of the Armenians in 1915," framing it as a wartime conflict with heavy casualties on both sides. Following these remarks, the Switzerland–Armenia Association filed a criminal complaint. The district police court convicted Perinçek of racial discrimination, which criminalises denying or trivialising genocides in a manner that violates human dignity. The court found his statements to be driven by "racist and nationalistic" motives. He was fined 100 Swiss francs per day for 90 days, with an alternative of 30 days' imprisonment if unpaid, and ordered to pay 1,000 CHF in damages to the Switzerland–Armenia Association. Perinçek's appeals were dismissed by the cantonal court, which upheld the genocide's recognition as a historical fact, and by the federal court, which reaffirmed the conviction and cited his racist motives. He lodged an appeal to the ECtHR on the grounds that his Article 10 right had been violated. In 2013, the ECtHR's Grand Chamber ruled that the conviction breached Article 10, finding that the Swiss courts had failed to demonstrate a 'pressing social need' or justify that the conviction was 'necessary in a democratic society' to protect the dignity of the victims' descendants. In 2014, the Swiss government requested a referral to the ECtHR's Grand Chamber. The Grand Chamber held that the applicant's remarks addressed a matter of public interest and did not amount to an incitement to hatred or intolerance. It further noted that the context in which the statements were made was not characterised by heightened social tensions and concluded that the comments did not infringe upon the dignity of Armenians to a degree warranting the application of criminal sanctions.

The Grand Chamber did not apply Article 17 to this case, in antithesis to Holocaust denial cases. In distinguishing this case from Holocaust denial cases, the Grand Chamber noted that Holocaust denial is a principal driver of anti-Semitism,[83] and that the facts related to Holocaust denial have, 'for historical and contextual reasons, invariably been presumed.'[84] The Court put forth several—unconvincing, in my opinion—factors for the differential treatment of the Armenian genocide. It looked at temporal and geographic elements,

83 *Perinçek v Switzerland* App no 27510/08 (15 October 2015) para 175
84 *Perinçek* (n 83) para 234

noting that the events in question had occurred approximately 90 years earlier and that the applicant's remarks were made in Switzerland concerning incidents that had taken place in the Ottoman Empire.[85] This contextual analysis contrasts sharply with the approach taken in cases involving National Socialism and Holocaust denial, where such considerations are notably absent. Further, the Court was influenced by the lack of legal consensus within Europe as to whether the denial of the Armenian genocide was punishable by national law.[86] Further, the Court did not agree with domestic courts that there was a 'general consensus' that the events in question fell under the framework of a genocide.[87] It did not provide any substantial evidence to support this position but, instead, noted:

> In any event, it is even doubtful that there can be a 'general consensus,' particularly among academics, about events such as those in issue in the present case, given that historical research is by definition subject to controversy and dispute and does not really lend itself to definitive conclusions or the assertion of objective and absolute truths.[88]

Recognising that the historical assessment of such events is inherently 'controversial and debatable' and not prone to 'definitive conclusions or objective and absolute truths,' the Court framed the discussion as a matter of public interest. This reasoning has never been applied in Holocaust-related cases in which the Court refers to 'clearly established historical facts.'[89] The Court justified its departure from prior rulings restricting Holocaust denial by asserting that Holocaust denial serves as a primary driver of anti-Semitism. In the Swiss case, however, it found that:

> Taking into account the overall thrust of his statements, [the Court] does not perceive them as a form of incitement to hatred or intolerance. The applicant did not express contempt or hatred for the victims of the events of 1915. . . . He did not call the Armenians liars, use abusive terms with respect to them, or attempt to stereotype.[90]

In Holocaust denial cases, the Court has never required such a contextual analysis to determine whether the speech constituted incitement to hatred or intolerance. Instead, it has consistently presumed a direct link between Holocaust denial and hatred, citing 'historical and contextual reasons'[91] for this automatic association. This contrasting approach underscores a significant

85 *Perinçek* (n 83)
86 *Perinçek* (n 83) para 229
87 *Perinçek* (n 83) para 116
88 *Perinçek* (n 83) para 117
89 *Perinçek* (n 83) para 243
90 *Perinçek* (n 83) para 233
91 *Perinçek* (n 83) para 235

inconsistency in the Court's treatment of genocides. Regarding the statements made in the Swiss case, the Court stated that the present case differs significantly from Holocaust denial cases, like *Robert Faurisson v France*, a case before the UN's Human Rights Committee. First, unlike Holocaust deniers, the applicant did not deny concrete historical events but questioned the legal classification of the Armenian genocide. This assertion is confusing since it says that the applicant did not deny any concrete historical events but, rather, questioned if what the Armenians experienced was a genocide. That, in itself, is a denial of a concrete historical event in that the applicants denied the historical event of the Armenian genocide. Second, Holocaust-related crimes were prosecuted under a clear legal framework established by the Nuremberg Tribunal. Third, the historical facts concerning the Holocaust were confirmed by an international court, giving them undeniable legal recognition.[92] The fact that the international community set up the Nuremberg tribunal but did not set up a tribunal for the genocide of the Armenian people is an issue marking the dysfunctionality of international law rather than a reality to be relied on by the highest court in Europe when discriminating amongst genocides. Further, there are several cases discussed previously where the applicants did not, *per se*, deny the genocide of the Jews but, instead, denied the involvement of Hitler and the Nazi Party in this genocide,[93] or the use of gas chambers in particular.[94]

The Court put emphasis on giving meaning to the use of Article 17, something which may not have occurred if it was dealing with a case involving the Holocaust. Particularly, it stated:

> Since the decisive point under Article 17—whether the applicant's statements sought to stir up hatred or violence, and whether by making them he attempted to rely on the Convention to engage in an activity or perform acts aimed at the destruction of the rights and freedoms laid down in it—is not immediately clear and overlaps with the question whether the interference with the applicant's right to freedom of expression was 'necessary in a democratic society,' the Court finds that the question whether Article 17 is to be applied must be joined to the merits of the applicant's complaint under Article 10 of the Convention.[95]

The Court acknowledged that determining whether the applicant's statements constituted an abuse of rights under Article 17 by inciting hatred or undermining Convention values cannot be easily separated from assessing whether restricting his speech was 'necessary in a democratic society' under Article 10,

92 *Perinçek* (n 83) para 117
93 *Witzsch* (n 58)
94 *Remer* (n 48); *Williamson* (n 64)
95 *Perinçek* (n 83) para 115

even though this separation can be seen in the preceding plethora of cases. When it comes to Holocaust denial, and based on previous case law, the hatred is, in fact, immediately clear to the Court, so the preceding paragraph may not be as relevant. The Grand Chamber did find an Article 10 violation after the application of Article 10(2) limitation grounds.

The previously described differentiation in treatment of the Armenian genocide effectively creates an implicit hierarchy of historical suffering, diminishing the recognition afforded to Armenian genocide victims compared to Holocaust victims. Judges Vučinić (Montenegro) and Pinto de Albuquerque (Portugal) expressed a similar concern in their joint partly dissenting opinion, criticising this unequal treatment by pointing out that

> the sufferings of an Armenian because of the genocidal policy of the Ottoman Empire are not worth less than those of a Jew under the Nazi genocidal policy. And the denial of Hayots Tseghaspanutyun . . . or Meds Yeghern . . . is not less dangerous than Holocaust denial.[96]

2.3 *Genocide Denial: Some Article 17 Commentary*

In light of the preceding text, while Article 17 is retained mostly for Holocaust cases in comparison to other hate speech cases which involve the targeting of protected characteristics, within the sphere of Holocaust denial cases, the ECtHR has adopted varying approaches, with some adjudicated under Article 17 and others a mix of both Articles 10 and 17. While Article 17 remains very central to the handling of Holocaust denial cases, what we do see over time is an Articles 10–17 blend. This blend reflects the Court's evolving method of addressing the most egregious forms of hate speech by using Article 17 not merely as an exclusionary mechanism but as a contextual lens for interpreting Article 10(2). However, this approach risks blurring the distinction between Articles 10 and 17, creating uncertainty about when Article 17 will serve as a strict exclusionary rule or as an interpretative aid. This lack of clarity may undermine predictability in the Court's free expression jurisprudence. For example, *Williamson* invoked Article 17 to reinforce its interpretation of Article 10(2) and support the necessity of state interference. This was recognised in *Pastörs*, where Article 17 was described as an interpretative aid to Article 10(2). This approach, while seemingly categorical, presents challenges when juxtaposed with the Court's broader jurisprudence on freedom of expression. In the context of the Armenian genocide, the Court has emphasised that 'it is an integral part of freedom of expression to seek

96 *Perinçek* (n 83) Joint Partly Dissenting Opinions of Judges Vučinić and Pinto de Albuquerque, para 22

historical truth,'[97] although maintaining that 'it is not its role to arbitrate the underlying historical issues.'[98] This tension highlights an inconsistency in the Court's stance, raising questions about the criteria for determining when historical commentary is protected and when it crosses into the realm of abuse precluded by Convention protection. The divergence suggests a heightened sensitivity to Holocaust-related expressions, reflecting the weight of historical atrocities and their resonance within the Convention's foundational values. While this sensitivity is understandable given the profound impact of the Holocaust on Europe's collective memory and the foundational backdrop of the Council of Europe, the Court has not extended comparable reasoning to other genocides, raising concerns about a hierarchy of historical suffering. The Court's enhanced sensitivity in Holocaust denial cases might be seen as a misguided yet well-intentioned effort to safeguard the memory of Holocaust victims and acknowledge the suffering of survivors. However, its treatment of the Armenian genocide reveals an inconsistent and arbitrary approach to historical accuracy and the protection afforded to victims. As discussed earlier, a striking example of this is *Perinçek*, where the Court found that prosecuting the applicant for describing the Armenian genocide as "an international lie" did not fall within the ambit of Article 17. The Court nevertheless found a violation of Article 10. In justifying this decision, the Court emphasised the absence of a legal consensus in Europe regarding the criminalisation of Armenian genocide denial, noting that historical classifications of such events remain subject to scholarly debate. This reasoning starkly contrasts with Holocaust denial cases, where the Court presumes incitement due to the unique historical and legal recognition of the Holocaust.

Moreover, the Court has consistently upheld restrictions, justifying them on the basis that Holocaust denial is a primary driver of anti-Semitism. In relation to this last point, it could be argued that the former EComHR and the ECtHR's jurisprudence on Holocaust-related cases is based on a presumption that the nexus between Holocaust denial and incitement to hatred or intolerance is not explicitly assessed but is instead 'invariably presumed'[99] due to 'historical and contextual reasons.'[100] However, the Court has not fully articulated the basis for this presumption. In antithesis to this, the Court, in *Perinçek*, invoked temporal and spatial distinctions, noting that the events in question occurred approximately 90 years earlier and that expressions denying the genocide were made in a different geographical and cultural context, far removed from the Ottoman Empire, where the events occurred. Such contextual distinctions and investigations are absent in case law concerning Holocaust denial. In this context, the Holocaust has been framed as a unique historical event, universally recognised and legally confirmed by the Nuremberg

97 *Perinçek* (n 83) para 223
98 *Perinçek* (n 83)
99 *Perinçek* (n 83) para 233
100 *Perinçek* (n 83)

Tribunal, justifying its categorical exclusion from Article 10 protection. However, the ECtHR's handling of *Perinçek* reflects a very different approach, where the Court emphasised the absence of a legal consensus on the Armenian genocide's classification as genocide and invoked the need for open historical debate. It argued that historical events, unless confirmed by international legal instruments, should remain subject to scholarly discussion. Whereas applications pertaining to Holocaust denial have systematically been considered inadmissible, triggering Article 17's exclusionary mechanism,[101] the application pertaining to the Armenian genocide prompted a more cautious legal and contextual analysis under Article 10. This divergence highlights key jurisprudential challenges and raises questions about the underlying principles guiding the Court's reasoning. One possible explanation for this differential treatment lies in the historical experiences of the Council of Europe's founding states, which were directly affected by the Holocaust, but less exposed to Soviet-era atrocities or the Armenian genocide. However, the selective application of Article 17 risks creating a hierarchy of historical suffering. Judicial protection should not depend on the geopolitical sensitivities or historical proximity of member states.

3 Violent Speech

The ECtHR has frequently addressed cases involving expressions related to violence, particularly in Turkish cases concerning the Kurdish issue. Since these cases fall more broadly into the spectrum of political speech, they are not dealt with extensively in this book. Nevertheless, this section provides an overview of some of the violent speech cases against Turkey and draws parallels, where relevant, with hate speech cases discussed earlier and in the previous chapters. Also, the section identifies an odd characteristic in some of these cases, namely, that the ECtHR has referred to 'hate speech' in several of them even when this involves anti-government/anti-establishment political speech rather than the targeting of protected characteristics. Hate speech, *per se*, should be limited to speech which directly or indirectly targets protected characteristics either through outright racism, for example, or through genocide denial, which, for the Court, by default, constitutes anti-Semitism. Even in cases with comparable facts examined in the section on violent speech, the Court has inconsistently characterised certain expressions as hate speech while refraining from doing so in others, adding to the confusion on the use of the term. The-already lacking definitional framework causes a variety of problems, as discussed in preceding chapters, with the incorporation of anti-government speech, whether violent or not, within that setting failing to contribute to some clarity. Cases such as *Erbakan v Turkey* (2006), which involved the targeting of

101 For example, in cases such as Garaudy, Witzsch and M'Bala M'Bala, the ECtHR has repeatedly invoked Article 17, deeming such expressions fundamentally incompatible with the Convention's democratic values

protected characteristics, and *IA v Turkey* (2005), which involved alleged religious hatred, are dealt with in more detail in the previous chapter. *Gündüz v Turkey* (2003) is also found in the previous chapter on hate speech directed at protected characteristics, since it laid the groundwork for the *Féret* paradigm of what the elements of hate speech are, as well as other Turkish cases which are particularly pertinent to the issues covered in the previous chapter.

Sürek v Turkey (1999) was an application made by the principal shareholder of a Turkish weekly who faced charges for publishing two readers' letters that referred to Kurdistan and depicted the PKK's[102] actions as a "national independence war." He was convicted for disseminating separatist propaganda and given a fine. Some of his statements include thus:

> In the face of the escalating war of national liberation in Kurdistan, the fascist Turkish army continues to carry out bombings. The "Şırnak massacre" which Gerçek journalists revealed at the cost of great self-sacrifice has been another concrete example this week.
>
> The TC (Republic of Turkey) murder gang is continuing its murders . . . on the grounds of 'protecting the Republic of Turkey.' But as people wake up to what is happening and become more aware, as they gradually learn to stand up for their rights and the idea that 'if they won't give, then we'll take by force' gradually germinates in people's minds and grows stronger day by day—as long as this continues, the murders will obviously also continue . . . [b]eginning of course with those who planted the seed in people's minds—according to the generals, imperialism's hired killers, and according to the double-chinned, pot-bellied, stiff-necked Turguts, Süleymans and Bülents.

The ECtHR determined that the letters contained hate speech and glorified violence. It dismissed the applicant's argument that he was merely a shareholder, holding that his role gave him sufficient influence over the publication's editorial direction. Consequently, the Court found no violation of Article 10. Its assessment considered the broader context of the volatile security situation and terrorism in southeastern Turkey.[103] The Court rendered the applicant responsible for the letters and their content even though he did not write them and even though he did not personally associate with them since he had

> provided their writers with an outlet for stirring up violence and hatred. The Court does not accept his argument that he should be exonerated from any criminal liability for the content of the letters on account of the fact that he only has a commercial and not an editorial relationship with

102 Kurdistan Workers' Party—PKK

103 *Sürek v Turkey* (1999) App no 26682/95 (ECHR, 8 July 1999) para 52

> the review. He was an owner and as such had the power to shape the editorial direction of the review.[104]

In *Karataş v Turkey* (1999), the applicant published a collection of poems about the Kurdish rebellion, for which he was prosecuted for spreading propaganda against the state's indivisibility. Segments of his poetry include thus:

> [L]et us go children of the unyielding we have heard there is a rebellion in the mountains can we hear and do nothing? let the festivities and celebrations begin let flames as high as the rooftops reach for the sky so that before the day's end the cannons fall silent venerable Kurdistan beautiful Kurdistan Kurdistan our friend.

The public prosecutor accused the applicant and his publisher for disseminating propaganda against the indivisibility of the state. The applicant was sentenced to one year and eight months' imprisonment and a fine of 41,666,666 Turkish lira (TLR). It also ordered the confiscation of the publications concerned. A new law was passed that led to the reduction of his prison sentence to one year, one month and ten days' imprisonment and increased the fine to TRL 111,111,110.

The ECtHR considered the security tensions in southeastern Turkey[105] but concluded that, despite some provocative language, the poems were artistic expressions[106] reflecting deep frustration rather than incitements to rebellion. The Court noted that 'the fact that they were artistic in nature and of limited impact made them less a call to an uprising than an expression of deep distress in the face of a difficult political situation.'[107] In light of the preceding text, and given their limited societal impact, the Court ruled that the conviction violated Article 10.

In *Gerger v Turkey* (1999), the applicant was a journalist who sent a speech to be read during the memorial ceremony of two of his friends who were sentenced to death for allegedly seeking to destroy the constitutional order by violence. Parts of his speech included thus:

> The spirit of resistance and revolt of those heroic years, a nightmare for the rulers, has been with the country for more than twenty years. The socialist flag, which was borne aloft at the time and is representative of the only system capable of replacing the incumbent capitalist system, is still flying. From the seeds of liberation of the Kurdish people sown in those days the guerrilla campaign in the mountains of Kurdistan was born.

104 *Sürek* (n 103) para 63
105 *Karataş v Turkey* (1999) App no 2316894 (ECHR, 8 July 1099) para 44
106 *Karataş* (n 105) para 49
107 *Karataş* (n 105) para 52

The applicant was charged with disseminating propaganda against the unity of the Turkish nation and the territorial integrity of the state. He was sentenced to one year, eight months' imprisonment and given a fine of 208,333,333 Turkish liras.

Several ECtHR judges emphasised that the intent behind speech and its potential to incite violence must be critically evaluated. Judge Bonello (Malta) stressed that incitement should pose a 'clear and present danger' to justify criminal punishment.[108] The ECtHR determined that the applicant's speech amounted to political criticism of the Turkish authorities.[109] Also, since the events at the Iraq border had already concluded, Turkey could not invoke them to justify restricting the speech.[110] Additionally, the speech was delivered at a memorial service, limiting its potential impact on public order.[111] The Court concluded that the speech did not incite violence, armed resistance or rebellion.[112] As such, it found, by a majority, that the applicant's rights under Article 10 had been violated.

In *Erdoğdu v Turkey* (2000), a periodical published a reader's article titled "The Kurdish Problem is a Turkish Problem." The public prosecutor initiated criminal proceedings against the publisher and the editor on the grounds that the article portrayed separatist terrorism in southeastern Turkey as "Kurdish National Resistance," referred to Kurdistan and called for support of this resistance. The defendant was charged with disseminating propaganda threatening the territorial integrity and indivisible unity of the Turkish state and fined TRL 50,900,000, which the Court decided to defer. The editor of the periodical filed an application at the ECtHR, arguing that his Article 10 right had been violated. The ECtHR agreed with him and, in finding such a violation, noted that the interviewee expressed moderate views on the Kurdish issue without endorsing violence, suggesting that the restriction aimed more at stifling political debate than curbing hate speech.[113] In fact, the Court noted that:

> Where a publication cannot be categorised as inciting to violence, Contracting States cannot with reference to the prevention of disorder or crime restrict the right of the public to be informed by bringing the weight of the criminal law to bear on the media.[114]

108 *Gerger v Turkey* App no 24919/94 (ECHR, 8 July 1999), Concurring Opinion of Judge Bonello
109 *Gerger* (n 108) para 48
110 *Gerger* (n 108) para 49
111 *Gerger* (n 108) para 50
112 *Gerger* (n 108)
113 *Erdoğdu v Turkey* (2000) App no 25723/94 (ECHR, 15 June 2020) para 62
114 *Erdoğdu* (n 113) para 71

The Court has also noted a positive obligation, or at least something close to that, when it comes to protecting freedom of expression in the framework of political speech. *Gündem v Turkey* (2000) involved *Özgür Gündem*, a Turkish daily published since 1992, which aimed to represent Turkish Kurdish perspectives. The applicants claimed that before its closure in 1994, the newspaper faced a state-backed campaign of violence, including journalist killings, disappearances and harassment, alongside seizures, fines, and prosecutions. They argued that authorities failed to provide protection or investigate effectively. The Turkish government countered that the newspaper served as a PKK propaganda tool and that restrictions targeted direct incitement to violence. The applicants lodged complaints under Article 10 for interference with freedom of expression in combination with Article 14 (non-discrimination). The ECtHR held that Turkey had not taken sufficient steps to safeguard the newspaper's ability to exercise its right to freedom of expression. It also ruled that actions like search-and-arrest operations were excessive and unjustified.[115] These circumstances ultimately forced the newspaper to cease publication, leading the Court to find a violation of Article 10. The Court noted that, even against a contextual background of an unsettled political situation in the particular region, promoting the idea of a separate Kurdish entity is not worsening the situation.[116] It recognised the tone and style of the articles, noting:

> While several of the articles were highly critical of the authorities and attributed unlawful conduct to the security forces, sometimes in colourful and derogatory terms, the Court nonetheless finds that they cannot be reasonably regarded as advocating or inciting the use of violence.[117]

This case is of particular importance when understanding the positive obligation arising from Article 10, something that marks only a few relevant cases. Specifically, the ECtHR held that:

> The Court recalls the key importance of freedom of expression as one of the preconditions for a functioning democracy. Genuine, effective exercise of this freedom does not depend merely on the state's duty not to interfere, but may require positive measures of protection, even in the sphere of relations between individuals. . . . In determining whether or not a positive obligation exists, regard must be had to the fair balance that has to be struck between the general interest of the community and

115 *Özgür Gündem v Turkey* App no 23144/93 (ECHR, 16 March 2020) para 80
116 *Özgür* (n 115) para 70
117 *Özgür* (n 115) para 70

> the interests of the individual, the search for which is inherent throughout the Convention.[118]

In *Medya FM Reha Radio v Turkey* (2006), the applicant, a radio broadcasting company, faced a suspension of its broadcasting authorisation due to remarks challenging the existence and independence of the Turkish Republic, as well as principles of national unity and state indivisibility. Although the Supreme Administrative Court overturned this decision, which was never enforced, national authorities later issued a warning after similar comments were aired. Following further broadcasts deemed by the regulatory authority to incite violence, terrorism or racial discrimination, the company's broadcasting rights were suspended twice for 30 days each and ultimately banned for 365 days, which was the maximum allowable penalty.

One such broadcast contained the following statement:

> Hey kid, pick up the ball, the stones. Exhaust your anger with stones. Do you know why you have to build up your anger? You saw the ruins of your village. Gather your anger in secret. Let your anger become the punch. Let the punch become revolt. Gather revolt, accumulate revolt. Let the revolt become the revolution.

The ECtHR determined that the speech amounted to hate speech, incitement to violence or an apology of violence,[119] placing it outside the protection of the ECHR, as it is incompatible with the fundamental values of justice and peace expressed in the convention. It held that Turkey had a broad margin of appreciation in regulating such expression.

In *Erdal Taş v Turkey (No. 5)* (2007), the applicant, an editor-in-chief of a daily newspaper, was convicted of disseminating propaganda against the indivisibility of the state due to publishing a statement from a terrorist organisation in an article titled "The Revolution of Kurds," which analysed the Kurdish issue. The State Security Court sentenced him to five months' imprisonment, later commuted to a fine of approximately EUR 800, and imposed a one-month publication ban on the newspaper.

Quotes from the article include:

> Those who, with the enthusiasm created by the development of the Kurdish National Movement, discovered Kurdish ancestors, or even learned to speak Kurdish again, this time, in order to go to rich Turkey, like millions of people in Eastern Europe now, would seek Turkish ancestors. . . . A defeated and losing Kurdish movement would not only

118 *Özgür* (n 115) para 43
119 *Medya FM Reha Radio v Turkey* (2006) App no 32842/02 (ECHR, 14 November 2006)

> imply the defeat of the Kurds but also that of the Turks. This would mean the end of Turkey's dream of Westernization.

The ECtHR found that the article was a critical discussion of the Kurdish question but did not constitute hate speech and did not call for violence. It unanimously found a violation of Article 10 and noted that:

> The Court observed that the contested article contained critical ideas on the Kurdish question which did not call for the use of violence, armed resistance or uprising, and that it was not a question of hate speech, which is, in the Court's view, the essential element to be taken into consideration.[120]

In *Temel v Turkey* (2011), the applicant, a political party leader, delivered remarks at a meeting addressing the Kurdish issue and advocating for a democratic resolution. Excerpts of the remarks include thus:

> If our country is not to be the victim of another period of confrontation, it is necessary to put an end to isolation practices in prisons as soon as possible. . . . Turkey's main problem, namely the Kurdish question, must form the basis of the peaceful democratic solution. . . . To remain silent today and to remain without acting amounts to having to bear tomorrow, morally, all responsibilities.
>
> The crowd, making the sign of peace, chanted the slogans "No to war" and "Let the dungeons be emptied, freedom for men." . . . The crowd dispersed, chanting the slogan "No to war."

The applicant received a ten-month prison sentence and a fine for promoting violence and supporting terrorist activities.

The ECtHR determined that the national courts had failed to consider the applicant's statements in their entirety, instead focusing selectively on certain excerpts to conclude that he was promoting violence and terrorism.[121] It extrapolated on the issue of violence, ruling that his remarks neither incited violence nor qualified as hate speech. Specifically, it stated:

> The Court also noted that the declaration read as a whole did not encourage the use of violence, armed resistance or uprising and—a fundamental element to be taken into account—it did not constitute hate speech either. The content of the declaration was also not likely

120 *Erdal Taş v Turkey* (No 5) (2007) App no 2984802 (ECHR, 29 July 2007) para 39
121 *Temel v Turkey* App no 16853/05 (ECHR, 1 May 2011) para 61

> to promote violence by instilling a deep and irrational hatred towards identified persons.[122]

More recent cases against Turkey which involve the Kurdish issue have, as many of the aforementioned, adopted a permissive stance to free speech. For example, in *Üçdağ v Turkey* (2021), an imam was convicted of disseminating propaganda for a terrorist organisation. The charges stemmed from two Facebook posts. One included an image of armed individuals allegedly linked to the PKK, while the other depicted a protest scene with a caption urging solidarity with residents of his area during a period of unrest. The assize court sentenced him to about one and a half years' imprisonment, suspended for five years. His appeal to the Turkish Constitutional Court was dismissed for procedural reasons, preventing substantive review. The ECtHR found a violation of Article 10. The ECtHR emphasised that the applicant's posts, though potentially provocative, did not constitute incitement to violence.[123] It also found that the domestic courts 'did not demonstrate in a sufficient manner how the applicant's posts were directly connected to the promotion of violence or constituted a threat to public order.'[124] Furthermore, the Court underlined that criminal sanctions, even if suspended, 'may have a chilling effect on the exercise of freedom of expression.'[125] The judgement highlights the importance of assessing both the context and the intent behind speech before imposing restrictions. The domestic courts, according to the ECtHR, failed to demonstrate a direct connection between the posts and any actual promotion of violence or threat to public order.[126] This omission rendered the interference with Üçdağ's freedom of expression disproportionate under Article 10.

The case of *Belek and Velioğlu v Turkey* (2015) concerned the owner and editor-in-chief, respectively, of a daily newspaper *Günlük Evrensel.* The newspaper published an article titled "Kadek Prisoners Call for a Democratic Solution," which included statements from imprisoned members of the KADEK (Kurdistan Freedom and Democracy Congress, a successor to the PKK). The article criticised prison conditions, called for amnesty laws, and referenced the treatment of Abdullah Öcalan, the organisation's leader. The Turkish authorities charged the applicants for publishing propaganda attributed to an illegal armed organisation. Both were fined, and *Günlük Evrensel* was temporarily banned from publication for three days. Their appeal to the court of cassation was unsuccessful, and although a subsequent legislative amendment lifted the publication ban, the fines remained enforceable. The ECtHR found a

122 *Temel* (n 121) para 62
123 *Üçdağ v Turkey* App no 23314/19 (ECHR, 31 August 2021)
124 *Üçdağ* (n 123) para 55
125 *Üçdağ* (n 123) para 60
126 *Üçdağ* (n 123) para 55

violation of Article 10. It noted that while the article discussed issues linked to KADEK, it contained no incitement to violence, armed resistance, or hatred, which are essential factors in determining whether a restriction is necessary in a democratic society. The ECtHR criticised the Turkish courts for failing to demonstrate how the article posed a threat to public order or security. It held that imposing fines and banning the publication constituted disproportionate interference with the applicants' freedom of expression. The Court emphasised that Article 10 protects not only favourable or neutral information but also content that may 'offend, shock, or disturb.'[127] It reiterated that restrictions on speech must be supported by 'sufficient and relevant reasons,'[128] which the Court considered were absent in this case.

A contrasting approach to many of the preceding cases was seen in *Leroy v France* (2009), which involved a cartoon about the September 11 attacks. Shortly after the attacks, a cartoonist published a drawing of the towers, accompanied by the caption "We have all dreamt of it. . . . Hamas did it." Following the publication of the drawing, the public prosecutor initiated proceedings against the applicant and the newspaper's publishing director on charges of complicity in condoning terrorism. The Court convicted both individuals, imposing a fine of EUR 1,500 on each. Additionally, they were ordered to publish the judgement at their own expense in *Ekaitza* and two other newspapers, as well as to cover the associated costs. Subsequent appeals against the conviction were rejected.

The ECtHR found no violation of Article 10, reasoning that the cartoon's proximity to the tragic event and the sensitive context of the Basque region made it likely to provoke violence and disrupt public order.[129] The link between the commentary and cartoon on the attacks in the United States and the sensitivities of the Basque region was not explained. Further, the ECtHR's decision was influenced by the caption accompanying the cartoon, observing that the applicant had conveyed moral support for those he believed to be responsible for the attacks.[130]

In *Stomakhin v Russia* (2018), it was essentially the principle of proportionality that played the central role in the outcome of this case. The applicant served as the editor, publisher and distributor of a monthly newsletter focused primarily on the war in Chechnya from 2000 to 2004. Authorities launched an investigation, accusing him of publishing content that incited extremism and promoted racial, national and social hatred. He was sentenced to five years in prison and banned from practising journalism for three years. After completing his sentence, he was released.

127 *Belek and Velioğlu v Turkey* App no 44227/05 (ECtHR, 6 October 2015) para 25
128 *Belek and Velioğlu* (n 127) para 26
129 *Leroy v France* App no 36109/03 (ECHR, 2 October 2008) para 45
130 *Leroy v France* App no 36109/03 (ECHR, 2 October 2008) para 43

The newsletter contained articles with statements such as:

> Let dozens of Chechen snipers take up their positions in the hills and the city ruins and hundreds and thousands of aggressors perish from their holy bullets! No mercy! Death to the Russian invaders!

In its analysis, the ECtHR considered the context of the ongoing conflict in the Chechen Republic.[131] It found that, while some of the applicant's statements justified terrorism and incited hatred, others fell within the bounds of permissible speech, reflecting legitimate discussion on the Chechen situation.[132]

> [The Court] reiterates in this connection that it is an integral part of freedom of expression to seek historical truth, and that a debate on the causes of acts of particular gravity which may amount to war crimes or crimes against humanity should be able to take place freely.[133]

It also noted that some political speech may be 'controversial and often virulent'[134] and, even though the statements contained 'hard-hitting criticism of official policy and communicated a one-sided view of the origin and responsibility of the situation . . . [cannot] . . . justify an interference with freedom of expression.'[135]

So the Court noted that not all the statements justified or incited hatred[136] and emphasised that the punishment imposed of five years' imprisonment and a three-year ban on the exercise of journalism was disproportionate, resulting in a violation of Article 10. It underlined that

> [a] fair balance should be struck between the individual's fundamental right to freedom of expression and a democratic society's legitimate right to protect itself against the activities of terrorist organisations.[137]

An interesting element in the preceding cases of violent speech which is by no means an extensive list but rather a well-rounded overview of what is out there is that Article 17 is not as prominent in the jurisprudence as one would except, particularly when compared with the previously discussed non-violent yet Holocaust-denying speech. A rare example of a violent speech case where Article 17 was used is *Roj TV A/S v Denmark* (2018). This case concerned convictions for terrorism-related offences stemming from the promotion

131 *Stomakhin v Russia* (2018) App no 52273/07 (ECHR, 9 May 2018) para 96
132 *Stomakhin* (n 131) para 124
133 *Stomakhin* (n 131) para 113
134 *Stomakhin* (n 131)
135 *Stomakhin* (n 131)
136 *Stomakhin* (n 131)
137 *Stomakhin* (n 131) para 96

of the PKK through television broadcasts. The broadcast featured heavily biased content, repeatedly urging viewers to engage in combat, join the organisation and glorify fallen guerrilla fighters as heroes. This was deemed propaganda for the PKK, a recognised terrorist group, rather than a mere expression of support. Additionally, the applicant company had received substantial financial backing from the PKK. The ECtHR held that the television station could not claim protection under Article 10, as the applicants had used it to advance aims incompatible with the core values of the Convention. The reasons for which the ECtHR employed Article 17 were set out by the Court as follows:

> The Court finds that, taking firstly account of the nature of the impugned programmes, which included incitement to violence and support for terrorist activity, elements extensively examined by the national courts, secondly, the fact that the views expressed therein were disseminated to a wide audience through television broadcasting and, thirdly, that they related directly to an issue which is paramount in modern European society—the prevention of terrorism and terrorist-related expressions advocating the use of violence—the applicant company's complaint does not, by virtue of Article 17 of the Convention, attract the protection afforded by Article 10.[138]

In conclusion, the first point to mention in relation to the preceding cases is to do with the term *hate speech*. In some cases, involving the Kurdish issue, the ECtHR refers to hate speech when assessing the protection (or not) of the speech in question. It is unclear why this is only done in some cases and not others which are factually very similar and deal with the same theme. More importantly, though, it is unclear why this speech qualifies as hate speech to begin with as it constitutes anti-establishment rhetoric with elements of violence at times but does not target protected characteristics. The targeting of such characteristics is a central element in defining hate speech, as outlined in the definitional framework established in Chapter 1 and reflected in the bulk of the ECtHR's jurisprudence. In cases such as *Erdal Taş*, where the ECtHR referred to the term hate speech, it did not elucidate why it did so or what elements would be required for the speech in question to count as hate speech. It is thus impossible to deduce the reasoning of the Court in integrating the term hate speech in some of the Turkish cases involving political violence.

In terms of comparison between cases, I find that the ECtHR's approach to violent speech cases reveals a jurisprudential duality shaped by contextual, political and historical factors. Turkish cases, predominantly involving the Kurdish issue, have prompted the Court to engage in detailed contextual

138 *Roj TV A/S v Denmark* (2018) App no 24683/14 (ECHR, 17 April 2018) para 47

assessments, balancing freedom of expression against national security and public order concerns. In these cases, the ECtHR has often highlighted the need for a pressing social need and a careful evaluation of whether the speech incited violence or merely expressed political dissent. Notably, in *Erdoğdu* and *Erdal Taş*, the Court underscored that critical political commentary on sensitive issues, such as the Kurdish question, could not be curtailed unless there was clear incitement to violence. Similarly, in *Temel* and *Gündem*, the ECtHR emphasised that the lack of direct incitement or hate speech warranted the highest protection under Article 10. These rulings establish that violent speech accusations require evidence of actual or imminent violence, placing a high threshold for state interference. However, in cases like *Sürek* and *Medya FM Reha Radio*, where speech was deemed to glorify violence or incite armed rebellion, the Court upheld state restrictions.

In fact, the distinction between classical hate speech jurisprudence, encompassing the targeting of protected characteristics, genocide denial and speech related to totalitarianism, and the primarily Turkish cases discussed earlier, which involve anti-government or anti-establishment expression, underscores a significant difference. In later cases, incitement to violence is a prerequisite for restricting speech, whereas this standard is not applied in hate speech cases. This is evident in rulings such as *Féret* (Islamophobic speech) and *Vejdeland* (homophobic speech), where the threshold for limiting expression was significantly lower. If the distinction arises from the principle that anti-government political discourse enjoys a higher level of protection, this is both reasonable and justifiable. However, it is crucial for this reasoning to be explicitly articulated by the Court. At the same time, such a distinction should not imply that speech targeting communities automatically falls at the opposite end of the spectrum in terms of protection. While several of the cases discussed in this section involve elements of violent speech, Article 17 is not invoked, nor is Article 10 protection categorically excluded. Instead, the ECtHR has often upheld Article 10 protections, reflecting the Court's recognition of the contextual and political nature of such speech rather than treating it as inherently abusive or inciting violence. However, the sporadic use of Article 17 in *Roj TV A/S* raises further questions about the Court's inconsistent application of this provision.

Lastly, while the ECtHR has recognised positive obligations to protect speech in contexts involving violence, such as in *Özgür Gündem v Turkey* and *Dink v Turkey*, this protective stance is absent in other speech categories. Instead, the Court has found positive obligations on states to punish hate speech where it involves revisionism and the obligation has been brought forth by the utterer of the speech, and where the applicant was a victim of hate speech either directly or indirectly as a member of a targeted group.

Conclusion

The ECtHR's jurisprudence on hate speech, as analysed in this chapter, highlights its complex and evolving struggle to reconcile the principles of freedom of expression with the imperatives of combatting ideologies that undermine democratic values. The Court's decisions reflect varying approaches across three primary categories, namely, totalitarianism, genocide denial and violent speech.

The Court has displayed consistency in its exclusion of Nazi propaganda and Holocaust denial from Article 10 protection, primarily through the invocation of Article 17, as evidenced in cases like *Kühnen v Germany* (1988) and *Schimanek v Austria* (2000). Here, the ECtHR underscored that National Socialism is incompatible with democratic principles and human rights, justifying blanket bans on Nazi symbols and propaganda. This strict approach aligns with the historical context of the ECHR's creation, reflecting Europe's collective memory of World War II and its commitment to preventing the resurgence of Nazi ideologies. However, the Court's treatment of symbols and expressions linked to other totalitarian regimes, such as Communism, has been less categorical. In *Vajnai v Hungary* (2008), the ECtHR found Hungary's ban on the red star symbol unjustified, emphasising the importance of contextual analysis and rejecting speculative risks. Similarly, in *Fáber v Hungary* (2012), the Court ruled in favour of the applicant for displaying a controversial symbol associated with a fascist regime, highlighting the absence of a clear and present danger to public order. These cases reflect the Court's nuanced and risk-based approach to totalitarian symbols, although inconsistencies persist. For instance, in *Nix v Germany* (2018), the Court upheld restrictions on the use of Nazi imagery in a public interest blog post, emphasising Germany's moral responsibility to distance itself from Nazi atrocities. This divergence in the Court's reasoning raises concerns about the consistency of its interpretive framework, particularly when historical sensitivity appears to justify disparate standards.

The Court has maintained a stringent stance on Holocaust denial, categorically excluding such speech from Article 10 protection through Article 17, as seen in *Garaudy v France* (2003) and *M'Bala M'Bala v France* (2015). These cases highlight the ECtHR's position that Holocaust denial constitutes a principal driver of anti-Semitism, undermines democratic values and poses a significant threat to public order. The Court has justified these restrictions by invoking the Holocaust's unique status as a 'clearly established historical fact' and its foundational relevance to the Convention's objectives of justice and peace. Conversely, the ECtHR's treatment of other genocides, such as the Armenian genocide, has been markedly different. In *Perinçek v Switzerland* (2015), the Court found that the applicant's denial of the Armenian genocide did not warrant Article 17's application and held that his conviction violated Article 10. The decision was predicated on the lack of a unified European stance on the Armenian genocide's classification and the contextual absence of heightened social tensions. This distinction reveals an implicit hierarchy of historical suffering within the Court's jurisprudence, raising critical questions about the uniformity of its principles. As Montenegrin judge Vučinić and Portuguese judge Pinto de Albuquerque observed in their dissenting opinion, such disparities risk devaluing the memory of non-Holocaust victims and undermining the Convention's commitment to equality. Moreover, the ECtHR's approach to hate speech reveals a pattern of implicit hierarchies and jurisprudential inconsistencies. While the Court's sensitivity to historical context, particularly in Holocaust-related cases, reflects its commitment to combatting anti-Semitism, its differential treatment of other genocides and totalitarian ideologies exposes a lack of principled consistency. The selective application of Article 17 and the varying thresholds for restricting expression raise concerns about the coherence of the Court's interpretative framework.

In cases involving violent speech, the ECtHR has oscillated between protecting political discourse and imposing positive obligations on states to address harmful expressions. For instance, in *Özgür Gündem v Turkey* (2000) and *Dink v Turkey* (2010), the Court recognised positive obligations on states to protect journalists and publications from violence, emphasising the importance of safeguarding democratic debate. However, this protective approach has not been extended to hate speech targeting protected characteristics. Instead, the Court has consistently upheld positive obligations to punish such speech, as seen in *Vejdeland v Sweden* (2012), where homophobic leaflets were deemed a serious threat to societal values, and *Atamanchuk v Russia* (2011), where xenophobic expressions warranted state intervention. While efforts to limit restrictions on anti-government speech are laudable and indispensable for the functioning of a democratic society, the previously described divergence needs some further extrapolation by the Court since, as it stands, classic hate speech jurisprudence demonstrates the Court's prioritisation of protecting victims of hate speech over safeguarding contentious speech. Analytical paradigms in cases where free speech has been effectively assessed and adjudicated, including *Fáber* and *Vajnai*, could start this off along with a reconsideration of thresholds of harms, with lessons learnt from the treatment of anti-establishment speech and an assessment of the kind of themes and issues that could also be integrated into other hate speech cases, such as low-threshold hatred cases, in order better to protect Article 10 and close the gap with *Handyside*.

The ECtHR's hate speech jurisprudence is marked by its efforts to balance freedom of expression with the protection of democratic values and historical memory. While the Court has shown robust protection for political discourse and nuanced evaluations in certain contexts, its differential treatment of symbols, ideologies and genocides underscores the need for a more principled and uniformed approach. To uphold its legitimacy as a guardian of human rights, the Court must strive for consistency in its application of Articles 10 and 17, ensuring that its decisions reflect the universality and impartiality of the Convention's foundational values.

Conclusion

1 The Low-Threshold Hatred Paradigm

The ECtHR's approach to the right to freedom of expression within the sphere of hate speech diverts from principles pertaining to the contours of expression in the name of prohibiting hate speech. In *Handyside v United Kingdom* (1976), the Court famously affirmed that freedom of expression includes speech that 'offends, shocks or disturbs.'[1] *Féret v Belgium* (2009)[2] is emblematic of the departure from *Handyside* principles, as it is the case which developed a paradigm which I refer to as the low-threshold hatred paradigm. *Féret* built on the pro-Sharia speech case of *Gündüz v Turkey* (2004), where the Court held that 'there can be no doubt that concrete expressions constituting hate speech, which may be insulting to particular individuals or groups, are not protected by Article 10 of the Convention.'[3] *Féret* involved an application by a far-right politician who distributed leaflets during an electoral campaign with statements such as "Stop the Islamization of Belgium" and allegations that a refugee centre "poisons the lives of residents." In upholding domestic restrictions on such speech, the Court equated insult, defamation and ridicule with hate speech that falls outside the protection of Article 10, denoting that incitement to violence is not a necessary prerequisite for hate speech. On this point, the Court highlighted that

> incitement to hatred did not necessarily require the calling of a specific act of violence or another criminal act. Attacks on persons committed through insults, ridicule or defamation aimed at specific population groups or incitement to discrimination, as in this case, sufficed for the authorities to give priority to fighting hate speech when confronted by the irresponsible use of freedom of expression which undermined people's dignity, or even their safety.[4]

1 *Handyside v the United Kingdom* App no 5493/72 (ECHR, 7 December 1976) para 49
2 *Féret v Belgium* App no 15615/07 (ECHR, 16 July 2009)
3 *Gűndűz v Turkey* App no 35071/97 (ECHR, 4 December 2003) para 41
4 *Féret* (n 2) para 73

DOI: 10.4324/9781003560548-7

Féret set a threshold precedent that would influence subsequent jurisprudence, in which the Court has systematically held that insults and/or defamation and/or prejudice and/or ridicule are enough to result in an Article 10 violation, even if they do not incite violence or other criminal acts. For example, in *Vejdeland v Sweden* (2012), the applicants distributed homophobic leaflets in a secondary school, criticising homosexuality as morally destructive and linking it to paedophilia. It was a positive development when the Court emphasised that 'discrimination based on sexual orientation is as serious as discrimination based on race, origin or colour.'[5] Nevertheless, continuing the low-threshold hatred paradigm and allowing for the prohibition of 'serious and prejudicial allegations'[6] continue to be problematic within the *Handyside* sphere and in free speech more broadly. Similarly, in *Lilliendahl v Iceland* (2020), the Court dealt with a case involving transphobic and homophobic comments on the comments section of an online news platform. Despite the speech's limited reach and no calls for violence, the Court nevertheless found it to 'promote intolerance and detestation'[7] of homosexuals. This judgement further entrenched the *Féret* paradigm, affirming that insult and ridicule can suffice to restrict speech, even in the absence of tangible harm and even if that harm is of low threshold.

Further, the *Féret* standard rests on an expansive conception of harm which includes negative emotions. The Court held that the applicant's statements were 'inevitably of such a nature as to arouse, particularly among the less informed members of the public, feelings of distrust, rejection or hatred towards foreigners.'[8] In a poignant dissenting opinion, Judge Sajó, joined by Judges Zagrebelsky and Tsotsoria, argued that the Court majority treated people as 'nitwits . . . incapable of replying to arguments and counterarguments, due to the irresistible drive of their irrational emotions.'[9] The Court's intention to protect marginalised groups from racism and ensure that 'less-informed' individuals are shielded from developing racist sentiments cannot reasonably be characterised as malicious. Nonetheless, this approach gives rise to significant concerns. It highlights the Court's inflexible paternalism as a regional judicial body and suggests a troubling deterioration of the right to freedom of expression.

In addition, the ECtHR has systematically emphasised the significance of political speech across a broad spectrum of case law, noting that restricting it requires strict scrutiny.[10] However, this is difficult to align with its rulings in cases such as *Féret*, *Le Pen v France* (2010)[11] and *Zemmour v France* (2022).[12]

5 *Vejdeland v Sweden* (2012) App no 1813/07 (ECHR, 9 February 2012) para 55
6 *Vejdeland* (n 5) para 54
7 *Lilliendahl v Iceland* (12 May 2020) App no 29297/18 (ECHR, 12 May 2020) para 38
8 *Féret* (n 2) para 69
9 *Féret* (n 2), Dissenting Opinion, Judge Sajó, joined by Judges Zagrebelsky and Tsotsoria
10 See, for example, *Wingrove v the United Kingdom* App no 17419/90 (ECHR, 25 November 1996)
11 *Le Pen v France* App no 187788/09 (ECHR, 20 April 2010)
12 *Zemmour v France* App no 64549/19 (ECHR, 20 December 2012)

In the latter two, the Court upheld restrictions on statements by far-right politicians that portrayed Muslims as a homogeneous and threatening group. While acknowledging the importance of political speech, the judgements emphasised the heightened responsibilities of politicians to promote social cohesion and avoid fostering hostility.

The previously described state of affairs raises concerns in relation to what speech is prohibited and who decides what can be prohibited and what not. In *Féret*, Judge Sajó warned that viewpoint-based restrictions risk suppressing dissent and privileging state-sanctioned narratives. Such restrictions not only undermine democratic debate but also create a dangerous precedent that authoritarian regimes can exploit to justify repression.[13] As such, the ECtHR's low-threshold hate speech paradigm, as exemplified by *Féret* and its progeny, highlights the Court's broad understanding of *harm*. On a basic level, while this framework reflects a laudable commitment to combatting discrimination and promoting social cohesion, Chapter 4 has demonstrated that many of the Court's judgements in the field of low-threshold hatred paradigm are marred by unsubstantiated narratives, which are accompanied by a fleeting disregard of free speech and its own *Handyside* principles. The book argues that the ECtHR must refine its jurisprudence to ensure that restrictions on hate speech really do meet the limitation grounds in Article 10(2). A more coherent approach grounded in a robust definitional framework, currently absent and informed by hate speech scholarship, which would facilitate the establishment of legitimate harm thresholds, would enable the Court to differentiate between hate speech and merely offensive or prejudicial speech. This would also allow for jurisprudential consistency which, as demonstrated in Chapters 4 and 5, is sometimes lacking.

2 Genocide Denial: Navigating Historical Memory

Rooted in the post-war consensus to combat anti-Semitism and Nazi propaganda, the Court's and the Commission's categorical exclusion of Holocaust denial from Convention protection through an application of Article 17 alone or as an interpretative aid to Article 10 has become a cornerstone of its jurisprudence. This stems from the Court's recognition of the enduring harm caused by the Holocaust and its denial not only to survivors, their descendants and groups but also to European democratic values. Chapter 5 contains a plethora of examples pertaining to Holocaust denial, a small sample of which is presented here. The ECtHR's strict stance in relation to the Holocaust and its denial was put forth in *Lehideux and Isorni v* France (1998), in which the Court ruled that there exists a 'category of clearly established historical facts—such as the Holocaust—whose negation or revision would be removed from the protection of Article 10 by Article 17.'[14] In *Garaudy v France* (2003),[15]

13 *Féret* (n 2), Dissenting Opinion, Sajó and others
14 *Lehideux and Isorni v France* App no 24662/94 (ECHR, 23 September 1998) para 47
15 *Garaudy v France* App no 65831/01 (ECHR, 25 June 2003)

the Court upheld the applicant's conviction for Holocaust denial, describing such speech as incompatible with the fundamental values of the Convention. Garaudy, a French philosopher, published a book alleging that the Holocaust was a "myth" fabricated to justify Zionist policies. The Court dismissed his application as manifestly ill-founded, emphasising that Holocaust denial constitutes a form of hate speech intended to incite anti-Semitism and undermine public order. These rulings illustrate the ECtHR's understanding of Holocaust denial, in itself and without any further examination, as a unique form of speech that transcends the boundaries of free speech and directly threatens the foundational principles of the Convention. It also demonstrates links between hate speech and anti-Semitism so it falls within the broader framework of protected characteristics. In the more recent case of *Pastörs v Germany* (2019), the Court extrapolated on when and how an Articles 10–17 blend can be used and underscored that, in cases concerning Holocaust denial, the decision to apply Article 17 directly and declare a complaint inadmissible or to assess the matter under Article 10 and invoke Article 17 during the necessity analysis of the alleged interference is determined on a case-by-case basis.[16] Article 17, however, is always fundamental in the judgements of Holocaust denial cases.

The ECtHR's approach to genocides and genocide denial becomes less consistent when addressing denial of genocides other than the Holocaust. In *Perinçek v Switzerland* (2015),[17] the Court faced the question of whether denial of the Armenian genocide warranted criminal sanctions akin to Holocaust denial. Perinçek, a Turkish politician, publicly denied the Armenian genocide during events in Switzerland, describing it as an "international lie." Swiss courts convicted him under laws prohibiting genocide denial. The ECtHR found that Perinçek had not committed an abuse of his rights within the meaning of Article 17 of the Convention, as is seen in Holocaust denial cases. As a result, the applicant was assessed under Article 10. While the case resulted in a finding of no violation, the fact remains that the case in question did not meet the severity required under Article 17, while Holocaust denial is systematically categorised as inherently harmful and abusive under Article 17, regardless of whether Article 10 is integrated in its analysis or not. The Court noted that, unlike the Holocaust, the Armenian genocide had not been universally recognised as genocide under international law, and Switzerland's connection to the events was deemed peripheral. The Court's use of historical consensus as a criterion for addressing cases of genocide denial risks reinforcing state-endorsed narratives while silencing alternative viewpoints. This approach raises concerns about the ECtHR's capacity to function as an impartial guardian of human rights. Furthermore, the Court's divergent treatment of the Holocaust and the Armenian genocide points to an emergence of a hierarchy in the recognition of genocides and historical memory, thereby challenging the universal

16 *Pastörs v Germany* (2019) App no 55225/14 (ECHR, 3 October 2019)
17 *Perinçek v Switzerland* App no 27510/08 (ECHR, 15 October 2015)

application of Convention safeguards in the Council of Europe region. This author contends that all speech cases, whether involving Holocaust denial or other forms of expression, should be assessed under Article 10(2) of the ECHR, unless the stringent criteria of harm, risk, and potential for destruction are demonstrably met based on the specific circumstances of the case. Such an assessment would also require examining the actual likelihood of this destruction materialising, as illustrated in the cases of *Vajnai v Hungary* (2008) and *Fáber v Hungary* (2012).

3 Totalitarianism: The Boundaries of Democratic Tolerance

The ECtHR has adjudicated on several cases regarding totalitarian ideologies as manifested in speech, including Nazism, Communism and country-based fascism, particularly in Hungary and Croatia. The ECtHR has frequently invoked Article 17 to exclude speech glorifying Nazism, which it categorises as inherently incompatible with the Convention's values. In *Kühnen v Germany* (1988),[18] the EComHR dismissed the applicant's claim that his conviction for advocating National Socialism violated Article 10. Kühnen was a member of a neo-Nazi group which distributed leaflets promoting the revival of Nazism. The Commission found that such speech constituted an abuse of rights under Article 17, precluding any protection under Article 10. The judgement emphasised that National Socialist ideology, with its emphasis on racial supremacy and violent overthrow of democratic systems, represents a direct threat to the democratic values enshrined in the Convention. Similarly, in *Schimanek v Austria* (2000),[19] the Court upheld Austria's decision to convict a far-right politician for distributing pro-Nazi materials. By invoking Article 17, the Court reaffirmed that speech glorifying Nazism falls outside the ambit of protected expression. This categorical exclusion reflects the Court's recognition of Europe's historical responsibility to combat the resurgence of Nazi ideologies and the harm they continue to inflict on groups and democratic institutions. These cases illustrate the ECtHR's consistent approach to Nazism, which it views as an existential threat to democracy and public order. By applying Article 17 in such cases, the Court avoids engaging in a proportionality analysis under Article 10(2), reflecting its determination to draw a clear line against anti-democratic speech.

The cases of *Vajnai v Hungary* (2008), *Fáber v Hungary* (2012), *Nix v Germany* (2018) and *Šimunić v Croatia* (2019)[20] demonstrate varying approaches to different forms of totalitarianism. In *Vajnai*, the ECtHR invalidated Hungary's restriction on the public display of the red star, underscoring that the applicant's use of the symbol did not pose an imminent threat to

18 *Kühnen v Germany* (1988) App no 12194/86 (EComHR, 12 May 1988)
19 *Schimanek v Austria* App no 32307/96 (ECtHR, 1 February 2000)
20 *Šimunić v Croatia* (2019) App no 20373/17 (ECHR, 22 January 2019)

democratic order or public safety. The Court highlighted the dual meaning of the red star, noting that although it represents Communism, it also serves as a symbol of the International Workers' Movement and lawful political parties in Europe. Also, the ECtHR rejected Hungary's reliance on speculative dangers to justify its restriction, reaffirming that offence or discomfort alone cannot curtail political expression under Article 10. The judgement reflects the adoption of a risk-based approach, with a contextual assessment of the symbol in question, setting a high threshold for restricting speech despite the emotional scars left by the Communist regime in Hungary.

The Court's judgement in *Fáber* extended the principles articulated in *Vajnai*, this time in the context of the display of the Árpád flag, a symbol associated with the fascist Arrow Cross regime, responsible for, *inter alia*, mass murders of Jewish people in the 1940s. It acknowledged that the flag was provocative and could cause 'uneasiness amongst past victims and their relatives who may rightly find such displays disrespectful.'[21] However, this was not deemed sufficient to set the limits of the expression, noting that intimidation was a necessary prerequisite for the speech's restriction. This position thereby echoes the contours of speech as set out by *Handyside*, in which even offensive, shocking or disturbing speech can be protected. It also adopts a harm-based approach, requiring that the speech cause a certain level of established harm, in this case, incitement. Unlike *Vajnai*, the judgement in *Fáber* raised additional complexities because of the symbol's direct association with the Arrow Cross regime responsible for mass atrocities and the fact that the applicant was standing at a place where a mass murder of Jews had occurred. These complexities arise given the way the Court deals with cases involving Nazism in Germany. Nevertheless, the ECtHR determined that the applicant's peaceful display of the flag, without engaging in abusive behaviour, did not justify the penalties imposed by Hungarian authorities. This judgement further solidified the Court's approach, requiring a context-specific, harm-based analysis that distinguishes between expression and conduct that undermines democratic values. However, to date, we have not seen the robust assessment of the two Hungarian cases being followed in other hate speech cases.

The ECtHR's reasoning in *Nix v Germany* (2018) marks a significant departure from its strict protection of Article 10 in *Vajnai* and *Fáber*. In *Nix*, the applicant used his blog to comment on problems his German-Nepalese daughter faced with the state employment office. In one of his posts, he included an image of Heinrich Himmler wearing Nazi symbols. Despite the absence of incitement, intimidation or any demonstrable harm, the Court upheld Germany's decision to convict the applicant under its blanket prohibition on Nazi symbols. In contrast to its nuanced assessment of context and harm in *Vajnai* and *Fáber*, the ECtHR deferred heavily to Germany's historical context, noting its unique moral responsibility to combat Nazism. The Court emphasised

21 *Fáber v Hungary* (2012) App no 40721/08 (ECHR, 24 July 2018) para 56

that the swastika, unlike the red star or Árpád flag, is unequivocally associated with Nazi ideology. By categorising the image as a 'gratuitous use of symbols,'[22] the ECtHR upheld Germany's restriction without engaging in a substantive analysis, effectively prioritising the symbolic harm of the swastika over the public interest of the applicant's blog, which sought to raise awareness on discrimination by German authorities. While the Court recognised that the blog was a public interest blog, it agreed with the national courts, which did not examine the particular post in question in light of other blog posts and the blog's purposes as a whole, thereby outrightly refusing to substantiate its approach, look at the context and adopt a harms-based approach. Its stance in *Nix* reflects that the Court has a different understanding of different symbols and moments in history, with a hierarchy of some events over others.

In *Nix*, the Court underscored Germany's unique historical responsibility to combat Nazism, applying a stringent threshold for freedom of expression. This contrasted sharply with its approach in *Vajnai*, where the Court recognised Hungary's Communist past but declined to uphold similar restrictions on the red star. As well as the dual nature of this symbol, the Court also justified its decision in the Hungarian case by citing the passage of time since the fall of Communist regimes, suggesting that the temporal distance diminished the risk associated with the symbol. However, this reasoning raises questions about the consistency of the ECtHR's approach to totalitarian legacies. While Germany's responsibility for Nazism is treated as an enduring and immutable justification for restrictions, Hungary's history with Communism is assessed through a more flexible temporal lens.

In *Šimunić v Croatia* (2019), at a football match, a Croatian football player chanted "For Home—Ready." As in the two Hungarian cases, this is a slogan with a dual meaning, one of a non-fascist nature and one related to the fascist Independent State of Croatia. The applicant was convicted for inciting hatred, with the ECtHR deeming his application under Article 10 to be inadmissible. The Court considered that *Šimunić*, a public figure, directly interacted with an audience that responded affirmatively to the chant. The Court viewed this as evidence of the applicant's intent to invoke a totalitarian ideology, justifying the restriction under Article 10(2). While the Court had before it an expert view which referred to the dual nature of the chant, one being of a fascist nature and one not, it still found this to be unprotected speech.

The ECtHR's approach to harm also varied significantly across the preceding cases. In *Fáber*, the Court required clear proof of a genuine threat to public order to justify restrictions. In *Vajnai*, it emphasised that speculative dangers or subjective feelings of discomfort were insufficient grounds for limiting expression under Article 10. In contrast, in *Nix*, the Court upheld Germany's restrictions without substantive evidence of harm, relying instead on the country's historical context to justify the prohibition. The *Šimunić*

22 *Nix v Germany* App no 35285/16 (ECHR, 13 March 2018) para 47

case introduces another dimension to the ECtHR's jurisprudence, illustrating the amplified impact of speech delivered by public figures. The applicant was a public person, a football player, whose chant was shouted to a large audience, in the charged public setting of a football match, and as such, the Court deemed that these factors could incite hatred and reinforce totalitarian ideologies. While taking into account the speaker's platform and audience is something we have seen in hate speech cases more generally, in this context, the fact that the element of the dual nature of the chant was disregarded by the ECtHR could potentially limit the overall impact of the speech in question.

In light of the preceding text, the Court, in *Vajnai* and *Fáber*, adopted an in-depth, harm-based, contextually apt assessment of the speech in question, avoided restricting expression on speculative grounds and also underlined that ill-feelings of victims of the past regimes did not meet the threshold of harm necessary to limit Article 10. However, the Court's approach in *Nix* and that in *Šimunić* are very different, with *Nix* in particular being legally perplexing as he was using the speech for symbolic and hyperbolic purposes to further his arguments on his public interest blog, which looked at the discrimination his German Nepalese daughter was experiencing with the authorities. The aforementioned inconsistencies shape a Court narrative on historical memory, retracting from its role as neutral arbiter and creating jurisprudential ambiguity. A more coherent framework grounded in necessity and uniform criteria, which are contextually applied, is needed to ensure the equitable and principled protection of freedom of expression across cases involving totalitarian symbols. One could make sense, based on the Court's previous jurisprudence, that Nazi symbols were ousted from protection, and others not. Moreover, here, we have a situation whereby a Communist symbol and a flag associated with a fascist regime, held up at a place of a mass extermination of Jews on a day of demonstrations, were both considered protected speech. On the other hand, Nazi symbols used in a public interest blog and a Croatian chant which has a dual meaning were considered unprotected speech. The need for clarity and predictability in the ECtHR's approach built on sound principles and precedents is of utmost importance to the beneficiaries of Convention rights.

4 Violent Speech

The ECtHR's treatment of violent speech cases reveals a jurisprudential tension shaped by the complex interplay of political and contextual factors. The majority of cases in this section are applications against Turkey on limiting the right to freedom of expression around the Kurdish issue. The ECtHR's treatment of violent speech cases frequently emanates from an assessment of the political and security contexts in which the speech occurs. In *Gerger v Turkey* (1999),[23] the ECtHR examined a speech delivered during a memorial ceremony that

23 *Gerger v Turkey* App no 24919/94 (ECHR, 8 July 1999)

lauded deceased individuals as Kurdish guerrilla fighters. The Court observed that the speech was presented solely to participants of the ceremony, thereby limiting its impact on public order. Additionally, it concluded that the speech did not amount to incitement to violence, despite references to terms such as "resistance." However, the Court refrained from elaborating on the contextual significance or articulating the precise rationale behind its finding of no incitement. This absence of detailed reasoning invites further scrutiny, as one might contend that memorial ceremonies inherently evoke heightened emotions, akin to the charged atmosphere observed in the football context of *Šimunić*. In *Sürek v Turkey* (1999),[24] the applicant, a principal shareholder of a weekly publication, faced charges for disseminating separatist propaganda through readers' letters that glorified the PKK's (Kurdistan Workers' Party) actions as a "national independence war." Despite the applicant's argument that he had no editorial responsibility for the letters, the ECtHR upheld his conviction. The Court reasoned that, as the publication's owner, he bore vicarious responsibility for its content and that the letters constituted hate speech and incitement to violence. The Court's decision in *Sürek* emphasised the volatile security situation in southeastern Turkey, where the PKK's activities posed a significant threat. However, it did not look at this issue more substantially to ascertain how and why the letters could cause harm or how they amounted to incitement to violence and hate speech, nor did it consider the public interest issue of allowing discourse on the matter. These two points are raised since, in several similar cases, the Court took a different view, finding a violation of Article 10, without the factual differences in cases being particularly clear. In *Karataş v Turkey* (1999),[25] the ECtHR found an Article 10 in addressing the conviction of a poet whose work, while provocative, was deemed to express frustration rather than incite rebellion. The Court ruled that the poems, which referred to the Kurdish struggle and "venerable Kurdistan," were artistic expressions reflecting deep distress rather than direct calls to violence. The Court noted that that poetry had a limited readership, was a less-accessible form of speech and, as such, had limited social impact. In this ambit, the Court focused on the difference between artistic expression and incitement. In *Erdoğdu v Turkey* (2000),[26] the Court dealt with a periodical that published an article titled "The Kurdish Problem is a Turkish Problem," which portrayed the Kurdish conflict as a national resistance movement. The ECtHR found that the article, while critical of the Turkish government, did not endorse violence and fell within the bounds of permissible political debate. The ruling reflected the Court's recognition that robust criticism of state policies is essential in a democratic society. Similarly, in *Erdal Taş v Turkey* (2007),[27] the ECtHR evaluated an arti-

24 *Sürek v Turkey* (1999) App no 26682/95 (ECHR, 8 July 1999)
25 *Karataş v Turkey* (1999) App no 2316894 (ECHR, 8 July 199)
26 *Erdoğdu v Turkey* (2000) App no 25723/94 (ECHR, 15 June 2020)
27 *Erdal Taş v Turkey* (No 5) (2007) App no 2984802, (ECHR, 29 July 2007)

cle analysing the Kurdish issue, which Turkish authorities claimed constituted propaganda against the state's indivisibility. The Court concluded that the article did not incite violence or qualify as hate speech, instead recognising it as a critical discussion of a politically charged topic. By affirming the applicant's Article 10 rights, the ECtHR reinforced the principle that political commentary, even when controversial or provocative, deserves heightened protection under the Convention.

The ECtHR has occasionally imposed positive obligations on states to safeguard freedom of expression in volatile contexts. *Özgür Gündem v Turkey* (2000)[28] serves as a landmark example, involving a pro-Kurdish newspaper subjected to state-backed harassment, including journalist killings and arbitrary prosecutions. This judgement marked a significant expansion of the ECtHR's Article 10 jurisprudence, establishing that states bear a dual obligation, namely, refraining from censorship and actively safeguarding free speech against threats from third parties. By recognising the importance of pluralistic media in conflict contexts, the Court affirmed its commitment to upholding democratic values, even in politically volatile environments.

However, not everything is clear-cut; the sporadic application of Article 17 in Kurdish cases further complicates the ECtHR's jurisprudence. In *Roj TV A/S v Denmark* (2018),[29] the Court invoked Article 17 to exclude protection for a television station accused of promoting the PKK through broadcasts inciting violence. The ECtHR found that the broadcasts, which glorified guerrilla warfare and encouraged viewers to join the PKK, violated the Convention's fundamental values and, thus, fell outside the scope of Article 10. However, in cases like *Medya FM Reha Radio v Turkey* (2006),[30] where broadcasts contained similarly inflammatory language, the ECtHR relied on Article 10(2) rather than Article 17, applying the test pertaining to Article 10(2) restrictions.

The ECtHR's approach to violent speech also reflects its emphasis on proportionality in assessing state-imposed penalties. In *Stomakhin v Russia* (2018),[31] the applicant, a journalist, was convicted of publishing inflammatory articles about the Chechen conflict. While the ECtHR acknowledged that some of his statements justified violence, it found the five-year prison sentence and three-year journalism ban disproportionate. By striking a balance between individual rights and state interests, the Court underscored the importance of tailoring penalties to the severity of the speech's impact.

In Turkish cases involving the Kurdish issue, the ECtHR has predominantly upheld Article 10 protections for speech, albeit with sporadic variations. The case of *Stomakhin v Russia* is rather notable since the Court itself

28 *Özgür Gündem v Turkey* App no 23144/93 (ECHR, 16 March 2020)
29 *Roj TV A/S v Denmark* (2018) App no 24683/14 (ECHR, 17 April 2018)
30 *Medya FM Reha Radio v Turkey* (2006) App no 32842/02
31 *Stomakhin v Russia* (2018) App no 52273/07 (ECHR, 9 May 2018)

acknowledged that some of the applicant's statements were of a violent nature. In most of the cases involving violent speech, the Court sets the bar high, requiring that incitement to violence is clearly present if Article 10 is to be restricted. Conversely, in cases such as *Féret v Belgium* and *Vejdeland and Others v Sweden*, the Court upheld restrictions on non-violent speech directed at ethnic or sexual minorities, applying a lower threshold for limiting expression. This difference may reflect the Court's strong emphasis on protecting anti-government speech, a protection which is emphatic for people's enjoyment of Article 10. This difference makes perfect sense, and anti-government speech needs to have very strong protections. However, this does not imply that other forms of speech, particularly those targeting protected characteristics, towards which the Court has demonstrated and admitted particular sensitivities, even when merely offensive, should be scrutinised less.

As noted at the start of this book, the choice to include the section on violent speech which is anti-government emanated solely from the fact that, in an array of these cases, the Court itself chose, without any explanation, to incorporate the term *hate speech* therein. While this can be considered as erroneous, their inclusion was therefore necessary. It is interesting, though, to see the Court in action, dissecting the cases before it, diluting margins of appreciation and ascertaining harm and context. For reasons of particular sensitivities extrapolated on in the book, it is unrealistic to expect the Court to afford the same level of protection to speech such as Holocaust denial or expressions targeting protected characteristics, as it does to anti-government speech. However, the framework and tools exist for the Court to develop greater nuance in its approach to classical hate speech cases, moving beyond the current narrative.

5 Extending Positive Obligations to Hate Speech

In *Beizaras and Levickas v Lithuania* (2020),[32] two men who posted a photograph of themselves kissing on Facebook were subjected to homophobic hate speech, including death threats, in the comments section under their post. Lithuanian authorities dismissed their complaints, citing the provocative nature of the post and the lack of criminal intent in the comments. The ECtHR found violations of Article 8 on the right to private and family life, in conjunction with Article 14, on non-discrimination, as well as Article 13, on the right to an effective remedy. The Court noted that such crimes which are fuelled by prejudices require heightened state scrutiny and that viewing them and treating them equally with ordinary offences would undermine the Convention and its objectives. By emphasising the discriminatory intent and violent undertones of the comments, the judgement affirmed the state's duty to protect individuals from hate speech and its psychological impact.

32 *Beizaras and Levickas v Lithuania* (2020) App no 41288/15 (ECHR, 14 January 2020)

The Court's approach to positive obligations on states to protect targets from hate speech was further evolved in cases involving group-based stereotyping. In *Behar and Gutman v Bulgaria* (2021)[33] and *Budinova and Chaprazov v Bulgaria* (2021),[34] the ECtHR addressed hate speech by a prominent politician targeting Jewish and Roma communities. The Court articulated a relatively detailed framework for assessing the impact of harmful expression, considering factors such as the vulnerability of the targeted group, the content and reach of the statements and the speaker's influence. In both cases, the ECtHR found violations of Article 8 in conjunction with Article 14, holding that the Bulgarian courts failed to balance the applicants' right to dignity against the speaker's right to freedom of expression. The Court concluded that the extreme negative stereotyping in the statements amounted to vilification, with the potential to harm the targeted groups' identity and dignity. These cases marked a significant expansion of positive obligations, moving beyond individual victims to address the broader impact of hate speech on targeted communities.

While the ECtHR has primarily invoked positive obligations under Article 8 in cases brought by the direct or indirect targets of hate speech, its application in Article 10 cases remains rare. *Özgür Gündem v Turkey* (2000) and *Dink v Turkey* (2010)[35] are notable exceptions, where the Court recognised states' responsibilities to safeguard freedom of expression. In *Özgür Gündem*, a pro-Kurdish newspaper faced a campaign of state-backed harassment, including journalist killings and arbitrary prosecutions, forcing it to cease publication. The ECtHR held that Turkey failed to fulfil its positive obligation to protect the newspaper's right to freedom of expression, emphasising that this right extends beyond non-interference to include proactive measures to ensure a safe environment for public discourse. Similarly, in *Dink*, the Court examined Turkey's failure to protect a journalist from threats and harassment following his articles on Armenian identity. The ECtHR stressed the state's duty to create an enabling environment for public debate, allowing individuals to express their opinions without fear. In *Nix*, the Court noted:

> [I]n the light of their historical role and experience, States which have experienced the Nazi horrors may be regarded as having a special moral responsibility to distance themselves from the mass atrocities perpetrated by the Nazis.[36]

While this approach aims to safeguard the rights and feelings of certain groups, it prompts significant concerns regarding the extent to which the

33 *Behar and Gutman v Bulgaria* App no 29335/13 (ECHR, 16 February 2021)
34 *Budinova and Chaprazov v Bulgaria* App no 12567/13 (ECHR, 16 February 2021)
35 *Dink v Turkey* App nos. 2668/07, 6102/08, 30079/08, 7072/09 et 7124/09 (ECHR, 14 September 2010)
36 *Nix* (n 22) para 47

Court allows for the restriction of speech. A key issue is the potential for state overreach, where the enforcement of positive obligations might allow governments to curtail dissenting or unpopular opinions under the guise of harm prevention. Moreover, the broad discretion afforded to states in defining harmful expression risks entrenching state-sanctioned narratives within hate speech regulations, thereby undermining pluralism and suppressing critical discourse.

6 The Role of Technology in Hate Speech Regulation

The digital age has fundamentally reshaped the communication landscape, introducing both significant opportunities and complex challenges for the protection and promotion of human rights in the realm of hate speech. Online platforms have magnified the reach and visibility of harmful rhetoric, yet they also serve as potent instruments for counterspeech, civic engagement and democratic participation. The jurisprudence of the ECtHR must evolve to reflect these realities, engaging with the structural dynamics of the digital ecosystem to ensure that hate speech regulation remains effective, equitable, and aligned with the principles of pluralism and equality. Digital intermediaries such as social media platforms, search engines and content-sharing websites have become central to modern public discourse. With cases such as *Delfi AS v Estonia* (2015),[37] the ECtHR has begun to grapple with the implications and complications of online hate speech and the liability of platforms. The Court upheld Estonia's decision to hold an online news portal liable for failing to remove defamatory comments on its platform. While this judgement emphasised the responsibility of digital intermediaries to prevent the spread of harmful content, it also raised concerns about the potential chilling effect on freedom of expression. Achieving an appropriate balance between platform accountability and protecting freedom of expression presents a significant challenge for the ECtHR, particularly as this domain represents a relatively new and evolving facet of its hate speech jurisprudence. Additionally, the Court will inevitably need to adapt its approach to address the growing concentration of power held by major technology corporations, a development with profound implications for the regulation of online speech. When the time comes, the ECtHR will need to keep in mind that platforms exercise substantial influence over public discourse through their content moderation policies, frequently operating with limited transparency and accountability. The ECtHR should critically examine the implications of this power imbalance, ensuring that hate speech regulation neither disproportionately affects marginalised communities nor suppresses legitimate dissent.

37 *Delfi AS v Estonia* App no 6459/09 (ECHR, 16 June 2015)

7 Hate Speech Cases Before the European Court of Human Rights: Toward a Principled Framework

A recalibrated approach to hate speech jurisprudence must rest on a principled framework that reconciles freedom of expression with the legitimate aim of combatting hate speech, which means a particular threshold of harm. The jurisprudence of the ECtHR, while aspiring to uphold the vital principles of equality and non-discrimination, is hindered by a lack of a coherent definitional framework, inconsistency in application, judicial overreach and a failure to draw sufficiently from available scholarly resources. A principled approach to hate speech regulation necessitates the adoption of a precise and universally applicable definition. Presently, the ECtHR often employs broad interpretations that categorise speech as hate speech merely because it insults or offends, without providing clear evidence of societal harm. By embracing a relatively narrowly tailored definition that systematically marks the conceptual framework of all its hate speech judgements, such as that proposed in Article 20(2) of the ICCPR and elaborated upon in the Rabat Plan of Action,[38] the Court could mitigate ambiguity and prevent the risks of excessive regulation. As such, a coherent definitional framework set forth by the Court could focus on speech that incites violence, discrimination or hatred, ensuring that only the most harmful expressions fall outside the protection of Article 10. To ensure that restrictions on hate speech are justified, the ECtHR must apply a sound definition and incorporate findings from scholarship to inform its analyses. The Court's rulings must articulate the specific harms posed by the impugned speech, drawing relevant scholarship. As illustrated throughout this book, the ECtHR frequently relies on abstract assertions regarding the societal harm posed by certain expressions, often without adequately substantiating these claims. For example, in *Vejdeland*, the Court upheld restrictions on the dissemination of homophobic pamphlets on the grounds of their prejudicial content yet offered minimal evidence to substantiate its reasoning. A more rigorous engagement with scholarly work on the nature and impact of hate speech, as well as its regulation, would enable the ECtHR more effectively to evaluate the necessity and proportionality of such restrictions. Such evidence-based reasoning would not only strengthen the Court's jurisprudence by establishing strong thresholds and clarity in terms of what hate speech is but also ensure that its rulings align with the realities of societal harm and democratic needs. A principled framework must also recognise the value of counterspeech as an alternative to censorship. Encouraging counterspeech initiatives, public education campaigns and robust protections for dissenting voices can mitigate the harms of hate speech without infringing on freedom of expression. While it is not

38 'Rabat Plan of Action on the Prohibition of Advocacy of National, Racial or Religious Hatred that Constitutes Incitement to Discrimination, Hostility or Violence' (2002) <https://www.ohchr.org/sites/default/files/Rabat_draft_outcome.pdf>

the role of the Court to set out the educational and counterspeech activities of contracting states, it can, through its jurisprudence, emphasise states' positive obligations under Article 10 to foster environments conducive to open and inclusive dialogue. The positive obligations we have seen put forth to date in the sphere of freedom of expression have pertained only to restrictions. While contextual sensitivity is vital in assessing hate speech, the ECtHR must guard against privileging certain narratives over others. For instance, the Court's differential treatment of Holocaust denial and Armenian genocide denial in *Perinçek* raised concerns about implicit hierarchies of historical memory.

The ECtHR's hate speech jurisprudence illustrates the difficulty of balancing the right to freedom of expression and the protection of convention values, public order, the rights and reputation of others, feelings and the list goes on. This is the route that Europe has chosen to take for historical reasons. While this book does not seek to call for a complete, unrealistic reshuffle of this reality, it does call for a more substantiated balancing between the aforementioned and a return to its *Handyside* principles, particularly in an era of rapid technological change and growing societal polarisation. The right to freedom of expression is a fundamental right, but it is not an absolute one. Its importance has been reiterated time and again by the ECtHR, but so has the possibility for its limitation. What the book has attempted to do is demonstrate that in the sphere of hate speech jurisprudence, apart from most of the cases of violent anti-government speech and some good practices, such as *Vajnai* and *Fáber*, the general approach the Court adopts is overreaching and, at times, disregarding of the fundamentality of speech, but also of the severe impact that restrictions, particularly of low-threshold hatred cases, can cause. The Court must set out a definitional framework and identify the thresholds of prohibitable speech which emanate from a sound definition, beyond the 'grave' and 'less grave' distinction in *Lilliendahl*. This would allow for the proper protection of the right to freedom of expression and the application of the *Handyside* principles, while simultaneously having a clear and coherent approach to hate speech, which comes in different forms and severity. It would further allow for its jurisprudence to be clear and consistent, which is a centrifugal point of departure for those benefitting from Convention rights as well as for contracting parties. The Court should, at the next opportunity, commence delving into the plethora of hate speech scholarship available that can guide it on conceptualising harm and further understanding the impact of restriction. In addition to these and, in fact, as a starting point, *Fáber* and *Vajnai* are the two cases to revisit. Most of all, if the Court does not seriously reconsider its stance on hate speech, adopting a permissive stance to viewpoint selective national prohibitions of hate speech, with no clear definition and no established, research-informed threshold of harm will, at some point, start deeply affecting the health of European democracy and result in quieting the decibels of dissenting and marginalised voices.

Index

FSC
www.fsc.org
MIX
Papier | Fördert gute Waldnutzung
FSC® C083411

Kolibri 360 GmbH
Ferdinand-Jühlke-Straße 7
99095 Erfurt, Deutschland
produktsicherheit@kolibri360.de